Thomas Crean | A
Integrali
A manual of politi

To our students

Thomas Crean | Alan Fimister

Integralism

A manual of political philosophy

Bibliographic information published by Deutsche Nationalbibliothek
The Deutsche Nationalbibliothek lists this publication in the Deutsche Nationalbibliographie;
detailed bibliographic data is available in the Internet at http://dnb.ddb.de

Our books are distributed worldwide by

EUROSPAN

USA & Canada
Eurospan
c/o Casemate Publishers
1950 Lawrence Road
Havertown, PA 19083
Tel: (610) 853-9131
Fax: (610) 853-9146
casemate@casematepublishers.com

U.K., Europe, Asia and Africa
Eurospan
Gray's Inn House
127 Clerkenwell Road
London EC1R 5DB
info@eurospan.co.uk

©2020 editiones scholasticae
53819 Neunkirchen-Seelscheid
www.editiones-scholasticae.de

ISBN 978-3-86838-226-6

Printed on acid-free paper

Printed in Germany
by CPI Buchbücher.de GmbH

Almighty everlasting God, who in Thy beloved Son, King of the whole world, hast willed to restore all things anew; grant in Thy mercy that all the families of nations, rent asunder by the wound of sin, may be subjected to His most gentle rule, who with Thee liveth and reigneth in the unity of the Holy Spirit, world without end. Amen.

(collect for the Feast of Christ the King)

Acknowledgements

It is with trepidation but in hope that we commit this manual to the public at large. It is the work of a layman and of a friar and priest and thus in its own small and halting way arises from some experience of the three principal aspects of the Church's life in this world. Although it is intended to guide the layman, yet as such guidance is the most important purpose of the clerical life after the divine cultus itself and a key aspect of the witness enjoined upon the religious, we pray that this manual will be of use to all three. As with such witness and guidance so with this text, blame for its limitations must be confined to the two authors, while credit for such merits as it possesses is far more widely dispersed. In the first place we should like to acknowledge the Order of Preachers and Mrs Colleen Fimister whose tireless support and encouragement for our work have made it possible. The work took root amidst the hospitality and tranquillity of Silverstream Priory and an English Carmelite community and the providential challenges afforded by the education of seminarians and undergraduates at Saint John Vianney Theological Seminary in Colorado, Thomas More College in New Hampshire and Newman College Ireland. More remotely but not less significantly it was born from our combined labours in the *otium sacrum* of the International Theological Institute's Indian summer. Our debt in this regard is expressed in the dedication but we would be remiss if we did not also thank Fr Yosyp Veresh of whose wisdom we are far more the recipients than the benefactors.

While countless passing victims have been compelled to express their views on this or that paragraph and turn of phrase, in what follows special mention must go to Dr John Joy of the Diocese of Madison (Wisconsin) and Pater Edmund Waldstein of the Abbey of Heiligenkreuz, who very generously agreed to read through the penultimate draft and pass on their observations, all of which have left an impression on the final text though not always as P. Edmund would have wished! To both men the text owes much more by way of their remote inspiration and insight. Mr Geoffrey Fimister very kindly examined the chapter on Political Economy and with heroic forbearance identified obscurities in an argument for the premises of which he has only very occasional sympathy.

* * *

In an ecclesiastical context the term Integralism (and its variant Integrism) is employed in two different but related ways. Firstly, it is used to denote an uncompromising adherence to the Social Kingship of Christ, that is, an insistence upon the moral duty of men and societies toward the true religion and toward the one Church of Christ. Secondly, it is applied to the tendency to see Scholasticism, and more specifically Thomism, no less than the imperishable Patristic Age, as a completed and indispensable stage in Catholic thought which must be assimilated and appropriated as one's own by any authentically ecclesiastical writer of a later age. As the great John Henry Newman, now happily raised to the altars, expresses it, "gradually and in the course of ages, Catholic inquiry has taken certain definite shapes, and has thrown itself into the form of a science, with a method and a phraseology of its own, under the intellectual handling of great minds, such as St Athanasius, St Augustine, and St Thomas; and I feel no temptation at all to break in pieces the great legacy of thought thus committed to us for these latter days." It is for this reason that the names of Leo XIII and Pius XI feature so prominently, as among the popes theirs were the greatest contributions to the work of properly scholastic thought in the *grand siècle* of Neo-Scholasticism. That is, it is as scholastic thinkers, not *per se* for their merely authentic magisterium, that they are principally cited. Absolute submission is naturally given to every pope and council in their infallible magisterium.

Reflecting on the possibility of progress in architecture beyond the sublime achievements of the *medium aevum*, A. W. N. Pugin remarked of the possibilities of development beyond that happy period: "I feel convinced that Christian architecture had gone its length, and it must necessarily have destroyed itself by departing from its own principles in the pursuit of novelty, or it must have fallen back on its pure and ancient models ... we cannot successfully suggest anything new, but are obliged to return to the spirit of the ancient work ... as the faith itself is perfect, so are the principles on which it is founded. We may indeed improve in mechanical contrivances to expedite its execution, we may even increase its scale and grandeur; but we can never successfully deviate one tittle from the spirit and principles of pointed architecture. We must rest content to follow, not to lead; we may indeed widen the road which our Catholic forefathers formed, but we can never depart from their track without a certainty of failure being the result of our presumption." It is in this spirit that we present to the reader *Integralism: A Manual of Political Philosophy* as an epitome of the *Via Antiqua* in its political aspect.

Feast of St Sylvester, AD 2019

Contents

Abbreviations

CIC: *Codex Iuris Canonici,* Rome, 1983.

CCC: *Catechism of the Catholic Church.* London: Geoffrey Chapman, 1994.

DH: *Compendium of Creeds, Definitions, and Declarations on Matters of Faith and Morals.* 43rd edition. Edited by Peter Hünermann and Heinrich Denzinger. San Francisco: Ignatius Press, 2012.

DTC: *Dictionnaire de Théologie Catholique.* Paris: Letouzey et Ané, 1907-51.

PG: *Patrologia Graeca,* 162 vols. Edited by Jacques Migne. Paris, 1857-66.

PL: *Patrologia Latina,* 221 vols. Edited by Jacques Migne. Paris, 1844-64.

STh: *Summa Theologiae.*

Chapter 1
Societies and the perfect society

The English word 'politics' comes from the Greek word πόλις (*polis*), which means 'city'. In ancient Greece, the *polis* or city-state emerged in the middle of the 6th century before our era as the principal community, a position which it retained until Philip of Macedon's victory at the Battle of Chaeronea in 338 BC. Since 'politics' refers in common speech to the activities of politicians, the phrase 'political philosophy' is often used to refer more precisely to the study of the *polis* and its successors.[1]

Political philosophy is therefore a branch of moral philosophy. Moral philosophy in general is the study of man's life, and of the good which strictly befits, or is proportioned to, man's nature: its goal is to show us how to attain this good on earth. Political philosophy, or politics, is the study of man's life insofar as he is united with his fellow men in a way that extends beyond the family. Since, as we shall see, the good that men may obtain by this union is greater than the good which they may obtain by their union in domestic society, which in turn is greater than the good which they may obtain as individual human beings, politics is *the study of the highest good, proportionate to human nature, which may be obtained on earth*. It is therefore the highest branch of moral philosophy.

Under the survey of political philosophy come: the nature of societies in general, and of the perfect or complete society in particular; the idea of the common good and of authority in general; the relation of the domestic society to external authority; the origin and scope of temporal authority; the nature and purpose of law; the goal or end of the temporal commonwealth; its economic organisation; the relations which different temporal commonwealths have with each other; and the relation of the temporal power to the ultimate end of human life.

Politics, like all moral philosophy, must be instructed by divine revelation. This is because, in contrast to speculative reason, the first principle in moral or practical philosophy is the final end: before deciding what to do, we must first know what to aim at. Revelation is necessary not simply because God has freely chosen to call man to a supernatural end; it would have been necessary in every

---

[1] The term 'political philosophy' (φιλοσοφία πολιτική) appears once in Aristotle's *Politics*, III.12.

order of providence.[2] Even if the end that God had assigned to man were merely proportionate to our nature, it would be impossible for us to know this fact by reason alone, and to exclude the possibility that we had been assigned a preternatural or supernatural end.[3] Thus, even in a hypothetical state of pure nature, man would require divine revelation.[4] Hence, to engage correctly in practical reasoning, man must learn by divine revelation where he is going and the way thereto.[5] "No one can arrive at any wisdom except by faith."[6]

The gospel teaches that our ultimate end is beatitude. This is available in heaven, and not on earth.[7] But only our life on earth can bring us to that end.

---

[2] By an 'order of providence' we understand the establishment by God's free choice both of an end for His rational creatures and of the means by which rational creatures must obtain this end. Pius XI uses the phrase in *Divini illius magistri*, 7: "In the present order of providence (*praesenti hoc rerum ordine Dei providentia constituto*), [...] God has revealed Himself to us in the person of His only-begotten Son."

[3] A preternatural end would have been one that surpasses the powers of human nature, for example the knowledge of angels. According to St Thomas, the Arab philosopher Averroes posited this as the summit of earthly felicity; see STh 1a 88, 1 and 1a 2ae 3, 7. A supernatural end is one that surpasses the powers of all created natures, actual or possible.

[4] Cf. Dionysius *The Divine Names*, 1; Girolamo Savonarola, *The Triumph of the Cross*, (Sands & Co.: London, 1901), 41. F.J. Sheed, *A Map of Life* (Sheed & Ward: New York, 1937), 15: "Even if human nature were fully understood with no shadow of error, the purpose of man's life could be deduced from it only if the purpose of man's life were contained in it - that is, if man's purpose simply meant the highest activity possible to his own nature. But supposing the purpose of human life is some activity or state higher than man's nature. Then we cannot find it simply by studying his nature. And God has in fact taught that He destines us not for something of which our nature is in itself capable (and which might, therefore, as I have said, be deduced from our nature) but for something to which He in His generosity chose to lift us; and this obviously cannot be deduced from any study of us: one may deduce the incidence of justice, but not of generosity."

[5] Cf. Jn. 14:4. Hence also St Thomas deduces the necessity of faith from the fact, true in all orders of providence, that rational creatures, unlike other beings, are immediately subject to God, and so to reach perfection must not simply unfold their own powers but also respond to His initiative; STh 2a 2ae 2, 3: "Wherever one nature is subordinate to another, we find that two things concur towards the perfection of the lower nature, one of which is in respect of that nature's proper movement, while the other is in respect of the movement of the higher nature [...] Now the created rational nature alone is immediately subordinate to God, since other creatures do not attain to the universal, but only to something particular, whether they partake of the Divine goodness either in 'being' only, as inanimate things, or also in 'living' and in 'knowing singulars', as plants and animals; whereas the rational nature, in as much as it apprehends the universal notion of good and being, is immediately related to the universal principle of being."

[6] St Thomas Aquinas, *Commentary on the Gospel of St John*, 771.

[7] Ex. 33:20.

A component, and in fact the most important component, of a good earthly life is therefore its being rightly directed to the life beyond. Therefore, since politics seeks to know the truth about the good earthly life, it must understand how man is directed toward beatitude, namely, by the teaching and the sacraments of the Catholic Church.[8]

Nature of society

Since politics studies human beings in society, the first question to consider is: 'What is a society?' At this stage we are not using the word as a synonym for what is normally called civil society, but in a more general sense. In this broader sense, the family is a society; so is a university, and a golf-club, and a trade union, and a multi-national corporation; so, on a higher plane, is the Catholic Church, and the religious institutes and other fraternities which she includes.

Yet not every grouping of human beings ranks as a society. Within a city or country, there may exist, for example, a certain number of brown-eyed or left-handed people, but they will not normally compose a society. The activity of none of these people need be affected by the fact that other people exist who share this physical characteristic. Nor need any reckon it as part of *his* good that others exist who share this characteristic.

A society exists when several beings so act that each makes it part of his aim that both he and those with whom he is grouped achieve something good by their activity. Since only intelligent beings can consciously intend an end as such, as opposed to acting for some particular end by simple instinct, only intelligent beings can strictly compose a society. We may therefore define a society as 'a union of intelligent beings acting for an end', or 'the conscious coordinated activity of persons for a common end'.[9]

---

[8] Cf. J. Maritain, *Science and Wisdom*, tr. B. Wall (New York: Scribner's, 1940), 162: "[Ethics] is *essentially* insufficient in the sense that no science directive of human conduct - no science pure and simple worthy of the name - can exist without taking into account the real and actual last end of human life."

[9] Some authors, speaking even more precisely, say that society *formally considered* belongs to the category of relation, since it is the union or ordering of many among themselves which constitutes society; that considered with reference to *material causality*, society is a multitude of intelligent beings; and that considered in its *complete entity*, society is this multitude together with the relation that orders them among themselves. Cf. H. Grenier, *Cours de Philosophie*, t. 2, 'Monastique-Economique-Politique', (Québec: 1942), para. 473.

Division of societies

While we may compare societies in many ways, the most important distinctions to draw pertain (i) to the end for which a society exists, and (ii) to the bond of union between its members.[10]

(i) Every created society exists for the sake of its end, and so the end is above all that by which the nature of a society is understood.[11] The end of a given society may be identical with man's ultimate end, beatitude, or it may be some lesser or partial end, such as happiness in this world, or the advance of learning, or the raising of children, or the pursuit of some trade or craft. This distinction gives rise to the distinction between perfect and imperfect societies, which, because of its importance, we shall consider separately below.

Again, still distinguishing societies by their ends, a society may be supernatural, when its specific goal exists by reason of God's elevation of mankind to a supernatural end; for example, a religious order which exists to communicate saving truth. Or it may be natural, when its specific goal does not depend on this elevation of mankind to the supernatural level; for example, a guild of teachers or physicians.

Again, the end of the society, and therefore the society itself, may be something *necessary*, whether in virtue of natural law, or of positive divine law, or even in virtue of some merely human law; or on the other hand, it may be an end which a man freely proposes to himself without being under any obligation. Thus the family, and the wider civil or political society are necessary by natural law; the Catholic Church is necessary by positive divine law; in time of war, the army may be necessary by human law for certain classes of people. On the other hand, a business or trade union or university or religious order, or a simple commercial contract entered into by a buyer and seller, are voluntary societies.[12]

Finally, we may also distinguish societies by reason of the relative dignity of their goals. In this respect, societies may be called equal or equivalent, when they have an end of the same worth, for example the United States of America

---

[10] Cf. A. Ottaviani, *Compendium Iuris Publici Ecclesiastici*, 4th edition (Rome: Vatican Press, 1954), 17-23.

[11] Hence the adage, *societates sunt ut fines*, "societies are as their ends are".

[12] It is characteristic of much modern political philosophy, following the example of Thomas Hobbes (1588-1679) and Jean-Jacques Rousseau (1712-1778), to ignore the essential distinction between voluntary and necessary societies and to treat all societies as voluntary. This distinction will be explained and justified when we consider the individual necessary societies.

and Malta, or two football teams; and unequal or non-equivalent, if one society has a specific goal which is worthier than another, for example Malta and the University of Oxford. If two equivalent societies are parts of some society that encompasses them both, like the States of the United States of America, or like two sovereign nations allied in a war, then they may be called co-ordinate societies. In the case of two non-equivalent societies, if one of them is part of another, like the University of Oxford and the United Kingdom, or if one exists for the sake of the other, like the civil service and the executive, then they are respectively subordinate and subordinating societies.

(ii) In virtue of the bond of union that unites its members, a society may be either juridical or non-juridical.[13] A society is juridical when membership of it implies rights and duties which must be recognised by law and which can therefore be upheld and enforced by those who enjoy authority either within it or within a wider society of which it is a part. Thus the United Kingdom is a juridical society; but so is a business, where one person contracts to work for another in return for pay. A group of friends who meet to discuss philosophy or to play darts is a non-juridical society. It is clear that every non-juridical society is also a voluntary society; however, not every juridical society is a necessary one.

Reason for society

Aristotle begins his *Politics* by noting that every society exists for the sake of some good. Why else would men associate if not to obtain something that will benefit them? Universal human experience manifests the desire for such association, and man's possession of speech suggests his aptitude for it, surpassing the aptitude of any other material creature for association with its fellows.[14] Hence, association among human beings is natural not only in the sense that each of us depends in fact for his existence, nurture and education on some prior association, but also in that it answers a desire of nature.

What is the deepest reason of this desire for association? All finite entities act toward ends established by their natures. By the very nature of a finite created entity, there is a real distinction within it between its existence (that it is) and

---

[13] Non-juridical societies are sometimes called 'friendly'. We prefer to avoid this word, since *every* society is a friendship. See below, pp. 15, 24.

[14] Cf. *Politics*, I.2: "For we assert that nature does nothing in vain; and man alone among the animals has speech."

its essence (what it is). It is this essence that limits and defines its being.[15] The absence of this distinction in God is the reason for His infinite and unlimited perfection.[16] As a consequence of the real distinction in creatures between essence and existence, the same essence can be realised in many ways and these many possible realisations express more or less perfectly the inherent perfectibility of each nature.[17] Although material perfections often exclude each other, yet all other things being equal, if two things are different one is better and the other worse.[18] Again, every created substance tends in virtue of its finitude and ontological dependence back into non-being,[19] but, in virtue of its act of being tends towards its continued existence, the continued existence of its kind and its own perfection in that kind.[20] The second and third of these three positive tendencies encompasses the preceding.

Since finite, creaturely perfection cannot include every perfection possible to the essence of the creature which attains it, the peace achieved by a creature will always be at best a merely relative bliss. Like a drowning man, the finite being reaches out to grasp the assistance of its fellow creatures to assist it in its threefold task of self-preservation, the preservation of its kind, and self-perfection. Nature supplies the love of the other by which this assistance will be granted:

> The very fact that two men are alike, having, as it were, one form, makes them to be, in a manner, one in that form [...]. Hence the

---

15 *Postquam sanctissimus,* 'Twenty-Four Thomistic Theses', Sacred Congregation of Studies, 1914, theses 1-3.

16 'Twenty-Four Thomistic Theses', thesis 23.

17 Among material things, the same essence may be simultaneously realised in many individuals. Among immaterial things, that is, angels, although only one individual of each species may exist, it does not in fact perform all of the actions of which it is capable. Cf. 'Twenty-Four Thomistic Theses', thesis 11.

18 St Thomas Aquinas, *Compendium Theologiae,* 73: "The basic diversity among things consists chiefly in diversity of forms. Formal diversity is achieved by way of contrariety; for genus is divided into various species by contrary differences. But order is necessarily found in contrariety, for among contraries one is always better than the other. Therefore diversity among things had to be established by God according to a definite order, in such a way that some beings might be more excellent than others."

19 St Athanasius, *De Incarnatione,* 4.

20 St Thomas Aquinas, *Compendium Theologiae,* 103: "The intellectual creature tends toward the divine likeness, not only in the sense that it preserves itself in existence, or that it multiplies its existence, in a way, by communicating it, but so that it may have in itself in act what by nature it possesses in potency."

affections of one tend to the other, as being one with him; and he wishes good to him as to himself.[21]

Thus arises friendship, which may be defined as 'the reciprocal willing of the good of another for the other's own sake'.[22] Since every society rests on the will that the other members enjoy with oneself the end for which that society exists, friendship is the foundation of every created society.[23]

Friendship seems indeed to be the highest 'complete' act available to a created being, insofar as it involves both an object of knowledge contained within the 'proper object' of the created intellect,[24] and also the highest form of love.[25]

To the created intellect, the existence of society thus appears to be a simple consequence of creaturely finitude. That man's need for and orientation to the other is also an intimation of the inner life of God is a truth entirely veiled from natural reason: the existence of the 'uncreated society' of the Most Holy Trinity is naturally unknowable to any created intellect. Yet not only does friendship offer to the created intelligence the possibility of compensating for the limitations of its own finite nature, albeit imperfectly; intelligent creatures also find a kind of ecstasy in the self-transcendence offered by friendship. This is an intimation of the truth revealed by the gospel, that friendship is a pure perfection, not a mixed one: that is, it is a perfection which implies no limitation in the one who possesses it.[26] For those who accept this revelation,

---

[21] St Thomas Aquinas, *Summa Theologiae* 1a 2ae 27, 3.

[22] Aristotle, *Nicomachean Ethics*, VIII.2: "Persons who wish another good for his own sake, if the feeling is not reciprocated, are merely said to feel goodwill for him: only when mutual is such goodwill termed friendship."

[23] Cf. Aristotle, *Nicomachean Ethics*, VIII.9: "In every society there seems to be some sort of justice, and some sort of friendship."

[24] The 'proper object' of a created intellect must be some creature at or below its own level of being; thus God and spiritual substances are not in this sense a proper object of the human intellect, being known only by analogy from material things. It is in this sense that natural knowledge and love of God (or of angels) are here described as 'incomplete'.

[25] St Thomas states that only the love of friendship is love simply speaking (*simpliciter*); the various forms of 'love of concupiscence', whether intellectual, sensible or natural, are love only 'in a certain respect' (*secundum quid*); cf. *Summa Theologiae*, 1a 2ae 26, 4. Creatures less than man also possess a certain gregariousness, for the reasons identified above, but they lack the conscious societal impulse which comes only with intelligence.

[26] Example of 'mixed perfections' are fluency in French or being a good runner of marathons: these perfections imply limitation in their possessor, since they can belong only to a bodily creature.

15

a society is possible in which friendship is not merely a remedy for creaturely finitude and deficiency but a participation in eternity.

What, then, are we to make of Aristotle's dictum that he who is no part of a city is either a beast or a god[27]; that is, as St Thomas glosses it, either bestial or else a 'divine man'?[28] Some vicious disposition may cause a person to shun company, but as with the other vices, this does not destroy the fundamental inclination of nature. Again, the Christian hermit who seeks solitude also retains this fundamental inclination: he renounces society not as if isolation were a good in itself, or a necessary concomitant of perfection, but for ascetic reasons, so that he may avoid the distractions by which the weakness of our fallen nature impedes the growth of charity. Yet he remains within the communion of saints, and he uses the solitude of a few years as an instrument to incorporate himself more firmly within that sempiternal society.

The perfect society

The phrase 'perfect society' is a translation of Aristotle's description of the city as κοινωνία τέλειος (koinonia teleios). This phrase may also be rendered 'complete community'. The city, he remarks, is the complete community which comes together from several villages. [29] Elsewhere he defines the city as "the community of families and villages in a complete and self-sufficient life".[30] Two things are thus included in the notion of the complete or perfect society: it has as its end the complete sufficiency of life, that is, a fullness of happiness for those who belong to it; and it possesses within itself all the means necessary for achieving that end.[31]

The opposite of a perfect society is an imperfect society. In calling a society 'imperfect', we do not mean that it is in some way faulty, but rather that its end is only some partial fulfilment of human life, and that it cannot contain within itself all the means necessary to ensure its end. For example, a trade union seeks not the complete temporal or eternal happiness of those who belong to it, but rather a just wage and decent conditions of work. Its end is thus something partial not complete, and so however excellent some trade union may be,

---

[27] *Politics*, I.2.

[28] *Summa Theologiae*, 2a 2ae 188, 8, ad 5.

[29] *Politics*, I.2.

[30] *Politics*, III.9.

[31] Grenier notes that older authors tended to define the perfect society by the first of these attributes, while those whom he calls moderns have tended to stress rather the second attribute; cf. H. Grenier, *Cours de Philosophie*, t. II, para. 476.

political philosophy will refer to it as an imperfect society. Again, such a society does not possess within itself all the means needed to acquire its end; for example, it cannot itself try and punish employers for injustice, but must rely on the courts of the wider society in which it operates.

Since an imperfect society has ends which it cannot wholly realise by its own resources, every imperfect society needs to exist within a perfect society, if it is not to be doomed to frustration. Hence, just as there is a natural inclination to live in society, so there is a natural inclination to belong to a perfect society. This also shows us that the notions of 'a society endowed with all the means needed to obtain its end' and 'a society whose end is the fullness of happiness' are co-extensive. If some society has an end which falls short of the fullness of happiness, its members will not be able to rest in their membership of it and peacefully pursue its proper activities until they believe themselves to form part of a society the end of which *does* encompass the fullness of happiness; hence the former society lacks the means whereby its members can suitably possess their end. Conversely, if a society lacks some of the means to obtain its end, its members will not be able to attain their end in that society alone, and hence that society alone will not be able to bring them to a fullness of happiness.

How many perfect societies exist in the world? The family is not such. Although in exceptional cases, a family may be able to survive in total isolation, such a life is liable to be materially and intellectually wretched.[32] For this reason, families have a natural inclination to unite in a higher unity, a desire which is frustrated by isolation.

What of the society that transcends the household, whether the Greek polis, or the modern 'sovereign state'?[33] Such societies may be called perfect in a certain respect, *secundum quid*.[34] After all, even if it is rare to find a country which furnishes its inhabitants with all the necessities of life directly by its own produce, most countries are able to do so by trading some of their produce, or at least by loans based on their likely future produce, and in this sense, they possess within themselves the *material* means which they need. Again, the very term 'sovereign' is used to express a fullness of power by which a country is

---

[32] A 20th century example is the Lykov family in Russia, which spent more than four decades in complete isolation.

[33] As mentioned above, Aristotle also postulates the 'village', as a natural society intervening between the family and the city; *Politics* I.2. See also below, p. 86.

[34] The phrase 'perfect society' is used to denote the *civilis congregatio* in Pius XI's encyclical, *Divini illius magistri* 12. See also STh 1a 2ae 90, 3 ad 3, where the *civitas* is called a *communitas perfecta* in comparison to the family, insofar as the father of the family lacks a strictly legislative power.

not intrinsically subordinate to any other county. Finally, the phrase 'perfect society' may be used of these entities to express the truth that there is within them a constant exercise of a power proper to itself which cannot be legally annulled by any higher power.[35]

However, this analysis is somewhat superficial. For as we have seen, in every order of providence, man would have needed divine revelation in order to have known his goal and therefore in order to have lived well on earth. Since man as a social animal desires to attain his goal in society, it follows that in every order of providence, there would have been some kind of 'church', that is, a society constituted and instructed by divine revelation, in which alone men could attain the divinely-appointed goal of their lives. Had man not sinned, there would have been in principle no reason why this 'church' need have been distinct from temporal society itself.[36]

We wish, however, to consider our race as it actually exists, fallen in Adam and redeemed by Christ. The purpose of the Incarnation was that, satisfaction being made for sin, man might be led to the supernatural end appointed to him by God, and to a life beyond this world. Yet without the spiritual power of teaching and sanctifying brought to earth by the Word incarnate, man lacks the intellectual and moral resources to attain even his natural end. This is for at least five reasons.

First, we have an absolute need from the moment that reason is awakened within us to know what our end is, and what the path is that leads to it, and this natural desire can be quenched only by revelation.

Secondly, without knowledge of his ultimate end, man cannot correctly pursue even those elements of his end which he is able to grasp by natural reason. For example, he is liable in pursuing the natural goal of education, to exhaust his time and energy in learning only natural truths while neglecting the study of sacred doctrine. Still more importantly, he is unable to fulfil what he can nevertheless know by reason to be his primordial duty, namely to offer acceptable worship to his Creator, since he must learn from God how God

---

[35] Pope Paul VI, *Sollicitudo omnium ecclesiarum*, 1969: "It is not to be denied that the ends proposed to the Church and to commonwealths (*rebus publicis*) are of different orders, nor that the Church and the city (*civitatem*) are perfect societies, each in its own order."

[36] Francisco Suarez (1548-1617) observed: "It would have been necessary [in the state of innocence] for men to have had some common and in fact external rule of faith, so that they might perpetually preserve the same faith and worship God in accordance with it, not only privately, but also by the public cultus of the whole community or Church"; *De opere sex dierum*, Bk. 5 c. 7, 6.

18

wishes to be worshipped. Since this is a matter that depends on the good pleasure of God, it cannot be discerned by human reason.

Thirdly, the disorder introduced into the human mind by the Fall means that men cannot in practice attain the intellectual perfection of which their nature, abstractly considered, is capable.[37]

Fourthly, without the spiritual power, men have not the moral resources to attain to the elements of their natural good which they discern by reason. Fallen man cannot exercise natural virtue consistently, or keep the commands of natural law entirely, by the power of nature alone.[38] To do these things, he must be justified, that is, endowed with sanctifying grace, which comes from the preaching of the word of God and the sacraments of the Church. Again, until he has been justified, he cannot fulfil the duty which he has under natural law of offering acceptable worship to God, since the worship offered by one at enmity with God cannot be called acceptable, even if the divine mercy does not leave such worship wholly unrewarded.

Fifthly, since according to the teaching of theology, each human being who reaches the age of reason is touched by actual grace, and thereby proportioned to a supernatural end,[39] no society generated by nature alone, even if it could *per impossibile* be enriched with every blessing and kept free from all fault, can in fact bring him complete fulfilment, and a happiness which he would experience as fully satisfying. Hence Aristotle, having sketched the life of the

---

[37] 1st Vatican Council, *Dei Filius*, cap. II: "It is to be ascribed to this divine revelation, that those things which in divine matters are of themselves not impenetrable to human reason, can, even in the present condition of mankind, be known by everyone with facility, with firm assurance, and with no admixture of error." This is true of man in society as well as of man as an individual, as St Thomas More sought to illustrate in *Utopia*. Cf. P. Duhamel, 'Medievalism in More's *Utopia*' in *Studies in Philology*, 52/2 (1955), 99-126.

[38] Cf. Council of Trent, *Decree on Justification*, can. 2: "If any one saith, that the grace of God, through Jesus Christ, is given only for this, that man may be able more easily to live justly, and to merit eternal life, as if, by free will without grace, he were able to do both, though hardly indeed and with difficulty; let him be anathema"; can. 22: "If any one saith, that the justified, either is able to persevere, without the special help of God, in the justice received; or that, with that help, he is not able; let him be anathema"; Leo XIII, *Testem benevolentiae*, January 22nd 1899: "To preserve in its entirety the law of the natural order requires an assistance from on high"; *Summa Theologiae*, 1a 2ae, 109, 4: "In the state of corrupted nature man cannot fulfil all the divine commandments without healing grace."

[39] Cf. St Thomas Aquinas, supplement to the *Summa Theologiae*, appendix 1, q. 1, a. 2: "Whether unbaptised children experience some spiritual affliction in their soul". The text is taken from the *Scriptum super Sententias*, II d. 33, 2, 2.

virtuous and lucky citizen, says wistfully that such people are "blessed - yet blessed as men are".[40]

What follows from this? Temporal society, meaning by this phrase, 'the widest community generated by nature', does not contain within itself all the means needed to obtain its end, as a perfect community must. Even in a hypothetical order of pure nature, man's perfect society would be a 'church', as already mentioned; but for fallen man, called to a supernatural end, temporal society is much less competent to be a perfect society in the strict sense of the term.

Hence only the Catholic Church is properly speaking and intrinsically a perfect society. For her end is beatitude: the vision of God in union with Christ and the saints. When attained, this brings complete fulfilment and a happiness experienced as wholly satisfying: first for the soul alone, and then, after the resurrection, for the whole man. Again, the Church contains within herself the means necessary to bring us to this end: the deposit of faith as guarded by an infallible magisterium, the indefectible apostolic succession, and the sacraments of grace. Since grace presupposes and perfects nature, the Church is also entitled to possess the natural resources necessary to sustain us in this mortal life as we seek for beatitude: hence her official organs have an indefeasible right, belonging to her by her constitution and not by the grant of any human government, to possess property,[41] to educate her baptised children,[42] to try by her own judges offences against her common good,[43] and to punish such offences either by her own officers or by calling on the

---

[40] Cf. *Nicomachean Ethics*, Bk. I.10: "μαχαρίους... μαχαρίους δ' ἀνθρώπους".

[41] CIC, canon 1259: "The Church can acquire temporal goods by every just means of natural or positive law permitted to others"; canon 1260: "The Church has an innate right to require from the Christian faithful those things which are necessary for the purposes proper to her."

[42] Pius XI, *Divini illius Magistri* 15-17: "Education belongs pre-eminently to the Church, by reason of a double title in the supernatural order, conferred exclusively upon her by God Himself; absolutely superior therefore to any other title in the natural order. The first title is founded upon the express mission and supreme authority to teach, given her by her divine Founder. [...] The second title is the supernatural motherhood, in virtue of which the Church, spotless spouse of Christ, generates, nurtures and educates souls in the divine life of grace."

[43] CIC 1401: "By proper and exclusive right the Church adjudicates: (1) cases which regard spiritual matters or those connected to spiritual matters; (2) the violation of ecclesiastical laws and all those matters in which there is a question of sin, in what pertains to the determination of culpability and the imposition of ecclesiastical penalties."

assistance of civil officers who recognise her authority.[44] This implies that she has the right to temporal power itself: not as if her ordained ministers were to wield the material sword or to judge of temporal matters, but in the sense that this temporal power must be held by baptised Catholics and put at the service of the highest common good. Rather than speak of 'Church and State' as two perfect societies, it is thus more exact to say that there is but one perfect society, the Church or city of God, in which two powers, spiritual and temporal, are hierarchically arranged. The very word 'State', suggesting as it does a complete society corresponding adequately to man's natural end, appears in fact fatally misleading.[45]

Within the one perfect society, we can speak of a temporal society or commonwealth which is made up of the same members, and hence is materially co-extensive with the Church, though formally distinct from her.[46] This temporal society is Christendom and the realms of which it is composed. These may be described as extrinsically perfect societies, in that as long as the Church resides within them with the fullness of her rights, they possess perfection: but it is a perfection which in order to possess they must submit to the higher power which transcends them. Conversely Christendom exists within the Church in that it exists only by this very ordering of the temporal power to the Church's spiritual power. Considered apart from this spiritual

---

[44] See below pp. 232-35, 250. Evidently, the Church does not always in fact enjoy the natural resources in question; she remains nevertheless a perfect society *de iure*, cf. A. Ottaviani, *Compendium* 27-28.

[45] The word forms no part of St Thomas's political theory. Likewise, although it is often used in English translations of the political writings of Leo XIII, he does not use the word *Status*, which is not classical in this sense. In *Immortale Dei*, one finds instead words and phrases such as *civitas, respublica, potestas publica, principatus, civilis hominum communitas, cives in societate, res civilis, potestas publica,* each of which is rendered as 'State' by one common English translation. The word is used in the *Syllabus of Errors* in its modern sense, but in order to condemn the proposition that 'the Church is to be separated from the state (*statu*) and the state from the Church' (no. 55).

[46] Cf. Leo XIII, *Immortale Dei*: "The Almighty, therefore, has given the charge of the human race to two powers, the ecclesiastical and the civil, the one being set over divine, and the other over human, things. Each in its kind is supreme, each has fixed limits within which it is contained, limits which are defined by the nature and special object of the province of each, so that there is, we may say, an orbit traced out within which the action of each is brought into play by its own native right."

21

power, it is not a distinct perfect society, but an impossibility.[47] Christendom may therefore be defined as the temporal aspect of the city of God.

Thus the ideal of which Plato dreamt, not without irony, of a republic in which the highest aspirations of man might be satisfied is achieved; but only as "that republic whose founder and ruler is Christ".[48]

---

[47] Speaking of the impossibility of a universal society which fails to meet the demands of the Church concerning the true religion and the one Church of Christ, Etienne Gilson (1884-1978) remarks: "Demain, dans un siècle, dans dix siècles, ils diront peut-être encore que le moyen qu'on leur propose est inacceptable, mais alors comme aujourd'hui ce ne sera toujours pour eux qu'une autre manière de dire qu'ils ne veulent pas véritablement la fin. Car c'est la fin qui commande. La cité des hommes ne peut s'élever, à l'ombre de la croix, que comme le faubourg de la Cité de Dieu" ("tomorrow, in a century, in ten centuries, they will perhaps still say that the means we propose are unacceptable, but just as today this will still only be another way for them to say that they do not truly desire the end. For it is the end which commands. The human city cannot be built, in the shadow of the cross, other than as the suburb of the City of God"); E. Gilson, *Les Métamorphoses de la Cité de Dieu*, (Paris: J. Vrin, 1952), 291.

[48] Cf. St Augustine, *City of God*, II.21.

Theses

(i)   Politics is the study of the highest good, proportionate to human nature, which may be obtained on earth.

(ii)   Politics must be instructed by divine revelation.

(iii)   A society is a plurality of intelligent subjects together with the relation which they have among themselves in acting for a common end.

(iv)   Societies may be compared either in respect of their different ends, or in respect of the bond of union between their members.

(v)   In respect of their different ends, societies are necessary or voluntary; natural and supernatural; perfect and imperfect.

(vi)   In respect of the bond of union between their members, societies are juridical or non-juridical.

(vii)   Friendship is the foundation of every created society.

(viii)   Divine revelation instructs us that friendship and life within society are pure perfections and not principally remedies for creaturely imperfection.

(ix)   A perfect society is one whose end is the complete good for man available within a given order of providence and which therefore contains within itself all the means necessary to achieve its end.

(x)   An imperfect society is one whose end is some partial good and partial happiness, and which does not contain within itself all the means necessary to achieve its end.

(xi)   In every order of providence, there would have been some kind of 'church', that is, a society constituted and instructed by divine revelation, either identical with or presiding over the society generated by the end proportionate to man's nature.

(xii)   In our order of providence, only the city of God, that is, the Catholic Church, is strictly a perfect society.

(xiii)   Christendom is not a distinct perfect society, but the temporal aspect of the city of God.

Chapter 2

The Common Good and Authority

Common and private goods

We may next consider the total activity of a given society. This is composed of the activities of each person within it, though only insofar as he is within it: for example, the work that a bank-clerk does in the bank forms part of the activity of the society which is the bank, but what he does at home generally does not. Hence, the achievement of the end of a given society may require very much less than the entire resources of each of its members. It is those actions that are ordered to that end, and that are undertaken on the basis of common interest and in friendship, which constitute the proper activity of that society as such. On the other hand, actions for that same end which are *merely* the 'instrumentalization' of some person's labour, for example, actions performed by an employee or slave against his own interests and simply to enrich his master, are not part of the proper activity of the society: for the master and the 'instrumentalized' person have as such no friendship, and hence no society.[1]

Closely related to the activity of a society is the notion of the common good. This notion is more restricted than that of 'shared good'. A common good is a good which can be shared *entirely* by several persons. Thus when several persons share a cake, the cake is not a common good, for no one person can have the whole of it. But when several persons enjoy together some work of art or philosophy, this work is a common good; the enjoyment which one person receives from the work does not lessen that of the others, and may even increase it. Hence, the notion of 'common good' applies directly to spiritual things, such as truth or beauty, which of their nature may be possessed by many without diminution. Common goods are not harmed as such by being shared and are often enhanced.[2] Since the spiritual good is attainable only by the intelligence, and since the intellect is man's highest faculty, man's highest goods

---

[1] Cf. *Nicomachean Ethics*, Bk. 8.11: "Where ruler and ruled have nothing in common, they have no friendship [. . .] insofar as he is a slave, then, there is no friendship with him."

[2] It should be noted, however, that the material conditions in which a common good is realised may mean that it is compromised by a disproportionate number of participants, for example, the truth which many people are discussing may be grasped less perfectly by each because people interrupt each other or talk at cross-purposes, or football, which like other games (although to a greater degree) may instantiate the spiritual good which is beauty, may be less perfectly realised by a team greatly exceeding eleven players.

are all common. Material things, by contrast, are always diminished by being shared.

It is because a common good is not diminished by being participated in by more than one person that it can be the end of a society. Only on the basis of such a good can one reciprocally will the good of another for the other's own sake. Were the good which is the end of a society to be something which *is* diminished by being shared, the participation in that good by one person would diminish it for the other participants and so harm them. As this is contrary to the identification of selves which is friendship and the ground of society, nothing less than a common, that is, a spiritual, good can ever be the basis of any society. Thus even a bank, if it is to be indeed a society simply speaking, and not a group of people who associate from avarice or necessity, must propose to itself some spiritual end, such as the rights of property or the just distribution of goods.

In contrast to the common good is the private good. This is a good which can only be fully possessed by one person, and so is directly diminished by being shared. Private good is therefore identical, in reality though not in concept, to material good. Material goods, as necessary to human life in the present age, must be provided if the higher goods of human life and human society are to be attained. On the other hand, to permit the private good to hold primacy over the common good would be to subordinate ends to means and reduce man and human society to a bestial condition.[3] It would also be fatal to human society and so to man himself. This is because private goods, being diminished by participation, generate irreconcilable opposition when sought for their own sake. Even some 'convention of civility'[4], such as the market, undertaken in order to facilitate the production and distribution of private goods could not survive the subordination of the common to the private; for if the members of

---

[3] Or indeed, to a diabolical condition. The devil fell by clutching at the common good of beatitude as if it could be his private good. Cf. St Augustine, *City of God* XII.1: "While some steadfastly continued in that which was the common good of all, namely, in God Himself, and in His eternity, truth, and love; others, being enamoured rather of their own power, as if they could be their own good, lapsed to this private good of their own (*ad propria defluxerunt*) from that higher and beatific good which was common to all."

[4] That is, some rules, which may be unspoken, by which parties elect for some further, possibly private, goal to treat each other as if they willed the other's good for his own sake, but which prescind from the question of whether they truly do so.

25

such a society sought only the private good, then they would sacrifice the common good to the private whenever they could do so with impunity.[5]

It is, of course, possible to use the phrase 'common good' in a different way. Some authors include within it all the things which are available in principle to be used by all the persons within some society; in this sense, highways, universities, libraries, the internet, parks, and so on, would be part of the common good of a country. Although such a notion of the common good is useful for certain purposes, for example judging the harmfulness of an act of criminal damage, it is a 'materialization' of the philosophical notion. Such material things which are in fact put at the disposition of all members of a society may be called 'public goods'.[6] They are however in the philosophical sense essentially private and not common, since they cannot be fully possessed by many.[7]

Extrinsic and intrinsic ends of society

The extrinsic end or good of a society is simply the end for which its members, as members, act. The intrinsic end or good of a society is the ordering which those who belong to the society have among themselves as they act for the extrinsic end. The intrinsic good of a society is the life of the society itself, which is shared without being diminished. However, this intrinsic common good cannot exist on its own because there must be some reason *this* society exists rather than *that* and this reason must itself be a common good, since otherwise the common good would be subordinated to the private, and the existence of the society itself become harmful to its members. The extrinsic common good generates the intrinsic, but also cannot survive without it.

For example, let us imagine two men playing chess, who associate with each other only for this reason, not even speaking the same language. A genuine society exists between them which is desired and delighted in for itself, in virtue

---

[5] A point rather eloquently expressed by Réginald Garrigou-Lagrange (1877-1964) in *The Three Ways of the Spiritual Life* (London: Burns, Oates and Washbourne, 1938), 3-4.

[6] *Gaudium et spes* seems to include such shared goods when it says that the common good is "the sum of those conditions of the social life whereby men, families and associations more adequately and readily may attain their own perfection"; GS 74; cf. GS 26.

[7] Is the virtuous act or habit of some person, e.g. John's knowledge of geometry or act of temperance, a common good or a private one? It is true that no one else can possess the numerically identical act or habit. However, such an act or habit is good only in the sense of causing John to participate in something which *can* be possessed by many, such as geometry or temperance. It therefore contributes to the common good: the society as a whole, and therefore all within it, are perfected thereby.

of the extrinsic common good of chess, that is, a beauty of a certain kind and range. Should one or both of these men lose interest in chess and cease to play it, their society would necessarily perish, having no other extrinsic common good. Doubtless, some further extrinsic common good might have been acquired meanwhile, for example, bridge or backgammon. In this way, the society between the two men might survive the loss of interest in chess; yet it will not be the same society.

Again, we may imagine two school friends who had lost touch for years, who meet again in the army in time of war. Little or nothing survives of what they had in common as boys but now they have the new common good of a just victory and, it turns out, much else besides. The war is won, and they return to civilian life, but their friendship endures because of the other things they discovered they had in common during their service. But the nature of their friendship – of the society between them – has differed through three distinct phases of their lives.

The most eloquent expression of the bond between the extrinsic and intrinsic ends of a society is marriage. So true is it that the common life of the spouses *qua* spouses is derived from the extrinsic common good which is the procreation and education of children, that two persons who exclude this good cannot validly contract the bond of matrimony or enjoy a familial life.

The correct pursuit of the extrinsic end ensures that its intrinsic end will be attained. Thus in a household where all carry out their duties of state, duties which flow from the very nature of the family, the parents, offspring, and siblings, and household-servants if there are such, are justly related one to another, each receiving from the others what is due to him. This just ordering, considered as enabling the members of the society to attain its extrinsic end by removing causes of quarrel between them and reasons for mental trouble within any one member, is called peace. It is in this sense that St Thomas can say that peace, defined by St Augustine as the tranquillity of order, is what rulers must chiefly pursue.[8] Again, considered as springing from the mutual

---

[8] *De Regno*, ch. 3. Cf. C. S. Lewis's inaugural lecture from the Chair of Mediaeval and Renaissance Studies at Cambridge University, *De Descriptione Temporum*, given in 1954: "In all previous ages that I can think of the principal aim of rulers, except at rare and short intervals, was to keep their subjects quiet, to forestall or extinguish widespread excitement and persuade people to attend quietly to their several occupations. And on the whole their subjects agreed with them. They even prayed (in words that sound curiously old-fashioned) to be able to live 'a peaceable life in all godliness and honesty' and 'pass their time in rest and quietness.' But now the organization of mass excitement seems to be almost the normal organ of political power. We live in an age of 'appeals,' 'drives,' and 'campaigns.'

willing of the good between members of the society, this just ordering may be called friendship. Hence Aristotle writes:

> Friendship would seem to hold cities together, and legislators would seem to be more concerned about it than about justice. For concord would seem to be similar to friendship, and they aim at concord among all, while they try above all to expel civil conflict, which is enmity.[9]

Each kind of society has its own specific ordering: for example, the order proper to a football team, or to a fire brigade. But a more general order will be common to all societies, because necessary for the common life of any society. Thus, all members of a society must recognise and pursue its extrinsic common good and the means essential to it; all must render unto each other their due, willing their good for their own sake and not seeking to appropriate each other's private good; all must develop a rational desire for private goods which is moderated by their actual needs and subordinated to the common good, since otherwise they will be unable to render to each his due, or to abstain from seeking to appropriate each other's private good. Lastly, as the willing of another's good for the other's own sake necessitates in principle the supreme sacrifice, it is not possible to belong securely to any society or possess any of the preceding dispositions unless one is willing at least in principle to exercise them to an heroic degree. Accordingly, no society can survive unless its members are willing to give their lives to defend their fellows. The dispositions known as prudence, justice, temperance and fortitude are accordingly intrinsically necessary elements of any friendship and society.

The common good and the good of the members

There are two ways of conceiving the relation of the good of a society to the good of its members. The first way, characteristic of the modern West, is to regard it as a merely 'instrumental' good. On this view, the good of the society is less valuable than the private good of those who compose the society, being merely an instrument to achieve these private goods. Thus, the bank would

---

Our rulers have become like schoolmasters and are always demanding 'keenness.' And you notice that I am guilty of a slight archaism in calling them 'rulers.' 'Leaders' is the modern word. I have suggested elsewhere that this is a deeply significant change of vocabulary. Our demand upon them has changed no less than theirs on us. For of a ruler one asks justice, incorruption, diligence, perhaps clemency; of a leader, dash, initiative, and (I suppose) what people call 'magnetism' or 'personality'."

[9] *Nicomachean Ethics*, VIII.1.

aim at its goal of extending a just affluence merely in order to enhance the individual wealth of its shareholders, or the army would aim at its goal of just victory in war solely in order to provide employment for low-skilled personages of violent temperament. This view, while clearly selfish or irrational in connexion with such societies as these, may appear correct in the case of civil society – does not civil society exist in order that individual people and families may be happy? Yet this objection is based on a misunderstanding. It rests in particular on what was called above a 'materialization' of the notion of the common good, whereby the latter is identified with the material goods generally available to the members of some society. Taken to its logical conclusion this distorted conception of civil society would imply that nepotism, far from being a social pathology, is the proper attitude of the individual to his 'public duties'.

The other view of the relation of the good of a society to that of its members is that of Aristotle and St Thomas, who hold that the former is necessarily higher than the latter. Hence the saying that the common good is better and more divine than the good of one.[10] This expression itself contains two truths. In one sense, it is a statement of the superiority of the common good over the private good, that is, of the spiritual over the material. In another sense, the 'good of one' includes the spiritual goods in which a given person participates, and the dictum that the common good is more divine indicates that it is better that many participate in them than one alone. In either sense, the term 'common good' never signifies a merely instrumental good. It is itself a 'noble' or 'virtuous good' and not merely a 'useful' one; a *bonum honestum* in St Thomas's language, and not merely a *bonum utile*; what Aristotle calls *kalon* or 'fine'.

Let us imagine a flourishing, independent city, such as Aristotle sketches at the end of his *Politics*, though without its pagan blemishes. The citizens are free, self-governing, physically healthy, possessed of a sufficiency but not an excess of material things, instructed in worthwhile knowledge, virtuous, and apt for noble friendships. The extrinsic common good of this city is the truth,

---

[10] Cf. *Nicomachean Ethics*, I.2: "While it is satisfactory to acquire and preserve the good even for an individual, it is finer and more divine to acquire and preserve it for a people and for cities"; St Thomas Aquinas, *Commentary on the Nicomachean Ethics*, Bk. 1 lect. 2: "This is said to be more divine because it shows greater likeness to God who is the ultimate cause of all good"; *Commentary on the Politics*, Bk. 1 lect. 1: "The common good [...] is better and more divine than the good of one individual, as is stated in the beginning of the Ethics." Cf. STh 1a 2ae 109, 3: "It is obvious that the good of a part is for the sake of the good of the whole."

goodness and beauty by knowing and loving which they are perfected. Its intrinsic common good is the ordering or life which they possess among themselves as they pursue these transcendent things. Composed thus of the happiness of all the citizens, this common good is something greater than the happiness of any one of them: this why any of its citizens, even if he be the wisest and most blessed among them, may virtuously give up his life in war to preserve the city.

The common good of a society is common not only in the sense of deriving from the activities of all the members, but also in the sense of belonging to them all. We should not imagine a society as if were somehow a being separated from the persons who compose it, and the common good as the good of a society imagined as such a separated being. Nor, evidently, should we suppose that the common good is the good proper to the governing element of the society. Precisely because it is the good of the society as such, it is the good of all the persons who compose it. If this were not so, then either the good in question would not genuinely be common or else the person in question would not genuinely be part of that society. Thus, in the flourishing city just mentioned, each of the citizens not only possesses his own share in knowledge and virtue, which will be greater and lesser in different citizens; each of them also possesses the excellence of the city as his own. The boy in such a city who is still learning his lessons and being instructed by his parents in the rudiments of civility possesses a certain perfection lacking to a fully virtuous man in a depraved society elsewhere: the perfection of being a part of an excellent whole.

What of the objection that political society, whether an ancient *polis* or a modern 'sovereign state', exists for the good of the persons and families within it, and hence that the common good is subordinated to their goods?[11] This forgets that an important part of the good life for persons and families consists precisely in belonging to a flourishing political society; indeed, insofar as the City of God is our supernatural *polis*, the *whole* of the good life for rational beings consists in belonging to a flourishing 'political' society.

While it is true that every temporal commonwealth exists by nature for the perfection of the families and persons within it, this happens not by subordinating the good of the whole to the good of a part, which would be absurd, but by enabling the part to be perfected by taking its proper place

---

[11] This appears to be the position of I. Gonzalez, author of the treatise on 'Ethics', in the comprehensive philosophy manual produced by the Spanish Jesuits in the 1950's; *Philosophiae Scholasticae Summa*, vol. 3: (Madrid: Biblioteca de Autores Cristianos, 1957), t. 2, 'Ethica', s. 3, c. 3, para. 1021-22, 1031.

within the whole. The good of a part as such lies in being well ordered toward its whole; hence the good of a person who belongs to a society, insofar as he belongs to it, is to tend toward its common good. As a naturally social animal, man can only attain his proper good in society. Hence, although he may form many associations which bring him only a very partial fulfilment, the good of that society which encompasses all others must be identical with the good of each of its individual members.

It is true that we can say, with Pope Pius XI, that 'the city is for man and not man for the city'.[12] This aphorism contains several truths. First, man is not for the city as if any society were an entity separated from the citizens who compose it, a sort of hypostasised tyrant whose good would be imagined simply as its private good, and not the common good of the members. Again, man is not for the city in the sense that citizens do not exist in order that there should exist parliaments, a civil service, a judiciary and so on; rather, these institutions exist in order that men should be perfected by them - yet not just as individual men, but rather as men forming an excellent society.[13]

Finally, this papal aphorism indicates that man has a supernatural end, which infinitely transcends the good of any natural society. Not even the most outstanding such society could have the right to preserve itself at the cost of the faith, hope or charity of a single citizen. Yet the principle of subordination of part to whole reappears on the supernatural level: the beatitude of each saint in heaven is a lesser good than the beatitude of the communion of saints, and each saint is perfected by belonging to the heavenly city and by possessing, in the manner proper to a part, this city's proper good. Moreover, each saint loves the good of the heavenly city more than his own good, and if *per impossibile* there could be occasion for him to renounce the latter for the sake of the former, he would not hesitate to do so.[14] Man is for the heavenly city.

---

[12] *Divini Redemptoris*, 29.

[13] "As long as we are thinking only of natural values we must say that the sun looks down on nothing half so good as a household laughing together over a meal, or two friends talking over a pint of beer, or a man alone reading a book that interests him; and that all economics, politics, laws, armies, and institutions, save insofar as they prolong and multiply such scenes, are a mere ploughing the sand and sowing the ocean, a meaningless vanity and vexation of spirit"; C.S. Lewis, 'Membership' in *Essay Collection: Faith, Christianity and the Church*, ed. L. Walmsley (London: HarperCollins, 2000).

[14] Cf. Rom. 9:3.

Nature and origin of authority

The co-ordinated activity of defectible persons toward a common good postulates some authority. Again, it is proper to man to come to know through the senses and to develop virtues by habituation, and hence, short of the unique episode of special creation, every man is preceded by the society of his parents which is in turn supported by the society that surrounds it. Education and discipline are thus intrinsic to human society and so there must be authority to legislate, enforce and judge. These are natural necessities, which therefore derive from the author of nature. In this sense, the authority which regulates human society, provided it take some form consistent with nature, derives from God, and those who resist it resist God. Were it not for the social nature of man, no human excellence would allow a person to assume government, or to have it bestowed upon him. As Pope Leo XIII asserts: "No man has in himself or of himself that whereby he may bind the free will of others by the bonds of command".[15]

Authority is often defined as a right to command,[16] although some authors prefer to say more precisely that the essence of authority is a certain elevation

---

[15] Cf. *Diuturnum* 11-12: "Nature, or rather God who is the Author of nature, wills that man should live in a civil society; and this is clearly shown both by the faculty of language, the greatest medium of intercourse, and by numerous innate desires of the mind, and the many necessary things, and things of great importance, which men isolated cannot procure, but which they can procure when joined and associated with others. But now, a society can neither exist nor be conceived in which there is no one to govern the wills of individuals, in such a way as to make, as it were, one will out of many, and to impel them rightly and orderly to the common good; therefore, God has willed that in a civil society there should be some to rule the multitude. And this also is a powerful argument, that those by whose authority the State is administered must be able so to compel the citizens to obedience that it is clearly a sin in the latter not to obey. But no man has in himself or of himself the power of constraining the free will of others by fetters of authority of this kind. This power resides solely in God, the Creator and Legislator of all things; and it is necessary that those who exercise it should do it as having received it from God. 'There is one lawgiver and judge, who is able to destroy and deliver'."

[16] For example, J. Gredt, *Elementa Philosophiae Aristotelico-Thomisticae*, vol. II, 'Metaphysica & Ethica' (Barcelona: Herder, 1946), para. 1007: "Auctoritas est ... potestas moralis (ius) praecipiendi" ("authority is the moral power (right) of commanding")'; A. Ottaviani, *Compendium Iuris Publici Ecclesiastici*, 32, defines authority as: 'Ius obligandi socios in ordine ad consecutionem finis" ("the right to command the members [of the society] in reference to attaining the end".

of one above another, and that the right to command is a property of it.[17] We need not delay on this question, which is more verbal than substantive.

The question of the origin of authority is one of the most important in political philosophy.[18] To answer it, we must first distinguish between authority in itself, and authority as existing in some ruler: that is, we must distinguish the questions, "How does authority of a certain kind come to be found in a certain kind of society, for example, in a family or a university?", and "How does *this* person come to possess the authority proper to this kind of society?"

In regard to the former question, since authority is necessary in every juridical society, the cause of that society is at the same time the cause of the authority proper to it.[19] Here we may recall the distinction made above between necessary and voluntary societies. When men form a voluntary, though juridical, society, their free will is the cause of the authority that exists within it, just as their free will, with no obligation of law, brings the society itself into existence. For this reason, they may give to their rulers as much or as little authority as they wish, and as is consistent with any other laws to which they may be subject. For example, if men come together to form a university, they may distribute the offices within it as they please.

When, by contrast, men form a society as being required to by some pre-existing law, whether the law be human, natural, or divine, then the nature of the authority that will exist in that society is defined by the pre-existing law. For example, a government that conscripts citizens to an army also establishes the ranks within it and the power that belongs to each. When primitive political societies merge into a larger *polis*, natural law establishes that there will now be within this new society an authority to enforce justice in their commercial transactions and to forbid at least the grosser public vices, since without such an authority, the end of the society could not be reached. When the Holy Spirit was sent upon the apostles at Pentecost, the law of Christ determined that there would be within the Church an authority to teach, sanctify and govern.[20]

---

[17] This is the position taken by Henri Grenier; cf. H. Grenier, *Cours de Philosophie*, t. II, 'Monastique-Économique-Politique', (Quebec, 1942), para. 477.

[18] We are speaking in this section of the authority of one person over another within a society. In a wider sense we talk about the authority of a book, a tradition, and so on.

[19] Cf. A. Ottaviani, *Compendium*, 33.

[20] Thinkers such as Hobbes and Rousseau, by rejecting the distinction between voluntary and necessary societies, and treating all societies as equally voluntary, make all authority to derive from the human will. Their position will be considered more fully later on.

As to how individual bearers of authority are determined, we must consider whether those who form the society are subject to some pre-existing claim which obliges them to recognise certain men as those whom they are to obey. In the case of a voluntary society, it is clear that they are not: since they were under no obligation to enter or create the society, but were able to fashion it according to their will, so they are able to fashion it as having this or that person as their ruler. In this case, the men who compose it transfer some part of their authority to govern themselves to those whom they select to rule them, and to those who will legally succeed these rulers.

In the case of a necessary society, a pre-existing right or the nature of the society itself sometimes determines who bears the authority within it.[21] For example, when Christ established the Catholic Church as a necessary society, He established St Peter and the apostles under him as its first rulers, and established that these rulers and their successors could to a certain extent establish the norms for choosing their successors until the end of the world. Likewise, by making the family a society necessary for the human race, at least in general, God appointed the husband as the ruler of the wife, and the parents as the rulers of their children. By contrast, when a distinct temporal society became necessary for man after the Fall, God did not make comprehensive provision for the appointment of its rulers; hence, when households, hitherto sovereign by default, come together to form such a society, the heads of these households may establish a sovereign as they will, and arrange the organs of sovereignty as they will. The *scope* of the sovereign's authority, however, is determined by natural law, and not by their free choice.[22]

As we have seen, man cannot in any order of providence reach even his natural end, even if this end be in fact his true final end in that order, without divine revelation. Hence the kinds of authority that derive from nature must be perfected by an authority instituted by such revelation, and they remain in some way only provisional without it.[23] This latter authority, in our order of providence, is called spiritual, and since the Fall, is distinct from temporal authority: since the first Pentecost it has belonged to the hierarchy of the Catholic Church.

---

[21] Cf. A. Ottaviani, *Compendium*, 35.

[22] For a fuller discussion of individual cases, see chapters 3 and 6.

[23] This fact is suggested by the celebrated letter of Pope Gelasius to the Emperor Anastasius I in which he refers to kings as possessing *potestas* and spiritual rulers as possessing *auctoritas*. See below, p. 72

Since authority exists to bring those under it to some good end, it is naturally loveable, and is, in fact, naturally loved.[24] Someone endowed with authority may abuse it, either by giving commands contrary to the commands of a higher authority, or by giving commands in matters which exceed his competence. In the former case, as happens whenever a man commands something contrary to natural or divine law, he must be disobeyed, or to speak more precisely, his command must not be executed, in order to preserve true obedience. In the second case, when a person simply gives a command outside his authority, for example, a teacher who tells his pupils to rise at a certain hour in the morning, his command may *per se* be lawfully either executed or not.

Rights and pseudo-rights

We have seen that activity for a common good requires that the members of a society possess the virtue of justice. When two people play chess, the common good which is chess cannot be attained if one of them moves the pieces when the other is not looking: to the extent that one of the players cheats, the game of chess does not exist. For any created society, the extrinsic end to be attained sets limits to the ways in which the members may act toward each other. The limits may be broad; thus, many legitimate moves are available to players of chess. The virtue of justice inclines each member to act within these limits so that the common goal may exist.

Since the goal of every society delimits the just relations that may exist between its members, this goal provides the foundation of all the genuine rights belonging to those within it. The term 'right' corresponds to the Greek *dikaion* and to the Latin *ius*. Both these terms, as used by Aristotle and St Thomas, refer to some *thing* or *act* which one person or group owes to another within a given society.[25] A simple example is the transitory 'society' of buyer and seller. If one person offers a loaf of bread for sale, and another person requests the loaf and gives to him the price of it, then that loaf becomes the latter's *ius* or right. Again, within a family, by virtue of its nature and natural end, acts of obedience from his son are the *ius* of the father, and acts of instruction from

---

[24] The view of authority entertained by the perennial philosophy is therefore to be sharply distinguished both from what might be called the 'liberal' conception of authority in which any good it affords is entirely outweighed by the good of liberty, such that each man should be free to do whatever he wills that does not impede another in the same freedom, and from what might be called the 'libertarian' position in which authority as such is an evil and should exist at all only when a necessary evil.

[25] Cf. *Nicomachean Ethics*, V.2-8; *Summa Theologiae* 2a 2ae, 57.

his father, performed personally or by proxy, are the *ius* of the son.[26] Since *ius* in this sense denotes something either existing independently of the members of the society, such as a loaf of bread, or at least observable by them, such as an act of teaching, it is sometimes called 'objective right' by modern authors. This is the primary sense of the word.

A second sense of the word 'right' may be legitimately derived from the first. If a loaf of bread is my *ius*, then I may justly claim the bread, and vindicate my claim if necessary before a court of law. By a natural development of language, the term *ius* or 'right' came to be applied to such a just claim. This is sometimes called a 'subjective right' by modern authors,[27] and may be defined as the moral power of doing, omitting or requiring something.[28] It is obvious that this is a secondary use of the term 'right'. If I *have* a right to one kind of thing or action rather than another, it is because that thing or action *is* my right, owed to me by some other member of my society. This thing or action is my right, meaning that only by receiving it from that person will I be related to him in such a way that the society to which we both belong may attain all or part of its goal. Only if I receive the loaf of bread for which I have paid will my society with the baker attain its goal, of ensuring to each of us equality in desirable goods. Only if the father receives obedience to his legitimate commands from his son, will the family have a perfection which its nature requires, of being the place where the father moves the son toward the son's and the family's good.

A fatal inversion occurs, however, when the notion of rights is detached from the notion of the common good. Rights now come to be conceived of as properties inherent in a person, akin to the powers of body and soul. Instead of the goal of a given society giving rise to a legitimate claim of one person on another to certain goods, persons are taken to possess inherent claims to certain goods, claims which are inevitably conceived of as being in themselves unlimited - for they supposedly exist independently of a person's ordering to the end of any society. Whereas in the former view, an innocent man has the right to life because anyone who kills him is harming the common good, of

---

[26] The *ius* of a member of a society need not be something which he will find desirable. Michel Villey pointed out that according to Roman law, the *ius* of a parricide was to be tied up in sack with a dog, a cockerel, a viper and an ape and thrown into the sea; quoted in J. Lamont, 'Conscience, Freedom, Rights: Idols of the Enlightenment Religion', *The Thomist*, 73 (2009), 210, n. 48.

[27] In technical language, it is called a relation of reason with a basis in reality (*cum fundamento in re*).

[28] A. Ottaviani, *Institutiones iuris publici ecclesiastici*, vol. II (Rome: Vatican Press, 1936), vol. 1, 1, note 1.

36

which an innocent man is an important part,[29] on the latter view, a man's 'right to life' flows from his human nature without reference to any society, somewhat as do his intellect, will, sense-powers, etc. The difficulty with this latter view is two-fold. First, no adequate reason is given for supposing that such a right does so flow, since unlike the intellect, will etc., its presence cannot be detected by experience, nor is it even possible to conceive what might *count* as detecting it. Defenders of this view often appeal to the notion of 'human dignity' as the basis of rights, and give the impression that human rights are 'intuited' in a quasi-angelic manner by contemplating this notion. But while human nature does indeed have a great dignity, as the Christian religion emphasises, the human mind does not intuit the properties of things, but discovers them by observation and reasoning. And the precedent once set of supposedly intuiting rights by contemplating human dignity, we see the rights grow ever more doubtful, evil and grotesque: from rights to life, liberty of speech and movement, and property, one passes through rights to clean water, and unemployment insurance, before arriving at rights to contraception, foeticide, and choice of 'gender'.

The second objection to a theory of rights which conceives them in this way as 'monadic properties', that is, as existing independently of the mutual relations of persons in some society, is that it is found in practice necessary to limit rights, even though they were conceived of as naturally unlimited. One recognises that freedom of speech, for example, must be curtailed for the sake of public order or that the right to property must bow to public exactions necessary to sustain the core functions of the civil power. In this way, political authority appears as something violent and contrary to nature, and political society appears as the realm wherein each citizen agrees to suffer some injustice in order to retain something of his own, like men ruled by *mafiosi*.[30]

Since rights conceived in this way are a corruption of the true notion of right, and have no place in a sound political philosophy, they may be called 'pseudo-rights'.[31] Unfortunately, such pseudo-rights have a leading place in the rhetoric

---

[29] Cf. STh 2a 2ae 64, 6: "The life of righteous men preserves and forwards the common good, since they are the chief part of the community. Therefore it is in no way lawful to slay the innocent."

[30] John Lamont, in his exposition of the work of Michel Villey, also gives as a reason for disbelieving in monadic rights "the fact that such rights were unknown to very many cultures, despite their supposedly flowing from the essence of human nature and being the basis for just social relations"; J. Lamont, 'Conscience, Freedom, Rights', 230.

[31] Cf. A. MacIntyre, *After Virtue* (London: Duckworth, 1985), 68-69: "By 'rights' [...] I mean those rights which are alleged to belong to human beings as such and which are cited

37

and imagination of modern times: the very phrase 'human rights' seems inevitably to evoke this false view.[32]

---

as a reason for holding that people ought not to be interfered with in their pursuit of life, liberty and happiness. […] they are supposed to attach equally to all individuals, whatever their sex, race, religion, talents or deserts, and to provide a ground for a variety of particular moral stances. It would of course be a little odd that there should be such rights attaching to human beings simply qua human beings in light of the fact […] that there is no expression in any ancient or medieval language correctly translated by our expression 'a right' until near the close of the middle ages: the concept lacks any means of expression in Hebrew, Greek, Latin or Arabic, classical or medieval, before about 1400, let alone in Old English, or in Japanese even as late as the mid-nineteenth century. From this it does not of course follow that there are no natural or human rights; it only follows that no one could have known that there were. And this at least raises certain questions. But we do not need to be distracted into answering them, for the truth is plain: there are no such rights, and belief in them is one with belief in witches and unicorns […] every attempt to give good reasons for believing that there *are* such rights has failed" (the author's disbelief in witchcraft reminds us that the prejudices of the Enlightenment are indeed hard to shake off.)

[32] A Catholic defender of the view of rights which we are criticizing may appeal to the language of important ecclesiastical documents, from Pius XI's *Divini Redemptoris* onwards. An exegesis of these documents is beyond the scope of this work; our reply in summary is that the evocation of subjective rights in these texts is set within the context of that universal human society generated by man's supernatural destiny. See especially Pius XII's 1939 encyclical *Summi Pontificatus*. For a fuller discussion of this question, see J. Lamont, 'Conscience, Freedom, Rights', 233-35.

Theses

(i)   Actions ordered to the end of a society, and undertaken on the basis of common interest and in friendship, constitute the proper activity of that society.

(ii)   A common good is a good which can be shared entirely by several persons.

(iii)   The extrinsic common good of a society is the end for which its members, as members, act.

(iv)   The intrinsic common good of a society is the peace which its members have among themselves in virtue of seeking the extrinsic common good.

(v)   Prudence, justice, temperance and fortitude are intrinsically necessary elements of any friendship and society.

(vi)   The common good is not a merely instrumental good.

(vii)   The common good is better and more divine than the good of one.

(viii)   The good of a person who belongs to a society, insofar as he belongs to it, is to tend toward its common good.

(ix)   The common good of a society is common not only in the sense of deriving from the activities of all the members, but also in the sense of belonging to them all.

(x)   Authority is that elevation of one above another within a society which consist in or gives the right to command in view of obtaining the end of that society.

(xi)   The cause of a society is the cause of the scope of the authority proper to it.

(xii)   The founders of a voluntary society determine the bearers of authority; the bearer of authority in a necessary society is sometimes determined by a pre-existing right or by the nature of the society itself.

(xiii)   The rights of rational creatures are not qualities intrinsic to them but derive from the extrinsic end of a society to which they belong.

Chapter 3

The family

Nature of the family

The family is the society constituted immediately by every fruitful marriage. To understand the family, it is therefore necessary first to understand marriage.

Since no human being can possess all the perfections accessible to human nature in the abstract; since it is connatural to man to learn from other members of his species; since friendship can properly speaking be had only for another and not for oneself; and since man, since the Fall and by his nature, is mortal, it is very fitting that human beings multiply. Since human gestation and maturation are lengthy and complex processes, they impose themselves as duties on those who procreate a new life, to whom also nature imparts a love of their offspring. Since procreation is a mutual work, and since the work of supervising maturation is burdensome, it is necessary that each of those two people who procreates a new life manifest to the other the firm intention of co-operating with the other so that maturation may occur. This contract is called marriage, and the family is the society generated by it.[1]

More fundamentally, as the end of man whether proportionate to his nature or absolutely final, cannot be attained without friendship, the indissoluble unity in friendship of his parents is the indefeasible moral right of any child. For without such an exemplar, the capacity of the individual to attain either of these ends is gravely injured from the first moments of his existence.

This institution of natural law has also been part of divine positive law from the beginning, its charter having been promulgated in these words: *Therefore a man shall leave father and mother and be joined to his wife, and they shall be two in one flesh,*[2] and re-promulgated by Jesus Christ as part of the Gospel. Since it

---

[1] In the absence of children, husband and wife may be said to have simply a marital society.

[2] "These words are not from Moses, as Calvin held, but from Adam, or rather from God, who confirms the words of Adam and draws from them the law of matrimony, ratifying it with His decree. For Christ attributes these words to God, in Matt. 19:5" (Cornelius à Lapide, *Commentary on Genesis,* chapter 2, verse 24). In the *Supplement* to the *Summa Theologiae,* we read: "As to Adam's words, he uttered them as having been inspired by God to understand that the institution of marriage was from God" (*Supplement,* 42, 2 ad 4).

possesses its nature and ends from natural law and not from the free will of its members, the family is a necessary and not a voluntary society.[3]

Since the marital contract consists in the mutual promise of fidelity in the work of procreation and education, it can subsist only between two persons able in principle to procreate together, that is, between a man and a woman. To claim therefore that two men, or a man and a brute, may marry each other, or ought to be allowed to do so, is akin to claiming that a man may, or ought to be allowed to, promise to change the past or to abolish the laws of geometry. Nothing which is impossible can be the object of a rational promise, and since it is impossible that any should procreate but a man and a woman, only a man and a woman can rationally promise fidelity in the mutual work of procreation.

Since carnal intercourse is the principle of procreation, the fundamental clause of the marital contract, on which the others depend, is the agreement by each spouse to pay the marital debt if requested by the other. Hence any man and any woman capable of such intercourse, and not otherwise impeded,[4] may marry. This applies even to a couple who are incapable of procreation, as when the woman is past the years of childbearing; such is however an atypical case, that is, not one to which one would point in order to make clear the nature of marriage.

While the procreation and education of offspring are the primary purpose of matrimony, it has also as secondary purposes friendship between the spouses[5] and the providing of a remedy for concupiscence.[6] The first of these secondary purposes is essential to marriage and arises from its nature, while the second is a consequence of sin and would not have existed in the state of innocence. The

---

[3] In a *tour de force* of disingenuous rhetoric, Karl Marx (1818-83) in his *Communist Manifesto* (1848), seeks to deflect the reader's attention from his doctrine of the community of wives while insinuating the very principle by alleging its universality. *De facto* he stands at the head of the modern movement to destroy the natural society of the family through the propagation of sexual immorality climaxing in the stupefying denial of the sexual difference itself.

[4] For example, by being near relations, or already married to another person.

[5] St Augustine, *On the good of marriage*, 3: "Concerning the good of marriage [...] there is good ground to inquire for what reason it be a good. And this seems not to me to be merely on account of the begetting of children, but also on account of the natural society itself in the different sexes. Otherwise it would not any longer be called marriage in the case of old persons, especially if either they had lost children, or had given birth to none. But now in good, although aged, marriage, albeit there has withered away the glow of full age between male and female, yet there lives in full vigour the order of charity between husband and wife." This good of marriage is called *fides*, fidelity.

[6] 1 Cor. 7:7-9.

primary goal excludes polyandry (the accepting of more than one husband), while the friendship between the spouses excludes all forms of polygamy.[7]

The husband has by natural right the authority to govern his wife so that the family may attain its end.[8] Since the souls of man and woman are in themselves by nature identical, the foundation for this authority lies in their bodily difference: since the woman gestates, bears and nourishes their children, the husband by his labour must defend and obtain the means to sustain the family, and so must be free to place it where he judges best, and to come and go in the knowledge that his children are under the supervision of their mother.[9] Since his wife is a rational being,[10] he ought in governing her to desire her counsel, and to explain the reasons for his decisions, as well as to recognise her right to accomplish her domestic tasks in the manner she judges best. If her domestic duties are not thereby harmed, the wife may by her husband's consent labour outside the home, although in a well-ordered society, this will not be necessary for the maintenance of the family.[11]

---

[7] It is generally held that since polygyny (the taking of more than one wife) is contrary only to the *secondary* end of marriage, it was possible for God to dispense this when there was need to multiply followers of the true religion, but that such dispensations were definitively ended by the promulgation of the gospel, owing to the unicity and universality of the Church after Pentecost; cf. STh *Supplement* 65, 2. Cf. Cant. 6:7-8.

[8] Eph. 5:22-23: "Let women be subject to their husbands, as to the Lord: because the husband is the head of the wife, as Christ is the head of the church"; John XXIII, *Ad Petri cathedram* 53: "Within the family, the father stands in God's place. He must enlighten and preside over the others not only by his authority but also by the example of his good life." Cf. St John Chrysostom, *Homilies on 1 Corinthians*, Homily 26.4: "But if any say, 'Nay, how can this be a shame to the woman, if she mount up to the glory of the man?', we might make this answer: 'She doth not mount up, but rather falls from her own proper honor.' For not to abide within our own limits and the laws ordained of God, but to go beyond, is not an addition but a diminution."

[9] The bodily differences between man and woman also for the most part give rise to psychological differences which favour the headship of the husband, where vicious social customs do not intervene. Aristotle and St Thomas held that the man has naturally greater aptness for decision; Aristotle, *Politics* I.13; St Thomas Aquinas, *Commentary on the Politics*, Bk. 1, lect. 10, n. 9.

[10] And, if both are baptised, a co-heir to the grace of life; 1 Pet. 3:7.

[11] Cf. Pius XI, *Quadragesimo anno*, 71: "Mothers, concentrating on household duties, should work primarily in the home or in its immediate vicinity. It is an intolerable abuse, and to be abolished at all cost, for mothers on account of the father's low wage to be forced to engage in gainful occupations outside the home to the neglect of their proper cares and duties, especially the training of children."

Without prejudice to the father's headship, the parents together govern their children until they reach the age of majority, and thus may command them in view of the goal of their common domestic society, requiring them to act in this or that way for the good order of the home.[12] On the other hand, they may not command them in matters that surpass the good of that society, and so the father may not oblige his son to choose one profession or trade rather than another, or to marry rather than remain celibate, or to take one bride rather than another.

Aristotle gives a descriptive, rather than an essential, definition of the family or household as "the community naturally constituted for daily purposes".[13] Men do not need to trade or fight every day, but they do need to eat and sleep each day, and in certain climates or at certain seasons, to warm themselves each day, and the family is the society within which they desire to do these things. He also distinguishes between the union of man and woman, which generates the family, and another kind of union which preserves the family, namely the union of the 'naturally ruling' and the 'naturally ruled'.[14] This is the distinction between those who are more inclined to direct others in bodily work than to carry it out themselves, and those who are more inclined to carry it out rather than to direct others in it. However, Aristotle, in considering this distinction, is unaware that it arises only from man's loss of the preternatural gifts[15]; and while the presence of domestic servants may be a perfection of a household, this very principle must itself be subordinated to the higher principle that it is a more perfect thing to found one's own family than to help to perfect another man's.

---

[12] 1 Tim. 5:8.

[13] *Politics*, I. 2: "ἡ μὲν οὖν εἰς πᾶσαν ἡμέραν συνεστηκυῖα κοινωνία κατὰ φύσιν οἶκός ἐστιν". The Greek contains no word that directly translates as 'purposes', saying literally that the domestic society is constituted by nature 'for every day". St Thomas in his commentary supplies the word 'actions'.

[14] Ibid.

[15] STh 1a 96, 4: "Mastership has a twofold meaning. First, as opposed to slavery, in which sense a master means one to whom another is subject as a slave. In another sense mastership is referred in a general sense to any kind of subject; and in this sense even he who has the office of governing and directing free men, can be called a master. In the state of innocence man could have been a master of men, not in the former but in the latter sense."

Priority of the family to the temporal commonwealth

Speaking of the friendship of man and woman, Aristotle observes: "Man is more inclined by nature to conjugal than to political society, inasmuch as the home is older and more necessary than the city."[16] Pope Leo XIII expressed the same thought, and drew an important consequence:

> Inasmuch as the domestic household is antecedent, as well in idea as in fact, to the gathering of men into civil society, the family must necessarily have rights and duties which are prior and founded more immediately in nature.[17]

The family is logically prior insofar as the idea of a city is that of a certain union of families, and prior in reality insofar as the establishment of a city requires that several families be already existing. As a natural reality existing before the city, the family therefore already has a certain goal or good independently of the city, and hence familial rights and duties cannot all derive from the city. The most basic of these are the spouses' mutual right and duty of cohabitation, and their right to procreate and educate children.

Incompetence of the temporal power

Since marriage is an ordinance of nature confirmed by divine positive law, and not an invention of man, the civil or temporal power cannot justly abolish marriage, or change its properties, or forbid marriage to those to whom natural and divine law permit it. Indeed, since human beings receive their freedom to marry from God and not from man,[18] and since entrance into the married state gives them the right to co-operate with God in causing new human life, the popes have described even those marriages which are not sacraments of the New Law as religious things, and, even as sacraments, albeit not grace-bearing

---

[16] *Nicomachean Ethics*, VIII.12: "ἄνθρωπος γὰρ τῇ φύσει συνδυαστικὸν μᾶλλον ἢ πολιτικόν, ὅσῳ πρότερον καὶ ἀναγκαιότερον οἰκία πόλεως."

[17] *Rerum novarum* 13: "Cum convictus domesticus et cogitatione sit et re prior, quam civilis coniunctio, priora quoque esse magisque naturalia iura eius officiaque consequitur."

[18] Hence Blessed Peter of Tarentaise OP (the future Pope Innocent V) wrote: "Since man and woman are fully subject to the dominion of God, it would not be licit for one to transfer his body to the dominion of another, unless it were approved by the will and authority of God"; *Super Sententias P. Lombardi*, IV d. 27 q. 2, quoted in F. Sola and J. Sagues, *Sacrae Theologiae Summa* (Biblioteca de Autores Cristianos: Madrid, 1956), t. 5, sect. 174.

ones.[19] Hence, since the Church has the supreme right to declare religious truth, she may judge the validity of the marriages not only of Christians but where necessary also of other persons.[20]

The temporal power may therefore not forbid married couples to procreate, nor may it sterilise those who seem likely to engender disabled or unhealthy children. For since an unmarried man and woman may, without requiring the permission of the temporal power, validly establish a matrimonial contract between themselves, a contract whose properties are fixed by nature, they cannot be prevented from exercising the rights and fulfilling the obligations which this contract involves. Nor can they be punished for procreating, for example, by a fine, since no one may justly be punished for exercising a right or fulfilling an obligation. At most, in exceptional circumstances, the civil power may advise a married couple to abstain from procreation. On the other hand, where populations are declining or threaten to decline, the civil power may offer inducements to married couples to have children.

Since the marital contract does not owe its nature to any created force, neither the spouses nor any human power can alter its essential properties. Indeed, when rulers attempt to do so, they are, insofar as lies in them, unlawfully forbidding their subjects to marry. Among these essential properties is

---

[19] Cf. Leo XIII, *Arcanum* 19: "Marriage has God for its Author, and was from the very beginning a kind of foreshadowing of the Incarnation of His Son; and therefore there abides in it a something holy and religious; not extraneous, but innate; not derived from men, but implanted by nature. Innocent III, therefore, and Honorius III, our predecessors, affirmed not falsely nor rashly that a sacrament of marriage existed ever amongst the faithful and amongst unbelievers. We call to witness the monuments of antiquity, as also the manners and customs of those people who, being the most civilized, had the greatest knowledge of law and equity. In the minds of all of them it was a fixed and foregone conclusion that, when marriage was thought of, it was thought of as conjoined with religion and holiness. Hence, among those peoples, marriages were commonly celebrated with religious ceremonies, under the authority of pontiffs, and with the ministry of priests: so mighty, even in the souls ignorant of heavenly doctrine, was the force of nature, of the remembrance of their origin, and of the conscience of the human race. As, then, marriage is holy by its own power, in its own nature, and of itself, it ought not to be regulated and administered by the will of civil rulers, but by the divine authority of the Church, which alone in sacred matters professes the office of teaching." St Thomas said of the marriages of unbelievers: "Such matrimony is in a certain way a sacrament habitually, even though it is not one actually, not being actually contracted in the faith of the Church" (*Scriptum super Sententias,* IV d. 39 q. 1 a. 2 ad 1). John Calvin (1509-64), by contrast, held that matrimony was no more a sacrament than are shoe-making or hairdressing; *Institutes,* IV. c.19. 34.

[20] Congregation for the Doctrine of the Faith, 2001, *Norms on the preparation of the process for the dissolution of the marriage bond in favour of the faith.*

indissolubility.[21] Friendship is naturally indissoluble because the friend is another self; thus it can be destroyed only by the loss of the extrinsic common good, the 'death' of the friend under the aspect whereby he was befriended. But the extrinsic common good of marriage is the good of the offspring, whose primary need, as mentioned above, is for an exemplary friendship. Thus the good of the offspring *is* the friendship of the parents. Hence in marriage, the indestructibility of the intrinsic common good is conferred upon the extrinsic common good, rendering the bond indissoluble by any human power.

Reason by itself discerns this fact in many ways. The angelic doctor mentions in the first place a man's natural desire that his son should inherit from him: the resulting solicitude which the father has until the end of his life for his children requires that he continue to dwell with their mother until the end, since otherwise he would be liable to contract new interests which would interfere with the proper exercise of his paternal instinct.[22]

> I reply that it should be said that matrimony, from the intention of nature, is ordered to the education of the children, not for a certain time only, but rather for the entire life of the children (which is the reason why, by the law of nature, parents are to lay up wealth for their children, and children should inherit from their parents). For that reason, since children are a common good of husband and wife, it is necessary according to the dictum of the law of nature that that association remain perpetually undivided. Thus, the inseparability of matrimony is based on the law of nature.[23]

Again, divorce does injustice to women. A woman, Aquinas writes, seeks a husband to have his protection, while the man takes a wife to raise up offspring, attracted by her fecundity and beauty. Hence:

> If any man took a woman in the time of her youth, when beauty and fecundity were hers, and then sent her away after she had reached an

---

[21] Since marriage cannot be dissolved by the spouses, it is said to possess 'intrinsic indissolubility'; since it cannot be dissolved by some other human power, it is said to possess 'extrinsic indissolubility'.

[22] Cf. *Summa contra Gentiles*, III.123.

[23] *Scriptum super Sententias*, IV d. 33 q. 2 a. 1: "Respondeo dicendum, quod matrimonium ex intentione naturae ordinatur ad educationem prolis non solum per aliquod tempus, sed per totam vitam prolis. Unde de lege naturae est quod parentes filiis thesaurizent, et filii parentum heredes sint; et ideo, cum proles sit commune bonum viri et uxoris, oportet eorum societatem perpetuo permanere indivisam secundum legis naturae dictamen; et sic inseparabilitas matrimonii est de lege naturae."

advanced age, he would damage that woman contrary to natural equity.[24]

Again, marriage is a friendship, and friendship exists in equality: hence, since the wife may not send away the one under whose authority she has put herself, neither must the husband be able to send away a wife who ceased to please him. Another reason is a man's natural desire to know who his children are, which may be frustrated by polyandry whether simultaneous or serial.[25]

Still other reasons may be drawn from the harm which the very possibility of divorce would cause to the relations between the spouses, and also between their families, and hence within society as such. Thus, "when they know that they are indivisibly united, the love of one spouse for the other will be more faithful". Again, "they will take greater care of their domestic possessions when they keep in mind that they will remain continually in possession of these same things". With regard to the wider society, "the sources of disagreements which would inevitably arise between a man and his wife's relatives, if he could put away his wife, are removed, and a more solid affection is established among the relatives".[26]

Such are some of the arguments from nature against divorce.[27] They are confirmed not only by divine revelation but also by history.[28] Nevertheless, so

---

[24] Ibid.

[25] Ibid.

[26] Ibid.

[27] *Syllabus of Errors,* condemned proposition 67: "By the law of nature, the marriage tie is not indissoluble, and in many cases divorce properly so called may be decreed by the civil authority."

[28] Cf. Leo XIII, *Arcanum* 29-30: "Truly, it is hardly possible to describe how great are the evils that flow from divorce. Matrimonial contracts are by it made mutable; mutual kindness is weakened; deplorable inducements to unfaithfulness are supplied; harm is done to the education and training of children; occasion is afforded for the breaking up of homes; the seeds of dissension are sown among families; the dignity of womanhood is lessened and brought low, and women run the risk of being deserted after having ministered to the pleasures of men. Since, then, nothing has such power to lay waste families and destroy the mainstay of kingdoms as the corruption of morals, it is easily seen that divorces are in the highest degree hostile to the prosperity of families and States, springing as they do from the depraved morals of the people, and, as experience shows us, opening out a way to every kind of evil-doing in public and in private life. Further still, if the matter be duly pondered, we shall clearly see these evils to be the more especially dangerous, because, divorce once being tolerated, there will be no restraint powerful enough to keep it within the bounds marked out or previously surmised. Great indeed is the force of example, and even greater still the might of passion. With such incitements it

47

unruly are the emotions of unregenerate man that "no law save Christ's has forbidden the divorcing of a wife".[29]

Rights of the temporal power

Although marriage, being a religious thing, does not of itself require the permission of temporal rulers for validity, it is not therefore wholly exempted from their authority. St Thomas writes:

> When something is directed to different ends, it needs different things to direct it to them, since the end matches the agent. Now, human generation is ordered to many things: to the perpetuity of the species; and to the perpetuity of some political good, such as to the perpetuity of a people in a given city; and to the perpetuity of the Church, which consists in the assembly of the faithful. Therefore human generation must be directed by several things. Insofar as it is ordered to the good of nature which is the perpetuity of the species, it is directed to its end by nature, which inclines to this end, and thus it is called an office of nature. Insofar as it is ordered to a political good, it is subject to the ordering of the civil law. Insofar as it is ordered to the good of the Church, it must be subject to ecclesiastical governance.[30]

Hence, temporal rulers have competence to determine the 'merely civil effects' of marriage, that is, to establish rights and duties in relation to marriage which do not flow from it as a sacrament of nature or of Christ, nor from the laws of

---

must needs follow that the eagerness for divorce, daily spreading by devious ways, will seize upon the minds of many like a virulent contagious disease, or like a flood of water bursting through every barrier."

[29] *Scriptum super Sententias* IV d. 33 q. 2 a.1 arg. 1; STh, *Supplement* 67, 1 obj. 1. Cf. Cf. E. Shestak, *Divorce and Remarriage in the Orthodox Churches of the Tradition of Kiev* (Lira: Uzhhorod, 2011) 154-155: "The first ecclesiastical collection which clearly recognised the validity of the divorce laws of Justinian was the second edition of the *Nomokanon in 14 Titles*, produced in about the year 883 in Constantinople, and which was known as the *Photian Nomokanon*." For other separated Eastern churches see: *DTC* 'Adultère', VI. Martin Luther alleged several justifying causes for divorce and remarriage in his 1522 sermon, 'Living as Husband and Wife', later published as *The Estate of Marriage*. Despite a certain squeamishness on the topic, the entity created by Henry VIII and his natural daughter is notoriously founded upon attempted divorce. John Locke (1632-1704) claimed that nothing in the nature of marriage required that it be a contract made until death; *Second Treatise on Government*, section 81. Wherever the reality signified by the indissoluble bond of matrimony perishes, the indissolubility of the bond is swiftly repudiated.

[30] *Summa contra Gentiles*, IV, 78.

the Church[31]; for example, to determine the extent of those privileges afforded to married persons under the tax system.

Temporal rulers are required by natural law to recognise and privilege marriage, given its necessity for the well-being of the realm; they are therefore required to ascertain that a marriage has occurred, and hence entitled to make such reasonable demands as will assist them in this duty, for example, requiring that a couple notify them of the witnesses before whom they intend to marry. However, they may not establish impediments to the forming of a marital bond, since this contract, insofar as it is a sacrament even in the natural order, falls exclusively under the authority of the Church. Nor may they judge of the validity of marriages already contracted where one or either party is baptised.[32]

Such rulers may, however, establish criteria by which they may reasonably discern validity for the marriages of the unbaptised, for example, establishing a minimum age for the bridegroom and bride by which they may be assumed to be capable of consent.[33] This right is not native to them,[34] but from necessity is lawfully assumed by them insofar as the unbaptised are not yet subject to that religious society to which the right properly belongs.[35] For the same reason it seems that they may also judge of the validity of marriages already contracted between unbaptised persons, except where the Church reserves such judgements to herself.[36]

The ways in which rulers are to privilege marriage are a matter for their own political prudence. For example, they may choose to impose lighter taxation upon married men. Other societies might choose to restrict certain honours, such as voting rights, or military duties, to citizens born in wedlock. Others have fostered friendship between the spouses by forbidding courts to compel

---

[31] Pius IX, *Letter to the King of Sardinia*, 1852.

[32] Council of Trent, Session 24, canon. 12: "If anyone shall say that matrimonial causes do not pertain to ecclesiastical judges, let him be anathema." Ottaviani remarks that it would be to distort the sense of this canon, as well as to ignore the practice of the Church to deny that it is affirming that *all* matrimonial cases (among the baptised) belong *only* to ecclesiastical judges; A. Ottaviani, *Institutiones iuris publici ecclesiastici*, vol. II (Rome: Vatican Press, 1936) 225, n. 50.

[33] Ibid. 222-23. For a more detailed examination of the question, see F. Sola and J. Sagues, *Sacrae Theologiae Summa* (Biblioteca de Autores Cristianos: Madrid, 1956), t. 5, sect. 292 ff.

[34] *Syllabus of Errors*, condemned proposition 74: "Matrimonial causes and espousals belong by their nature to civil tribunals."

[35] Hence it is called a *ius devolutivum*, a right that devolves to them.

[36] As she may do, for example, in the case of a pagan who wishes to be baptised.

one spouse either to testify against the other, or to reveal confidential communications made between them.

Education of children

The next right and duty of the married couple is to educate their children.[37] Parents, as causes of their children, have by nature authority over them within the domestic society.[38] "A father is the principle of generation, of education, of learning and of whatever pertains to the perfection of human life."[39] Aristotle observes that parents love their children as being a something of themselves,[40] on which St Thomas comments: "The son is as it were a separated part of the father."[41] Hence the parents fitly seek their own good by seeking that of the children. Again, the family, like other living natures, falls short of its proper perfection for as long as it is unable to generate something like itself. For these reasons, parents must cause their children to reach maturity, that is, a state where they are themselves able to marry and assume the parental task.

The process by which parents cause their children to reach such maturity is called education. This is the raising of children to the level of complete adulthood, and so comprises bodily training, intellectual instruction, and formation in prudence and the virtues directed by prudence. The authority by which the parents may do this does not derive from the community, but comes to them immediately from God. They can, if they wish, exercise it at least in part by proxy, employing tutors and teachers, but should they do so, they cannot dispense themselves of the duty to supervise the work done. This is also true should they choose to avail themselves of help offered by the temporal power.[42]

---

[37] The right of acquiring property will be considered later on, as it is does not belong only to the family.

[38] Cf. Leo XIII, *Rerum novarum* 13-14. In accordance with his denial of natural law in the true sense of the word, that is, as based on a good and evil in things themselves, Hobbes was forced to deny this, and to make the parental authority dependent on a contract between parents and children; *Leviathan*, chapter 20, 'Of dominion paternal, and despotical'.

[39] STh 2a 2ae 102, 1.

[40] *Nicomachean Ethics*, VIII.12: "οἱ γονεῖς μὲν γὰρ στέργουσι τὰ τέκνα ὡς ἑαυτῶν τι ὄντα."

[41] "Filius est quodammodo pars patris ab eo separata".

[42] *Divini illius Magistri* 32: "The family therefore holds directly from the Creator the mission and hence the right to educate the offspring, a right inalienable because inseparably joined

As the parents beget their children to a natural life, they have from God the power to educate them for natural perfection. They may therefore not be prevented against their will from accomplishing this task by any merely human power, even for the sake of achieving some greater good.

> On this point the common sense of mankind is in such complete accord, that they would be in open contradiction with it who dared maintain that the children belong to the city before they belong to the family, and that the city has an absolute right over their education. Untenable is the reason they adduce, namely that man is born a citizen and hence belongs primarily to the city, not bearing in mind that before being a citizen, man must exist; and existence does not come from the city, but from the parents.[43]

Just as an innocent man may resist a public official seeking to amputate one of his limbs, so may he resist, even with bodily force, an official who seeks to remove the children from his home, especially if it be to place them where they will be imbued with infidelity or instructed in the techniques of perversion. Indeed, rather than send their children to such schools, parents would do well to let them grow up unlettered.

For the same reason, an unbaptised child may not be taken from its parents in order to be made a Christian:

> A child is by nature a part of its father: thus, at first, it is not distinct from its parents as to its body, so long as it is enfolded within its mother's womb; and later on after birth, and before it has the use of its free-will, it is enfolded in the care of its parents, which is like a spiritual womb. For, so long as a child has not the use of reason, he differs not from an irrational animal; so that even as an ox or a horse belongs to someone who, according to the civil law, can use them

to the strict obligation, a right anterior to any right whatever of the civil society and commonwealth, and therefore inviolable on the part of any power on earth." The Supreme Court of the United States upheld this principle in the 1925 case of Pierce v. Society of Sisters: "The fundamental theory of liberty upon which all governments in this Union repose excludes any general power of the State to standardize its children by forcing them to accept instruction from public teachers only. The child is not the mere creature of the State; those who nurture him and direct his destiny have the right, coupled with the high duty, to recognize and prepare him for additional obligations." See also CIC 793.

[43] Ibid. 35. Pope Pius XI protested against the Fascists' usurpation of the right to education; *Non abbiamo bisogno*, 52: "A conception of the State which makes the rising generations belong to it entirely, without any exception, from the tenderest years up to adult life, cannot be reconciled by a Catholic either with Catholic doctrine or with the natural rights of the family."

when he likes, as his own instrument, so, according to the natural law, a child, before coming to the use of reason, is under his father's care. Hence it would be contrary to natural justice, if a child, before coming to the use of reason, were to be taken away from his parents' custody, or anything done to him against his parents' wishes.[44]

When a child is born again in baptism to a supernatural life, the Church as mother of this new child of God has the right to educate the child for beatitude.[45] Since this end is immeasurably more important than any other, this right of the Church cannot cede to any other right.[46] Hence, even in schools which have been erected by Catholic citizens acting on their own authority, the Church has the duty to watch over the moral and religious instruction imparted there, and to require that teachers of scandalous life be removed; within Christendom, this right of the Church is enforced by the temporal power. In extreme circumstances, the authorities of the Church may take a baptised child even from its parental home if its religious education cannot otherwise be secured. The practical application of this principle must however be governed by the truth that the love between parents and children is the best soil for the theological virtues, as well as by the general principle that evils should be tolerated where this is necessary to achieve some greater good or avoid some greater evil.[47]

---

[44] STh 2a 2ae 10, 12. Canon law excepts the case when a child is in imminent danger of death, and hence is no longer tending toward any earthly goal; CIC 868§2. "Scotus in book 4 [of his *Commentary on the Sentences of Peter Lombard*], dist. 4, q. 9, no. 2, and in questions related to no. 2, thought that a prince could laudably command that small children of Hebrews and unbelievers be baptised, even against the will of the parents, provided one could prudently see to it that these same children were not killed by the parents …. Nevertheless, the opinion of St Thomas prevailed … it is unlawful to baptise Hebrew children against the will of their parents"; *Postremo mense,* Benedict XIV (DH2553-4).

[45] Pius XI, *Divini illius Magistri,* 15-17: "First of all education belongs pre-eminently to the Church, by reason of a double title in the supernatural order, conferred exclusively upon her by God Himself; absolutely superior therefore to any other title in the natural order. The first title is founded upon the express mission and supreme authority to teach, given her by her divine Founder. [...] The second title is the supernatural motherhood, in virtue of which the Church, spotless spouse of Christ, generates, nurtures and educates souls in the divine life of grace."

[46] Ibid. 18: "The Church is independent of any sort of earthly power as well in the origin as in the exercise of her mission as educator, not merely in regard to her proper end and object, but also in regard to the means necessary and suitable to attain that end."

[47] Cf. Romanus Cessario OP, 'Non Possumus' in *First Things,* February 2018.

The parents and the Church therefore have between them priority in the work of education.[48] Given the complexity of the task of education it appears normal that families should unite to carry it out, and hence that at least part of the education of children will be accomplished in common.[49]

The family as a part of the city

Aristotle states near the beginning of the *Politics* that 'the city is by nature prior to the household and to each of us'.[50] How is this compatible with his assertion in the *Ethics* that the family is prior to the city? St Thomas remarks in his commentary on the *Politics* that the city is prior in the way that any whole is prior to its parts, namely 'in the order of nature and of perfection'. As we saw in a previous chapter, the city has a more excellent end than the family, and thus is 'prior in perfection'. Again, since families are naturally inclined to gather themselves into cities, the city is 'prior in the order of nature', that is, families tend toward the preservation of the city even more than toward their own preservation, as when the father leaves his home to fight in a war. For every part tends toward the preservation of the whole more than toward its own.[51]

Thus, although the family, unlike other parts of the city, such as parliaments, trades unions, businesses, and universities, can have an existence anterior to the city and freedoms which it retains intact when it enters it, it nevertheless also has duties which belong to it as a part of the city. Thus the direct right of parents to educate their children includes the duty to educate them in those virtues such as patriotism by which the good of the city will be preferred to that of the family and in the specific duties imposed by citizenship in their own polity. Again, once a family is part of a city, the city has the right to intervene should the parents gravely neglect the task of education, since it is her own

---

[48] Pius XI, *Divini illius Magistri*, 40: "The mission of education regards before all, above all, primarily the Church and the family, and this by natural and divine law."

[49] This was the judgement of Pius XI; ibid., 77: "Since the younger generations must be trained in the arts and sciences for the advantage and prosperity of civil society, and since the family of itself is unequal to this task (*sola ad id familia minime sufficeret*), public schools (*gymnasia*) took their rise. But let it be borne in mind that this institution owes its existence to the combined activity of the family and of the Church, long before it was undertaken by the republic."

[50] I.2: "πρότερον δὲ τῇ φύσει πόλις ἢ οἰκία καὶ ἕκαστος ἡμῶν ἐστιν."

[51] A principle often invoked by Aquinas under various forms, for example, STh 2a 2ae 26, 3: "Unaquaeque pars naturaliter plus amat commune bonum totius quam particulare bonum proprium" ("any part naturally loves the common good of the whole more than its proper and particular good.")

53

future which is now at stake. The father has a duty to the city to educate his son for citizenship; should he refuse to do this, for example leaving his son in a feral and illiterate condition or training him as a thief, the authorities of the city may take the son from him. In this sense, we may say that education, while naturally and directly the task of the parents pertains also naturally and indirectly to the city.[52] Thus Aristotle observed that the superintendence of education should be common and not merely private, though without suggesting, as Plato had done, that the city should confiscate children for the sake of their education.[53]

In our order of providence, it is only the City of God, that is, the Catholic Church, which fully realises the notion of the 'city' as pure philosophy conceives it. Hence the following theses summarise the relative authority of the parents, and of the city in its spiritual and temporal rulers, over education:

(a) this City has a direct right to educate the children for their ultimate end, which is supernatural: this implies the right to teach not only the truths of faith but also all that is necessary for understanding and practising these truths[54]; (b) although this supernatural education, like all communication of saving truth, is done by the authority of the bishops,[55] these latter may not take this task from the parents except when the parents are gravely neglecting it, because of the harm to the supernatural life that this very separation would be liable to cause;

---

[52] *Divini illius Magistri*, 44-45: "It is the right, or to speak more correctly, it is the duty of the republic to protect in its legislation, the prior rights, already described, of the family as regards the Christian education of its offspring, and consequently also to respect the supernatural rights of the Church in this same realm of Christian education. It also belongs to the city to protect the rights of the child itself if ever the work of the parents, whether owing to their inactivity, their incompetence or their unworthiness (*ob eorum vel inertiam vel imperitiam vel indignitatem*), should be found wanting either physically or morally. For, as We have said above, their right to educate is not an absolute and despotic one (*non absolutum est atque imperiosum*), but dependent on the natural and divine law, and therefore subject alike to the authority and judgement of the Church, and to the vigilance and care of the city in view of the common good." See below, p. 111.

[53] Cf. *Politics*, VIII.1: "ἀναγκαῖον ... ταύτης τὴν ἐπιμέλειαν εἶναι κοινὴν καὶ μὴ κατ᾽ ἰδίαν".

[54] *Divini illius Magistri*, 21: "With full right the Church promotes letters, sciences, and the arts in so far as necessary or helpful to Christian education, in addition to her work for the salvation of souls"; cf. Leo XIII's encyclical of 1897, *Militantis Ecclesiae*: "It is necessary not only that religious instruction be given to the young at certain fixed times, but also that every other subject taught be permeated with Christian piety. If this is wanting, if this sacred atmosphere does not pervade and warm the hearts of masters and scholars alike, little good can be expected from any kind of learning, and considerable harm will often be the consequence."

[55] Hence parents must have received the sacrament of confirmation.

(c) the parents have the direct right to educate their children for their natural end as individual men and women; (d) this right derives neither from the authority of the bishops nor that of the temporal rulers, yet the latter retain the right to intervene if the parents gravely neglect their task.

The family and the Fall of man

Material perfections, including those pertaining to the 'interior senses', often exclude each other.[56] For this reason, human society is essentially organic. Just as some persons are inherently more suited to running a marathon rather than a sprint, or vice versa, so also skills necessary to certain intellectual pursuits of a speculative or practical nature will belong more to one person than another in virtue of peculiarities of their imagination, sense-memory, cogitative power or 'common sense'.[57] A naturally gifted architect may have no aptitude for chemistry, and a talented chemist no skill in designing buildings. This is not because the light of reason shines more brightly in one but because it is 'refracted' differently through the corporeal instruments at its disposal. St Thomas holds that some such difference would likely have been found among men even before the Fall.[58] On the other hand, the capacity for the fundamental moral reasoning in which, among other things, politics consists, does not vary among men, unless there be some positive malady. For the intellectual capacity operative in all men who have attained to the age of reason equips us for moral before technical or scientific judgments. Since in its essence it is not operating through a material organ it is the same in all men and far less reliant on the particular disposition of the interior senses. In some, indeed, the interior senses may be injured and the light obscured, but that light is still in itself undimmed.

In the beginning man was created with sanctifying grace, preternatural gifts and the capacity to transmit both by natural generation. Moreover, Adam was endowed with infused knowledge of all natures and given the revelation of man's supernatural end.[59] Had it not been for the Fall, it would have been

---

[56] For the interior senses, see STh 1a 78, 4.

[57] That is, the *sensus communis*.

[58] STh 1a 96, 3: "Nothing prevents us from saying that, according to the climate, or the movement of the stars, some would have been born more robust in body than others, and some larger and fairer and with better temperaments than others; yet in such a way that in those who were thus surpassed, there would have been no defect or fault of either soul or body."

[59] Ibid. 1a 94, 3; cf. 2nd Vatican Council, *Dei verbum* 3.

unnecessary for man to form a society beyond this family to survive and attain perfection. The relative moral perfection of man and the lucidity of his intellect would have meant that political *potestas* or dominion, that is, the right to coerce obedience, as opposed to *auctoritas* or principality, the simple right to obedience, would have existed only in God, in parents with regard to their minor children, and in men with regard to beasts.

St Thomas comments:

> Mastership has a twofold meaning. First, as opposed to slavery, in which sense a master means one to whom another is subject as a slave. In another sense, mastership refers in general to any kind of subject; and in this sense even he who has the office of governing and directing free men can be called a master. In the state of innocence man could have been a master of men, not in the former but in the latter sense [...]

> A man is the master of a free subject, by directing him either towards his proper welfare, or to the common good. Such a kind of mastership would have existed in the state of innocence between man and man [...] If one man surpassed another in knowledge and virtue, this would not have been fitting unless these gifts conduced to the benefit of others, according to 1 Peter 4:10, 'As every man hath received grace, ministering the same one to another.' Wherefore Augustine says (De Civ. Dei xix, 14): 'Just men command not by the love of domineering, but by the service of counsel': and (De Civ. Dei xix, 15): 'The natural order of things requires this; and thus did God make man.'[60]

The proper deference due to one's elders and progenitors, and their own experience, would have indicated why one person rather than another should have undertaken governmental responsibilities in prelapsarian society. Hence, although the persons to undertake *ministerial* responsibilities would have been

---

[60] STh 1a 96, 4. St Gregory the Great affirms that even after the Fall, just men exercised only the latter form of mastery: "Our ancient fathers are said to have been not kings of men, but shepherds of flocks. And, when the Lord said to Noe and his children, *Increase and multiply, and replenish the earth*, He at once added, *And let the fear of you and the dread of you be upon all the beasts of the earth*. Thus it appears that, whereas it is ordered that the fear and the dread should be upon the beasts of the earth, it is forbidden that it should be upon men. For man is by nature preferred to the brute beasts, but not to other men; and therefore it is said to him that he should be feared by the beasts, but not by men; since to wish to be feared by one's equal is to be proud against nature"; *Pastoral Rule*, Book II, c. 6.

56

selected by natural aptitude, it may be supposed that society itself would have been an hereditary principality by primogeniture.[61]

The loss of original justice, rendering man far more dependent upon technology and entirely dependent upon external channels of grace, means that the family is no longer materially sufficient to obtain securely the necessary means of human subsistence, and that the elder cannot be indiscriminately entrusted with supreme governmental functions without fear either of idiocy, because of the imperfect dominion of the soul over the body, or of moral corruption, because of the loss of sanctifying grace. Furthermore, the delinquency of the subject means that the ruler must possess dominion and not merely principality over those subject to him.

At the same time, the essential *moral* equality of all men continues to find legitimate and often desirable expression not only in such institutions as the jury and universal franchise, but also in institutions such as hereditary citizenship, nobility and monarchy, which, being in effect appointment by lot, are based on no special excellence of character, achievement or physique.

Social units

The family is thus antecedent to the civil power and is placed in different hands from the temporal commonwealth and from the Church only in consequence of sin. The temporal power exists because the family has fallen from its original dignity and the Church has not yet attained to its full stature. Again, when the Church attains to its full stature, familial ties will be superseded.[62] Human procreation persists in order to replenish a mortal race and make up the number of the elect but the faithful walk in the "hope of life everlasting, which God, who lieth not, hath promised before the times of the world" (Titus 1:2) and the faithful as "children of the resurrection" marry only by exception (Mt. 19:11-12). Indeed, St Augustine teaches us that were all the faithful to embrace perfect continence the number of the elect would be made up in that

---

[61] "I believe that if we had not fallen, Filmer would be right, and patriarchal monarchy would be the sole lawful government"; C.S. Lewis, 'Membership' in *Essay Collection: Faith, Christianity and the Church*, ed. L. Walmsley (London: HarperCollins, 2000). Robert Filmer (c. 1558-1653) was an intellectual antagonist to Charles I's parliamentary opposition.

[62] Cf. STh 2a 2ae 26, 13: "The entire life of the blessed consists in directing their minds to God; hence the entire ordering of their love will be ruled with respect to God, so that each one will love more and reckon to be nearer to himself those who are nearer to God."

generation.[63] The individual and not the family is thus the basic unit of ecclesiastical society.

The reverse is true in regard to civil society.[64] The civil power is generated by the family to supply its wants and is ordered to it. As Leo XIII teaches:

> If the citizens, if the families on entering into association and fellowship, were to experience hindrance in a commonwealth instead of help, and were to find their rights attacked instead of being upheld, society would rightly be an object of detestation rather than of desire. [...] True, if a family finds itself in exceeding distress, utterly deprived of the counsel of friends, and without any prospect of extricating itself, it is right that extreme necessity be met by public aid, since each family is a part of the commonwealth. In like manner, if within the precincts of the household there occur grave disturbance of mutual rights, public authority should intervene to force each party to yield to the other its proper due; for this is not to deprive citizens of their rights, but justly and properly to safeguard and strengthen them. But the rulers of the commonwealth must go no further; here, nature bids them stop.[65]

It is thus exclusively as the head of a family, whether as an actual head, that is, as a father or widowed mother, or as a potential head, that the individual operates within civil society and beyond the precinct of his own family, and is thus subject to civil power. Hence within the family, property can be transmitted subject to the authority of its head without any right of the civil

---

[63] *On the Good of Marriage*, 10: "I know what some murmur. What is it? They say: 'If all people were to abstain from all sexual intercourse, how would the human race remain?' Would that all people did so refrain, provided only it be done 'in charity out of a pure heart, and good conscience, and faith unfeigned'; much more speedily would the City of God be filled, and the end of the age hastened."

[64] Pope John XXIII, in *Pacem in terris* 16, stated that the family is "the first and natural seed of human society" (*"tamquam humanae societatis primum et naturale semen"*). Cf. St Augustine, *On the City of God*, XV.16: "Copulatio igitur maris et feminae, quantum adtinet ad genus mortalium, quoddam seminarium est civitatis" ("the union of male and female, in respect to the race of mortals, is a kind of seed-bed of the city.") Leo XIII, for his part wrote in *Sapientiae Christianae* 42: "The family may be regarded as the cradle of the republic, and it is in great measure within the circle of family life that the destiny of cities is determined. Whence it is that they who would tear cities away from Christian principles go to the root of things, and plot to corrupt family life."

[65] *Rerum novarum*, 14.

power to tax it.[66] It therefore fittingly manifests the truth that the family is the basic unit of society, when civil society vests in families rather than merely in individuals, those offices which call upon the essential moral equality of all men, for example, hereditary citizenship, nobility and kingship.

The proprietary immunity of the family raises the danger of great concentrations of landed wealth accumulating in the hands of one family and of the power and legitimate interests of such families distorting the structure and governance of the commonwealth. Under the Old Law, this possibility was recognised and avoided by a strict system of land tenure. By this system, a leasehold only (of not more than fifty years) could be granted to his ancestral lands by the head of any family. This would lapse in every jubilee year, restoring the original division of territory.[67] This arrangement, however, relied upon the exclusive marriage laws of the Jewish people, which excluded the problem of assimilating new populations to land ownership. It lapsed with the passing of the Mosaic covenant and cannot legitimately be restored for the Jews or any other people, since no divine law now restricts the natural freedom of marriage. As concentrations of landed property cannot be avoided without violating the rights of the family, the formal investiture of hereditary political rights and duties in heads of large landed families, subject to forfeiture for misuse, is a legitimate means of regulating and turning to the common good such power and legitimate interests.[68]

It is concomitantly natural for such hereditary rights and duties to lapse when a society develops in a preponderantly mercantile direction. Such a development, however, is not desirable:

> If the citizens themselves devote their life to matters of trade, the way will be opened to many vices. Since the foremost tendency of tradesmen is to make money, greed is awakened in the hearts of the citizens through the pursuit of trade. The result is that everything in the city will become venal; good faith will be destroyed and the way

---

[66] St Thomas, *Scriptum super Sententias*, IV d. 33 q. 2 a. 1: "Matrimony, from the intention of nature, is ordered to the education of the children, not for a certain time only, but rather for the entire life of the children (which is the reason why, by the law of nature, parents are to lay up wealth for their children, and children should inherit from their parents)." Thus, whatever the specific provisions of positive law, parents are effectively the trustees of their property for their children and must dispose it for their benefit, transferring legal possession upon death unless there is a grave reason to the contrary. See also below, p. 193 n. 43.

[67] STh 1a 2ae 105, 2 ad 3.

[68] Ibid. 95, 4. Cf. St Isidore of Seville, *Etymologies*, V.10.

opened to all kinds of trickery; each one will work only for his own profit, despising the public good; the cultivation of virtue will fail since honour, virtue's reward, will be bestowed upon the rich. Thus, in such a city, civic life will necessarily be corrupted.[69]

---

[69] *De Regno,* II.3.

Theses

(i)   The family is the necessary society constituted immediately by every fruitful marriage.

(ii)   The efficient cause of marriage is the promise of mutual fidelity in the work of procreation and education of offspring.

(iii)   Marriage can be contracted by any man and any woman capable of carnal intercourse, and not otherwise impeded, and only by such.

(iv)   The husband has the natural right to govern his wife so that their family may attain its end, though he ought to desire her counsel and aid in his government.

(v)   The parents have the natural right to govern their children in view of the goal of their common domestic society until these reach the age of majority.

(vi)   Marriage is both intrinsically and extrinsically indissoluble.

(vii)   The temporal power cannot abolish marriage, or change its properties, or forbid it to those to whom natural and divine law permit it.

(viii)   Temporal rulers are required by natural law to recognise and privilege marriage, and hence may make such reasonable demands upon a couple as will allow them to determine that a marriage has occurred.

(ix)   The family is prior to the temporal commonwealth in notion and in reality and hence has rights and duties which are independent of it.

(x)   The city is prior to the family in perfection and as a whole is prior to its parts, and hence can oblige the family to fulfil its duties toward the city.

(xi)   The temporal power may not forbid married couples to procreate, nor may it sterilise those who seem likely to engender disabled or unhealthy children.

(xii)   Education is the raising of children to the level of complete adulthood, and comprises bodily training, intellectual instruction, and formation in prudence and the virtues directed by prudence.

(xiii)	The temporal power may not interfere with the education which the parents give to their children, unless the parents gravely neglect their duty.
(xiv)	No one may baptise children against the will of the parents, except when the children are in danger of death.
(xv)	In extreme circumstances the spiritual power may take a baptised child even from its parental home if its religious education cannot otherwise be secured.
(xvi)	The need for non-patriarchal rule derives from the Fall of man.
(xvii)	The family and not the individual citizen is the basic unit of the temporal commonwealth, and hence it is fitting to vest certain offices in families and not merely in individuals.

Chapter 4
Servitude

Nature of servitude

Servitude, or slavery, is the ownership of one person's labour by another.[1] As such it is not contrary to natural law but it is an undesirable state.[2]

Although not *per se* sinful,[3] it is a consequence of sin.[4] The most obvious instance of this is when servitude is imposed as a punishment for crime. However, mortality and frailty too are consequences of the fallen state of man

---

[1] *Instruction* of the Sacred Congregation for the Propagation of the Faith, 20th June 1866: "Dominium enim illud, quod domino in servum competit non aliud esse intelligitur quam ius perpetuum de servi operis in proprium commodum disponendi, quas quidem homini ab homine praestari fas est" ("for that dominion which a master has over a slave is to be understood as the perpetual right of disposing, for his own benefit, of those toils of the slave which it is lawful to be performed by one man for another.")

[2] Leviticus 25:39-42; Philemon *passim*; STh 1a 2ae, 105, 4 ad 1: "As the children of Israel had been delivered by the Lord from slavery, and for this reason were bound to the service of God, He did not wish them to be slaves in perpetuity. [...] Consequently, since they were slaves, not absolutely but in a restricted sense, after a lapse of time they were set free."

[3] *Instruction* of the Sacred Congregation for the Propagation of the Faith, 20th June 1866: "Etsi Romani Pontifices nihil intentatum reliquerint quo servitutem ubique gentium abolerent, iisdemque praecipue acceptum referri debeat quod iam a pluribus saeculis nulli apud plurimas christianorum gentes servi habeantur; tamen servitus ipsa per se et absolute considerata iuri naturali et divino minime repugnat, pluresque adesse possunt iusti servitutis tituli quos videre est apud probatos theologos sacrorumque canonum interpretes" ("although the Roman pontiffs have left nothing untried in order that they might abolish slavery from all nations, and although it must be principally attributed to their efforts that there have been no slaves among very many Christian nations now for many centuries, nevertheless slavery itself considered abstractly and in itself is by no means contrary to natural and divine right, and many just titles to it can exist, which can be studied in the writings of approved theologians and commentators on the sacred canons.")

[4] St Augustine, *De civitate Dei*, XIX.15: "He did not intend that His rational creature, who was made in His image, should have dominion over anything but the irrational creation, - not man over man, but man over the beasts. And hence the righteous men in primitive times were made shepherds of cattle rather than kings of men, God intending thus to teach us what the relative position of the creatures is, and what the desert of sin; for it is with justice, we believe, that the condition of slavery is the result of sin. And this is why we do not find the word 'slave' in any part of Scripture until righteous Noah branded the sin of his son with this name. It is a name, therefore, introduced by sin and not by nature."

and these too may result in slavery without the personal sin of the one reduced to this state.

St Isidore declared: "Slavery alone is the most extreme of all evils; for free people it is worse than every kind of punishment, for where freedom is lost, everything is lost with it."[5] Of course, he is undoubtedly thinking here of perpetual slavery. Strictly speaking, whenever a person is employed by another for payment, he is in some sense that person's servant or slave. Indeed, the coercive aspect of government, whether parental, civil or ecclesiastical, is a form of servitude to at least one of which almost all are subject.[6] Even in the commonplace sense of paid employment, slavery is undesirable, for the paradigmatic form of ownership is where the labourer owns his own means of production.[7] This is more attuned to the nature of man, whom God has "left in the hand of his own counsel".[8] It is also a greater perfection, insofar as it is better, other things being equal, to move oneself to a certain goal than to be moved to it by another. It is in view of self-sufficiency and emancipation that the servant, that is, the man labouring for another in exchange for remuneration, labours. The condition of servitude is therefore of its very nature infantilising.[9]

Beyond this, St Isidore is no doubt also thinking of the fact that a man or woman reduced to perpetual servitude will very often, given man's fallen state, find that his master employs his labour for an end not common to slave and master, or to employee and employer, but privately advantageous to the latter and prejudicial to the former. This tyrannical relationship, sometimes called 'chattel slavery', finds pseudo-legal expression in the idea that the master owns the person rather than merely the labour of the slave. The potentially valid legal relationship of perpetual ownership of another's labour, already undesirable in itself, is rendered sinful when the master employs this labour for his own private good to the prejudice of the good of the slave. The pseudo-legal

---

[5] St Isidore of Seville, *Etymologies*, V.xxvii.32. St Thomas likewise writes: "There is nothing from which man by his natural inclination more shrinks than slavery"; *Liber de perfectione spiritualis vitae*, 10.

[6] Cf. St Augustine, *De civitate Dei*, 19.14-15; also STh 1a 96, 4.

[7] *Rerum Novarum* 46-47. See below, p. 187. Aristotle observed that "the skilled craftsman has a kind of delimited slavery (ἀφωρισμένην τινὰ ἔχει δουλείαν)"; *Politics*, I.13.

[8] Ecclesiasticus 15:14.

[9] Galatians 3:23-4:7; John 15:15.

approbation of this use of the slave by the master is directly contrary to natural law[10] and hence such a purported state of servitude is null and void.[11]

Origins of servitude

Given that non-penal but voluntary servitude, where the master owns only the labour of the slave, while a potentially valid legal relationship is nevertheless undesirable, how can it arise? If we speak of temporary servitude, which might be called servitude *secundum quid*, the answer is obvious. An individual does not own or possess the resources or opportunity to purchase the means of production necessary for his own fruitful labour and so he sells that labour to another to obtain the resources necessary to sustain himself and his dependants and to set aside enough in order eventually to acquire ownership of the means of production himself. If the remuneration for a full day's labour is insufficient to meet these needs, while the owner of the means of production enjoys a superfluity, this is a sign that some exceptional circumstances or the dishonest practices of an unscrupulous employer are depriving the labourer of the just remuneration of his toil and the civil magistrate may need to intervene, without respect of persons.[12]

---

[10] St Thomas Aquinas, *Scriptum super Sententias*, IV dist. 36, q. 1 a. 2; STh *Supplement*, 52, 2: "Positive law arises out of the natural law, and consequently slavery, which is of positive law, cannot be prejudicial to those things that are of natural law"; ad 1: "A slave is his master's chattel (*res domini*) in matters superadded to nature, but in natural things all are equal. Wherefore, in things pertaining to natural acts, a slave can by marrying give another person power over his body without his master's consent."

[11] St Augustine, *De sermone Domini in monte*, 1.59: "For a Christian ought not to possess a slave in the same way as a horse or money: although it may happen that a horse is valued at a greater price than a slave, and some article of gold or silver at much more."; *On the Sermon on the Mount*, William Findlay (tr.), Nicene and Post-Nicene Fathers, First Series, Vol. 6, ed. Philip Schaff (Buffalo, NY: Christian Literature Publishing Co., 1888). Cf. STh 1a 2ae, 57, 2 ad 2: "A son, as such, belongs to his father, and a slave, as such, belongs to his master; yet each, considered as a man, is something having separate existence and distinct from others. Hence in so far as each of them is a man, there is justice towards them in a way: and for this reason too there are certain laws regulating the relations of father to his son, and of a master to his slave; but in so far as each is something belonging to another, the perfect idea of 'right' or 'just' is wanting to them."

[12] In the most ancient body of Roman laws we find the following declaration: "Privilegia, sive leges in privos aut singulos homines, ne serantur, ad privatam alicuius iniuriam, contra ius, quod civibus commune est omnibus: et quo singuli, cuiuscunque sunt ordinis, recte utuntur" ("let not privileges, or laws for particular individuals, be established to the harm of some other particular person, contrary to the right which is common to all citizens, and

In some cases perpetual servitude, or servitude *simpliciter*, arises from an extreme version of the same conditions, often, although not necessarily, including dishonest practice. An individual cannot provide for himself because he lacks the resources or opportunity to possess the means of production and he is offered perpetual remuneration in exchange for perpetual employment. The judicial precepts of the Old Law allowed for indentured servitude for a term of years not exceeding that remaining before the next Jubilee, hence a maximum of fifty years. The Jubilee would also bring about the restoration of the original lands assigned to the twelve tribes at the conquest of Canaan so ensuring the possession by each family of its own means of production. Thus, not only the state of slavery but its external causes would lapse every fifty years.[13] Nevertheless, it was permitted for the Israelite slave in the land of promise to reject his periodic emancipation and voluntarily reduce himself, though not his descendants, to perpetual servitude.[14]

Indentured servitude of a term of years was often used as a means of obtaining passage across the Atlantic and a smallholding in the new world by emigrants from the British Isles. This is an extreme form of paid employment that might be justly offered instead of the more familiar contract of employment in circumstances, such as colonisation,[15] where the termination of such a contract might face the employer with disastrous, even life-threatening, consequences. In other similarly isolating and life-threatening circumstances such as civilizational collapse, where a contraction of technological horizons and a break-down in long-distance exchange reduces a population to subsistence agriculture, such indentured servitude could be rationally accepted as lifelong or even hereditary - the state known as serfdom. These circumstances are *ex hypothesi* extreme and this state is, as St Isidore indicated, highly undesirable in itself. If the slave or serf were prevented from owning property, or from enjoying marriage, privacy, weekly rest or worship, this would be a sign that he was subject to individual abuse on the part of the master or that the state to

---

which each person, whatever his rank may be, rightly enjoys"); Johann Nicolaus Funck, *Leges XII tabularum suis quotquot reperiri potuerunt fragmentis restitutae* (Rinteln, 1744), 378. Some speculative reconstruction is involved in this collection.

[13] Leviticus 25:10.

[14] Exodus 21:1-11.

[15] We do not here consider the legitimacy of the settlement itself which may be challenged by prior claims of existing inhabitants, but are only considering the challenges of cultivating in putative isolation supposedly virgin territory at vast distances from the original society of the settlers.

which he had been reduced was chattel slavery and therefore null and void.[16] Again, just as the payment of a wage to a contracted employee that was inadequate to permit him to set aside enough eventually to acquire ownership of the means of production himself would be a sign of some injustice requiring the attention of the civil magistrate, so too if a slave or serf cannot choose to labour additionally to the hours reasonably demanded by his master in order to accumulate the resources necessary to purchase his own redemption, this is normally a sign of concealed chattel slavery.

As it is slavery and not liberty which departs from man's natural state the burden of proof as to the legitimate title of a master to the perpetual or inherited servitude of any individual lies upon the master. If he finds a flaw in the title or is unable to meet that burden of proof he must immediately emancipate the individual and compensate him.[17] Should he fail to do so, the falsely imprisoned person (for such he is) may take such steps as he judges prudent, including necessary but proportionate force, to restore his freedom. Where there is a just title the master must nevertheless employ the slave's labour towards the common good of both, respect the other conditions so far mentioned and never alienate his title to another where he has good reason to

---

[16] St Thomas Aquinas, STh 2a 2ae 104, 5 "[T]here are two reasons, for which a subject may not be bound to obey his superior in all things. First on account of the command of a higher power. For as a gloss says on Romans 13, 'They that resist the power, resist the ordinance of God', 'If a commissioner issue an order, are you to comply, if it is contrary to the bidding of the proconsul? Again if the proconsul command one thing, and the emperor another, will you hesitate, to disregard the former and serve the latter? Therefore, if the emperor commands one thing and God another, you must disregard the former and obey God.' Secondly, a subject is not bound to obey his superior if the latter command him to do something wherein he is not subject to him. For Seneca says in *De Beneficiis* III: 'It is wrong to suppose that slavery falls upon the whole man: for the better part of him is excepted. His body is subjected and assigned to his master but his soul is his own.' Consequently, in matters touching the internal movement of the will man is not bound to obey his fellow-man, but God alone. Nevertheless man is bound to obey his fellow-man in things that have to be done externally by means of the body: and yet, since by nature all men are equal, he is not bound to obey another man in matters touching the nature of the body, for instance in those relating to the support of his body or the begetting of his children. Wherefore servants are not bound to obey their masters, nor children their parents, in the question of contracting marriage or of remaining in the state of virginity or the like. But in matters concerning the disposal of actions and human affairs, a subject is bound to obey his superior within the sphere of his authority; for instance a soldier must obey his general in matters relating to war, a servant his master in matters touching the execution of the duties of his service, a son his father in matters relating to the conduct of his life and the care of the household; and so forth."

[17] Innocent XI, *Response of the Congregation of the Holy Office*, n. 230, March 20th, 1686, in *Collectanea S.C. de Propaganda Fide*, 1907, Rome, I, 2100, no. 4-6.

suspect these conditions will not be met, or to an infidel.[18] Aristotle himself, while considering widespread slavery a normal feature of human life, also held that to be just it must be mutually beneficial, and that in such circumstances there could be a kind of friendship between master and slave, even considered as such.[19] However, this belief was based on the false conception of 'natural slaves' unable to direct themselves to their own good. Except in the case of a physical impairment to the brain or of minors there are no such persons.[20] In

---

[18] "But with respect to that slave, if he is being educated and ruled by you as his master, in a way more upright, and more honourable, and more conducing to the fear of God, than can be done by him who desires to take him away, I do not know whether anyone would dare to say that he ought to be despised like a garment. For a man ought to love a fellow-man as himself, inasmuch as he is commanded by the Lord of all"; St Augustine, *On the Sermon on the Mount*, William Findlay (tr.), Nicene and Post-Nicene Fathers, First Series, Vol. 6, ed. Philip Schaff (Buffalo, NY: Christian Literature Publishing Co., 1888), translation partly corrected.

[19] *Politics*, Bk. I.6. This friendship however could only be friendship 'in a certain respect', not simply speaking, since his conception of 'just servitude' requires that the enslaved person have so diminished a power of reason as to be capable only of virtue 'in a certain respect'; *Politics* I.13. In the *Nicomachean Ethics*, Bk. VIII.11, by contrast, Aristotle had stated that the master and slave could have friendship with each other insofar as they were men, and not insofar as they were master and slave. We can perhaps reconcile these passages by supposing that in the *Ethics* he is considering simply what is implied by the relation of master and slave as such, and abstracting from the justice of a given case.

[20] Paul III, *Sublimis Deus*: "[S]ince man, according to the testimony of the sacred scriptures, has been created to enjoy eternal life and happiness, which none may obtain save through faith in our Lord Jesus Christ, it is necessary that he should possess the nature and faculties enabling him to receive that faith; and that whoever is thus endowed should be capable of receiving that same faith. Nor is it credible that anyone should possess so little understanding as to desire the faith and yet be destitute of the most necessary faculty to enable him to receive it. Hence Christ, who is the Truth itself, that has never failed and can never fail, said to the preachers of the faith whom He chose for that office 'Go ye and teach all nations.' He said all, without exception, for all are capable of receiving the doctrines of the faith. The enemy of the human race, who opposes all good deeds in order to bring men to destruction, beholding and envying this, invented a means never before heard of, by which he might hinder the preaching of God's word of Salvation to the people: he inspired his satellites who, to please him, have not hesitated to publish abroad that the Indians of the West and the South, and other people of whom We have recent knowledge, should be treated as dumb brutes created for our service, pretending that they are incapable of receiving the Catholic Faith. We, who, though unworthy, exercise on earth the power of our Lord and seek with all our might to bring those sheep of His flock who are outside into the fold committed to our charge, consider, however, that the Indians are truly men and that they are not only capable of understanding the Catholic Faith but, according to our information, they desire exceedingly to receive it. Desiring to provide ample remedy for these evils, We define and declare by these Our letters … that, notwithstanding

the case of perpetual or inherited servitude, given that charity itself demands that he will the good of his slaves for their own sake, there will need to be perduring exceptional circumstances to explain at any given time why a Christian master has not emancipated his slaves.

Servitude, even perpetual, is a legitimate punishment for the gravest criminal offences or for a person taken prisoner in pursuit of an unjust war. In fact, no temporal polity could endure if this were not the case, as the capacity to incarcerate criminals and wage just war is essential to the existence of a temporal polity and conversely the execution of all criminals and a refusal to take prisoners in combat would be incompatible with natural justice.

Given the immense scope for the abuse of perpetual and hereditary servitude, it would seem prudent for the civil magistrate to forbid these arrangements by positive law, outside the exceptional circumstances of civilizational collapse, widespread subsistence agriculture or colonial settlement mentioned above.[21] Involuntary non-penal enslavement is contrary to natural law and is null and void.[22] The attempt to reduce anyone to this condition should be punished by the civil magistrate most severely. The laws should in general favour and encourage economic autonomy over employment, although employment will remain a necessary mechanism, not least pedagogically, at some stage in life for many people in almost all societies.

In the pursuit of measures favouring economic autonomy the civil magistrate must take great care not to compromise the equality of his subjects before the

---

whatever may have been or may be said to the contrary, the said Indians and all other people who may later be discovered by Christians, are by no means to be deprived of their liberty or the possession of their property, even though they be outside the faith of Jesus Christ; and that they may and should, freely and legitimately, enjoy their liberty and the possession of their property; nor should they be in any way enslaved; should the contrary happen, it shall be null and have no effect." *Sublimis Deus* was promulgated in 1537.

[21] Cf. St Gregory the Great, *Epistles,* Book 6, epistle 12; PL 77, 803-804: "Since our Redeemer, the Author of all life, deigned to take human flesh, that by the power of His Godhead the chains by which we were held in bondage being broken, He might restore us to our first state of liberty, it is most fitting that men by the concession of manumission should restore to the freedom in which they were born those whom nature sent free into the world, but who have been condemned to the yoke of slavery by the law of nations." See also Leo XIII, *In plurimis*, 2.

[22] Paul III, *Sublimis Deus*. Magisterial documents sometimes use the term 'slavery' to refer exclusively to that servitude which has its root in involuntary non-penal enslavement or in which the 'owner' purports to dispose of the person and not merely the labour of the slave; cf. 2nd Vatican Council, *Gaudium et spes*, 27. In either of these senses the condition is violent and evil in itself.

law, as this would convert the temporal power itself into a private economic actor and reduce its subjects simply as subjects to a form of servitude on the very pretext of its eradication. For in regulating the disposal of the private goods of its subjects apart from the law common to all citizens, the civil power effectively assumes to itself an interest in those goods and makes itself judge in its own cause. "There shall be no difference of persons, you shall hear the little as well as the great: neither shall you respect any man's person, because it is the judgment of God."[23]

The legalization of usury is also, by converting the potential labour of all the subjects of a particular government into a commodity available for a consideration within its jurisdiction, a covert form of enslavement.[24]

> And the kings of the earth, who committed fornication and were wanton with her, will weep and wail over her when they see the smoke of her burning; they will stand far off, in fear of her torment, and say,

> 'Alas! alas! thou great city, thou mighty city, Babylon! In one hour has thy judgment come.'

> And the merchants of the earth weep and mourn for her, since no one buys their cargo any more, cargo of gold, silver, jewels and pearls, fine linen, purple, silk and scarlet, all kinds of scented wood, all articles of ivory, all articles of costly wood, bronze, iron and marble, cinnamon, spice, incense, myrrh, frankincense, wine, oil, fine flour and wheat, cattle and sheep, horses and chariots, and slaves, that is, human souls.[25]

---

[23] Deuteronomy 1:17. See also Henry de Bracton, *De Legibus et Consuetudinibus Angliae*, III.6.

[24] Leo XIII, *Rerum novarum*, 3: "[B]y degrees it has come to pass that working men have been surrendered, isolated and helpless, to the hard-heartedness of employers and the greed of unchecked competition. The mischief has been increased by rapacious usury, which, although more than once condemned by the Church, is nevertheless, under a different guise, but with like injustice, still practiced by covetous and grasping men. To this must be added that the hiring of labour and the conduct of trade are concentrated in the hands of comparatively few; so that a small number of very rich men have been able to lay upon the teeming masses of the labouring poor a yoke little better than that of slavery itself." For usury, see below, pp. 191-93.

[25] Apoc. 18: 9-13.

Theses

(i)   Servitude, or slavery, is the ownership of one person's labour by another.

(ii)   Life-long ownership of one person's labour by another is servitude simply speaking.

(iii)   Temporary ownership of one person's labour by another is servitude, in a certain respect.

(iv)   Servitude, while not *per se* contrary to natural law, is a highly undesirable state.

(v)   'Chattel slavery' is a tyrannical relation, based on the false claim that one man may own the person and not simply the labour of another.

(vi)   While extreme social conditions may justify life-long or even hereditary non-penal servitude, in the absence of such conditions, this state is fittingly proscribed by positive law.

(vii)   The burden of proof as to the legitimate title of a master to the perpetual or inherited servitude of any individual lies upon the master.

(viii)   The presence of a just title does not abrogate the master's duty to will the good of the slave or employee for the latter's own sake and hence to desire his emancipation.

(ix)   Servitude, even perpetual, is a legitimate punishment for the gravest criminal offences or for a person taken prisoner in pursuit of an unjust war.

Chapter 5
Temporal authority (I): its origin

I saw in my vision by night, and behold the four winds of the heaven strove upon the great sea. And four great beasts, different one from another, came up out of the sea. The first was like a lioness, and had the wings of an eagle: I beheld till her wings were plucked off, and she was lifted up from the earth, and stood upon her feet as a man, and the heart of a man was given to her.[1]

Nature of temporal power

Since man possesses a nature composed of potency and act, he has some goal proportionate to his nature, and may attain this goal by action. He desires to do this not only by using society as an instrument, and from material necessity, but *within* society, attaining thereby higher goods which being shared are not thereby diminished. Indeed, he is more excellent in society insofar as he possesses in some way the excellences of all within it.

Since the legitimate power (right to coerce) of the parents ceases when it has reached the goal for which it is given, of raising children to physical and moral manhood, there is need of another power which though by nature posterior to that of parents, is not delegated by them, and which is broader in scope than theirs. This is what is often referred to as civil or political power; but since, as we have argued, in our order of providence only the Catholic Church intrinsically instantiates the notion which political philosophers have framed of the *civitas* or *polis* as a perfect society, it will here be called temporal power. This name suggests its native and proximate purpose: to bring men to the goal assigned by human nature and attainable in time, that is, in this life. Among fallen men temporal life must be guided not only by *auctoritas*, in the sense of the simple right to govern, but also *potestas*, in the sense of governance with coercion.[2]

---

[1] Dan. 7:2-4.

[2] For the distinction between *auctoritas* and *potestas* see Augustus, *Res Gestae* 34 and St Gelasius I, Epistle 8, *Famuli vestrae pietatis*, written in AD 494; PL 59:42. This epistle is sometimes known as *Duo sunt*, because these are the opening words of that section within it normally excerpted in collections of canon law.

Aristotle sketched man's natural earthly goal in the *Nicomachean Ethics* and the *Politics*. Man's greatest good, as there set forth, which is identical to his natural happiness, consists in the activity of the soul according to virtue,[3] principally the virtue of speculative wisdom which finds its highest act in the contemplation of God, secondarily the virtues of practical wisdom and character,[4] practised in the company of friends, supported by a healthy body and by the minimum sufficiency of material goods, as a free citizen of a free and self-sufficient city where all the citizens know one another, a city possessing peace within and security without. Since this is the social good assigned to man by his human nature it is incorrect to claim that political authority exists principally to secure for each person the greatest possible exercise of liberty compatible with the liberty of others.[5] This doctrine, commonly called 'liberalism', and dominant in the West since the French Revolution, tacitly assumes that free will, or else free action, is itself the highest human good. This is absurd: a faculty, such as the will, cannot be the highest good, since it exists for the sake of something else, namely its own activity; and a creature's free action as such cannot be its highest good, since this action can

---

[3] Aristotle often mentions pleasure as a property of happiness, e.g. *Nicomachean Ethics* VII.13: "Everyone thinks that a happy life is a pleasant one; and understandably they associate pleasure with happiness, for no perfect activity is impeded. But happiness is a perfect good. Therefore the happy man needs goods of the body and external goods of fortune so that he may not be impeded in his activity. People who say that a virtuous man is happy even when broken on the wheel and overcome by great misfortune talk nonsense either willingly or unwillingly."

[4] It is often disputed whether Aristotle has a consistent doctrine about the respective place of *sophia* (speculative wisdom) and the other virtues in happiness. Although the question cannot be pursued here, it seems that his various comments can be reconciled if one allows that in itself, activity according to the wisdom of the speculative intellect, that is, the contemplation of God, is sufficient to constitute *eudaimonia*, while in the conditions of man as Aristotle understood him to exist, unable to perceive the essence of God, this happiness remains incomplete without being supplemented by the activity of the other virtues. Hence St Thomas argues that only in heaven is there a happiness according to the speculative intellect alone; STh 1a 2ae 3, 5: "The last and perfect happiness, which we await in the life to come, consists entirely in contemplation. But imperfect happiness, such as can be had here, consists first and principally in contemplation, and secondarily in an operation of the practical intellect directing human actions and passions, as stated in *Ethics* X.7, 8." Cf. STh 1a 2ae 4, 8 ad 3: "If there were but one soul enjoying God, it would be happy, though having no neighbour to love."

[5] Such a claim is strongly suggested by John Stuart Mill (1806-73) in his highly influential work *On Liberty*. In more recent times it has been explicitly formulated among others by John Rawls (1921-2002); J. Rawls, *A Theory of Justice* (Belknap Press: Cambridge MA, 1971), 60-65.

be evil. It is quite conceivable, and indeed often the case, that human beings freely render themselves miserable.

Aristotle in his portrait of man's happiness was sketching unconsciously a distant image of the heavenly city, to which we must be brought by another kind of power, called spiritual. The relation of the temporal and spiritual powers is one of the principal questions of political philosophy.

Need for temporal power

Since powers are specified by their objects, some power distinct from that of parents over their children would always have been necessary. Would temporal and spiritual power have been distinct in an unfallen world? Even in this state, adult human beings would have needed ruling.[6] It would have been possible for God to have ruled each person directly; yet outside the state of beatitude, where He makes rational creatures gods by participation, this is unfitting, since "according to the Blessed Dionysius, it is a law of the divinity that the lowest things reach the highest place by intermediaries".[7] Hence by causing all other human beings to exist from Adam, God intimated that there was to be a hierarchy of power among them.[8] There would certainly have been an exercise of spiritual authority among unfallen men. Some would have had the right to instruct others about revealed truths and about all matters pertaining to public worship, such as sacred rites and holy times and places. For men in that state were able to sin, and would therefore have required to be reminded with authority about their duties.

Some small degree of temporal authority directing man to the end proportionate to his nature and attained in this life, would perhaps have been necessary to preserve unity among them. For example, we can imagine that even in the paradisal state some public authority might have existed to solve doubts about ownership, or to assist in communication as mankind spread out across the face of the earth. However, there would have been no need for spiritual and temporal authority to have been placed in different hands.

---

[6] STh 1a 96, 4: "Man is naturally a social being, and so in the state of innocence he would have led a social life. Now a social life cannot exist among a number of people unless under the presidency of one to look after the common good; for many, as such, seek many things, whereas one attends only to one." Cf. also St Robert Bellarmine, *Controversiae*, 'On the members of the Church', bk. 3, ch. 7. The 'one' who presides need not in all cases be a single human being, but can be a single institution. See below, 'Forms of Polity'.

[7] Boniface VIII, *Unam sanctam*.

[8] STh 1a 92, 2.

Principle of all other human beings, replete with wisdom and virtue, the first Adam would have fitly been both high priest and universal king. Even if prelapsarian philosophers had mentally distinguished a temporal authority from the spiritual, no one in such a world would have thought of himself as belonging to two societies, temporal and spiritual. Why would they? At peace with each other as they aspired toward beatitude, and receiving no commands except those which would make the path thither more pleasant and expeditious, their society would have been far more united than any we shall experience here below.

After the Fall of man, the spiritual and temporal powers seem at first to have been generally still united in the same person. This is the testimony first of all of Holy Scripture. Melchisedek is both king and priest; and commenting on the words of Jacob, *Ruben, my firstborn, thou art my strength*[9] St Jerome puts these words into the father's mouth: "You ought according to the order of your birth to have received the inheritance due to the first born, both the priesthood and the kingdom".[10] Moses, likewise, exercises both spiritual and temporal power over the people of Israel, and somewhat later Eli is presented as not only high priest but also as 'judge' for forty years.[11] Much later still, successive members of the Maccabean dynasty united the two powers.[12] Among pagan witnesses, Aristotle states that in the heroic age, kings "had authority over matters related to the gods", and offered sacrifices.[13]

The Fall, however, not only caused the heavier weight of temporal power to be applied to Adam's sons, but also furnished reasons why this power might be placed into other hands than wield the spiritual. Accordingly, not only did the judges and the seventy elders ruling the people with Moses not have to be drawn exclusively from the tribe of Levi,[14] but the Mosaic Law recognised a

---

[9] Gen. 49:3.

[10] *Hebrew Questions on Genesis*, PL 23: 1056B: "Debebas iuxta ordinem nativitatis tuae, haereditatem, quae primogeniti iure debebas, et sacerdotium accipere et regnum." Bellarmine, for his part, notes that while Cain founded the first material city, the *politicum regimen* did not begin with him: "It cannot be denied that Adam's sons and grandsons were subject to him"; *Controversiae*, 'On the members of the Church', bk. 3, ch. 7.

[11] 1 Sam. 4:18.

[12] The union of the powers was decided in favour of Simon Maccabeus in 140 BC; cf. 1 Mach. 14 and Josephus's *Antiquities of the Jews*, Book 12.

[13] *Politics* III.14. However, he recognises a certain distinction even at this early period, since he remarks that these kings offered only those sacrifices which did not require priests.

[14] Num. 11:16.

future kingship among the Jews distinct from the Levitical priesthood,[15] and when that kingship was later instituted by God, the offices of king and of high priest always belonged to different men.[16] When King Uzziah attempted to usurp the priestly office, he was stricken with leprosy.[17]

Under the New Law, Pope Gelasius I laid down an important principle:

> Christ, mindful of human frailty, regulated with an excellent disposition what pertained to the salvation of his people. Thus he distinguished between the offices of both powers according to their own proper activities and separate dignities, wanting his people to be saved by healthful humility and not carried away again by human pride, so that Christian emperors would need priests for attaining eternal life, and priests would avail themselves of imperial regulations in the conduct of temporal affairs.[18]

The *supreme* temporal ruler, therefore, should under the New Covenant not be a priest. This does not exclude the possibility of some spiritual and temporal power, even under the gospel, belonging to the same man.[19] Most obviously, it is very desirable that the pope not be subject, even *de facto*, to any temporal sovereign. St Robert Bellarmine likewise held that it was by divine providence that certain bishops in Germany were also temporal princes, since otherwise the Reformation would have swept all before it in that land. Nevertheless, under the New Covenant, the wielder of the spiritual power has as such no title to *the use* of the temporal power and indeed is apparently forbidden to make use of it save in necessity.[20] Where the Roman empire persisted in Byzantium,

---

[15] Deut. 17.18.

[16] Again, while Moses performs certain priestly functions, it is not he but Aaron who is the high priest. In this way the two brothers appear as at least archetypes of the distinction of temporal and spiritual powers.

[17] 2 Chron. 26.

[18] 'On the bond of the anathema', PL 59:109 In the same place, St Gelasius indicates that since Christ came, as both true king and true high priest, it would now be an impossible presumption for any fallen man to attempt to exercise both offices.

[19] Cf. *Syllabus of Errors*, condemned proposition 27: "The sacred ministers of the Church and the Roman pontiff are to be absolutely excluded from every charge and dominion over temporal affairs."

[20] Cf. Jn. 18:11: "Jesus therefore said to Peter: Put up thy sword into the scabbard." The collapse of the temporal power in the west after the fall of the Western Empire and of the Carolingian Empire, and the subsequent elision of property ownership and civil authority, frequently provoked such cases of necessity, which nevertheless remained *per se* exceptional.

clergy did not exercise such power, and in modern canon law the holder of spiritual power is in general forbidden to do so.[21] Bellarmine himself allows that "absolutely speaking, it would perhaps be better for pontiffs to deal only with spiritual things, and kings only with temporal ones".[22] St Gelasius indicated the reason. As well as the sheer difficulty of wielding both swords on behalf of a numerous people, the occasions for avarice and pride offered by supreme temporal power and the urgent need for humility and detachment in those who exercise spiritual power, especially now the higher perfection of the New Covenant has been given us to pursue, suggest that the two powers should not be combined in the same men where no pressing cause exists.[23] This distinction also serves to remind men of the distinction between natural and supernatural things.[24]

Temporal power is subject to spiritual power

Some arts, Aristotle remarks at the very beginning of the *Nicomachean Ethics*, are subordinate to others, since some products of art are chosen for the sake of others. Athletic vestments, for example, are chosen for the sake of running or jumping, and hence the maker of such vestments must consider principally, not whatever material or shape most please his eye, but whatever will best suit the competition for which they will be worn. His art is subordinate to the athlete's. More generally we can say that the subordination of ends implies the subordination of means.

Can we apply this to the relation of the temporal and the spiritual power? Yes, since the temporal good of some society of men is of its nature subordinate to their eternal good; that is, temporal good, though good in itself and hence not a mere means, would no longer deserve to be loved by men if it became an

---

[21] CIC 285§3: "Officia publica, quae participationem in exercitio civilis potestatis secumferunt, clerici asssumere vetantur" ("clerics are forbidden to assume public offices which entail a participation in the exercise of civil power.")

[22] *Controversiae*, 'On the Supreme Pontiff', bk. 5, ch. 9. A prelate who possesses temporal authority is not freed from the restrictions that pertain to him by reason of holy Orders, and hence he may not personally shed blood; STh 2a 2ae 64, 4 ad 3.

[23] For example, simony would be far more prevalent if the same men exercised both powers.

[24] Cf. *De Regno*, 1.15, where St Thomas remarks that kings have not been given the governance of the Church, *ut a terrenis essent spiritualia distincta* ("so that spiritual things might be distinguished from earthly ones"). The opinion that kings or other temporal rulers have supreme power in religious matters is called Erastianism, after the Swiss physician Thomas Lieber (1524-83), who after the fashion of the time hellenized his surname as Erastus.

obstacle to their eternal good. Likewise, its highest value lies in disposing them to eternal good: "It is not the ultimate end of an assembled multitude to live virtuously, but through virtuous living to attain to divine fruition".[25] Hence, the end to which the temporal ruler directs the multitude can only be correctly pursued when it is subordinated to the higher goal which is eternal life. Most especially does this apply to the highest naturally knowable good, that of religion, and the fulfilment of our most fundamental naturally knowable duty, namely to worship our Creator according to the manner that He has appointed: for without submitting to an authority based on revelation, the temporal power cannot know in what this good and this duty concretely consist and order its actions accordingly.

Indeed, outside the state of sanctifying grace, fallen men are unable consistently to keep even those elements of the natural law which they can correctly discern, and for this reason too the natural end of man cannot be obtained unless the supernatural end is loved more than it.

Thus, since the ordering of agents among themselves flows from the ordering of ends,[26] the temporal power must be subordinated to the spiritual. "The king must be subject to the dominion and government administered by the office of the priesthood."[27] Since Pentecost, this means that all temporal rulers must be subject to the authority of the Catholic Church.[28] St Thomas writes as follows:

> The ministry of this kingdom [sc. the Church] has been entrusted not to earthly kings but to priests, and most of all to the chief priest, the successor of St Peter, the vicar of Christ, the Roman Pontiff. To him all the kings of the Christian people are to be subject as to our Lord Jesus Christ Himself. For those to whom pertains the care of

---

[25] *De Regno*, I.1.

[26] A principle often invoked by St Thomas, e.g. ibid. 15: "We always find that the one to whom it pertains to achieve the final end commands those who execute the things that are ordained to that end."

[27] Ibid. 16.

[28] Pius XI instituted the feast of Christ the King in part to affirm this principle; cf. *Quas primas* 18: "All men, whether collectively or individually, are under the dominion of Christ. In him is the salvation of the individual, in him is the salvation of society [...] If, therefore, the rulers of nations wish to preserve their authority, to promote and increase the prosperity of their countries, they will not neglect the public duty of reverence and obedience to the rule of Christ."

intermediate ends should be subject to him to whom pertains the care of the ultimate end, and be directed by his rule.[29]

According to St Robert Bellarmine, this obligation is incurred when a temporal ruler receives baptism:

> When kings and princes come to the Church to be made Christians, they are received with the agreement, either express or tacit, to submit their sceptres to Christ and to promise to preserve and defend the faith of Christ, even under pain of losing their realm. [...] For whoever is not ready to serve Christ, and to lose for His sake whatever he has, is not suitable for the sacrament of baptism.[30]

By the same reasoning, the obligation to put one's temporal power at the service of the Church is also incurred when an already baptised person first acquires such power.

The need for the temporal power to be subjected to the spiritual can be proved in another way, not now from the perspective of man who has to be brought to his due end, but from that of God who has the right to be worshipped by His creatures. Human societies, deriving from nature and thus from the author of nature, are among these creatures which have the duty to worship God, and therefore those who rule them must offer this worship as representatives of them; and thus rulers are obliged, as a condition of ruling rightly, publicly to profess that faith by which God is rightly worshipped,[31] and publicly to participate in the rites which express that faith.[32] Since God wills to be worshipped not only as Creator but also as a Trinity of persons of whom the Word has been made flesh, uniting to Himself a Church as His mystical body, those who hold temporal power over men have been obliged since Pentecost to worship God according to a lawful rite of the Catholic Church.

---

[29] *De Regno*, 15.

[30] *Controversiae*, 'On the Supreme Pontiff', bk. 5, ch. 7: "Quando reges et principes ad Ecclesiam veniunt ut Christiani fiant, recipiuntur cum pacto expresso vel tacito ut sceptra sua subiciant Christo, et polliceantur se Christi fidem servaturos et defensuros sub poena regni perdendi [...] Nam non est idoneus sacramento baptismi qui non est paratus Christo servire, et propter ipsum amittere quidquid habet."

[31] Cf. *The Athanasian Creed*: "Fides autem catholica haec est: ut unum Deum in Trinitate, et Trinitatem in unitate veneremur" ("the Catholic faith is this: that we worship one God in Trinity, and Trinity in Unity".)

[32] These rites, moreover, cannot be of man's devising, lest man appear to claim the power to give from himself an adequate response to God's gifts, something which is impossible on account of the absolute asymmetry of the relationship and the gratuity of the end that God grants to man.

Only a Catholic polity is simply speaking legitimate

Temporal power which is possessed or exercised without subjection to the rightful spiritual power therefore cannot be called simply speaking "legitimate", that is, "in accordance with law". Insofar as its bearer may have nonetheless, as we shall see, a right and duty to wield it, and others the duty to obey, it may be called legitimate in a certain respect: in this sense, Alexander did not differ from the pirate chief only by the number of his men.[33] Yet insofar as temporal power unsubject to the rightful spiritual power cannot direct man either to his supernatural or to his natural end, societies so ruled are depicted by the word of God as destructive wild beasts.[34] Thus Babylon under King Nebuchadnezzar is seen by the prophet as a winged lioness. Yet because the king would eventually come to acknowledge the true God and recognise Daniel as His spokesman, the prophet also saw a dramatic change occur: "I beheld till her wings were plucked off, and she was lifted up from the earth, and stood upon her feet as a man, and the heart of a man was given to her". Even so do human societies enjoy a change from a bestial to a human state insofar as the temporal power recognises the superior rights of the spiritual.[35]

Institution of the temporal authority

Since temporal power cannot be simply legitimate unless subordinated to the spiritual, the spiritual power must in some way establish it. The principle that

---

[33] While the earliest source for the story is Cicero, it is best known in St Augustine's version: "When that king had asked the man what he meant by infesting the sea, the latter answered with bold pride, 'The same as you do by infesting the whole earth; but because I do it with a petty ship, I am called a robber, and because you do it with a great army, you are called an emperor'" (*On the City of God*, IV.4).

[34] Dan. 7. Cf. *CCC* 2244: "Only the divinely revealed religion has clearly recognized man's origin and destiny in God, the Creator and Redeemer. The Church invites political authorities to measure their judgments and decisions against this inspired truth about God and man: societies not recognizing this vision or rejecting it in the name of their independence from God are brought to seek their criteria and goal in themselves or to borrow them from some ideology. Since they do not admit that one can defend an objective criterion of good and evil, they arrogate to themselves an explicit or implicit totalitarian power over man and his destiny, as history shows."

[35] The truly human community is not realised in Daniel's vision until the coming of the human figure who represents the Messiah and His mystical body: "I beheld therefore in the vision of the night, and lo, one like the son of man came with the clouds of heaven" (Dan. 7:13).

the temporal power is instituted by the spiritual was stated by Hugh of St Victor in his treatise *De sacramentis.*

It belongs to the spiritual power both to institute the earthly power, so that it may exist, and to judge it if it be not good. It was itself instituted by God to be first, and if it should go wrong, it can be judged by God alone, as it is written: *The spiritual judges all things, and is itself judged by none* (1 Cor. 2). That the spiritual power is, in regard to its divine institution, both first in time and greater in dignity is clearly declared in the ancient people of the Old Testament, where first of all the priesthood was instituted by God, and afterwards, the royal power was ordained by the priesthood, at the command of God. For this reason, in the Church, the priestly dignity still consecrates the royal power, both sanctifying it by a blessing, and forming it by an act of instituting.[36]

A generation later, St Thomas Becket boldly made the same assertion in writing to King Henry II of England.[37] It is likewise implied by Innocent III's comparison of the priestly power to the sun and the kingly to the moon[38], since the moon derives its light from the sun.[39] Boniface VIII's dogmatic bull *Unam sanctam* made use of Hugh's very words:

The spiritual power surpasses in dignity and in nobility any temporal power whatever, as spiritual things surpass the temporal. This we see very clearly also by the payment of tithes, by benedictions and consecrations, by the reception of power itself and by the very government of things. For truth bears witness that the spiritual power must institute the earthly one and judge it if it be not good;

---

[36] PL 176: 418. Hugh died in 1141.

[37] Letter 74, PL 190: 652: "Certum est reges potestatem suam accipere ab Ecclesia, non ipsam ab illis, sed a Christo" ("it is certain that kings receive their power from the Church, and that she receives power not from them but from Christ.")

[38] *Decretals*, Bk. 1, tit. 33, c. 76: "Ad firmamentum coeli, hoc est universalis Ecclesiae, fecit Deus duo magna luminaria, id est, duo instituit, dignitates, quae sunt Pontificalis auctoritas et Regalis potestas. Sed illa quae praeest diebus id est spiritualibus, maior est, quae vero carnalibus, minor: ut quanta est inter solem et lunam, tanta inter Pontifices et Reges differentia dignoscatur" ("in the firmament of the heaven, that is, the universal Church, God made two great lights, that is, He instituted two dignities, which are the pontifical authority and the royal power. But that which presides over the days, that is, over spiritual things, is greater, and that which presides over carnal things is lesser; so that as great a difference may be seen between pontiffs and kings as between the sun and the moon.")

[39] A fact known to mediaeval astronomy; cf. STh 1a 109, 3 obj. 2. Boniface VIII would make the same comparison in a discourse of 1303 recognising Albert of Austria as emperor.

thus with the Church and the ecclesiastical power is fulfilled the prophecy of Jeremiah, *Behold, I have set thee today over nations and kings* (Jer. 1).[40]

What does 'institution' mean here? Certainly not simply 'teach', as some authors, appealing to the second sense of the Latin *instituere* have suggested. Clearly also, it is something much greater than the mere recognition by the Holy See of some foreign power as an entity with which it desires to have normal diplomatic relations. Yet institution by the spiritual power does not mean that popes and bishops must choose temporal rulers, nor that these rulers must take instruction from the spiritual power in purely temporal matters, that is, ones which do not in themselves require revelation or grace to accomplish, for example, the best manner to build a road or train an army. It means that the temporal power, to exist in a well-ordered manner and to be legitimate *simpliciter* must be put at the service of the spiritual power, so that it may play its part in bringing men to heaven.[41] For the temporal power is united to the spiritual, according to the ancient metaphor, as body to soul, or as matter to spirit, when the Church exists in her normal state[42]; and "whenever two

---

[40] "Spiritualem autem et dignitate et nobilitate terrenam quamlibet praecellere potestatem, oportet tanto clarius nos fateri quanto spiritualia temporalia antecellunt. Quod etiam ex decimarum datione, et benedictione, et sanctificatione, ex ipsius potestatis acceptione, ex ipsarum rerum gubernatione claris oculis intuemur. Veritate testante, spiritualis potestas terrenam potestatem instituere habet et judicare, si bona non fuerit, sic de Ecclesia et ecclesiastica potestate verificatur vaticinium Hieremiae, 'Ecce constitui te hodie super gentes et regna'."

[41] *De Regno*, I.16: "It pertains to the king's office to promote the good life of the multitude in such a way as to make it suitable for the attainment of heavenly happiness."

[42] Cf. St Gregory Nazianzen, Oration 17.8, where the bishop addresses the prefect in these terms: "The law of Christ puts you under my jurisdiction and authority, for we too are rulers ourselves; and, I might add, our rule is of a more important and perfect nature; else the spirit must yield to the flesh, and the things of heaven to the things of earth"; St John Chrysostom, *Homilies on the 2nd Epistle to the Corinthians*, 15.5: "There is yet another rule, higher than the political rule. And what is this? That in the Church.[..] As great then as the difference between soul and body, is that which separates this rule from that one"; St Isidore of Pelusium, spiritual father to St Cyril of Alexandria, to Isidore the deacon, PG 78:928: "By priesthood and kingship are things held together, though they differ much from each other. For the one is like the soul, and the other like the body, yet do they look both toward one goal, the salvation of their subjects"; St Robert Bellarmine, *Controversiae*, 'On the members of the Church', bk. 3, ch. 18: "The temporal and spiritual power in the Church are not two disjoined and separate things, like two political kingdoms, but they are conjoined so as to make one body; or rather, they are related as are the body and the soul in one man"; Leo XIII, *Immortale Dei*, 14: "There must, accordingly, exist between these two powers a certain orderly connection, which may be compared to the union of the soul

things come together to form one, one of them is formal [i.e. determining] in respect to the other".[43] Just as "the human soul subsists by itself, and is created by God whenever it can be infused into a sufficiently disposed subject"[44] so the acceptance of the easy yoke of Christ by the public law of any realm constitutes a substantial change and a new creation. This is well expressed by the tradition by which each King of France on assuming his crown would return to the place of Clovis's baptism and by the image of St Æthelberht's baptism which hangs above the British throne in the House of Lords.

Hence to be fully legitimate, the temporal power must be recognised by the spiritual as its material correlate.

> Kingship not instituted through priesthood, therefore, was either not kingship, but brigandage (*latrocinium*), or was united with priesthood. For even before Saul was instituted and appointed as king through Samuel as through a priest of God, Melchizedek was king of Salem. But this Melchizedek, while he was a king, was also a priest.[45]

This recognition or institution of the temporal power is fitly manifested by outward ceremony, for example by the coronation and anointing of an emperor or king by a pope or archbishop.[46] The temporal ruler within Christendom thus receives his right to rule from the apostolic hierarchy of the Church, yet in such a way that the pope or relevant bishop has the duty to

---

and body in man." Earliest of all is the 2nd century *Epistle to Diognetus*, chapter 6: "What the soul is in the body, Christians are in the world [...] The soul dwells in the body, yet is not of the body; and Christians dwell in the world, yet are not of the world. The invisible soul is guarded by the visible body, and Christians are known indeed to be in the world, but their godliness remains invisible." Certain distinctions need to be made between the Church and the ecclesiastical hierarchy and between the temporal community and its political organs and the way in which these correspond with the soul-body analogy. These will be pursued in chapter eleven.

[43] STh 1a 2æ, q. 13, a. 1. Aristotle had said: "Whenever from several things, some one, common thing emerges [...] the ruler and the ruled appear in all cases"; *Politics* I.5.

[44] *Postquam sanctissimus*, 'Twenty-Four Thomistic Theses', Sacred Congregation of Studies, 1914, 15.

[45] Giles of Rome, *On Ecclesiastical Power*, tr. R. W. Dyson (New York: Columbia University Press, 2004), 25.

[46] Leo XIII, *Diuturnum* 21: "When republics had Christian princes, the Church insisted much more on testifying and preaching how much sanctity was inherent in the authority of rulers. [...] On this account she wisely provides that kings should commence their reign with the celebration of solemn rites."

confer it,[47] when the temporal ruler has come legally to the seat of power. The manner of coming to the seat of power is decided by the temporal law of a given society, a law which like other laws could only be declared null by pope or bishop if it were perverse.[48] Hence, a pope could not, for example, legally confer a crown on a personal friend rather than on the true heir, or on the duly elected candidate.[49]

Cause of temporal authority outside Christendom

What we have just described is the normal case. Does it follow that where this does not occur, that is, outside Christendom, there can be no rightful use of temporal power, that is, no right of one man to command with coercion and no duty of another man to obey him? Such a view would sit ill with St Paul's instruction to the Romans that they must obey the higher powers "not only for wrath, but also for conscience's sake" (Rom. 13:5), and with the constant attitude of the faithful toward the pagan Roman emperors. In what then consists the right to command among heathens? Should we suppose with Thrasymachus in Plato's *Republic* that it is merely a matter of having the power to enforce one's orders? This is a notion repugnant to human self-respect and condemned by the Church.[50]

It is instructive to compare temporal society with marriage.[51] Natural law gives a man and a woman the power to form a union which will possess a nature and properties fixed independently of their wills. Of course, a man and a woman can form any number of societies in virtue of their own contingent wishes, for example a society for collecting stamps or for mining coal; but in marriage they unite not as two persons with contingent wishes but precisely as man and woman. When they unite in this way, the society thus formed has a primary end independent of their free will, the procreation of children, and

---

[47] This was not the case in regard to the Holy Roman emperor, where the pope, in virtue of the emperor's special prerogatives as head of the laity, and his association with the city of Rome itself had a positive role in the approval of the candidate selected by the imperial electors.

[48] See below, 'The Two Swords'.

[49] Hence Innocent III, writing to Philip Augustus, recognises that the latter has his sword, that is, his authority, from God, from whom comes all power; Letter 7, PL 215:527: "Gladius, quem Dominus tibi tradidit a quo est omnis potestas".

[50] *Syllabus of Errors*, condemned proposition 60: "Authority is nothing else but numbers and the sum total of material forces."

[51] The idealised account of the origin of temporal authority which is given here for the sake of simplicity is completed by the later section on the usurpation of power.

properties also independent of it, for example, the fact that it cannot be dissolved by the choice of the spouses or by any higher earthly power. Since human maleness and femaleness are certain natures with certain properties, so is the marital society.

Likewise, natural law gives to families the duty and hence the power to unite with other families into a new society.[52] Again, we are speaking here not of a union based on contingent shared aims or interests, as when families unite to run a school or to raise money for charity, but of a union of families as such. Since the family is a thing of a certain fixed nature, deriving from the nature of man and woman, the new society which is produced when families as such unite, that is, temporal or civil society, is itself a thing with a certain nature and properties independent of the wills of its members. Thus, temporal society has for its goal the complete fulfilment of human nature possible in this life, and among its properties a power to oblige those who belong to it to observe certain laws.

Hence, just as nature, or God as author of nature, gives to a man and woman the power to forge a union which they cannot afterwards dissolve, so nature, or God as author of nature, gives to families the power to bring into existence a constitutional order to which they will themselves be subject. Both powers are given by nature, as being necessary to attain ends assigned by nature. Hence, the continued authority through time of the rulers over their subjects does not depend on the continued consent of the subject, just as the husband's authority over his wife does not depend on his wife's continued consent to it.

Indeed, original, civil authority was derived from Adam and Noah, but whether by estrangement of distance, or usurpation, this legitimate line was lost except among the Hebrews; and *patres familias* seeking to reinstate legitimate temporal power derived thereafter their provisional title to do so from nature. Even if there were but one family in existence, temporal authority would still be present as flowing from human nature, since required by natural law. In these circumstances, the father would have the right to the temporal governance of his adult children while they remained in his territory; for as the first cause of the multitude, it would pertain to him to bring it to perfection. Later, with the multiplication of descendants, and as the organs of society, become more developed and distinct, postulated a more fitting institutional head, he could

---

[52] Leo XIII, *Diuturnum*, 11: "Sane homines in civili societate vivere natura iubet seu verius auctor naturae Deus" ("indeed, nature, or more truly God, the author of nature, bids men live in civil society".)

renounce this temporal authority and allow the several households to put themselves under some new constitution.[53]

This is not the so-called 'social contract' imagined in different ways by Hobbes, Locke and Rousseau.[54] It differs from that imaginary contract, not only because temporal society is forged between families and not between individual persons. It differs also because those authors failed to see the essential distinction between a necessary and a voluntary society. Lacking a conception of natures, they did not see that families can by their union produce something of a new nature, which has properties inscribed in it not by the will of man but by the wisdom of God, and hence that civil society is not simply the largest of the societies that men choose to construct. We do not need a theory, as these authors imagined, to explain how men pass from a 'state of nature' into a 'state of civil society', since men are subject to temporal authority, and hence part of a society, in virtue of natural law itself.[55]

---

[53] Aristotle implicitly recognises this temporal authority of the father in the absence of other constitutional arrangements when he presents the village as a natural intermediary between the family and the *polis*. Cf. *Politics*, I.2: "By nature the village seems to be above all an extension of the household. Its members some call 'milk-mates'; they are 'the children and the children's children'. [...] Every household is under the eldest as king, and so also were the extensions [of the household making up a village]."

[54] For Hobbes, civil society must be created by each man saying to his fellow about some sovereign person or body: "*I authorise and give up my right of governing myself to this man, or to this assembly of men, on this condition; that thou give up, thy right to him, and authorise all his actions in like manner*" (*Leviathan*, ch. 17, 'Of the causes, generation, and definition of a commonwealth'). From this renunciation of rights vis-à-vis the sovereign, Hobbes excepts only the right to defend one's person. For Rousseau, people enter into a civil state by "the total alienation of each associate, together with all his rights, to the whole community" (*The Social Contract*, Bk. 1, ch. 6), in such a way that the community as a whole is the sovereign. These rights include the right to life itself, which henceforth becomes "no longer a mere bounty of nature, but a gift made conditionally by the State" (ibid., bk. 2, ch. 5). For John Locke, civil society is created when a group of men in a state of nature "give up all the power, necessary to the ends for which they unite into society, to the *majority* of the community, unless they expresly agreed in any number greater than the majority" (*Second Treatise on Government*, 99). Since the 'ends' in question are the protection not only of life but also of property (ibid. 95), he concludes that no tax can be levied on a community unless the majority agree to it (ibid. 140) – whence the slogan of the dissident American colonists, "no taxation without representation", transformed from being a principle of fundamental English public law (*Magna carta*, 12) into a supposed precept of nature.

[55] The same objection applies to the so-called 'invisible hand' account of the origin of temporal power, which seeks to explain how a state would arise if human beings in a 'state of nature' acted simply from rational self-interest and without any of them intending to

A further problem with such theories is that they imagined political authority as coming into being through a *delegation* of power: that same power which I had previously over myself, I now give to this terrible or benign Leviathan to exercise over me on my behalf.[56] Yet to delegate another person to act on my behalf is not to put myself under his authority, but rather the reverse.

The popes therefore found fault with the social contract. St Pius X pointed out the absurdity of claiming that authority is delegated by those over whom it is to be exercised to those who are to exercise it over them. It is in the nature of delegation to descend not to ascend, and hence for legates not to have authority over their principals.[57] Authority delegated at will may be revoked at will and so, when the one conferring it is supposed to be also its subject, it is no authority at all.

Pope Leo XIII had intimated a similar criticism in his encyclical *Diuturnum* of 1881. Speaking of the so-called social contract, he asserted that it could not be the foundation of human society, since it would have "no authority to confer on political power such great strength, dignity, and firmness as the safety of the State and the common good of the citizens require". He pointed out that it was also manifestly fictitious.[58]

Temporal authority comes from God, in that He has given to families the power to form societies, and these societies possess as one of their properties the distinction between authority and subjection:

---

establish a state. This is the thesis of Robert Nozick (1938-2002) in his 1974 work, *Anarchy, State, and Utopia*.

[56] The notion of delegation is more evident in Rousseau, who draws from it the conclusion that the citizens may withdraw the authority of the rulers at any time. Hobbes refuses this conclusion, and yet he also asserts that the relation of subjects to rulers is that of principals to agents; cf. *Leviathan*, ch. 18, 'Of the rights of sovereigns by institution': "Because every subject is by this institution author of all the actions and judgements of the sovereign instituted, it follows that whatsoever he doth, can be no injury to any of his subjects; nor ought he to be by any of them accused of injustice. For he that doth anything by authority from another doth therein no injury to him by whose authority he acteth: but by this institution of a Commonwealth every particular man is author of all the sovereign doth; and consequently he that complaineth of injury from his sovereign complaineth of that whereof he himself is author."

[57] *Notre charge apostolique*: "Il est anormale que la délégation monte, puisqu'il est de sa nature de descendre".

[58] *Diuturnum*, 12: "Pactum, quod praedicant, est aperte commentitium et fictum, neque ad impertiendam valet politicae potestati tantum virium, dignitatis, firmitudinis, quantum tutela reipublicae et communes civium utilitates requirunt."

As regards political power, the Church rightly teaches that it comes from God [...] A society can neither exist nor be conceived in which there is no one to govern the wills of individuals, in such a way as to make, as it were, one will out of many, and to impel them rightly and orderly to the common good; therefore, God has willed that in a civil society there should be some to rule the multitude.[59]

Hence all bearers of temporal authority rule in the name of God, whether or not they claim to do so.[60]

This is not to say that no temporal ruler can be chosen by the people:

Those who are to be set over a commonwealth may in certain cases be chosen by the will and decision of the multitude, with no opposition or contradiction from Catholic doctrine. Now, by this choice, the ruler is designated, but the rights of ruling are not conferred (*quo sane delectu designatur princeps, non conferuntur iura principatus*).[61]

If families coalesce into a society, then the heads of household are free to establish who shall rule it, and how his successor shall be determined; in other words, to produce a constitution. They are not thereby delegating their power, but using the power they have to produce a new kind of entity, whose principal properties are determined not by themselves but by natural law, and in so doing, they are free to decide who will wield the temporal power within it. We may say that they make a contract with the ruler or ruling body that he or it shall rule them, provided it is distinguished from the 'social contract' discussed

---

[59] Ibid. 8, 11; cf. St Thomas Aquinas, *Scriptum super Sententias*, II dist. 44 2, 2: "Ordo praelationis a Deo descendit" ("the order of prelacy descends from God"). Note that even in a pure democracy, where all possessed an equal share of the rule, the distinction between 'having the right to rule' and 'having the duty to obey' would still be found.

[60] Ibid. 13: "The power of the rulers of a city, if it be a certain communication of divine power, will by that very reason immediately acquire a dignity greater than human"; cf. Leo XIII, *Sapientiae Christianae*, 9: "Hallowed, therefore, in the minds of Christians is the name of public power, in which they recognize some likeness and symbol as it were of the divine majesty, even when it is exercised by one unworthy"; *CCC*, 2238: "Those subject to authority should regard those in authority as representatives of God, who has made them stewards of his gifts."

[61] *Diuturnum*, 6. Cf. St. John Chrysostom, *On Romans*, Homily 21: "What are you saying? Is every ruler appointed by God? No, that is not what I mean, he says, for I am not now talking about individual rulers, but about authority as such. My contention is that the existence of a ruling authority - the fact that some should command and others obey, and that all things not come about as the result of blind chance - this is a provision of divine wisdom"; PG 60: 615.

above. Analogously, a woman, when she marries, freely makes a contract with her husband for him to govern her, but he does not thereby become her delegate whose decisions she may revoke; nor do they have the right to decide that marriage, for them, will not be ordered to the procreation of children, to mutual aid, and to the alleviation of concupiscence.

St Robert Bellarmine taught that temporal authority differs from spiritual in that the latter descends immediately from God to its possessor, whereas the former descends from God to the multitude, and must then be transferred by them to some person or persons "since the commonwealth (*Respublica*) cannot exercise this power through itself".[62]

This is not in itself the theory of authority reprobated by Leo and Pius, in which the people are supposedly the source of all authority, and hence are not truly subject to the authority of their rulers.[63] Yet Bellarmine's account needs some qualification. First, the 'multitude' in question must be a multitude not of individuals but of families. Secondly, the heads of these families would confer temporal authority only when it is a question of establishing a new constitutional order, that is, of creating some society for the first time, perhaps after a civilizational collapse. Yet such a constitutional order, once created, would not derive its authority 'mediately' from God through the people, but rather immediately from God. Again, once constitutional order had been created, authority would not again revert to the people, for example at the death of a king or at the expiration of the term of office of a president. The existence of an abiding constitutional order renders this unnecessary.[64] Thirdly,

---

[62] *Controversiae*, 'On the members of the Church', bk. 3, ch. 6. Marsilius, or Marcellus, of Padua (c. 1275-1342) erroneously held that both spiritual and temporal power passed from the community to the rulers.

[63] Cf. St Pius X, *Notre charge apostolique*: "Authority, so they concede, comes from God, but it resides primarily in the people and expresses itself by means of elections or, better still, by selection. However, it still remains in the hands of the people; it does not escape their control. [...] The Sillon places public authority primarily in the people, from whom it then flows into the government in such a manner, however, that it continues to reside in the people. But Leo XIII absolutely condemned this doctrine in his encyclical *Diuturnum illud*."

[64] Hence we reject the theory according to which the people would be the 'immediate subject of power', who supposedly alienate their power while some ruler is in office but who regain it after he ceases to be so, being then obliged to alienate it again. As Ottaviani remarks, it would be strange if the immediate subject of power were obliged by natural law to transfer it straightaway so some other subject; *Institutiones* vol. 2, 32. Furthermore, if this were the case, the franchise for the election of a president or legislature would be limited by natural law to the heads of households and any election in which this restriction was not observed would be illicit. For further discussion, see also C. Journet, *Church of the Word Incarnate*, tr. A. Downes (Sheed & Ward: London and New York, 1955), 485-90.

although temporal authority confers a right to command and creates a duty to obey, yet outside Christendom, all such authority is dislocated. It needs to be instituted by the spiritual power so that it may attain its native goal, and its separation from the spiritual power is a mark of sin, at least original. Hence a multitude of families aspiring to society may put themselves under a new constitutional order only provisionally, awaiting this institution.

Putting aside exceptional circumstances requiring or suggesting the creation of a new constitutional order, men have no natural right to select those by whom they are to be governed, both because rulers are by definition not delegates, and because the goal of society can be obtained without such selection. Yet for a given society at a given time it may be highly desirable that "those set over a commonwealth [...] be chosen by the will and decision of the multitude".

Division of temporal authority

It is customary to divide temporal authority into executive, judicial and legislative power.[65] The legislative power is the power to enact laws binding on the citizens or on some legitimately restricted group of them.[66] The judicial power is the power to judge those charged with infringing the laws, which implies also the power to interpret their meaning.[67] The executive power may be defined negatively, as all temporal authority not possessed by the legislature or the judiciary. Positively it might be defined as the power to conform society to the laws, to administer the common material goods of the realm and ultimately to direct society to the common good by concrete commands apart

---

[65] This tripartite division is often attributed to Baron de Montesquieu (1689-1755). In fact it is equivalently found in Aristotle's *Politics* IV.14: "There are, then, three parts in all constitutions (ἔστι δὴ τρία μόρια τῶν πολιτειῶν πασῶν). [...] Of these three, one is that which deliberates about common matters (τὸ βουλευόμενον περὶ τῶν κοινῶν); the second concerns the offices (δεύτερον δὲ τὸ περὶ τὰς ἀρχάς), what they should be and over what matters they should have authority, and what the manner of choosing them must be; the third is the judiciary (τρίτον δὲ τί τὸ δικάζον)." This passage states in effect that a constitution (this appears to be the best translation on this occasion of πολιτεία) must provide for a legislature, a functioning executive and a judicial power.

[66] A. Ottaviani defines it as the 'right of determining in an obligatory manner the things which are necessary and useful for attaining the end of the society'; *Compendium Iuris Publici Ecclesiastici*, 4th edition (Rome: Vatican Press, 1954), 43.

[67] A. Ottaviani defines it as 'the right of declaring and proposing in an obligatory manner which concrete acts of subjects are conformed or contrary to right, and the legitimate effects of this conformity or contrariety'; *Compendium*, 49.

from general precepts[68]: like all created authority it is limited by the good for which it is instituted, the temporal happiness of the citizens as subordinated to their eternal beatitude.

What is the deepest reason for this three-fold division? Since human authority exists to achieve what is just, we may seek the reason in the distinction of the three principles of just order in society as apprehended by the human mind, known respectively as *ius naturale, ius gentium,* and *ius civile.*[69]

Temporal authority, being the power to direct men in society toward their natural end, must fulfil the demands of natural law. Natural law (*lex naturalis*) is the expression in human nature of the eternal law insofar as it relates to man, that is, of God's knowledge of Himself as imitable in human nature. *Ius* is our participation, whether in the mind or in things, of that knowledge. Natural law first of all instructs man to pursue certain goods which he sees as choiceworthy without the need for reasoning, such as existence itself, offspring, life in society, and indeed all the things for which he has a natural inclination.[70] Since we must pursue them according to reason, they are not to be pursued when they are contrary to higher goods, and they need not be pursued when they make the acquisition of higher goods more difficult. These goods which can be seen without the need for deliberation as fitting are referred to as *ius naturale,* or the 'naturally just'.[71] The authority to command vested in man in virtue of the *ius naturale* is intrinsically discretionary, that is, it neither should nor can be reduced to general rules or expressed as universal precepts. It remains human authority but it flows directly into the particular command unmediated by propositional laws (*leges*). The particular decision to open fire on this concrete enemy position, to apply this particular punishment to a disobedient child, to declare this person the beneficial owner of some property, or to visit the

---

[68] Or as the "right of enforcing the application of laws and sentences, of directing persons or of disposing of things, and of removing all obstacles which impede the full possession of the social end"; ibid., 61. The executive power itself may be divided into a power of governance, in regard to persons, and of administration, in regard to things. The power of coercion, which is sometimes mentioned as a third part of the executive power, is therefore rather an aspect of the power of governance.

[69] St Thomas takes this distinction from St Isidore of Seville, cf. STh 2a 2ae 57, 3.

[70] STh 1a 2ae 94, 2 ad 2: "All the inclinations of any parts whatsoever of human nature, such as the concupiscible and irascible parts, in so far as they are ruled by reason, belong to the natural law."

[71] Although some authors use *ius naturale* to mean natural law itself, this is not St Thomas's preferred sense for the phrase.

baker's at 2pm may in each case be a legitimate exercise of authority incapable of being reduced to a general rule by a finite intellect.

However, the existence within us of reason allows us in many other instances profitably to formulate general rules or universal precepts from the natural law, and this in two ways: "first, as a conclusion from premises, secondly, by way of determination of certain generalities".[72] An example of the first way of deriving a precept is to reason from the desirability of life with others to the precept not to kill the innocent. An example of the second way of deriving a precept is deciding that the rate of tax will be so many pence in the pound, or that the punishment for a certain offence will be to be put in the stocks and pelted with rotten fruit, or to be fined a fixed sum of money. Those precepts which reason sees to be just in the first way are derived from the *ius gentium*, literally, 'the right of nations', so called because, being derived from human nature as conclusions from premises, it is the same for all nations, and so these precepts are followed in large part everywhere.[73] The precepts which are derived as determinations of more general precepts which could be determined justly in various ways are collectively known as 'civil law', so called because it ought to vary according to the conditions of time and place of each temporal commonwealth.[74] That which it declares to be just is thus known as the *ius civile*.

Although natural law tells us to seek the *ius naturale*, it does not tell us the circumstances in which it may be lawfully pursued. Since circumstances are infinitely various, the human mind cannot furnish in advance a complete list of precepts that will enable us to attain these natural goods in the right way. For example, food is naturally fitting for every animal as something necessary

---

[72] STh 1a 2ae 95, 2.

[73] The phrase *ius gentium* is also used by some authors, and also by St Thomas when he is quoting these authors, to mean the '*law* of nations', in the sense of the *laws* which are common to all or nearly all nations, to protect that which reason has seen to be just by reasoning from the first precepts of the natural law. Again, the term *ius gentium* has been extended to cover positive determinations of the natural law which happen to be the same for all (or nearly all) nations such as the convention that pirates may be killed without trial on the open seas. All three senses of the phrase *ius gentium* must be distinguished from 'international law' in the modern sense of a body of law ruling the relations between independent States, and which contains precepts derived from natural law both by inference and determination. 'International law' in this sense is obviously related to the last sense of *ius gentium* but is now so elaborate as really to constitute the emerging civil law of a nascent world state.

[74] This is not to be confused with 'civil law' in the sense in which this is distinguished in some legal systems from criminal law, where it refers to that part of the law which governs relations between private citizens rather than being mainly concerned with the public good.

for survival. Natural law therefore obliges a man to take food. However, human law cannot furnish him in advance with a complete list of the precepts which someone must fulfil in order to accomplish this duty, for example, telling him what food he must eat and when, and when he must forego it for some greater good such as alms-giving or asceticism, in such a way that he would need to make no decisions for himself. *Ius naturale¸* in other words, is decreed by natural law, but by that part of the natural law which cannot be reduced to propositional form by a human mind, because the matter in question is too complex and variable. The *ius naturale* is to be achieved by the authority of parents over their children and the 'authority' of a man over himself.

Similarly, *ius naturale* is what is achieved by the 'executive' authority of civil rulers. For example, 'adequate defence' is naturally fitting for every realm. It is not possible to specify in advance the precepts which realms must follow to achieve this, and so the attainment of it is not a matter of simply formulating or of applying precepts but of acting until the goal is achieved, with laws being a merely negative constraint on one's activity. It belongs therefore not to a legislative or judicial body, but to the executive. *Ius naturale* is also found in the discretionary authority of judges exercised when the law has failed in particulars but a new precedent would worsen rather than remedy such difficulties.[75]

The authoritative derivation of human laws from natural law, as mentioned above, can take the form of a conclusion drawn from premises. Owing to the complexity of human life and the nature of the human intellect as the least of intellects, advancing through time from potentiality to act, these conclusions will often first be drawn only when they become relevant to judgements of good and evil here and now. For example, the principle that, owing to the common destination of material goods by their Creator, the taking by a starving man of the surplus goods of his neighbour against that neighbour's will does not constitute theft, might be overlooked by a legislature in drawing up laws, and discerned only by a judge before whom such a case is brought. The *ius gentium* is thus the origin of laws that have been 'discerned', that is, derived as conclusions from premises in judging a case here and now.[76] Since the authority of these laws derives directly from the natural law without the intervention of human decision, but only of human reasoning and insight, the *ius gentium* is the source of a distinctive power, namely the judicial power of human rulers.

To the legislative body, for its part, there falls the determinations of that which natural law itself both leaves undetermined and requires to be determined, and

---

[75] This belongs to that part of English Law known as equity.

[76] This gives rise to the branch of English law known as common law.

in this way it constructs the body of civil law. Here alone does the human legislator legislate in his own right. This involves therefore a distinctive human legislative power.[77]

Of these three branches, the legislative enjoys a certain priority, since it belongs to the legislature to set limits to the judicial and executive power. Hence the person or body which possesses legislative power may be called the sovereign, or sovereign power within a given society.[78] It is consequently highly desirable that the sovereign power comprise within it persons charged with executive and judicial as well as merely legislative responsibilities (relating only to the *ius civile*). A complete separation of powers, such that no one person possesses any share of more than one of these three kinds, seems impossible in practice and unnecessary in principle. Impossible in practice, since the possession of legislative and judicial authority implies the right to put into motion some part of the executive: a judge could hardly exercise his judicial authority unless he could call on officers of the court to take a convicted criminal to punishment. Unnecessary in principle, since there are advantages to be gained by having at least some of those who must administer according to law and of those who must judge according to law to have some share in making the law, since they will have a special motive for preventing the passage of foolish or hasty measures.[79] However, some degree of separation will usually be necessary as a safeguard against corruption. For example, if there were no separation between the judicial and executive branches, or the judiciary and the legislature, then criminal wrongdoing in the executive and the legislature would be harder to prosecute with success. If there were no separation between the legislature and the executive, the temptation would be great to legalise any use of executive power that would serve the private interests of its possessors.

This partial separation is thus to some extent a consequence of creaturely finitude and the organic nature of society and to some extent a consequence of sin, although not so as to be unnecessary in a state of innocence. Just therefore as Christ divine and sinless is both Priest and King so He also unites

---

[77] This gives rise to the branch of English law known as statute law.

[78] Alexis de Tocqueville (1805-59) made the same observation; A. de Tocqueville, *Democracy in America*, tr. J. Schleifer (Indianapolis: Liberty Fund, 2010), vol. 1, 205 "Strictly speaking, sovereignty can be defined as the right to make laws."

[79] Cf. A. Ottaviani, *Compendium Iuris Publici Ecclesiastici*, 54. In England for many centuries the highest court was composed of members of the Upper House of Parliament; likewise, members of the cabinet are chosen from the two Houses of Parliament.

all the powers: "For the Lord is our judge, the Lord is our lawgiver, the Lord is our king: he will save us".[80]

Non-constitutional change of temporal rulers

Every adequate constitution provides for the peaceful passing of temporal power from one to another, for example by the succession of the eldest son on the death of the king or by the election of new representatives at the end of a fixed number of years. The question arises of whether non-constitutional change of temporal rulers can be just. We prefer not to speak of 'revolution', as this word since 1789 strongly suggests erroneous doctrines about the source of authority and the nature of society.[81]

A subject as such is not permitted to displace his ruler, since the one who displaces must have authority over the one displaced, and a subject by definition has no authority over his ruler. If those who govern were merely delegates of the governed, then the latter could replace them at will at any moment; but if, as follows from the nature of temporal society, those who govern possess authority over the governed, they cannot be so replaced.[82]

Authority, however, is conceded by the author of nature for the good of the governed. Authority belongs to the one who has lawfully come to the seat of power, therefore, only on condition that he intend the good of the governed. When someone acts as a tyrant, habitually manifesting his intention not to govern for their good, he no longer has the right to use his power, which may therefore be placed in other hands against his will.

---

[80] Isaiah 33:22.

[81] Cf. Leo XIII, *Vigesimo quinto anno*, 1902: "Far from oppressing the State, history clearly shows when it is read without prejudice, that the Church like its divine Founder has been, on the contrary, most commonly the victim of oppression and injustice. The reason is that its power rests not on the force of arms but on the strength of thought and of truth. It is therefore assuredly with malignant purpose that they hurl against the Church accusations like these. It is a pernicious and disloyal work, in the pursuit of which above all others a certain sect of darkness is engaged, a sect which human society these many years carries within itself and which like a deadly poison destroys its happiness, its fecundity, and its life. Abiding personification of the revolution (*personificazione permanente della rivoluzione*), it constitutes a sort of retrogressive society whose object is to exercise an occult suzerainty over the established order and whose whole purpose is to make war against God and against His Church."

[82] The 63rd of the propositions condemned in the *Syllabus of Errors* is this: "It is lawful to refuse obedience to legitimate princes, and even to rebel."

This may not be done by the initiative of any private citizen, or by any group of private citizens united for the task, just as no private citizen may punish any other malefactor. It may be done by those who, though not the sovereign, have by their office some duty of care for the whole commonwealth.[83] St Thomas considers two possibilities:

> If to provide itself with a king belongs to the right of a given multitude, it is not unjust that the king be deposed or have his power restricted by that same multitude if, becoming a tyrant, he abuses the royal power. It must not be thought that such a multitude is acting unfaithfully in deposing the tyrant, even though it had previously subjected itself to him in perpetuity, because he himself has deserved that the covenant (*pactum*) with his subjects should not be kept, since, in ruling the multitude, he did not act faithfully as the office of a king demands.

If, on the other hand, it pertains to the right of a higher authority to provide a king for a certain multitude, a remedy against the wickedness of a tyrant is to be looked for from him.[84]

An example of the first case, familiar in the 13th century, would be the city whose representatives had voted to bring in a ruler from another city to be impartial between their own factions.[85] Even though the representatives had promised perpetual allegiance to him, yet should he rule unjustly they might eject him. They had made with him a contract to put themselves under his authority for as long as he should seek their good, and hence they were free from obligation to him when he became a tyrant. For all those who place someone over themselves make such a contract at least implicitly, since they cannot give a person the right to rule unjustly; therefore in accepting his authority they accept it insofar as he rules justly.

The second case is also clear. If someone rules a multitude only at the pleasure of some higher power, then the multitude can through its representatives appeal to that higher power to be rid of him if he abuses them.[86]

---

[83] Cf. St Thomas Aquinas, *De Regno* Bk. 1.7: "To proceed against the cruelty of tyrants is an action to be undertaken, not through the private presumption of a few, but rather by public authority." In 1415, the Council of Constance, in its 15th session, condemned this proposition: "Any vassal or subject can lawfully and meritoriously kill, and ought to kill, any tyrant."

[84] *De Regno,* Bk. 1.7.

[85] This was the function of the Podestà in certain Italian cities.

[86] Cf. Lateran IV, can. 3.

One might ask, what of a third case, where the ruler has neither been chosen by the community or its representatives, nor imposed from above, but holds power by some other title, such as hereditary right? In fact, this case is reducible to the first. If the ruling family truly possessed power in a lawful fashion, this must be because this family was in the past accepted by the heads of household. In accepting to put themselves under the rule of this hereditary house, they made the agreement that they and their offspring should be governed by it for as long as it sought their good; a pact which did not include this last clause at least implicitly would not have been lawful, and hence would have been invalid. Hence if the hereditary ruler turn tyrant, he may be ejected as having violated his side of the pact.[87] This is not revolution, just as it is not murder to kill a man when this is necessary to preserve one's own life:

> To trouble a regime of this kind is not a form of revolution (*non habet rationem seditionis*), except perhaps when the regime of the tyrant is troubled in so disordered a way that the subject multitude suffers greater harm from the consequent trouble than from the tyrant's regime. Rather, the tyrant is the revolutionary (*seditiosus est*), who foments discord and revolts among the people so that he may dominate them more safely. For this is tyrannical, being ordered to the personal good of the one who presides, with harm to the multitude.[88]

Hence those who justly eject a ruler in a non-constitutional way are rightly called counter-revolutionaries.

To avoid the 'private presumption' which both St Thomas and Leo XIII tell us is contrary to apostolic doctrine,[89] such action would have to be undertaken

---

[87] Although one must not obey him, one cannot rise up against a tyrant when the usurpations of which he is guilty are confined to divine (rather than natural) law as this would constitute coercive conversion which is itself forbidden by divine law. Hence Catholics in a pagan state may not eject their ruler because he forbids them to acknowledge the authority of the Pope.

[88] STh 2a 2ae 42, 2 ad 3.

[89] *De Regno* 1.7: "If the excess of tyranny is unbearable, some have been of the opinion that it would be an act of virtue for strong men to slay the tyrant and to expose themselves to the danger of death in order to set the multitude free. [...] This opinion is not in accord with apostolic teaching. For Peter admonishes us to be reverently subject to our masters, not only to the good and gentle but also the froward (1 Pet. 2): 'For if one who suffers unjustly bear his trouble for conscience's sake, this is grace.' Wherefore, when many emperors of the Romans tyrannically persecuted the faith of Christ, a great number both of the nobility and the common people were converted to the faith and were praised for patiently bearing death for Christ"; Leo XIII, *Diuturnum*, 20: "Even under these

97

by the most authoritative non-tyrannical body within the society, for example, a chamber of deputies or a regiment of the army, or even an *ad hoc* collection of such public persons. To be just, such action would have also to meet the criteria of any just war.[90]

Usurpation of temporal power

Doubtless, when power changes hands in some non-constitutional way, this has often been not by the just action of public persons, but by unjust violence and usurpation.[91] The question therefore arises of whether a successful usurpation by itself may confer the right to rule. St Thomas lays down these principles:

---

circumstances, they were so far from doing anything seditious or despising the imperial majesty that they took it on themselves only to profess themselves Christians, and declare that they would not in any way alter their faith. But they had no thought of resistance, calmly and joyfully they went to the torture of the rack, in so much that the magnitude of the torments gave place to their magnitude of mind." We may add that the loyalty of the faithful to the pagan Roman emperors had also another motive, namely the belief that the Roman *imperium* prevents the final emergence of the antichrist, e.g. Tertullian, *Apology*, 32: "We know that a mighty shock impending over the whole earth - in fact, the very end of all things threatening dreadful woes - is only retarded by the continued existence of the Roman empire."

[90] Cf. *CCC* 2243: "Armed *resistance* to oppression by political authority is not legitimate, unless all the following conditions are met: 1) there is certain, grave, and prolonged violation of fundamental rights; 2) all other means of redress have been exhausted; 3) such resistance will not provoke worse disorders; 4) there is well-founded hope of success; and 5) it is impossible reasonably to foresee any better solution." The catechism does not cite any earlier authority for its teaching, although Sixtus V in 1589 bestowed great praise upon the Dominican lay brother Jacques Clement for the tyrannicide of Henry III of France: "[A] work famous, memorable, and almost incredible, a work not wrought without the special providence and government of the almighty; a Monk hath slain a King, not a painted King, one figured out upon a piece of paper or upon a wall, but the King of France, in the middle of his army, being hedged in with his camp and guard on every side, which indeed is such a work, and so brought about as no man will believe it when it shall be reported, and the posterity perhaps will repute it for a fable." *Consistorial address of the Supreme Pontiff Sixtus V in praise of the assassination of King Henry III of France by Br. Jacques Clement OP.*

[91] John Henry Newman, 'Sanctity the token of the Christian Empire' in *Sermons on Subjects of the Day* (Longmans, Green & Co.: London, 1902) 242: "Earthly kingdoms are founded, not in justice, but in injustice. They are created by the sword, by robbery, cruelty, perjury, craft, and fraud. There never was a kingdom, except Christ's, which was not conceived and born, nurtured and educated, in sin. [...] What monarchy is there but began in invasion or usurpation? What revolution has been effected without self-will, violence, or hypocrisy?"

The one who seizes dominion by violence does not become truly the superior or lord; and therefore where there is the possibility, one can drive off such dominion, unless perhaps afterwards he is made truly lord either through the consent of the subjects or through the authority of a superior.[92]

The one who has been dispossessed of power does not thereby lose authority, that is, the right to rule. He can lose it by publicly renouncing it, explicitly or tacitly, for since he holds it on condition of intending to rule for the good of his subjects, he holds it by his own free will and therefore has the power of abdication. If he does not so renounce his authority, he may seek to wrest power back from the usurper, for as long as the evil of such conflict is outweighed by the good to be achieved by success, something determined by the superiority of his principles to those of the usurper, and the number, excellence and power of the subjects who would welcome him. If however he foresees that the evil of conflict would outweigh the good, and this, according to all probability, whether the attempt be made now or else later by those who would otherwise be his legitimate successors, for example because the preponderating part of the people had willingly accepted the usurper, then he should renounce his claim, for if he continued to intend to regain his power he would no longer be intending the common good of the people, and hence would himself become a tyrant. If he sees that the good of conflict may probably at some future time outweigh the evil, as when the people only reluctantly acquiesce in the usurper, then he may retain his claim, and wait his moment to return. The Catholic families of Spain, for example, when they were overrun by the Moors, did not, we may presume, consent to the usurpers; whence the lawfulness of the *Reconquista*. If he does not assert his intention to return when he was free to do so, he may be taken to have abdicated.

When after a usurpation the rightful ruler abdicates, or when it ceases to be probable that the good of conflict would outweigh the evil, the usurper does not possess by that very fact the right to rule, for that would make of theft a title of ownership. Rather, the temporal society now strictly speaking ceases to exist, being deprived of its head. The heads of household, or, if they do not protest when they could, a body speaking in their name, may therefore reconstitute that society by using their authority to establish a new constitution.[93] Given the great evil which would be the decomposition of the society, and given the difficulty in any large society of the heads of household

---

[92] *Scriptum super Sententias*, II dist. 44, 2, 2.

[93] Given what has been said above, this new constitution and its rulers, in order to be legitimate simply speaking will require recognition by the Church. See below, p. 242.

conferring in person, a body, such as a parliament or senate, which till then has had some charge of the common good will rightly be taken as having from the heads of household a mandate to speak in their name, unless there be some evident reason why it should not do so.

If the heads of household, in person or through a body speaking in their name, choose in establishing a new constitution, or in re-establishing the old one, the new *de facto* ruler as their sovereign, then he will now possess the right to rule.

Finally, while the usurper holds his *de facto* sway, although he does not possess the right to govern, and the people may have neither the right nor duty to recognise his authority, they may nevertheless have the duty to obey individual laws or commands which he gives, for example a command about how to act in the face of some natural disaster, where someone must take charge, and no one else but he is an immediate position to do so. "It is more beneficial to the Republic to have a bad prince than to have none."[94]

---

[94] St Robert Bellarmine, *Controversiae*, 'On the members of the Church', bk. 3, ch. 4.

Theses

(i)   Temporal authority, which is essentially distinct from parental, has as its native and proximate purpose to bring men to the goal assigned by human nature and attainable in this life.

(ii) The distinction in title to temporal and spiritual authority results from the Fall of man.

(iii) Under the New Covenant, spiritual and temporal authority are not to be held by the same person except by necessity.

(iv) The subordination of temporal good to eternal good requires the subordination of the temporal to the spiritual power.

(v)   Man's inability, in every order of providence, to know his end without revelation, requires the subordination of the temporal to the spiritual power, where these are concretely distinct.

(vi) Fallen man's inability to obey the natural law without grace also requires the subordination of the temporal to the spiritual power.

(vii) The right of God to be honoured by every natural society also requires the subordination of the temporal to the spiritual power.

(viii) Only a Catholic polity is simply speaking legitimate.

(ix) The spiritual power institutes the temporal power and hence makes it fully legitimate by receiving the assistance of the latter in bringing mankind to beatitude.

(x)   In any given society the spiritual power cannot annul the law that determines the manner in which temporal power is obtained, unless that law be perverse.

(xi) God as author of nature, gives to families the power to bring into existence a constitutional order to which they will themselves be subject, and in this sense even outside Christendom temporal authority, though provisional, is from God.

(xii) The authority of a temporal ruler is not delegated to him by individuals or by families.

(xiii) Men do not have a natural right to be governed in either temporal or spiritual matters only by those whom they have themselves chosen.

(xiv) Temporal authority is divided into a legislative, judicial and executive power; among these, the legislative power enjoys priority.

(xv)   The legislative power is the power to enact laws binding on the citizens or on some legitimately restricted group of them.

(xvi)   The judicial power is the power to judge whether citizens have infringed rights, which implies the power to interpret the meaning of the laws.

(xvii)   Executive power is the power to confirm society to the laws and to administer the common material goods of the realm and ultimately to direct society to the common good by concrete commands apart from general precepts.

(xviii) The primary precepts of natural law give rise to executive power; man's ability to draw conclusions from these primary precepts gives rise to judicial power; his need further to determine these precepts and conclusions gives rise to legislative power.

(xix)   A complete separation of these powers is not necessary; a partial separation is required by man's finitude and by his fallen state.

(xx)   Subjects may not depose their rulers at will.

(xxi)   A temporal ruler who habitually manifests his intention not to govern for the good of a society loses the right to govern and may be replaced by the action of the most authoritative non-tyrannical body within the society.

(xxii)   Usurpation, even if prolonged, by itself confers no title to rule.

(xxiii) The one whose power is usurped may seek to expel the usurper, for as long as the evil of such conflict is outweighed by the good to be achieved by success.

(xxiv)   When the one whose power is usurped renounces his right to rule or can no longer justly seek to regain power, the heads of household, or a body speaking in their name, must reconstitute the society.

Chapter 6

Temporal authority (II): its scope

Hear therefore, ye kings, and understand: learn, ye that are judges of the ends of the earth. Give ear, you that rule the people, and that please yourselves in multitudes of nations: For power is given you by the Lord, and strength by the most High, who will examine your works, and search out your thoughts: Because being ministers of his kingdom, you have not judged rightly, nor kept the law of justice, nor walked according to the will of God. Horribly and speedily will he appear to you: for a most severe judgment shall be for them that bear rule. For to him that is little, mercy is granted: but the mighty shall be mightily tormented. For God will not except any man's person, neither will he stand in awe of any man's greatness: for he made the little and the great, and he hath equally care of all. But a greater punishment is ready for the more mighty. To you, therefore, O kings, are these my words, that you may learn wisdom, and not fall from it. For they that have kept just things justly, shall be justified: and they that have learned these things, shall find what to answer.[1]

Duties of temporal rulers

Since the proximate purpose of earthly society is natural happiness, temporal authority does not exist only to protect the bodies and property of the citizens. It exists also, and primarily, to promote the life of virtue among them.[2] We

---

[1] Wis. 6:2-12.

[2] Cf. Leo XIII, *Sapientiae Christianae*, 2: "If a city strives after external advantages only, and the achievement of a cultured and prosperous life; if, in administering the commonwealth, it is wont to put God aside, and show no solicitude for the upholding of moral laws, it turns woefully aside from its right course and from the injunctions of nature; nor should it be accounted as a society or a community of men, but only as the deceitful imitation or appearance of a society"; Pius XI, *Quadragesimo anno*, 118: "According to Christian teaching, man, endowed with a social nature, is placed on this earth so that by leading a life in society and under an authority ordained of God he may fully cultivate and develop all his faculties unto the praise and glory of his Creator; and that by faithfully fulfilling the duties of his craft or other calling he may obtain for himself temporal and at the same time eternal happiness"; Pope John XXIII, *Pacem in terris*, 42: "We consider that we should remind Our sons that the common good has to do with the whole man, that is, with his needs of both

have seen above why it cannot adequately guide man even to natural moral and intellectual virtue without divine revelation[3]; and, in particular, that the temporal power needs to be instructed about how men are to accomplish the primordial duty of rational creation, namely to worship the Creator in the manner He has appointed.[4]

> Government is also to help create conditions favourable to the fostering of religious life, in order that the people may be truly enabled to exercise their religious rights and to fulfil their religious duties, and also in order that society itself may profit by the moral qualities of justice and peace which have their origin in men's faithfulness to God and to His holy will.[5]

Since the content of these duties cannot be known without divine revelation, every ruler, not only as a private man but also as a ruler, is subject to the divine positive law given in this revelation and must therefore seek to incorporate it within the law of his society as supreme over all other laws.[6]

Since the revealed law of God tells us that the Word incarnate is sovereign over all other sovereignties, the only normal state of temporal society is to exist as a province of Christendom, that is, as a realm wherein the sovereignty of Christ

---

body and of soul. Therefore, the rulers of the commonwealth should take thought to obtain this good by suitable ways and stages, and so, while keeping to the right order of things, they must supply the citizens with goods of the soul along with goods of the body." St Augustine, in the *City of God* II. 20, gives a vivid description of a society where pleasure and possessions, rather than virtue, are reckoned by rulers and people alike to be the aim of politics.

[3] See above, 'Societies and the perfect society'.

[4] Cf. Leo XIII, *Sapientiae Christianae*, 3: "When Christian institutions and morality decline, the main foundation of human society goes together with them. Force alone will remain to preserve public tranquillity and order. But force is very feeble when the bulwark of religion has been removed, and, being more apt to beget slavery than obedience, it bears within itself the germs of ever-increasing troubles. The present century has encountered memorable disasters, and it is not certain that some equally terrible are not impending." Pope Leo was writing in 1890.

[5] 2nd Vatican Council, *Dignitatis humanae*, 6.

[6] Leo XIII, *Annum sacrum*, 3, concerning consecration to the Sacred Heart: "This world-wide and solemn testimony of allegiance and piety is especially appropriate to Jesus Christ, who is the Head and Supreme Lord of the race. His empire extends not only over Catholic nations and those who, having been duly washed in the waters of holy baptism, belong of right to the Church, although erroneous opinions keep them astray, or dissent from her teaching cuts them off from her care; it comprises also all those who are deprived of the Christian faith, so that the whole human race is most truly under the power of Jesus Christ."

is publicly proclaimed and where His law is therefore recognised within that society's constitution.

Although the exercise of temporal authority outside Christendom is abnormal, it seems better in expounding the duties of temporal rulers to consider this case first, so that what derives from nature may be more clearly distinguished from what derives from grace. We shall afterwards consider the duties incumbent upon them once they have submitted their sceptres to the reign of Christ.

Again, we have seen that it is the family rather than the individual which is the basic unit subject to temporal power. Hence in speaking of the duties of temporal rulers we may distinguish (a) their duties to God; (b) their duties to families; and (c) their duties to the associations which families or their members freely form among themselves.

Duties of temporal rulers outside Christendom

(a)   *Duty of rulers to God*

God is in many ways the cause of the society which the temporal ruler governs: He is the efficient cause of its parts, that is, of human beings and families, and thereby of the authority under which they are united; He is likewise the cause of the many things which they must use to obtain their end; and He is the final cause for which they are united, since all perfections of the society that they form are attempted approximations of the divine excellence.[7] For all these reasons, men united in society owe to God that tribute of gratitude which is worship. Leo XIII declared this in clear terms:

> It cannot be doubted but that, by the will of God, men are united in civil society; whether its component parts be considered; or its form, which is authority; or the object of its existence; or the abundance of the vast services which it renders to man. God it is who has made man for society, and has placed him in the company of others like himself, so that what was wanting to his nature, and beyond his attainment if left to his own resources, he might obtain by association with others. Wherefore, civil society must acknowledge God as its Founder and Parent, and must obey and reverence His power and authority (*potestatem dominatumque vereatur et colat*).[8]

---

[7] Cf. STh 1a 44, 4.

[8] *Libertas praestantissimum donum*, 21; Cf. *Immortale Dei* 6: "Nature and reason, which command every individual devoutly to worship God in holiness, because we belong to Him

Where this duty is ignored, a society is willing its own demise:

As there is nothing good in nature which is not to be referred to the divine goodness, every human society which does its utmost to exclude God from its laws and its constitution, rejects the help of this divine beneficence, and deserves, also, that help should be denied it. Rich, therefore, and powerful as it appears, that society bears within itself the seeds of death, and cannot hope for a lengthy existence.[9]

As Leo's words make clear, this is a duty even under natural law, although the ruler cannot fulfil it adequately until he has accepted divine revelation and incorporated this into the public law of his people.

Comprehensively secular societies therefore are inevitably of short duration, and prepare the way for their own replacement by new cultural and social forms imbued with a greater vigour and religiosity (whether of an authentic or a distorted character).

His obligations toward God likewise oblige the temporal ruler to forbid crimes directly contrary to the honour of God, such as blasphemy and the public proclamation and propagation of false doctrines about the divine nature. Again, without the light of divine faith he cannot adequately know the scope of this duty; yet even while unenlightened, and while his people remain under natural and human law alone, he should forbid those things which reason itself can know to be false or blasphemous, for example the doctrines that God is evil, or bodily, or subject to necessity or to change, or that He is not one, and

---

and must return to Him, since from Him we came, bind also the civil community by a like law. For men living together in society are under the power of God no less than individuals are, and society, no less than individuals, owes gratitude to God who gave it being and maintains it and whose ever-bounteous goodness enriches it with countless blessings"; St Pius X, *Vehementer Nos* (letter to the French bishops): "The Creator of man is also the Founder of human societies, and preserves their existence as He preserves our own. We owe Him, therefore, not only a private worship, but also a public one."

[9] Leo XIII, *Nobilissima Gallorum gens*, 2. Pope John XXIII expressed the same thought in his first encyclical, *Ad Petri cathedram*. "There is one truth especially which We think is self-evident: when the sacred rights of God and religion are ignored or infringed upon, the foundations of human society will sooner or later crumble and give way." Benedict XV in *Ad beatissimi apostolorum* 11 observed: "Sad experience proves that human authority fails where religion is set aside. The fate of our first parent after the Fall is wont to come also upon nations. As in his case, no sooner had his will turned from God than his unchained passions rejected the sway of the will; so, too, when the rulers of nations despise divine authority, in their turn the people are wont to despise their authority."

all forms of cult which are based on these doctrines. He should likewise remind his people of their duty to worship the one God.

> All who rule, therefore, must hold in honour the holy name of God, and one of their chief duties must be to favour religion, to protect it, to shield it under the credit and sanction of the laws, and neither to organize nor enact any measure that may compromise its safety. This is the bounden duty of rulers to the people over whom they rule.[10]

It is a heathen error, St Robert Bellarmine tells us, to suppose that the civil magistrate must have no care for religious truth, provided only that public peace be not disturbed.[11]

What freedom in religious matters must that ruler grant to his subjects, who has not yet publicly subjected his power to the law of Christ? Since in this case the law may not forbid anything which is neither forbidden by natural law, nor is contrary to a determination of natural law which human rulers have the power to make, no monotheistic cult may be forbidden, unless it involves elements contrary to natural law.[12] In theory, men in such circumstances could band themselves into different religions, each teaching or emphasising different divine attributes, or worshipping God according to different ceremonies. Some of these religions might also include false doctrine, but which could be known as false only by revelation, and hence they cannot in these circumstances be forbidden.[13] While his society remains under natural and human law alone, no ruler can forbid this plurality of religions,[14] even if

---

[10] *Immortale Dei*, 6.

[11] *Controversiae*, 'On the members of the Church', bk. 3, ch. 18.

[12] For example, human sacrifice or ritual prostitution.

[13] It is true that reason itself even prior to receiving faith can attain moral certainty of the truth of the Christian revelation and the duty to embrace it; but this is not a duty that can be enforced by the civil power because of the positive divine law forbidding coerced conversion (Matt. 10:14).

[14] Cf. *Dignitatis humanae*, 2nd Council of the Vatican, 2, 4: "All men are to be immune from coercion on the part of individuals or of social groups and of any human power, in such wise that no one is to be forced to act in a manner contrary to his own beliefs, whether privately or publicly, whether alone or in association with others, within due limits. [...] Provided the just demands of public order are observed, religious communities rightfully claim freedom in order that they may govern themselves according to their own norms, honor the Supreme Being in public worship, assist their members in the practice of the religious life, strengthen them by instruction, and promote institutions in which they may join together for the purpose of ordering their own lives in accordance with their religious principles." We take this *Declaration on Religious Liberty* to refer to the rights and duties of

one of these religions be dominant within society,[15] or even if he already himself possesses divine faith and hence knows which is the true religion. A ruler who does not possess such faith ought to pray and bid his people pray for messengers who would teach them what form of worship is right, and he should be disposed to welcome missionaries claiming a revelation from God, unless and until he had ascertained that their claim were repugnant to natural reason.

(b) Duties to families

Even outside Christendom, the ruler is bound to enforce natural law upon those subject to his sway. For it is in virtue of their nature as human beings and therefore as seeking the fulfilment of it that they are subject to temporal authority.

Temporal rulers have jurisdiction primarily over actual and potential heads of families for the sake of the common good. They have jurisdiction over those subject to the ruler of a household, that is, though in essentially different ways, wives and minor children, only insofar as these are not adequately governed by

---

rulers and citizens under natural law, since it apparently intends to abstract from "the traditional Catholic doctrine on the moral duty of men and societies toward the true religion and toward the one Church of Christ", which doctrine it mentions not to expound but only to declare it left intact (*Dignitatis humane* 1). Hence, we agree with Professor Thomas Pink that it leaves to one side the jurisdiction of the Church over the baptised, and the consequent rights of the ecclesial authorities to use coercion over such persons, whether acting directly or through the 'secular arm'. Cf. T. Pink, 'The Interpretation of *Dignitatis Humanae*. A Reply to Martin Rhonheimer', *Nova et Vetera*, English Edition, Vol. 11, No. 1 (2013): 77–121. Furthermore, its decision to restrict itself to questions of natural law means that it does not give a full account of the rights and duties proper to the temporal ruler within Christendom, where some of the precepts of natural law have been more precisely specified by revelation, for example, that the 'unworthy persuasion' mentioned in *Dignitatis humanae* 4 must include all attempts to induce Catholics to abandon their faith, since this is necessarily an attempt to make them subordinate supernatural faith to natural reason. For further discussion, see below, 'The Two Swords'. For a full survey of the possible orthodox interpretations of *Dignitatis humanae*, see T. Crean and A. Fimister (ed.), *Dignitatis Humanae Colloquium*: Dialogos Institute Collection, vol. 1 (Dialogos Institute: 2017).

Dignitatis humanae, 6: "If, in view of peculiar circumstances obtaining among peoples, [speci]al civil recognition is given to one religious community in the constitutional order of [society], it is at the same time imperative that the right of all citizens and religious [commu]nities to religious freedom should be recognized and made effective in practice."

the head of a household and commit offences harmful to the common good of the society.

Since even by natural reason the ruler can know that man is ordered toward some kind of knowledge and love of God,[16] to be sought through virtuous living and sustained by virtuous friendships, he must above all seek to direct his subjects to the common possession of this good. Other things being equal, therefore, he should prevent the propagation within society of errors contrary to the truth not only, as we have seen, about God, but also about human nature, virtue and the goal of human life, as far as these things are knowable by reason: for example, the doctrine that man has no immortal soul.[17] Likewise, all external actions contrary to natural law are of themselves apt to be prohibited, as turning his subjects away from their common earthly good. Insufficient therefore is the opinion that no action should be forbidden which is not contrary to the will of some other citizen, a doctrine which would permit usury, sodomy and necromancy.

Temporal authority confers the right to oblige subjects, by moral and physical means, to act in view of the common good. Since their authority derives from God, rulers bind their subjects not only under pain of a penalty, but in conscience and under pain of sin. Leo XIII observes that this ability to compel under pain of sin is necessary, no doubt so that citizens will have sufficient motive to obey.[18] St Paul likewise told the Romans that they must obey the higher powers "not only for wrath, but also for conscience's sake". [19] Bellarmine remarks that political power and civil laws are called temporal because they have to do with temporal things, but that in themselves they are spiritual, in that they can bind in conscience.[20]

---

[16] Cf. Leo XIII, *Sapientiae Christianae*, 1: "To contemplate God, and to tend toward Him, is the supreme law of the life of man. Created in the divine image and likeness, they are strongly impelled by nature itself to attain their Author. [...] For, indeed, God is the first and supreme truth, and only the mind is nourished by truth. God is perfect holiness and the sovereign good, to which only the will can aspire to and approach, with virtue as its guide."

[17] 5th Lateran Council, Eighth Session; Leo XIII, *Humanum genus*, 17.

[18] *Diuturnum*, 11: "Those by whose authority the commonwealth is administered must be able so to compel the citizens to obedience that it is clearly a sin in the latter not to obey."

[19] Rom. 13:5.

[20] *Controversiae*, 'On the members of the Church', bk. 3, ch. 11. He is responding to John Calvin, who had maintained that the general duty to honour magistrates did not imply that human law could by itself bind under pain of sin; cf. *Institutes of the Christian Religion*, bk. IV.10, section 5.

Since the duty to restrict error and vice exists for the common good of the society, it is suspended whenever it appears that a greater good could be obtained or a greater evil prevented by toleration. As Leo XIII explains:

> God Himself in His providence, though infinitely good and powerful, permits evil to exist in the world, partly that greater good may not be impeded, and partly that greater evil may not ensue. In the government of cities, it is not forbidden to imitate the ruler of the world; and, as the authority of man is powerless to prevent every evil, it has, as St. Augustine says, to overlook and leave unpunished many things which are punished, and rightly, by divine providence. But if, in such circumstances, for the sake of the common good, and this is the only legitimate reason, human law may or even should tolerate evil, it may not and should not approve or desire evil for its own sake; for evil of itself, being a privation of good, is opposed to the common welfare which every legislator is bound to desire and defend to the best of his ability. In this, human law must endeavour to imitate God, who, as St. Thomas teaches, in allowing evil to exist in the world, "neither wills evil to be done, nor wills it not to be done, but wills only to permit it to be done; and this is good." This saying of the angelic doctor contains briefly the whole doctrine of the permission of evil.[21]

Yet, in contradiction with the modern, incoherent praise of 'tolerance' as something desirable for its own sake, he continues:

> But, to judge aright, we must acknowledge that, the more a city is driven to tolerate evil, the further is it from perfection; and that the tolerance of evil which is dictated by political prudence should be strictly confined to the limits which its justifying cause, the public welfare, requires.[22]

It is sometimes supposed that the right of the ruler to restrict error pertains only to the public sphere. As we have seen, St Thomas teaches in accordance with Catholic tradition that the ruler may not remove children from the care of their father so that they may be baptised and raised as Christians.[23] However, since the family is part of society and the manner in which the children are

ertas praestantissimum donum, 33.

*., 34.

other magisterial and theological references, see C. Journet, *The Church of the Word
e, vol. 1, 228-31.

raised is of great importance for its future good,[24] the parents are obliged to educate their children for their future life as adult citizens of a society governed by natural and human law. Hence, if parents are gravely neglecting or harming their children physically or mentally, for example starving or burning them, or instructing them in theft or idolatry or sexual perversion, thus manifesting their intention not to obtain the goal for which their natural freedom in regard to the temporal power exists, then the temporal power, or a third party acting subject to ratification by the same, may take up the duty and rights thus cast aside. In this way the parents may be deprived permanently or for a time of their guardianship of the children.[25]

The temporal power has a native right to found educational institutions which bear directly on matters of public interest, such as military schools.[26] Normally, however, the task of the temporal power in regard to education is a supplementary one, offering help to families or to groups of families who have united for this task. In the exceptional cases where children must be taken from their parents, it must seek some other family in which education will occur, since orphanages and similar artificial institutions cannot be reckoned

---

[24] Cf. Leo XIII, *Sapientiae Christianae*, 42: "It is in great measure within the domestic walls that the destiny of cities is determined."

[25] Cf. *Divini illius Magistri*, 45: "It belongs to the city to protect the rights of the child itself if ever the work of the parents, whether owing to their inactivity, their incompetence or their unworthiness (*ob eorum vel inertiam vel imperitiam vel indignitatem*), should be found wanting either physically or morally. For, as We have said above, their right to educate is not an absolute and despotic one (*non absolutum est atque imperiosum*)."

[26] Cf. ibid, 49: "This does not prevent the State from making due provision for the right administration of public affairs and for the protection of its peace, within or without the realm. These are things which directly concern the public good and call for special aptitudes and special preparation. The State may therefore reserve to itself the establishment and direction of schools intended to prepare for certain civic duties and especially for military service, provided it be careful not to injure the rights of the Church or of the family in what pertains to them. It is well to repeat this warning here; for in these days there is spreading a spirit of nationalism which is false and exaggerated, as well as dangerous to true peace and prosperity. Under its influence various excesses are committed in giving a military turn to the so-called physical training of boys (sometimes even of girls, contrary to the very instincts of human nature); or again in usurping unreasonably on Sunday, the time which should be devoted to religious duties and to family life at home. It is not our intention however to condemn what is good in the spirit of discipline and legitimate bravery promoted by these methods."

equivalent or superior to the natural society of the family, any more than an artificial limb can be equivalent or superior to a natural one.[27]

The temporal power may establish schools to aid parents in their work, but may not lawfully establish secular schools, since this would be to imbue the future citizens with irreligion.[28] Hence, outside Christendom, its schools must teach the truths about God that can be known by reason. Again, it cannot forbid the construction of religious schools by private initiative, unless it be a question of religions forbidden for the reasons given above. Nor can it tax parents to pay for schools their children cannot morally attend, which would be a form of theft.

(c)   Duties to other bodies

Temporal authority is not the source of all rights, since both the individual and the family have, independently of it, the right to seek their perfection by following God's laws and counsels.[29] As part of this quest for perfection, individuals and families may unite for various ends without requiring the permission of their rulers, for example, in schools, universities, businesses, trades unions, hospitals and clubs of every kind. Those who govern must protect the rights of individuals and families to seek their perfection by such unions, encouraging and protecting private initiative, directing it toward the common good and completing it only if it be otherwise insufficient. They can recognize such groups as juridical persons, able to receive new rights from the temporal power and to represent themselves at law.

Temporal rulers, and in general those who exercise authority in higher associations, must not take to themselves tasks that can be accomplished by lower ones. For example, the rulers of a country may not take it upon themselves to organise the growth and distribution of crops, where private agriculture and commerce suffice for the people to be fed. This principle, often

---

[27] Cf. ibid. 45: "In such cases, very rare no doubt, the city does not put itself in the place of the family, but merely supplies deficiencies, and provides suitable means, always in conformity with the natural rights of the child." On this point, Plato in the *Republic* erred though an insufficiently enlightened zeal for education.

id, 79: "The so-called 'neutral' or 'lay' school, from which religion is excluded, is ary to the fundamental principles of education. Such a school moreover cannot exist tice; it is bound to become irreligious."

yllabus of Errors, condemned proposition 39: "The State, as being the origin and of all rights, is endowed with a certain right not circumscribed by any limits."

called the 'principle of subsidiarity' is a root of the natural right of property and is validated by experience.[30]

Duties of temporal rulers within Christendom

What does it mean for a temporal ruler as such, and not as a private individual, to recognise the reign of Jesus Christ? It means first that he publicly affirms that the Catholic Church alone is the accredited representative of God on earth, infallibly teaching the truth about man's final end and providing through her sacraments the necessary means to attain it; and secondly that he publicly pledges to exercise his power above all to help the citizens to attain this end by these means. These two affirmations, made by the sovereign person or body within a society, and accepted by the hierarchy of the Church in Christ's name, make that society to be formally Catholic, and a province of Christendom; part of the City of God and no longer of the City of man and of the devil. The law of Christ is now part of the public law of that realm, the highest part and immutable.

As with individuals, so with nations. These, too, must necessarily tend to ruin if they go astray from the Way. The Son of God, the Creator and Redeemer of mankind, is King and Lord of the earth, and holds supreme dominion over men, both individually and collectively. "And He gave Him power, and glory, and a kingdom: and all peoples, tribes, and tongues shall serve Him" (Dan. 7: 14). "I am appointed King by Him . . . I will give Thee the Gentiles for Thy inheritance, and the uttermost parts of the earth for Thy possession" (Ps. 2: 6, 8). Therefore, the law of Christ ought to prevail in human society and be the guide and teacher of public as well as of private

---

[30] *Quadragesimo anno*, 79-80: "Just as it is gravely wrong to take from individuals what they can accomplish by their own initiative and industry and give it to the community, so also it is an injustice and at the same time a grave evil and disturbance of right order to assign to a greater and higher association what lesser and subordinate organizations can do. For every social activity ought of its very nature to furnish help to the members of the body social, and never destroy and absorb them. The supreme authority of the republic ought, therefore, to let subordinate groups handle matters and concerns of lesser importance, which would otherwise dissipate its efforts greatly. Thereby it will more freely, powerfully, and effectively do all those things that belong to it alone because it alone can do them: directing, watching, urging, restraining, as occasion requires and necessity demands. Therefore, those in power should be sure that the more perfectly a graduated order is kept among the various associations, in observance of this principle of 'supportive duty' (*subsidarii officii*) so will authority within society be stronger and more effective, and the commonwealth itself more prosperous and glad."

life. Since this is so by divine decree, and no man may with impunity contravene it, it is an evil thing for the common weal wherever Christianity does not hold the place that belongs to it.[31]

In some circumstances, it may not be feasible for a believing temporal ruler to incorporate his realm within Christendom, namely when he foresees that the attempt is likely to cause greater harm than good. For example, he may perceive that such a declaration would cause him to lose his power, which would then come into the hands of a less worthy person. Or he may perceive that such a declaration would so agitate the minds of so many of the citizens that the continued existence of the society as a united body would be at stake: for grace must build on nature, though fallen.

In such cases, he can subject his power to the spiritual power only *in praeparatione animi*, 'in preparedness of mind', as married people practise the evangelical counsels or as a poor man practises the virtue of magnificence; that is, as being ready to do so when the occasion comes. Provided his decision derives from true political prudence and not from pusillanimity, he does not thereby sin against the sovereignty of the Son of God. Yet he must also seek by lawful action to help the right occasion to arise, and if he is asked about his wishes, he must not deny that he desires his society to be a part of Christendom, that is, of Christ's dominions, in the way described. For "the common good is to be procured by such ways and means which not only are not detrimental to man's eternal salvation but which positively contribute to it."[32]

How may a believing ruler prepare a society to be incorporated into Christendom? Such a change presupposes the prayer and apostolic activity of the Church, which where not clogged by the sins of her members are always fruitful: *the earth of itself bringeth forth fruit, first the blade, then the ear, afterwards the full corn in the ear.*[33] As the number of Catholics in a society increases, and the risk of endangering public peace accordingly decreases, the sovereign should, while the society is still under only natural and human law, make the human law to correspond ever more perfectly to the natural. For example, the sovereign may forbid those who are not monotheists, or who deny the immortality of the human soul, or who live in concubinage, from becoming representatives of the people, or judges, or from voting. In so acting he does no injustice to the citizens thus disqualified, for they are all inescapably subject

<hr>

[31] Leo XIII, *Tametsi futura*, 8.

[32] Pope John XXIII, *Pacem in terris*, 59.

[33] Mk. 4:28.

to natural law, and therefore obliged to assent to naturally knowable truths about God and man; and his task is to enforce the obligations of natural law whenever this can be done without causing some greater evil or harming some greater good. In this way a still secular society can be justly disposed to become a formally Catholic one.

Such a situation, however long it last, is abnormal. The normal situation is for the ruler to submit his sceptre to Christ not only in preparation of mind, but in act. This is the baptism of his society.[34] Henceforth he rules in the name of Christ and by His authority, and must therefore enforce Christ's law. Although as temporal ruler he is charged primarily with the natural common good of the people whom he rules, yet in promoting this good according to the law of Christ, he must bear in mind two revealed truths about our order of providence: firstly, that for fallen man this natural good requires sanctifying grace, whose normal channel is the sacraments of the Church, since fallen man cannot while in a state of sin consistently keep the divine commandments[35]; and secondly, that this natural good, to be correctly pursued, must be pursued in subordination to the supernatural end.

Again, being now not only a "minister of God', as were even the heathen emperors,[36] but a minister in the Kingdom of God and of Christ, he rightly concerns himself, though in due subordination to the apostolic hierarchy, with the common good of that Kingdom.[37]

Hence the ruler, both in his own name, that is, to fulfil the charge proper to a temporal ruler, and also in the name of the Church, as a minister within a supernatural kingdom, must preserve the sources of grace, and must not pursue the temporal good of his realm in any way that could obstruct the citizens' pursuit of their final end. He must therefore now seek to keep his realm free not only from doctrines which reason itself sees to be gravely contrary to the truth, but also from all the doctrines which Christ's law forbids,

---

[34] "France, Fille aînée de l'Eglise, es-tu fidèle aux promesses de ton baptême?" ("France, eldest daughter of the Church, are you faithful to the promises of your baptism?"), asked Pope John Paul II when he visited that country in 1980.

[35] As Pope St Leo I wrote to the Empress Pulcheria: "Human affairs cannot stand secure, unless both the royal and the priestly authority defend the things that belong to the profession of the divine faith"; Epistle 60, PL 54: 873-74: "Res humanæ aliter tutæ esse non possunt, nisi quæ ad divinam confessionem pertinent, et regia et sacerdotalis defendat auctoritas."

[36] Cf. Rom. 13:4, where St Paul calls the Emperor Nero θεοῦ διάκονος, 'minister of God'.

[37] Cf. Wis. 6:5. The temporal ruler's *ministerial* role in regard to the Church is discussed below in chapter 11, 'The Two Swords'.

115

that is, from all heresies and other opinions solemnly condemned by the Church.[38] This doctrine was dogmatically defined by Pope Pius IX in 1864, when he taught that it is "against the doctrine of Scripture, of the Church, and of the holy Fathers, [...] to assert that 'that is the best condition of civil society, in which no duty is recognized, as attached to the civil power, of restraining by enacted penalties, offenders against the Catholic religion, except so far as public peace may require'."[39] Again, he must foster the splendour of divine worship and the salvation of souls, for example by building churches, endowing seminaries, religious houses and Catholic schools,[40] by recognising and granting exemption to sacred persons and places, where this does not exist,[41] and by patterning the civil calendar on the ecclesiastical.[42]

He must however be careful not to usurp the spiritual authority of the bishops by enforcing his own opinions about disputed matters of doctrine which have not been settled by the Church, by determining the liturgical forms to be used by his subjects, or by claiming either to create new ecclesiastical offices or to install or depose the holders of existing offices.[43]

---

[38] St Francis de Sales considered this a gravely binding duty. When he saw, in 1598, that Duke Charles-Emmanuel of Savoy was being advised by his counsellors to permit Protestant ministers to exercise functions in his domains, he said to him: "Alas, Sire, to permit ministers in this country is to lose your dominions and to lose Paradise besides, of which the span of one foot is worth more than all the world". Quoted in Fr. Pierre-Marie, *Religious Liberty* (Association of St Dominic: Edinburgh, 1994), 11, from Lajoinie, *Saint François de Sales*, 348ff.

[39] *Quanta cura* 3. See also Council of Trent, Session 7, decree 'On Baptism', canon 14.

[40] Leo XIII, *Militantis Ecclesiae*, 50.

[41] Cf. Pope Pius IX, *Syllabus of Errors*, condemned propositions 30: "The immunity of the Church and of ecclesiastical persons derived its origin from civil law", and 31: "The ecclesiastical tribunal for the temporal causes of clerics, whether civil or criminal, ought by all means to be abolished, even without consulting and against the protest of the Holy See."

[42] Cf. Eusebius, *Life of Constantine*, IV.23: "A statute was also passed, enjoining the due observance of the Lord's day, and transmitted to the governors of every province, who undertook, at the emperor's command, to respect the days commemorative of martyrs, and duly to honor the festal seasons in the churches."

[43] St Athanasius, *History of the Arians*, 6.44, quotes the address of Hosius to Constantine the Great: "God has put into your hands the kingdom; to us He has entrusted the affairs of His Church; and as he who would steal the empire from you would resist the ordinance of God, so likewise fear on your part lest by taking upon yourself the government of the Church, you become guilty of a great offence"; St John Damascene, *2nd Oration on Holy Images*: "We are obedient to you, O King (βασιλεῦ), in things concerning our daily life, in tributes, taxes, and payments, which are your due; but in ecclesiastical government we have our pastors, preachers of the word, and exponents of ecclesiastical law." The opinion that

Position of non-Catholics within Christendom

Since in any province of Christendom the gospel is recognised as necessary for the common temporal good of the society, it must also be recognised that no one can simply speaking will this good who does not profess the gospel. Since a citizen simply speaking is a subject endowed with certain rights and duties within a society because of his presumed willing of that society's common good, only someone who professes the gospel, as taught by the Church, can be a citizen simply speaking within Christendom. Hence baptism confers full citizenship, while the crimes of heresy and schism in a baptized person, declared by the Church, cause citizenship to be suspended until they have been absolved in the public forum.[44]

Since the flesh lusts against the spirit and the spirit against the flesh, it is not possible for any province of Christendom to stand unless temporal power be generally by law restricted to those who are themselves submissive to the gospel. Thus in a formally Catholic society, not only idolaters and atheists must be generally excluded from the legislature, and from the higher executive and judicial offices, but also all the unbaptised, as well as all adherents of heretical and schismatic bodies. A partial exception may be made for those selected to represent the interests of a non-Catholic body recognised by that society, since the restricted number of such representatives and the public nature of their allegiance would prevent them from subverting the religion of the realm. Such a provision is however an act of toleration, made to prevent greater evil or to foster greater good, not the recognition of a natural right to such representation supposedly possessed by such groups.

Unbaptised persons are not subject to the jurisdiction of the Church.[45] Dwelling within a province of Christendom, they are, however, subject to the kingship of Christ as proclaimed by the temporal ruler, and hence can be prevented in their public actions from harming the Christian character of the realm. Since the law of Christ forbids both hatred, and suasion toward baptism by temporal threats, the unbaptised must be placed by law at no disadvantage

---

temporal rulers, even within Christendom, may establish laws about the manner of divine worship is sometimes called 'Josephinism', after Joseph II, Holy Roman Emperor from 1765 to 1790.

[44] Since the question of the duties of the temporal ruler toward those in heresy and schism is closely connected to that of his relation to the hierarchy of the Church, it will be considered in chapter 11.

[45] Council of Trent, Session XIV, *De Poenitentia*, cap. II: "The Church never passes judgement on anyone who has not yet come into her by the door of baptism."

save that which is necessary to preserve the Catholic harmony of the realm, and outrages against them must be severely punished.

Unbaptised persons, capable of a partial willing of the common good, may receive certain civil rights, although not citizenship *per se*, while groups of such persons can receive particular law. The temporal ruler of the commonwealth in framing particular law must will the good of the group for which it is framed, governing them as persons subject to natural law. However, unlike the situation of a temporal ruler outside Christendom, he may justly in this governance make use of the knowledge he has from revelation of the contents of the law of Christ, in order to prevent them from doing harm to his realm, in which they are dwelling.

What must be the religious content of such particular law? In accordance with the tradition of the Church, the ruler must grant freedom of worship to Jewish residents in his realm, because the testimony to Christ of their rites and inspired Scriptures is the more powerful as coming from those who do not profess faith in Him.[46] In this way he fitly also shows gratitude to the people from whom the Word took flesh, and honours God's promise that the future ingrafting of the branches to their native olive tree will be life from the dead.[47] However, neither they nor any other group may seek proselytes among the baptised, as this would be contrary to the fundamental law of the realm, which professes Christ as the only Saviour.

St Thomas contrasts the tolerance of Christendom for Jewish worship with its attitude to other non-Christian cults:

> The rites of other unbelievers, which bring nothing of truth or of benefit, are by no means to be tolerated, except perhaps in order to avoid some evil, for example some scandal or disturbance that might ensue, or some hindrance to the salvation of those who if they were unmolested might gradually be converted to the faith.[48]

A distinction should doubtless be drawn between idolatrous and monotheistic cults. The former, as we have seen, are justly subject to suppression even outside Christendom, and they should be even more firmly reprobated within

---

[46] STh 2a 2ae 10, 11. The immunity of Jewish worship and of Jewish property was laid down under pain of excommunication in the bull *Sicut Iudaeis*, promulgated in the 12th century, and confirmed by many subsequent popes.

[47] Cf. Rom. 11:15-29.

[48] STh 2a 2ae 10, 11.

it, not least for the demonic activity they foster.[49] Other forms of non-Christian and non-Jewish public, monotheistic worship which bring something of truth or of benefit are more likely to benefit from the reasons for toleration mentioned by the angelic doctor, unless practised by bodies which have a history of violent opposition to Christianity or of aggressive proselytism. The reality or even the appearance of coercive proselytism must be assiduously avoided, nor must a power to police the interior acts of its subjects be inadvertently attributed to the temporal power. For nothing must be enacted by the temporal power which impedes the right of all men to discover and embrace the true religion.[50]

Finally, the question arises of religious education within non-Christian and non-Jewish families and schools. The ruler of course retains the right, possessed even outside Christendom, to remove children whose parents are gravely failing in their duties under natural law to will the moral or physical good of their offspring. He cannot forbid them to instruct their children in religions which are not excluded by natural law. He can however in assessing the gravity of sinful instruction take into account contrariety not only to natural law but also to the Christian commonwealth which he is charged to protect.[51]

---

[49] Ibid., obj. 2: "Christian princes at first caused the temples of idols to be closed, and afterwards, to be destroyed, as Augustine relates (*On the City of God*, 18.54)."

[50] Thus the right to religious freedom is not reducible to a mere act of tolerance because it corresponds to a real limitation of the scope of the temporal power laid down by natural law, to wit, that it may not impede the conscientious efforts of its subjects by the exercise of reason to discover and embrace the true religion, i.e. to fulfil their duty to worship God. Nevertheless, every time this right is exercised *indirectly* through the conscientious but erring pursuit of a false religion whose erroneous character is merely probable by the light of natural reason then the restraint of the Christian temporal power is concretely an act of tolerance, although it is adopted for the sake of the inviolable natural right.

[51] Hence, for example, a parent instructing his children to steal consecrated hosts could be treated not only as someone who had violated a duty under natural law but also as an enemy to the commonwealth as a Christian commonwealth.

Theses

(i) Men united in society owe to God that tribute of gratitude which is worship.

(ii) Even outside Christendom, the temporal ruler should seek to forbid the propagation of doctrines about God which reason itself can see to be false.

(iii) Outside Christendom, the temporal ruler may not forbid the practice of religions which contain no elements contrary to natural law.

(iv) Temporal rulers have jurisdiction primarily over actual and potential heads of families.

(v) Temporal rulers should seek to prevent the propagation within society of errors contrary to the truth about human nature, virtue and the goal of human life, as these things are knowable by reason.

(vi) Temporal rulers can bind their subjects under pain of sin.

(vii) The duty to restrict error and vice is suspended whenever it appears that a greater good could be obtained or a greater evil prevented by toleration.

(viii) Even outside Christendom, the temporal power may not establish non-religious schools.

(ix) Since temporal authority is not the source of all rights, individuals and families may unite for various ends without requiring the permission of the temporal ruler.

(x) Those who exercise authority in higher associations must not take to themselves tasks that can be accomplished by lower ones.

(xi) When the sovereign has publicly affirmed that the Catholic Church alone is the accredited representative of God on earth, and publicly pledged to exercise the sovereign power to help the citizens to attain their final end by the means declared necessary by the Church, the society becomes a province of Christendom.

(xii) If a believing temporal ruler foresees that the attempt to incorporate his realm into Christendom is liable in present circumstances to cause greater harm than good then he must do so only 'in preparedness of mind'.

120

N.B. The following theses pertain to Christendom only.

(xiii) Acting both in his own name, that is, to fulfil the charge proper to a temporal ruler, and also in subordination to the apostolic hierarchy, as a minister within the kingdom of God, the temporal ruler must preserve the sources of grace, and seek to keep his realm free from all the doctrines which Christ's law forbids.

(xiv) Baptism confers citizenship; the crimes of heresy and schism in a baptized person, declared by the Church, cause citizenship to be suspended; unbaptised persons may receive certain civil rights.

(xv) Only Catholics are generally eligible for the legislature, and for the higher executive and judicial offices.

(xvi) The unbaptised must be placed by law at no disadvantage save that which is necessary to preserve the Catholic peace of the realm.

(xvii) Groups of unbaptised persons may enjoy representation and be governed by particular law.

(xviii) The temporal ruler must grant freedom of worship to Jewish residents in his realm.

(xix) The public practice of other non-Christian religious bodies, although in itself an evil, is not to be impeded in such a way as to obstruct the discovery and adoption of the true religion which is the prevailing right of all men.

(xx) Children may not be taken from non-Christian parents to be baptised or educated, unless these parents explicitly or implicitly renounce the care of those children.

Chapter 7

Law

Nature of law and natural law

The purpose of law is to bring those subjects to it to their proper end. "For as man is the best of the animals when perfected," observes Aristotle, "so he is the worst of all when sundered from law and justice."[1] Likewise, Clement of Alexandria wrote: "Legislation, inasmuch as it presides over and cares for the flock of men, establishes their virtue, by fanning into flame, as far as it can, what good there is in humanity."[2]

St Thomas defines law as "an ordinance of reason for the common good, made by him who has care of the community, and promulgated".[3] So far as lies within its power it excludes those actions and omissions incompatible with the end of that community, commands those actions and omissions indispensable for that end, and permits those which are neither.[4] The final end of all created reality, the common good of the entire universe, is God Himself. The highest law from which all others are derived is therefore God's own understanding of His governance of creatures, which is identical with His own substance.[5] Because each existing substance is constituted in its own nature[6] specified by its end,[7] there is for each species a law corresponding to its nature which stipulates the instrumental and constitutive means necessary for perfection. The same holds true for man and this law, proper to man's nature, is what we call the natural law. As God Himself is extrinsic formal cause of each creature, and as each creature possesses a nature, which is its intrinsic formal cause, so the natural law of man is an image and a participation of the eternal law which is God Himself. The natural law stands midway between the eternal law and the laws of men. No purported human law contrary to natural law has the true nature of law; rather, it is an act of violence:

---

[1] *Politics*, I.2.

[2] *Stromata*, I.26.

[3] STh 1a 2ae, 90, 4.

[4] Ibid. 92, 2.

[5] "In God all is one except there be opposition of relation"; Council of Florence, Session 11, 4th February 1442, *Cantate Domino*, Bull of union with the Copts.

[6] Genesis 1:11-12, 21, 24-25; 2:19.

[7] Wisdom 11:20.

There is a true law, a right reason, conformable to nature, universal, unchangeable, eternal, whose commands urge us to duty, and whose prohibitions restrain us from evil. Whether it enjoins or forbids, the good respect its injunctions, and the wicked treat them with indifference. This law cannot be contradicted by any other law, and is not liable either to derogation or abrogation. Neither the senate nor the people can give us any dispensation for not obeying this universal law of justice. It needs no other expositor and interpreter than our own conscience. It is not one thing at Rome and another at Athens; one thing today and another tomorrow; but in all times and nations this universal law must forever reign, eternal and imperishable. It is the sovereign master and emperor of all beings. God himself is its author, its promulgator, its enforcer. He who obeys it not, flies from himself, and does violence to the very nature of man. For his crime he must endure the severest penalties hereafter, even if he avoid the usual misfortunes of the present life.[8]

Need for human law

According to the ancient Roman historians, human communities were ruled first by the decisions of princes rather than by laws.[9] St Thomas, drawing on Aristotle's discussion, summarises the reasons why it is desirable that political societies be under the rule of law.

As the Philosopher says in *Rhetoric* I, "it is better that all things be regulated by law, than left to be decided by judges", and this for three reasons. First, because it is easier to find a few wise men competent to frame right laws, than to find the many who would be necessary to judge aright of each single case. Secondly, because those who make laws consider long beforehand what laws to make; whereas judgment on each single case has to be pronounced as soon as it arises: and it is easier for man to see what is right, by taking many instances into consideration, than by considering one solitary fact. Thirdly, because lawgivers judge in the abstract and of future events; whereas those who sit in judgment of things present, towards which

---

[8] Marcus Tullius Cicero, *De Republica*, 3.22.33. Cf. *CCC* 1956.
[9] *City of God*, IV.6. St Augustine refers to Trogus Pompeius and Justinus, without vouching for their accuracy.

they are affected by love, hatred, or some kind of cupidity; wherefore their judgment is perverted.[10]

Aristotle remarks that the third reason is the weightiest, and speaks of it also in the *Politics*:

He that recommends that the law shall govern seems to recommend that God and intellect alone shall govern, but he that would have man govern adds a wild animal also; for desire is like a wild animal. Also, spiritedness warps the rule even of the best men. Therefore the law is intellect without appetite.[11]

In the *Nicomachean Ethics*, the philosopher mentions another reason for the same conclusion: people tend to be hostile to a man who opposes them, but not to a law.[12]

In the state of innocence, human laws might have been directive only and not coercive: that is, not enjoined under threat of punishment. Fallen man, however, requires coercion in order to become good, and human law helps to fulfil that office for some of Adam's sons:

As to those young people who are inclined to acts of virtue by their good natural disposition, or by custom, or rather by the gift of God, paternal training suffices, which is by admonitions. But since some are found to be depraved, and prone to vice, and not easily amenable to words, it was necessary for such to be restrained from evil by force and fear, in order that, at least, they might desist from evil-doing, and leave others in peace, and that they themselves, by being habituated in this way, might be brought to do willingly what hitherto they did from fear, and thus become virtuous. Now this kind of training, which compels through fear of punishment, is the discipline of laws.[13]

Punishment may be defined as an evil imposed by public authority, according to the norm of law, on account of a crime which has disturbed the just ordering of society.[14] Its ultimate end is therefore to restore this just, social order. If I break a civil law which forbids usury, and lend money to another person for

---

[10] STh 1a 2ae 95, 1 ad 2.

[11] *Politics*, III.16. 'Desire' and 'spiritedness' are in St Thomas's vocabulary the concupiscible and irascible appetite respectively.

[12] *Nicomachean Ethics*, X.9.

[13] STh 1a 2ae, 95, 1.

[14] Cf. A. Ottaviani, *Institutiones Iuris Publici Ecclesiastici*, vol. 1, 135-36.

interest, then I have not only taken some of his property unjustly, I have also enjoyed an unjust power over him. I can therefore be punished not only by being made to restore the interest which I took, but also by being deprived of some power, by a fine or imprisonment. In this way, a just order within society is established anew.

In achieving this end, punishment also serves four other ends, called preservative, emendatory, expiatory, and exemplary. By weakening the criminal in some way, it makes him less likely to offend again, and hence preserves society from future harm. By instructing him about the evil of his action, it disposes him to improve. By inflicting evil upon the criminal, it allows him, if he freely accepts his sentence, to expiate his debt to the society which inflicts it. By showing others what they would suffer if they copied his example, it encourages them to observe the laws.

The ultimate, retributive end of punishment limits the pursuit of the other ends. Hence one may not punish a criminal, to improve him or to protect society, more severely than his offence warrants.[15]

In the case of crimes of the highest gravity and where the preservation of life cannot otherwise be assured because either the individual or the offender as a category cannot easily be contained, recourse to the death penalty may be morally and practically necessary.[16] Where the offender has sought to inflict irreversible and severe harm, for example by murder or treason, it may be impossible to restore the order of justice without subjecting him to capital

---

[15] Cf. C. S. Lewis, 'The Humanitarian Theory of Punishment', in *God in the Dock,* ed. W. Hooper (William B. Eerdmans: Grand Rapids, 1970).

[16] *CCC* 2267 (1997) "Assuming that the guilty party's identity and responsibility have been fully determined, the traditional teaching of the Church does not exclude recourse to the death penalty, if this is the only possible way of effectively defending human lives against the unjust aggressor."

punishment.[17] Whether the conditions necessary for the use of the death penalty have been realised is a judgement reserved to the laity.[18]

St Thomas describes the objection that execution deprives the wrongdoer of the opportunity to repent as 'frivolous':

> The fact that the evil, as long as they live, can be corrected from their errors does not prohibit the fact that they may be justly executed, for the danger which threatens from their way of life is greater and more certain than the good which may be expected from their improvement. They also have at the critical point of death the opportunity to be converted to God through repentance. And if they are so stubborn that even at the point of death their heart does not draw back from evil, it is possible to make a highly probable judgment that they would never come away from evil to the right use of their powers.[19]

Punishment for offences against merely human law may not be applied retrospectively, for this would be an injustice as the defendant could have had no knowledge of his transgression at the point at which it is alleged and therefore would not have transgressed. In regard to those offences against natural law which ought to be embodied in human law, punishment may and indeed should be applied retrospectively because the natural law is written on the hearts of all men and if a delinquent civil power omitted to apply it and the defendant took advantage of this fact to violate the precept, this greatly

---

[17] *Catechism of the Council of Trent*, 'On the fifth commandment': "Another kind of lawful slaying belongs to the civil authorities, to whom is entrusted power of life and death, by the legal and judicious exercise of which they punish the guilty and protect the innocent. The just use of this power, far from involving the crime of murder, is an act of paramount obedience to this Commandment which prohibits murder. The end of the Commandment is the preservation and security of human life. Now the punishments inflicted by the civil authority, which is the legitimate avenger of crime, naturally tend to this end, since they give security to life by repressing outrage and violence. Hence these words of David: *In the morning I put to death all the wicked of the land, that I might cut off all the workers of iniquity from the city of the Lord.*"

[18] This is because it is a technical question relating to temporal conditions and not a universal moral judgment but also because the shedding of blood by the one who offers sacrifice is unfitting and traditionally causes the person inflicting death to incur irregularity. "His a quibus Domini sacramenta tractanda sunt, iudicium sanguinis agitare non licet" ("those who are to handle the Lord's sacraments may not carry out the judgement of blood"); 11th Council of Toledo, c. 6.

[19] *Summa Contra Gentiles* III.146. For a thorough treatment of this topic see: E. Feser & J. Bessette, *By Man Shall His Blood Be Shed: A Catholic Defense of Capital Punishment* (San Francisco: Ignatius, 2017).

compounds both the guilt of the offender and the harm done.[20] We see this principle applied to the atrocities of the Third Reich after its defeat and assuredly it should be applied to those physicians who at this time make use of the vulnerability of the unborn in the happy event that the protection of the laws is once more restored to them.

Wherever some commonwealth is so constituted that its ruler is placed above its laws as regards coercion, as is often the case in regard to sovereigns and heads of state, he remains nevertheless subject to the laws as regards the obligation in conscience to obey them.

> The authority of a wise man says: "Obey the law that thou thyself has made". The Lord also reproaches those who "say and do not"; and who "bind heavy burdens and lay them on men's shoulders, but with a finger of their own they will not move them", as is said in Matt. 23. Hence, in the judgment of God, the ruler (*princeps*) is not exempt from the law, as to its directive force; but he should fulfil it of his own free-will and not of constraint.[21]

In the same way, observes St Robert Bellarmine, clergy, though by divine law exempt from temporal jurisdiction, must obey the laws of the land in which they dwell as citizens, and yet they cannot rightly be coerced to do so.[22]

The prerogative of pardon attaching to the sovereign or head of state is a manifestation of his moral responsibility before God to make provision for those occasions where general law fails in particulars.[23]

---

[20] For example, in a situation in which the civil power has been disabled, a person who decides to break a shop-window and steal some items displayed there sins far more gravely than would an ordinary shop-lifter because he is likely to trigger a general bout of looting.

[21] STh 1a 2ae 96, 5. The wise man in question is Dionysius Cato, the author of the 3rd or 4th century work *Distichs*. Suarez explains that while the legislator is not subject to himself, he is subject to the precept of the natural law which requires that one obey a law that one has made; *de Legibus*, III.XXXV.13.

[22] *Controversies*, 'On the members of the Church', I.28; cf. Council of Trent, Session 25, 'On Reformation', cap. 20.

[23] STh 2a 2ae 67, 4: "The ruler who has full authority in the commonwealth, can lawfully remit the punishment to a guilty person, provided the injured party consent to the remission, and that this do not seem detrimental to the public good."

Origin of Human Law

In the temporal order human law, that is, laws actually formulated and promulgated by men, performs two functions: it communicates the natural law in propositional form and it determines indifferent questions necessary for human communal life, the determination of which the natural law requires without specifying the nature of that determination - such as which side of the road to drive on or how many pennies there should be in the pound. It is only in this latter respect that the human legislator truly acts as a legislator rather than an expositor of law. Such laws, originating in human ingenuity, are called human positive laws. Hence Aristotle, though lacking a developed doctrine of natural law, wrote that "one part of what is just within the city is natural (φυσικόν), the other part is legal (νομικόν)".[24]

Not every requirement of the natural law should be transposed into human law. This is for three reasons. First, some elements will be unenforceable by third parties (such as the prohibition against rash judgements). Secondly, while others might be enforced this would be at the cost of an intrusion into the autonomy of the subject so infantilising or despotic as to be a greater evil than the evil proscribed. Finally, the level of perfection demanded might be so exalted as to be beyond the concrete capacity of the greater part of fallen men and so the attempt to enforce such a law would hold the law up to ridicule.

> The purpose of human law is to lead men to virtue, not suddenly, but gradually. Wherefore it does not lay upon the multitude of imperfect men the burdens of those who are already virtuous, viz. that they should abstain from all evil. Otherwise these imperfect ones, being unable to bear such precepts, would break out into yet greater evils: thus it is written (Proverbs 30): "He that violently bloweth his nose, bringeth out blood"; and (Matthew 9) that if "new wine", i.e. precepts of a perfect life, "is put into old bottles," i.e. into imperfect men, "the bottles break, and the wine runneth out", that is, the precepts are despised, and those men, from contempt, break into evils worse still.[25]

Man has been elevated from the beginning of human history to an end infinitely surpassing the end merely proportionate to his nature. This elevated end subsumes and perfects man's nature without destroying it. Since natural

---

[24]*Nicomachean Ethics*, V.7. The claim that human laws do not rest on natural law but only on the decision of the human legislator is called legal positivism. Aristotle noted that "some people think everything just is merely legal"; ibid.

[25] STh 1a 2ae, 96, 2 ad 2.

law is the law merely proportionate to man's nature, there exists another law, which is also proper to man, but which is above natural law. This is the divine law, also called divine positive law.[26] There can be in principle no conflict between the natural and divine laws just as there is no conflict between the natural and supernatural ends. However, man, who would have received the supernatural habits necessary for him to attain this surpassing end at conception, forfeited these endowments owing to the rebellion of our first parents. God does not abandon man but offers to everyone who attains the age of reason a supernatural motion by which he is able in principle to turn to the due end.[27] This motion elicits in human nature a desire for the uncreated and infinite good.[28] Because man is not conceived with a proportion to this good this unleashes a conflict within him, manifesting the 'wounds of the fall': ignorance, malice, weakness and concupiscence.[29] For this reason, at least from the time of Moses, divine law bifurcated human authority into a spiritual power charged with the supernatural end and a temporal power charged with the attainment of the natural end.

The temporal commonwealth is the community constituted by the end proportionate to man's nature. But Satan's rebellion, in which he implicated our first parents, consisted precisely in the claim that the absolutely final end is proportionate to the nature of every intellectual creature; in other words, that created persons are owed beatitude by God, and should not have to receive it as a gift on God's terms.[30] For the City of the world, that is, for all those outside the Church and her own dead members, united by the love of self to the point of contempt for God, the very existence of the Church is thus an affront to the dignity of man as an intellectual creature. The temporal community is the object or at least the locus of their hopes and aspirations. The essence of the intellectual creature's rebellion against God consisting essentially in the claim that man's objectively final end is proportionate to his nature, the inevitable frustration of the attempt to attain to that end without

---

[26] Even before the Law of Moses, individual precepts were given to the human race; cf. Gen 2:17, 9:4.

[27] STh 1a 2ae 89, 6.

[28] Cf. St Thomas Aquinas, *Supplement to the Summa*, appendix 1, q. 1, a. 2.

[29] For these 'wounds of nature', see STh 1a 2ae 85, 3.

[30] STh 1a 63, 3: "He sought to have final beatitude of his own power, whereas this is proper to God alone."

grace leads him, individually and as a society, to transfer his ideals progressively from the vanity of pagan virtue to gross and sensual objects.[31]

Since it is thus necessary for God's honour and man's happiness that the transcendence of the spiritual end be manifest, the titles to spiritual and to temporal power must be separate and, where possible, those actually exercising the two powers must be distinct.[32] This is necessary also because of the ever present temptation to the first of all heresies: simony. Simony asserts a proportion between the temporal and the spiritual, since it sells spiritual for temporal goods or purchases spiritual goods by means of temporal ones.

There are thus two parallel systems of human law: that issued by the temporal power, namely, the civil law, and that issued by the spiritual power, namely, the canon law.[33] There ought to be no conflict between these, but as in their essence as human law they bear upon indifferent questions, the possibility of conflict between laws promulgated in good faith in each order and not in conflict with natural or divine law, cannot be excluded in the abstract.[34] How can it be avoided in practice?

The attainment of the goods of this life, the proper object of the temporal power, requires the propitiation and impetration of the Almighty - something which only the spiritual power can accomplish. Thus, without prejudice to its infinitely more important task of procuring the salvation of souls, the spiritual power has a place in temporal society definable by temporal law and without which temporal society falls short of its proper perfection, just as the Sun serves as the source of the Moon's light, while also ruling the day by its own splendour. So long as this place is respected by the temporal rulers, and a wholesome deference is extended by them to their fathers in Christ, and so long as the spiritual rulers do not stray into the merely technical considerations proper to the temporal order, conflict can be avoided.

---

[31] This is the decline traced by St Augustine in the *City of God* climaxing in his description of the hedonistic pagans of his own day. "Here, then, is this Roman republic, which has changed little by little from the fair and virtuous city it was, and has become utterly wicked and dissolute. It is not I who am the first to say this, but their own authors, from whom we learned it for a fee" (II.19). See *City of God* XIV.3 for St Augustine's account of this decline within the individual.

[32] See chapter 5, 'Temporal authority: its origin'.

[33] 'Canon law' in the sense of the *Code of Canon Law* also contains some provisions which are of divine law, for example regarding the matter of the sacraments or the rights of the Roman pontiff.

[34] For example, if a day of public celebration were to be declared which coincided with a day of fasting and abstinence.

The right to judge and to declare when a civil law, because it transgresses the natural or divine law, is null and void, belongs of right to the spiritual power. If no definitive judgment is forthcoming from the spiritual power, through moral cowardice on the part of the hierarchy or some other impediment, each man must follow his conscience in this regard.

> [T]he Church was not given the commission to guide men to an only fleeting and perishable happiness but to that which is eternal. "Indeed, the Church holds that it is unlawful for her to mix without cause in these temporal concerns"; however, she can in no wise renounce the duty God entrusted to her to interpose her authority, not of course in technical matters (*iis quae artis sunt*) for which she is neither suitably equipped nor endowed by office, but in all things that are connected with the moral law.[35]

Unjust laws

"He that resisteth the power resisteth the ordinance of God. And they that resist purchase to themselves damnation".[36] Since human legislators, both spiritual and temporal, act with the authority of God, they have the power to promulgate laws that bind their subjects 'in the tribunal of conscience'. Yet they do not have the authority to abuse this power by enacting unjust laws.

Human good requires that acts of governance have a proper end, a proper form, and a proper author. A 'law' which lacked any of these would not of itself bind the subjects under pain of sin.[37] Some simple examples may serve to illustrate this.

Laws have a proper end when the ruler is acting for some general benefit and not from private desire or vainglory. For example, if a ruler taxed the citizens for the express purpose of building a fleet of luxury yachts for himself and his friends or to fund the pursuit of a manifestly unjust war, that would not be a true law, and so one need not pay the tax.

Laws lack a proper form if they distribute some benefit or burden unequally over the community without a proper cause. Hence, a parliament could not pass a law requiring that all brown-haired people pay tax at a higher rate than others, even if that rate were not in itself inequitable, since there is no

---

[35] Pius XI, *Quadragesimo anno*, 41. Internal quotation from the same pope's encyclical *Ubi arcano*.

[36] Rom. 13:2.

[37] STh 1a 2ae 96, 4.

connection between the colour of one's hair and one's duty to pay for public amenities.

Thirdly, a law must have a proper author, which means that the subject matter on which it bears must be one in which the law-giver is competent. Hence, for example, a king or president may not pass a law requiring all families in his domain to eat dinner at a certain time; for by natural law each man's household is under his own sway.

These three requirements correspond to three parts of justice. General justice, the virtue by which all virtuous acts are directed to the common good of the society in which one is acting, requires that a law have a right end. [38] Distributive justice, by which tasks are distributed among the members of a society in accordance with their abilities, requires that a law have a proper form, in the sense explained. Commutative justice, by which a man does not seek an unfair advantage in his transactions, prevents one from seeking obedience from those who do not owe it.[39]

Even though unjust laws of this kind do not of themselves bind under pain of sin they can become binding in certain circumstances, "to avoid scandal or disturbance, for which cause a man should even yield his right".[40]

Finally, a purported law which is contrary not only to the rights of those on whom it is imposed but also to the rights of God may never be obeyed: for example, a law purporting to command a pharmacist to sell abortifacients or a registrar to register marriages between persons of the same sex.

---

[38] STh 2a 2ae 58, 5 and 6. St Thomas holds that general justice, also called 'legal justice' since it inclines a person to obey all just laws, is a virtue distinct from others, and not simply a name given to moral virtue as a whole. See also his *Commentary on the Nicomachean Ethics*, Book V, lecture 2, no. 912, where he shows how this may be reconciled with Aristotle's treatment of legal justice.

[39] Suarez, *de Legibus*, I.IX.13.

[40] STh 1a 2ae 96, 4. The so-called 'merely penal law', even though it does not *per se* oblige a person to perform a certain act under pain of sin, nevertheless obliges him under pain of sin to accept the penalty which may be imposed if he fails to perform it. Such are, for example, some of the laws included in the constitutions of religious orders; STh 2a 2ae 186, 9. Cf. STh 2a 2ae 108, 4 ad 2: "A man may be condemned, even according to human judgment, to a punishment of forfeiture, even without any fault on his part, but not without cause". Suarez suggests that signs of a law's being merely penal are that it relates to a matter which is not of great moment for society and that it is punished by a relatively light penalty; *de Legibus*, V.V.12. Cf. Clement V, *Exivit de paradiso*.

Custom

Natural law provides for a secondary source of positive law, apart from the express decree of a legislator: custom. St Isidore of Seville defined custom as a "right instituted by practice, which is taken as law when law is lacking".[41] The angelic doctor explains how custom may come to be equivalent to written law:

> Just as human reason and will, in practical matters, may be made manifest by speech, so may they be made known by deeds: since seemingly a man chooses as good that which he carries into execution. But it is evident that by human speech, law can be both changed and expounded, in so far as it manifests the interior movement and thought of human reason. Wherefore by actions also, especially if they be repeated, so as to make a custom, law can be changed and expounded; and also something can be established which obtains force of law, in so far as by repeated external actions, the inward movement of the will, and concepts of reason are most effectually declared; for when a thing is done again and again, it seems to proceed from a deliberate judgment of reason. Accordingly, custom has the force of a law, abolishes a law, and is the interpreter of the laws (*consuetudo et habet vim legis, et legem abolet, et est legum interpretatrix.*)[42]

As repetition of similar acts by an individual man, notes Suarez, may give rise to a *habitus* within him, so repetition of similar acts by a society may give rise to a right or duty within itself.[43] St Thomas distinguishes two cases:

> The people among whom a custom is introduced may be of two conditions. For if they are free, and able to make their own laws, the consent of the whole people expressed by a custom counts far more in favour of a particular observance, than does the authority of the ruler, who has not the power to frame laws, except as representing the people. Wherefore although each individual cannot make laws, yet the whole people can. If however the people have not the free power to make their own laws, or to abolish a law made by a higher authority, nevertheless with such a people a prevailing custom obtains force of law, in so far as it is tolerated by those to whom it belongs to make laws for that people: because by the very fact that

---

[41] *Etymologies* V.3: "Consuetudo autem est ius quoddam moribus institutum, quod pro lege suscipitur, cum deficit lex."

[42] STh 1a 2ae 97, 3.

[43] *De Legibus*, VII.I.4.

they tolerate it they seem to approve of that which is introduced by custom.[44]

Applying this distinction to modern representative legislatures, we may say that the rulers themselves may by repeated actions introduce a custom having the force of law, for example the constitutional convention in the United Kingdom that the Prime Minister shall be an individual capable of commanding an absolute majority of seats in the House of Commons.[45] Again, if the majority of people owning television sets ceased to pay for a licence, then even if the first people so to act would apparently do wrong, yet if the courts chose not to prosecute, then custom would have achieved a change in the law.[46]

The repeated actions must be performed with at least the implied intention of asserting a right or assuming a duty, for the custom to be able to gain the force of law.[47] Evidently, also, to gain the force of law, a custom is subject to the same limitations as written law: it must not be contrary to natural or divine law, nor must it be in some other way 'unreasonable', for example, by making too great a demand on human powers.

Written law may itself govern custom, in the sense that a legislator may decree that when any custom has prevailed in a population for a specified period of time then it obtains the force of law[48]; independently of this, however, natural law itself ordains that a custom obtains the force of law whenever it has prevailed long enough to manifest the mind of the legislator that it should be so binding. The legislator may also choose to promulgate a law ordering the subjects to observe a custom which has itself already obtained the force of law: in this case, the practice in question now enjoys a double strength.[49]

---

[44] STh 1a 2ae 97, 3 ad 3.

[45] Such a custom is said to be 'beside the law' (*praeter legem*), since it does not contradict any existing law.

[46] Such a custom is called 'contrary to law'. Something like this seems to occur in the case of 'jury repeal'.

[47] Suarez gives the example of going to bed between one's evening meal and receiving Holy Communion at Mass next day. Although this is the customary practice of those who receive Holy Communion, it is not done with the purpose of instituting a binding custom, but arises simply from the ordinary manner of human living; *de Legibus*, VII.XIV.5.

[48] For example, the current *Code of Canon Law* in the Latin church ordains that legitimately observed customs obtain the force of law after thirty continuous years; CIC 26. The 1917 *Code*, in canon 28, prescribed forty years.

[49] Suarez notes that in such circumstances, if the law itself is later removed, the rights and duties arising from the custom remain intact; *de Legibus*, VII.III.3-4. This apparently

Custom is of great power in ensuring the efficacy of a legal order as it constitutes, as it were, the internalisation of the laws by a people. If the laws are subjected to revision on frivolous pretexts or indeed for less than a grave and pressing cause, the potency of the law in general and its power over the minds of men will be seriously weakened to the detriment of the weak and the poor and the common good of all. For this reason St Thomas strongly counsels against amending laws even when their limitations are quite significant:

> Human law is rightly changed, in so far as such change is conducive to the common weal. But, to a certain extent, the mere change of law is of itself prejudicial to the common good: because custom avails much for the observance of laws, seeing that what is done contrary to general custom, even in slight matters, is looked upon as grave. Consequently, when a law is changed, the binding power of the law is diminished, in so far as custom is abolished. Wherefore human law should never be changed, unless, in some way or other, the common weal be compensated according to the extent of the harm done in this respect. Such compensation may arise either from some very great and every evident benefit conferred by the new enactment; or from the extreme urgency of the case, due to the fact that either the existing law is clearly unjust, or its observance extremely harmful.[50]

Nor did this insight originate with St Thomas, as the ancient Greeks had already perceived the great dangers inherent in legal novelty. As Demosthenes observes:

> I should like, gentlemen of the jury, to give you a description of the method of legislation among the Locrians. It will do you no harm to hear an example, especially one set by a well-governed community. In that country the people are so strongly of opinion that it is right to observe old-established laws, to preserve the institutions of their forefathers, and never to legislate for the gratification of whims, or for a compromise with transgression, that if a man wishes to propose a new law, he legislates with a halter round his neck. If the law is

---

abstruse point of legal theory came to have great practical importance in the Church after the promulgation by Pope Paul VI of the apostolic constitution *Missale Romanum* in 1969.

[50] STh 1a2ae, 97, 2. Cf. Aristotle, *Politics*, II.8. We may recall here the aphorism of Tacitus, "corruptissima re publica plurimae leges" ("in a debased commonwealth there is a plethora of laws"); *Annals*, III.27.

accepted as good and beneficial, the proposer departs with his life, but, if not, the halter is drawn tight, and he is a dead man.[51]

Equity

Since no merely human legislator can foresee all chances, and since the attempt to incorporate a multitude of foreseeable chances into a body of law would render it cumbersome, the observance of some positive, human law may in certain circumstances lead to some evil. For example, a man who obeys traffic regulations when driving a dying man to hospital may be guilty of folly. In such a case, we speak of a 'partial cessation' of the law, which loses its obligatory force while the circumstances remain.[52]

For this reason, a special virtue exists, called *epikeia* or 'equity', by which one may justly set aside a positive law in such circumstances.[53] Hence Aristotle defines *epikeia* as "rectification of a law insofar as the universality of the law makes it deficient" (ἐπανόρθωμα νόμου ᾗ ἐλλείπει διὰ τὸ καθόλου). St Thomas describes it as "a kind of higher rule of human actions", and a superior part of human justice.[54] It is exercised by the one who has charge of the society, who "is empowered to dispense in a human law that rests upon his authority", but when there would be danger in delay, the private citizen himself may exercise this virtue, as in the example given above.[55] *Epikeia* is not to be confused with the interpretation of the meaning of a doubtful law, which is something belonging to public authority and not to the private citizen.

---

[51] *Against Timocrates*, 24.149. Ronald Reagan alluded to this practice in a speech of July 20th, 1974, given to 'Young Americans for Freedom'. Other cities employed less lethal mechanisms against innovation in the public counsels: "It is their custom to deliberate about the gravest matters when they are drunk; and what they approve in their deliberations is proposed to them the next day, when they are sober, by the master of the house where they deliberate; and if, being sober, they still approve it, they act on it, but if not, they drop it. And if they have deliberated about a matter when sober, they decide upon it when they are drunk." Herodotus on the Persians, in *Histories*, I.133.

[52] Suarez, *de Legibus*, VI.VI.1.

[53] See *Nicomachean Ethics*, V.10; STh 2a 2ae 120.

[54] He refers to the corresponding *intellectual* virtue by the Greek word *gnome* (γνώμη), noting that it implies 'a certain perspicacity of judgement'; STh 2a 2ae 51, 4. Cf. *Nicomachean Ethics*, VI.11, where Aristotle defines *gnome* as the 'correct judgement of the decent [or equitable] person'.

[55] STh 1a 2ae 97, 4.

Common and Civilian legal systems: historical background and philosophical significance

Two legal systems dominate the western world and much of the world beyond: the Civilian and Common law systems.[56] Both grew fundamentally from Roman Law, whose origins stretch back into legendary antiquity, to the time of the Roman Kings and the first years after the deposition of Tarquin the Proud in 509 BC. The Roman Law underwent a fundamental change in the sixth century after Christ when it was codified by the Emperor Justinian. This created the 'Civilian' tradition. The Common Law system emerged out of the kingdom of England, which was welded together from the Anglo-Saxon kingdoms whose conversion was accomplished at the initiative of St Gregory the Great, a little over half a century after the codification of Justinian. In a famously suggestive passage St Bede wrote:

> Among other benefits which he [Æthelberht, the first king converted by Gregory's mission] conferred upon the nation, he also, by the advice of wise persons, introduced judicial decrees, after the Roman model; which, being written in English, are still kept and observed by them.[57]

Whatever these judicial decrees after the Roman model were, they had nothing to do with the codex of the Emperor Justinian, which was unknown to the West until the eleventh century, but which thereafter became the main rival legal system to the Anglo-Saxon Common Law. What an educated Latin in the barbarian West would have known about Roman Law in the late sixth and early seventh century was largely theoretical rather than substantive and is exemplified by the fifth book of St Isidore of Seville's *Etymologies*, entitled *De legibus et temporibus* and based on the *Institutes* of Gaius, a manual of legal theory.[58] Although Gaius's *Institutes* were an important source for Justinian's, they lack one crucial and highly influential passage which is possibly original to Justinian. For after Justinian has listed the ancient sources of Roman Law (the people, the senate, both together, magistrates etc.) he is faced with the inconvenient fact that by the sixth century, none of these is in reality any longer a source of law, especially now the whole legal corpus has been abrogated, reformed and re-promulgated by himself. The embarrassment is covered over with the concept of the *Lex Regia*: "The pleasure of the emperor [Justinian writes] has the vigour and effect of law, since the Roman people, by the royal

---

[56] Common Law accounts for a third of the world's population, Civilian Law slightly more.

[57] St Bede, *Ecclesiastical History of the English People*, 2:5.

[58] Gaius's *Institutes* are dated to c. AD 160-70.

law, have transferred to their prince the full extent of their own power and sovereignty."[59]

Justinian himself meant the *Lex Regia* as a statement of a mechanism in Roman positive law by which the institutions of the Republic were permanently suspended in favour of the legislative power of the emperor at the beginning of each new reign.[60] However, after the Western rediscovery in the eleventh century of his recension of the Civil Law, and especially after the rise of nominalism in the fourteenth century, with the consequent inability to base authority on human nature, the belief took hold that the *Lex Regia* describes the fundamental means by which civil legitimacy as such is constituted.[61] From this arises the distinctively modern contractualist account of the origin of civil legitimacy, which makes the temporal commonwealth an artificial, not a natural, society.[62]

The classical and Christian understanding of civil legitimacy (including, in his defence, Justinian's) is quite different. It is well expressed by St John Chrysostom, commenting on Romans chapter 13,

> 'For there is no power', [St Paul] says, 'but of God'. What say you? It may be said; is every ruler then chosen by God? This I do not say, he answers. Nor am I now speaking about individual rulers, but about the thing in itself. For that there should be rulers, and some rule and others be ruled, and that all things should not just be carried on in one confusion, the people swaying like waves in this direction and that; this, I say, is the work of God's wisdom. Hence he does not say, 'for there is no ruler but of God'; but it is the thing he speaks of, and says, 'there is no power but of God. And the powers that be, are ordained of God'. Thus when a certain wise man says, 'It is by the Lord that a man is matched with a woman' (Proverbs 19:14, LXX), he means this, God made marriage, and not that it is He that joins together every man that comes to be with a woman.[63]

From this conception of the temporal commonwealth as a natural reality with properties independent of human will, there flows a threefold idea of human

---

[59] Institut. l. i. tit. ii. No. 6. s. In fairness, this embarrassment had in practice been covered over since the second century, and in some sense since the death of Augustus.

[60] Anthony Kaldelis, *The Byzantine Republic: People and Power in New Rome* (Harvard University Press: Cambridge MA, 2015).

[61] Alexander Lee, *Humanism and Empire* (OUP: Oxford, 2018), 356.

[62] See above pp. 86-87.

[63] *On Romans*, Homily 21; PG 60: 615. See p. 88.

law, described by Isidore and Justinian both.[64] All legitimate commands backed up by native authority and coercive power[65] can be assigned to one of these three forms of right. First, there is the *Ius Naturale* which is that irreducibly discretionary part of legitimate human authority which, while real, cannot be reduced to a propositional form: this comprises the authority of a man over himself, of parents over their children, discretionary judicial power and the executive power of governments. Secondly, there is the *Ius Gentium*, that part of the natural law which *can* be reduced to propositional form and is thus, in principle, the same for all peoples. Finally, there is the *Ius Civile*, that part of human law which concerns matters indifferent in themselves but which the natural law, i.e. human nature, demands be determined one way or another for the sake of communal life, which is the proper life of man.

Under the influence of this conception, and separated from that of Justinian's system by the chauvinism of the English lawyers, the English legal system has spontaneously developed a parallel threefold structure. Equity, the discretionary power to depart from precedent in a way that does not establish precedent,[66] exists in order to give effect to the *Ius Naturale*. The Common Law, which rests exclusively upon natural justice and precedent,[67] gives effect to the *Ius Gentium*. The Statute Law which consists of univocal written legislation (being, as we have seen, the only part of the system in which man publicly legislates in his own right) creates the *Ius Civile*. These in turn correspond to the threefold structure of the public law of England, now widely if imperfectly imitated. The King, through his Chancellor, once known as 'the keeper of the King's conscience', dispenses Equity; the House of Lords is the

---

[64] See the more general discussion of this topic in chapter 5.

[65] A parent, court, or sovereign (and their agents if they delegate this power) possess such native authority and may immediately restrain or punish those who resist. In contrast, an employer or an agent of the temporal power or parents to which such authority is not delegated will have to have recourse to the courts or the parents to vindicate a legitimate demand.

[66] For example, where legal ownership of property cannot be challenged without upsetting the structure of the law but the moral ownership lies elsewhere, the English courts constitute the moral owner as the 'beneficial owner' for whose interests the legal owner must exercise his rights.

[67] For example, there is in England no statute of murder, the offence being defined and governed in its essence entirely by precedent grounded ultimately upon natural law.

highest court of Common Law[68]; for particular and indifferent matters the consent of the Commons is required.[69]

The implication of the Common Law system is that societies are natural entities with properties independent of the will of man, and that the ruler reigns by the grace of God, the author of nature, but is also correspondingly limited by divine and natural Law. Government being natural rather than conventional, the temporal polity is a juridical person in natural law with same sort of obligations towards God and towards His revealed will as the individual man.[70] Indeed, the juridical personhood in natural law of temporal society, with the corresponding obligation of public worship in the manner God has appointed, means that the existence of a divine, revealed law is implied by the very structure of the Common Law system. The *Ius Gentium* is necessarily established through the analogous mode of precedent because the human intellect is inadequate to know human nature comprehensively and so cannot but fail in particulars. The likelihood of this is diminished by the use of precedent rather than statute for the *Ius Gentium* and the consequent appeal to the standard of the reasonable man. But the possibility of failure in particulars cannot be eradicated, hence Equity. Indifferent matters are susceptible to univocal human legislation precisely because they are human creations, whose artificial 'natures' can be known comprehensively by the human mind.

Not so are the civilian jurisdictions, not so. For them all is Civil Law: all matters, criminal as well as civil, are legislated for by man and codified. The Civilian system thus implies the deity, and hence the secularity, of the state, which comprehends all reality and legislates for it in a univocal code. As its creator, the Civilian state exists before society, and the individual and the family exist under license from the Civilian state. The subject of the Common Law has *liberties* empowering him to do everything that has not been positively forbidden by reason or statute. The temporal power constituted by natural law is limited by natural and divine law. When the ruler commands something contrary to these laws his command is null and void. When he seeks to compel his ostensible subject to violate God's law he is to be resisted, by the grace of

---

[68] At least until recent highly regrettable and hopefully transient innovations.

[69] For a fuller treatment of these topics see the articles of the late Sir Roger Scruton, 'The Fundamental Principle of Common Law' and 'The Law of the Land', available on his website www.roger-scruton.com/

[70] To this day the accession of the British monarch depends upon his or her adherence to the true religion (unfortunately the true religion is misidentified.)

God.[71] The subject of the Civilian Code, in contrast, has 'rights': a list of things he is allowed to do by the 'State'. For everything else he must ask permission.[72] The subject of the contractualist Civilian state has agreed in advance to all that Leviathan wills. The denial of this subjection is a threat to the very existence of the beast, as is the claim that any sort of society, pre-eminently the family, is natural. For to admit the existence of any natural society is to strike a fatal blow at the foundation myth of the Leviathan. In the first instance Leviathan must institute divorce (that is, in effect, prohibit marriage); ultimately, it must deny even the objective reality of the sexual difference itself.

Without foreseeing all the horror of modernity (although he did imply that the time of the antichrist would be marked by unashamed sodomy)[73], St Thomas sees no difficulty in balancing various sources of law against each other, and touches upon the parallel between the divisions of private law[74] and the structures of public law in asking, 'Whether Isidore's division of human laws is appropriate?'

> In the notion of human law, many things are contained, in respect of any of which human law can be divided properly and of itself. For in

---

[71] "Christian liberty bears witness to the absolute and most just dominion of God over man, and to the chief and supreme duty of man toward God. It has nothing in common with a seditious and rebellious mind; and in no title derogates from obedience to public authority; for the right to command and to require obedience exists only so far as it is in accordance with the authority of God, and is within the measure that He has laid down. But when anything is commanded which is plainly at variance with the will of God, there is a wide departure from this divinely constituted order, and at the same time a direct conflict with divine authority; therefore, it is right not to obey." Leo XIII, *Libertas* (1888) 30.

[72] A single example, commonplace to the civilian but shocking to the anglophone, serves to illustrate the point. In Common Law countries there are no mandatory state identification cards. Civilian Law countries almost inevitably have these. In Civilian jurisdictions one must register one's residence with the local authorities if one remains more than a few days in the same place. If one walks more than a few metres from this registered abode without one's state identification card, one commits an offence. If one refuses to produce this card on demand by a policeman, one commits an offence. In England, if a policeman so much as requires a man to tell him his name without reasonable grounds to suspect him of an offence, the policeman commits an offence.

[73] *Commentary on the 2nd Letter to the Thessalonians*, cap. 2, lect. 2.

[74] See: Justinian, *Institutes*, 1.1.4: "There are two branches of this study [jurisprudence], namely: public and private. Public Law is that which concerns the administration of the Roman government; Private Law relates to the interests of individuals. Thus Private Law is said to be threefold in its nature, for it is composed of precepts of Natural Law, of those of the Law of Nations, and of those of the Civil Law."

the first place, it belongs to the notion of human law to be derived from the law of nature, as explained above. In this respect, positive law is divided into the *ius gentium* and *ius civile*, according to the two ways in which something may be derived from the law of nature (*a lege naturae*), as stated above. Because, to the law of nations belong those things which are derived from the law of nature, as conclusions from premises, e.g. just buyings and sellings, and the like, without which men cannot live together, which is a point of the law of nature, since man is by nature a social animal, as is proved in *Politics* I. But those things which are derived from the law of nature by way of particular determination belong to the civil law, according as each city decides on what is best for itself.

[...]

It belongs to the notion of human law, to be framed by that one who governs the community of the city, as shown above. In this respect, there are various human laws according to the various forms of government. Of these, according to the Philosopher in *Politics* III, one is 'monarchy,' i.e. when the city is governed by one; and then we have 'Royal Ordinances' (*constitutiones principum*). Another form is 'aristocracy,' i.e. government by the best men or men of highest rank; and then we have the 'Authoritative legal opinions' (*Responsa Prudentum*) and 'Decrees of the Senate' (*Senatus consulta*). Another form is 'oligarchy,' i.e. government by a few rich and powerful men; and then we have 'Praetorian', also called 'Honorary', law. Another form of government is that of the people, which is called 'democracy', and there we have 'Decrees of the commonalty' (*Plebiscita*). There is also tyrannical government, which is altogether corrupt, which, therefore, has no corresponding law. Finally, there is a form of government made up of all these, and which is the best: and in this respect we have 'Law' (*lex*) sanctioned by the 'Lords and Commons' as stated by Isidore. [75]

The ideal of the threefold polity created by the Romans and adopted by the Englishmen of the high Middle Ages was well expressed by a chastened Charles I in 1642:

> There being three kindes of Government amongst men, Absolute Monarchy, Aristocracy and Democracy, and all these having their particular conveniencies and inconveniencies, the experience and

---

[75] STh 1a 2ae 95, 4. The concluding reference is to St Isidore's *Etymologies*, V. 4.

wisdom of your Ancestors hath so moulded this out of a mixture of these, as to give to this Kingdom (as far as human prudence can provide) the conveniencies of all three, without the inconveniencies of any one, as long as the Balance hangs even between the three Estates, and they run jointly on in their proper Chanell (begetting Verdure and Fertilitie in the Meadows on both sides) and the overflowing of either on either side raise no deluge or Inundation. The ill of absolute Monarchy is Tyrannie, the ill of Aristocracy is Faction and Division, the ills of Democracy are Tumults, Violence and Licentiousnesse. The good of Monarchy is the uniting a Nation under one Head to resist Invasion from abroad, and Insurrection at home. The good of Aristocracie is the Conjuncion of Counsell in the ablest Persons of a State for the publike benefit. The good of Democracy is Liberty, and the Courage and Industrie which Libertie begets.[76]

[76] Charles I, *Propositions Made by Both Houses of Parliament ... with His Majesties Answer Thereunto*, 18th June, 1642.

143

Theses

(i)   Law is an ordinance of reason for the common good, made by the one who has charge of the community, and promulgated.

(ii)   The purpose of law is to make men good.

(iii)   The acts of law are to command, to forbid, to permit and to punish.

(iv)   Eternal law is God's knowledge of Himself as ordering all things to their end in accordance with His wisdom.

(v)   Every other law is law insofar as it derives from the eternal law.

(vi)   Natural law, which is the rational creature's share in the eternal law, is grasped by man inasmuch as human nature tends to its own perfection.

(vii)   It is better to be under the rule of law than under the rule of men.

(viii) The principal end of punishment is to restore a just social order.

(ix)   The other ends of punishment are to protect society, to amend the criminal, to enable him to expiate his crime and to deter others.

(x)   Capital punishment may be used in retribution for crimes when the preservation and security of human life require this because the gravity of such crimes does not allow the just social order to be restored in another way.

(xi)   Crimes against natural law may be punished retroactively.

(xii)   Those placed above the laws of their society as regards coercion are nevertheless obliged to obey them.

(xiii) Human laws derive from natural law either as conclusions from premises or as something more specific from something more general.

(xiv)   Requirements of natural law should be included within human law when they are enforceable, unless this tends to an evil greater than that forbidden.

(xv)   Divine positive law directs man to his supernatural end.

(xvi)   As civil law facilitates the fulfilment of natural law, canon law facilitates that of divine positive law.

(xvii) Laws bind in conscience unless they are opposed to divine or human good.

(xviii)	A 'law' contrary to divine good may not be obeyed.
(xix)	A 'law' contrary to human good by its lack of a proper end, form or author need not be obeyed.
(xx)	Custom can have the force of law, can abolish law, and is the interpreter of law.
(xxi)	Custom cannot prevail over natural or divine law.
(xxii)	A just law should not always be replaced by a better one, since a change of law is itself an evil.
(xxiii)	A merely human law may be dispensed by the law-giver, or where there is danger in delay by a private man, where its observance would lead to evil.
(xxiv)	It is better to incorporate natural law into human law by discernment in concrete cases and by precedent, than by attempting to foresee all possibilities.
(xxv)	The common-law system is connatural to Christendom.

Chapter 8
Forms of Polity

Principle of division

The word 'polity', like the Greek *politeia* from which it comes, has several meanings. It can be used 'concretely' to mean a political society, and so we can speak of the French or German polity. We use it here more abstractly, with the sense assigned by Aristotle in book III of his *Politics*: "The ordering of a city in respect of its various authorities, and especially of the one that is supreme over all matters."[1] In this sense, a polity is established by the constitution or fundamental law of a political society.

Aristotle famously asserted that there are three general kinds of just polity, and that each of them has its corresponding 'deviation' or 'corruption' which arises when the ruling element in the society seeks its private good rather than the common good.[2] By a translation or transliteration of Aristotle's Greek terms, the three just forms are normally called monarchy[3] or kingship, aristocracy[4] and timocracy[5], while their corresponding corruptions are named tyranny, oligarchy[6] and democracy.[7] However, the vicissitudes of history have lent to many of these terms a sense somewhat different from that which they bore for the Stagirite. For example, *monarchia* is not in his mind necessarily linked to hereditary rule. Our first task therefore is to clarify his meaning.

What 'principle of division' distinguishes one kind of polity from another? The question is not as simple as it may appear, since at times Aristotle speaks of the

---

[1] "Ἔστι δὲ πολιτεία πόλεως τάξις τῶν τε ἄλλων ἀρχῶν καὶ μάλιστα τῆς κυρίας πάντων."

[2] *Politics* III.12; *Nicomachean Ethics* VIII.10. The Greek term translated as 'deviation' is παρέκβασις.

[3] Literally, rule by one (*monos*).

[4] Literally, rule by the best (*aristoi*).

[5] In the *Nicomachean Ethics*, VIII.10, Aristotle explains that this word comes from the term τίμημα (*timeema*), property, and denotes rule by many people who nevertheless each possess a specified amount of property. He notes that such a system is normally called by the name of the genus, and termed a 'polity'. In the *Politics*, he conforms to this common but confusing practice.

[6] Literally, rule by a few (*oligoi*).

[7] Literally, rule by the people. For his summary of these six possibilities, see *Politics* III.7, IV.2 and *Nicomachean Ethics* VIII, 10.

number of the rulers, either one, few or many, as if it were the key, while at other times he appears to suggest that the wealth or poverty of the governing element is the most basic reason for the distinction.[8] For enlightenment, we may consider his statement that "one may find resemblances to these polities, and patterns (παραδείγματα) of them, so to speak, in households".[9] The orderly rule of a father over his children, he asserts, offers a pattern for kingship, that of a husband over his wife, a pattern for aristocracy, and the governance of a household by brothers, for timocracy.

This comparison between the family and the city indicates that the number of those who rule does not furnish the essential difference between polities: the father and husband is but one man, and yet his rule is called kingly in one case, and aristocratic in the other.[10] The difference between his rule over his children and over his wife is that in the latter case, "he commits to his wife what is fitting for her".[11] If he tried to rule everything (ἁπάντων δὲ κυριεύων) he would corrupt the household. By contrast, no such area of self-governance exists for the children.

This suggests that the essential difference between polities, for Aristotle, lies in whether, and to what extent, the ruling element governs the society independently of the governed. In the domestic society, the father governs independently of the children, in such a way that there is no part of their common life where they may justly assert their will against him; and he may justly annul any agreements they make amongst themselves. Hence paternity resembles, or rather models, pure kingship, for the king governs his subjects justly indeed, yet in such a way that his subjects may not in the public life of their society assert their will against his, having no temporal authority of their

---

[8] Hence R. Robinson claims that 'the one-few-many scheme is dropped as soon as stated'; *Aristotle, Politics III and IV*, Clarendon Aristotle Series, General Editors J. Ackrill and L. Judson (Oxford: Clarendon Press, 1995), 26-27.

[9] *Nicomachean Ethics*, VIII.10. That he considers the households to offer the pattern for the city rather than conversely confirms that he thought of the family as naturally prior to the city. See above p. 53.

[10] St Thomas, it is true, seems to understands the reference to aristocracy in this place differently, as meaning that the husband and wife together rule their children 'aristocratically', since he writes: "The authority by which a husband and a wife govern a household is aristocratic"; *Commentary on the Nicomachean Ethics*, VIII, lect. 10. However, Aristotle does not mention children in this context. His words are literally: 'Of husband and wife it appears aristocratic' (ἀνδρὸς δὲ καὶ γυναικὸς ἀριστοκρατικὴ φαίνεται). Irwin inserts 'the community' into the beginning of the sentence, while Ross has 'the relation'. St Thomas's Latin version was, as usual, a verbal translation of Aristotle's elliptical Greek.

[11] *Nicomachean Ethics*, VIII.10.

own, and such that he may, subject to the demands of natural law, over-rule any agreements they may have made among themselves.[12]

By contrast, the husband does not justly govern independently of his wife the whole of the marital society which he enjoys with her. Within her own sphere of domestic duties she sets her priorities and executes her plans. An aristocracy resembles this, since in such a polity the rulers distribute what pertains to the city, such as its offices, to the people in accordance with the people's worth, rather than keeping them all to themselves as in an oligarchy.[13] Thus in a pure aristocracy, although those who choose and are eligible for the highest temporal authority will be a class apart, this ruling class will entrust other citizens with some authority in the public life of the society, for example in trying lesser legal cases and exercising regional executive power, and members of the ruled class will be able to establish binding contracts among themselves. That Aristotle understands the relation of husband and wife to be analogous to that between the higher and lower classes within an aristocracy is confirmed by the fact that he uses the same phrase, "contrary to worth" (παρὰ τὴν ἀξίαν) to describe the activity both of oligarchs and of the excessively controlling husband.

Finally, when adult brothers share a house, since the 'ruling element' here means all the brothers taken together, it governs no part of the life of their society independently of any of those who are ruled. All decisions, that is, which affect their common life, are made by all of them, and no brother has authority independently of the 'laws' which they have thus established in common, whether by simple majority or by unanimity, to govern any part of the life of any of his brethren. A pure 'timocracy' resembles this, since in such a society, laws, office-holders and decisions affecting the city are determined by the whole people in their assembly, and legal cases are tried by a jury of all the citizens.

This distinction of regimes according as the governing element governs all or none or some of the life of the society independently of those governed appears to be the most formal distinction, even if it is not made fully explicit by Aristotle. It explains how two such different societies as the family and the *polis* have exactly corresponding regimes. The other manners of distinguishing the regimes appear to be either 'material', that is, not based on the very

---

[12] It is clear that Aristotle in making this comparison between the father and the king has in mind not every form of kingship which has existed, but kingship in its purest form. See the second and especially the fifth of the five forms of kingship which he distinguishes in *Politics*, III.14-17.

[13] *Nicomachean Ethics*, VIII.10.

structure of authority, as when the regimes are distinguished in virtue of the different social class which is dominant, or by reason of the numbers of those who possess power[14]; or else to indicate conditions necessary for the different just regimes to exist, as when Aristotle speaks of the rulers as needing to possess outstanding virtue, or complete virtue, or simply military virtue, for kingship, aristocracy and timocracy respectively.

Lawfulness of each kind of polity

Pure monarchy and pure timocracy are 'limiting cases' among men, that is, polities to which a society may make an ever closer approach, but which it can never reach. Even the most timocratic of Greek city-states would not assemble all its citizens to judge every petty larceny. Even the most autocratic of kings must leave some room to his ministers for their own judgement and initiative. But using human words humanly, we may speak of societies as pure monarchies or pure timocracies, insofar as the monarchic or timocratic principle tends as far as possible to govern everything within them.

Pure monarchy, pure aristocracy and pure democracy is each a lawful regime.[15] In each case the governing element may intend the common good and subject itself to natural and divine law. Leo XIII often taught that the Church's opposition to the French Revolution does not contradict this principle.

> The Church, the guardian always of her own right and most observant of that of others, holds that it is not her province to decide which form of government (*forma civitatis*) is most desirable, or by what institutions the civil affairs of Christian nations are to be conducted, and amid the various kinds of commonwealth she does not disapprove of any, provided religion and the observance of good morals be upheld.[16]

---

[14] In theory, a 'ruling class', as defined above, could consist of one person, and still be an aristocracy, while several persons, if they necessarily had but one will, would be a monarchy.

[15] Henceforth, to conform to a long-established custom we shall drop the term 'timocracy', and use 'democracy' to refer to lawful rule by the people over themselves.

[16] *Sapientiae Chistianae*, 28; cf. *Libertas* 44: "Of the various forms of government (*ex variis reipublicae generibus*), the Church does not reject any that are fitted to procure the welfare of the subject"; *Au milieu des sollicitudes,* to the Church in France, 1892: "Various political governments have succeeded one another in France during the last century, each having its own distinctive form: the Empire, the Monarchy, and the Republic. By giving one's self up to abstractions, one could at length conclude which is the best of these forms, considered in themselves; and in all truth it may be affirmed that each of them is good,

The same doctrine was taught by Pope Pius XI:

> Universally known is the fact that the Catholic Church is never bound to one form of government more than to another, provided the divine rights of God and of Christian consciences are safe. She does not find any difficulty in adapting herself to various civil institutions, be they monarchic or republican, aristocratic or democratic.[17]

Possibility of mixed polities

The aspiration to a 'mixed polity' is an ancient one. Already Aristotle noted that "some say that the best constitution is a mixture of all the constitutions (τὴν ἀρίστην πολιτείαν ἐξ ἁπασῶν εἶναι τῶν πολιτειῶν μεμειγμένην)".[18] The phrase however has been variously used, sometimes to refer to a constitution giving a stake in the city to all the social classes, sometimes to refer to a separation of the organs of government. Here we use it to refer to a polity which possesses elements of more than one of the three 'pure' polities. This yields four new possibilities: a mixture of all three pure polities, a mixture of monarchy and aristocracy, of monarchy and democracy, and of aristocracy and democracy. Hence we may speak of seven basic forms of polity, as St Robert Bellarmine remarks.[19]

Thomas Hobbes declared that a mixed polity is an impossible chimaera. Either one of the men or bodies bearing authority has the right to control the others, in which case that man or body is alone the sovereign; or else no man or body has the right to control the others, in which case the realm is not one realm, but an unstable alignment of independent factions. Any society with discrete bearers of authority, one of whom could not limit the others at will, would thus necessarily be in a permanent state of war, either open or concealed.

provided it lead straight to its end - that is to say, to the common good for which social authority is constituted; and finally, it may be added that, from a relative point of view, such and such a form of government may be preferable because of being better adapted to the character and customs of such or such a nation. In this order of speculative ideas, Catholics, like all other citizens, are free to prefer one form of government to another precisely because no one of these social forms is, in itself, opposed to the principles of sound reason nor to the maxims of Christian doctrine."

[17] *Dilectissima nobis*, written to the Church in Spain in 1933.

[18] *Politics*, II.6. F. Wormuth remarks that "in the time of Aristotle the idea of the mixed state seems to have been a commonplace"; *The Origins of Modern Constitutionalism* (New York: Harpers & Brothers, 1949), 19.

[19] *Controversiae*, 'On the papacy', bk. 1, ch. 1.

Discounting the claim that authority is indeed divided in England between the King, the Lords, and the Commons, he affirms that such government would not be government at all, but rather "division of the Commonwealth into three factions."[20]

Likewise, an elective kingship, where the people have the right to choose another king after the death of the present one, was to Hobbes not a mixed monarchy, but a simple democracy, since the sovereignty in such a case clearly remains, he held, in the people. "That king whose power is limited", he asserts, "is not superior to him, or them, that have the power to limit it; and he that is not superior is not supreme; that is to say, not sovereign". One cannot share in sovereignty: one possesses it whole, or not at all.

Hobbes's doctrine of the 'indivisibility of sovereignty' is a consequence of holding that temporal authority arises through the will of all the citizens to yield all their right of governing themselves to a single person or body. If temporal authority within human society is constituted by a prior agreement to submit to everything willed by the recipient of that authority then by definition there can be only one such authority, for were its scope to be limited in some way then the judge of those limitations would simply be the irresponsible final authority. More fundamentally, Hobbes's view rests on his belief that a man's action is necessarily determined by his strongest passion. On this view, no bearer of authority can do anything but follow where his or its dominant passion leads, which will be to a private goal that can only accidentally and hence unstably be the same as the goal of some other bearer of authority: it will not be to the good of a society as such.[21] This view in turn reflects his belief that 'good' is only a name which a man gives to something to express the fact that he desires it.[22]

But Hobbes's view is incorrect: we do not believe something to be good because we desire it, we desire it because, at least in some respect, we believe it to be good. Someone whose perception is correct will therefore desire a

---

[20] *Leviathan,* chapter 29.

[21] Cf. St Thomas Aquinas, *Commentary on the Nicomachean Ethics,* Book VIII, lecture 5: "Passion, since it belongs to the sensitive appetite, does not go beyond the particular good of the one loving."

[22] *Leviathan,* chapter 6: "Whatsoever is the object of any man's appetite or desire, that is it which he for his part calleth good; and the object of his hate and aversion, evil; and of his contempt, vile and inconsiderable. For these words of good, evil, and contemptible are ever used with relation to the person that useth them: there being nothing simply and absolutely so; nor any common rule of good and evil to be taken from the nature of the objects themselves."

greater good more than a lesser good, and hence a common good more than a private one. For this reason a truly mixed polity, in which sovereignty is divided among several bearers, none of which has a power over the others limited only by natural and divine law, is possible. For all may intend as the good that specifies their action, the common end to which they all contribute.

Nature of mixed polities

Without admitting that a mixed polity is a chimaera, we can agree that the terms 'monarchy', 'aristocracy', and 'democracy' do not have the same sense when they are used to designate a mixed rather than a pure constitution. In a mixed monarchy, for example, the monarch will clearly not be the sole bearer of temporal authority. Just as a chemical compound does not have the same properties as the elements of which it is composed, so it is with a mixed or composite polity. In this case, the terms 'monarchy', and 'aristocracy' are used to denote something which is secondary to them when they are used to refer to pure polities, namely authority as possessed by one person or by several.

All composites have a formal and a material component.[23] This must therefore be true of a mixed polity. Since the highest part of temporal authority is the legislative power, therefore within a mixed polity, an element is formal insofar as it is or determines this power. The most formal element naturally gives its name to the regime. From this it follows that the four species of mixed polity distinguished by Bellarmine contain within themselves twelve principal sub-species. Since the point is of some importance, we shall set this out by simplified examples, despite the inevitable appearance of pedantry.[24]

We shall speak only of the legitimate forms, i.e. we assume that in each case those who govern intend to do so for the common good, but without claiming that each form is likely to be feasible.

First, there are four forms of mixed monarchy.

(1) An assembly, not chosen by the people, may propose laws but they must be approved by one man not chosen by the people. While this is a mixture of monarchy and aristocracy, it is a mixed monarchy, rather than a mixed aristocracy.

---

[23] STh 1a 2æ, q. 13, a. 1.

[24] Aristotle states in *Politics* VI.1 that as well as investigating each of the basic regimes, part of the task of the political philosopher is to investigate "combinations (συναγωγὰς) of all the modes".

(2) The people by referenda which they have themselves initiated may propose laws but they must be approved by one man. While this is a mixture of monarchy and democracy, it is a mixed monarchy, rather than a mixed democracy.

(3) An assembly, elected by the people, may propose laws but they must be approved by one man. Here all the elements are mixed, while the 'material element', i.e. initiating power, is constituted more by the assembly than by the people. Since one man must approve what is proposed, the polity is monarchical.

(4) An assembly may propose laws for popular vote, a vote that must be approved by one man. Here again the elements are all mixed, with the material element being constituted more by the people than by the assembly. But again, since one man must approve what is proposed, the polity is monarchical.

Likewise, four forms of mixed aristocracy can be imagined:

(5) One man, not chosen by the people, can propose laws, but they must be approved by an assembly not chosen by the people, for example by heirs of noble families. This is a mixed aristocracy rather than a mixed monarchy, even though both elements are present.

(6) The people by referenda which they have themselves initiated may propose laws but these must be approved by an assembly not chosen by them. Here the democratic element is material, while the aristocratic is again formal, and so this is a kind of aristocracy.

(7) One man, elected by the people, can propose laws, but they must be approved by an assembly. While all three elements are present, the most formal is the aristocratic one.

(8) One man may propose laws for popular vote, a vote that must be approved by an assembly. Again, the most formal element here is aristocratic.

Finally, we may imagine four forms of mixed democracy:

(9) One man, not chosen by an assembly, may propose laws which must be approved by popular vote. Here the monarchical element is material, the democratic, formal.

(10) An assembly, not chosen by one man, may propose laws which must be approved by popular vote. Here the aristocratic element is material, the democratic formal.

(11) One man, chosen by an assembly, may propose laws which must be approved by popular vote.

(12) An assembly, chosen by one man, may propose laws which must be approved by popular vote.

Still considering only the legislative power, we may see that even these twelve forms admit of variation: for example, in (1) the 'monarch' might be chosen by the assembly or might be a hereditary king, and in the former case, while the polity would still be a mixed *monarchy*, the aristocratic element in it would be more pronounced than in the latter case. If we consider also that the executive and judicial elements might in theory be monarchical, aristocratic, or democratic, or mixed in many different ways, the sub-species of mixed polity are beyond easy reckoning. In fact, they are strictly innumerable, with the infinitude of matter, since there is no limit to the ways in which human affairs may be ordered.[25]

Ranking of polities

"The soul delights to compare one thing with another, for the comparison of one thing to another is the proper and connatural act of the human reason."[26] The question therefore naturally arises, which polity is best? Aristotle acutely remarks that the enquiry may cover several quite different questions.[27] St Robert Bellarmine distinguishes three such questions at the start of his discussion of regimes: (i) 'which of the three pure polities is best?'; (ii) 'which of the seven polities, including both mixed and pure, is best for fallen human beings?'; and (iii) 'which of the seven polities is best in itself?'[28] We may consider each question in turn.

In attempting to rank polities, people sometimes compare not their innate fitness to bring society to its goal, but rather certain consequences that they are judged likely to produce in the characters of the people. Thus St Thomas himself remarks that in a monarchy, it often happens that people "strive more sluggishly for the common good", since they imagine that the common good is a benefit not to themselves but to the one person in whose charge it is

---

[25] 158 descriptions of different constitutions are attributed in ancient lists to Aristotle and his school. None survives, except for part of the *Constitution of the Athenians*, discovered at the end of the 19th century.

[26] STh 1a 2ae 32, 8.

[27] *Politics*, IV.1. For his own discussion, see below, pp. 164 ff.

[28] *Controversiae*, 'On the papacy', Bk. 1, ch. 1. The context of his discussion is a defence of the institution of the papacy as the predominant, monarchic element within the mixed constitution of the Church.

placed.[29] One may in this way suggest both advantages and disadvantages which could follow each kind of polity. Thus, monarchy could remind the subjects of the unity of God; the separation between the monarch and everyone else in the society would effectually impress on the minds of the subjects the awesome truth that he is God's minister; his having, in a pure monarchy, the fullness of temporal power in his hands, might aid them in growing in the virtue of humility. On the other hand, monarchy might occasion servility in the souls of the subjects; or again, the monarch's pre-eminent place might cause them to slight the superior, spiritual authority of their bishop. Next, aristocracy, with its distinction between a ruled and ruling class might also favour both humility and servility among the ruled, and both magnanimity and pride among the rulers. As for democracy, it might be praised for manifesting the truth that each man bears the image of God in his soul, and for encouraging each citizen to proper initiative and self-respect; or it might be blamed for occasioning the belief that the rulers are not only chosen by the people, but also are the ministers of the people alone, and therefore need not enforce God's law; and for spreading throughout society a general distaste for hierarchy and obedience of all kinds.[30]

While such comparisons have an undoubted fascination, they do not seem able to solve our question. In general, things designed for an end should be ranked rather by their fitness for that end than by their accidental advantages, unless these latter be both certain and very differing in perfection.

Monarchy is the best of the pure polities

St Thomas in comparing the three pure forms thus begins his enquiry "from the very purpose of governance", *ex ipso fine regiminis.*[31] He has in mind the intrinsic end of human society:

The welfare and safety of a multitude formed into a society lies in the preservation of its unity, which is called peace. If this is removed, the

---

[29] *De Regno*, I.5.

[30] This was Plato's view; *Republic*, VIII: "I must add that no one who does not know would believe, how much greater is the liberty which the animals who are under the dominion of man have in a democracy than in any other State: for truly, the she-dogs, as the proverb says, are as good as their she-mistresses, and the horses and asses have a way of marching along with all the rights and dignities of freemen; and they will run at anybody who comes in their way if he does not leave the road clear for them: and all things are just ready to burst with liberty."

[31] *De Regno*, I.3.

benefit of social life is lost and, moreover, the multitude in its disagreement becomes a burden to itself. The chief concern of the ruler of a multitude, therefore, is to procure the unity of peace.[32]

One man, rather than several or many, is best able to achieve this goal, for "what is itself one can more efficaciously bring about unity than several", just as anything which has an attribute in itself is a more efficacious cause than what has that same attribute in dependence on another. Just as the teacher, having mastered a subject, can more effectively communicate it to others than can his student who has not yet made the subject his own and who thus repeats the half-understood sayings of his master; or just as land, being valuable in itself, makes a man wealthier than does money, which has value only in relation to other things; so one person is best able to effect unity in a group, being himself one. This, says the angelic doctor, is "manifest". As he further argues, any ruling group is only able to rule insofar as it is united and not factious; but if it is union among the rulers that we are seeking, what could be more united than a single man? A society, in fact, is only *one* society because it has one principle of unity, for "every multitude is derived from unity". Nature itself, he affirms, leads us to the same conclusion, since gregarious animals, like bees, have a monarch, "and a work of art is better according as it attains a closer likeness to what is in nature". Experience does the same, since "provinces or cities which are not ruled by one person are torn with dissensions and tossed about without peace". Nor is a single ruler *per se* most apt to bring about only unity and peace: *any* end is more efficaciously achieved, when the cause aiming at it is more united.[33]

True, the corruption of the best is the worst, and hence tyranny, that is, one man ruling for his private good, is the worst regime.[34] Yet this in itself is not a sufficient argument against monarchy, for two reasons: a single ruler is unlikely to act as a tyrant continuously, never willing the public good in any of his actions, especially as it is hardly possible for one man to enslave a group wholly against their own interests, whereas by contrast in a group of supreme rulers it is likely that one of them at any given moment will be subordinating the common welfare to himself; and secondly, a good monarchy is less likely to deteriorate into a tyranny than is a polyarchy, where the need to jockey for position will often end with one man oppressing the rest: "Almost every regime

---

[32] Ibid.

[33] *De Regno,* I.4.

[34] Ibid.

156

of many rulers has ended in tyranny".[35] Hence "it is best for a human multitude to be ruled by one man."[36]

We should, however, note that neither in the *De Regno* nor elsewhere does St Thomas speak of the 'rex' as a *hereditary* monarch; he seems even to assume the opposite, speaking of him as either having been chosen by the people or as having been given to them by a higher authority.[37]

The doctrine of the *De Regno* is taught more briefly in the *Summa contra Gentiles*, in regard to the papacy:

> No one should doubt [...] that the government of the Church has been established in the best way, since He has disposed it by whom "kings reign, and lawmakers decree just things" (Prov. 8:15). But the best government of a multitude is rule by one, and this is clear from the purpose of government, which is peace; for peace and the unity of his subjects are the purpose of the one who rules, and one is more fit to cause unity than many.[38]

St Robert Bellarmine begins his examination of the question with arguments from authority: all the ancient Hebrew, Greek and Latin writers, he observes, whether theologians, philosophers, orators, historians or poets, agree in preferring monarchy. Again, the divinely instituted polity of the chosen people is the greatest authority, and this was always monarchical:

> The rulers (*principes*) among the Hebrews were first the patriarchs, such as Abraham, Jacob, Juda, and others; then leaders (*duces*), such as Moses and Josue; then judges, such as Samuel, Samson, and

---

[35] Ibid., I.6.

[36] Ibid., I.3. Writing of the papacy, Chesterton argued in a different way for the thesis that aristocracy is more like than monarchy to be tyrannical: "It is not the people who would be the heirs of a dethroned Pope; it is some synod or bench of bishops. It is not an alternative between monarchy and democracy, but an alternative between monarchy and oligarchy. And, being myself one of the democratic idealists, I have not the faintest hesitation in my choice between the two latter forms of privilege. A monarch is a man; but an oligarchy is not men; it is a few men forming a group small enough to be insolent and large enough to be irresponsible. A man in the position of a Pope, unless he is literally mad, must be responsible. But aristocrats can always throw the responsibility on each other; and yet create a common and corporate society from which is shut out the very vision of the rest of the world"; *The Thing* (Sheed and Ward: London, 1946), 238.

[37] See above, p. 96.

[38] IV.76.

others; afterwards kings, such as Saul, David and Solomon; finally leaders once more, such as Zorobabel and the Maccabees.[39]

While God found fault with the Jews for requesting a king, this was not because something is wrong with desiring one visible ruler, since Samuel was already acting as such; it was because they asked for a king who would be like the kings of the nations, ruling the realm, that is, as if it were his own possession which could therefore be passed to his offspring, rather than ruling as vice-gerent of God.[40]

Among many other ancient witnesses, Christian and pagan, the Jesuit doctor cites St Jerome:

> Bees have princes, and cranes fly after one of their number in the shape of a Y. There is but one emperor and each province has but one judge. Rome was founded by two brothers, but, as it could not have two kings at once, it was inaugurated by an act of fratricide.[41]

Bellarmine then moves on to his own arguments. Monarchy is the most orderly of the pure polities, for order is not discerned among equals but among superiors and inferiors, and in a monarchy there is no one who is not subject to someone, with the sole exception of the monarch. Again, it is easier to find one good man than several, or many. Again, a republic with many rulers is like a household where the same kind of task is assigned to many servants: "The work is carried out in a slovenly manner, because each one leaves their common duty to someone else."

Finally, experience chimes in with both authority and reason. History shows how monarchies tend to be more stable and to last longer than any other form of regime. [42]

A mixed polity is better than a pure monarchy

In 1 Maccabees 8, the ambassadors of Judas Maccabeus extol the constitutional arrangements of the Romans as a mixed monarchy. That the ambassadors admired the system they described and the reasons they admired it are both telling:

---

[39] *Controversiae*, 'On the papacy', book 1, c. 2.

[40] Ibid.

[41] *Letter* 125, 'To Rusticus', 15. St Jerome is urging Rusticus not to pursue the religious life by himself, but under the authority of an abbot.

[42] *Controversiae*, 'On the papacy', book 1, c. 2.

And none of all these [the Romans] wore a crown, or was clothed in purple, to be magnified thereby. And that they made themselves a senate house, and consulted daily three hundred and twenty men, that sat in council always for the people, that they might do the things that were right. And that they committed their government to one man every year, to rule over all their country, and they all obey one, and there is no envy, nor jealousy amongst them.[43]

St Thomas too does not favour a pure monarch, that is, a man untrammelled except by natural and divine law, whose ministers would be merely his delegates. Writing to the king of Cyprus, he warns him that the monarch's power must be so 'tempered' that it cannot easily become the instrument of a tyrant.[44] This points in the direction of the 'mixed' regime which he elaborates in the *Summa,* in a discussion of the constitution given to ancient Israel:

Two points are to be observed concerning the right ordering of rulers in a state or nation. One is that all should take some share in the government: for this form of constitution ensures peace among the people, commends itself to all, and is most enduring, as stated in *Politics* II. The other point is to be observed in respect of the kinds of government, or the different ways in which the constitutions are established. For whereas these differ in kind, as the Philosopher states in *Politics* III, nevertheless the first place is held by 'kingship', where the power of government is vested in one; and 'aristocracy', which signifies government by the best, where the power of government is vested in a few. Accordingly, the best form of government is in a city or kingdom, where one is given the power to preside over all; while under him are others having governing powers: and yet this governing power pertains to all, both because all are eligible to govern, and because the rulers are chosen by all. For this is the best form of polity, being partly kingship, since there is one at the head of all; partly aristocracy, in so far as a number of persons are set in authority; partly democracy, i.e. government by the people, in so far as the rulers can be chosen from the people, and the people have the right to choose their rulers.

Such was the form of government established by the divine law. For Moses and his successors governed the people in such a way that

---

[43] 1 Maccabees 8:14-18. The description is reported speech and so the question of its historical accuracy does not implicate the inerrancy of scripture.

[44] *De Regno,* I.7: "Simul etiam sic eius temperetur potestas, ut in tyrannidem de facili declinare non possit."

each of them was ruler over all; so that there was a kind of kingship. Moreover, seventy-two men were chosen, who were elders in virtue: for it is written: "I took out of your tribes wise and honourable, and appointed them rulers" (Deut. 1:15), so that there was an element of aristocracy. But it was a democratic government in so far as the rulers were chosen from all the people; for it is written: "Provide out of all the people wise men" (Ex. 18:21); and, again, in so far as they were chosen by the people; wherefore it is written: "Let me have from among you wise men" (Dt. 1:13). Consequently, it is evident that the ordering of the rulers was well provided for by the Law.[45]

The justification for the democratic element is paradoxically similar to that for the monarchic element; it will promote civil peace.[46] The justification for the 'aristocratic element' seems to be simply the fact that it is by definition composed of 'the best'.

St Robert Bellarmine likewise favours a regime mixed from the three elements, and describes it thus:

This form of governance requires that there be some supreme ruler (*princeps*) in the commonwealth, who commands (*imperet*) all others and who is himself subject to none. Yet those who govern the provinces or the city are not vicars of the king, or judges sitting for one year, but true rulers (*principes*), who both obey the command of the supreme ruler and who at the same time, govern their province or city not as another's but as their own. In this way there will be room in the commonwealth both for a royal monarchy and for an aristocracy of the best rulers.[47]

He continues:

If we add to this that neither the supreme king nor the lesser rulers acquire their positions by hereditary succession, but that rather whoever is best is elevated to those positions, then democracy also would have its own place within the commonwealth.

---

[45] STh 1a 2ae 105, 1.

[46] He does not specify which passage in Book II of the *Politics* he has in mind, but the Leonine editors refer us to chapter 6, where Aristotle says that "the regime that is composed out of more is better". The context suggests that Aristotle is thinking rather of more kinds of influence than simply of more people.

[47] *Controversiae*, 'On the papacy', book 1, c. 3.

Like St Thomas, Bellarmine considers that the divinely furnished example of ancient Israel shows this to be the best polity for mankind in this mortal life. He argues that it not only possesses the advantages of a pure monarchy, but is also clearly more profitable and pleasant. It is more pleasant because "all people prefer that form of regime in which they participate."[48] It is more profitable, because any human monarch will have to govern through intermediaries of some kind, and these will fulfil their task more diligently if they each govern what pertains to themselves as a *princeps*, rather than governing as a *vicarius* what pertains to another.[49] As for this polity possessing the advantages of a pure monarchy, this is evident, he writes, since it contains a true and proper monarchy.[50]

In their sketch of the well-tempered polity, both these authors emphasise the monarchic element. They do not, however, fill in the details sufficient for us to judge whether their ideal polity is formally a monarchy in the sense defined above, since they appear to be thinking above all of the executive power. It seems in fact that the executive is the most naturally monarchical of the three parts of temporal power. Since the executive power proceeds all the way to the individual act, it has itself a greater need of unity than the legislative power, which terminates in general decrees. We may therefore suppose that it is normal for the legislative power to be shared by many, even though to secure the unity of the commonwealth it seems advisable for the supreme *princeps* to share in this power, whether as the one who initiates new laws or as the one who confirms them or both.[51] As for the judicial power, concerning itself as it does with numerous discrete events, it is naturally exercised by many, though acting individually. It is also naturally aristocratic as its exercise requires great learning.

---

[48] Cf. Leo XIII, *Libertas* 45: "Unless it be otherwise determined, by reason of some exceptional condition of things, it is expedient to take part in the administration of public affairs. And the Church approves of everyone devoting his services to the common good, and doing all that he can for the defence, preservation, and prosperity of his country."

[49] A *princeps*, or ruler, acts according to his own judgement, even though he may have a superior who is free to dismiss him; a *vicarius* must strive to learn and fulfil the judgement of his superior.

[50] Someone might object that the pure monarchy would be even better at achieving unity; Bellarmine does not address this point but would presumably reply that such an advantage would be outweighed by the other factors which he mentions.

[51] The legislative power of English monarchs and more modern executives seem to be modelled on the *tribunicia potestas*, held by the ancient tribunes of the people, and later by Augustus and his successors. It included both the power to initiate and veto legislative proposals.

Finally, what of Bellarmine's third question: which of the seven polities is best in itself, as opposed to 'best for fallen men'? The Jesuit doctor answers that it must be pure monarchy, for such is the empire of God and of Christ.[52] Those who rule the Church on earth do so as vicars, obliged to put into practice the will of Christ as they understand it; while our Lord Himself does not hold His kingship "from hence".[53]

Supreme authority in the Church

St Robert Bellarmine remarks that all Catholic doctors agree that the Church's polity is principally monarchical, though tempered by aristocracy and democracy.[54] Old Israel, considered as a religious society, had been a monarchy at least since the time that Moses had consecrated Aaron as pontiff, subjecting to him the other priests and Levites; and "thenceforth until the time of Christ, there was never lacking one ruler of the priests who governed all the synagogues of the entire world."[55] Since this was a perfection in the Synagogue by which it reflected the rule of the one God over creation, and since perfections found in a figure must be found also, and more distinctly, in the reality prefigured, the Church must have a visible monarch, acting as 'pro-rex' for Christ in heaven.[56]

---

[52] *Controversiae*, 'On the papacy', book 1, c. 4. Although the question cannot be pursued here, we note in passing some words of Pius XII in his encyclical letter, *Ad caeli reginam*: "Mary, too, as Mother of the divine Christ, as His associate in the redemption, in his struggle with His enemies and His final victory over them, has a share, though in a limited and analogous way, in His royal dignity (*temperato modo et analogiae ratione* [..] *regalem participat dignitatem*)."

[53] Jn. 18:36. However, God's government might also be characterised as a mixed monarchy insofar as the position of the faithful is essentially different from that of the subjects of any merely human king: God moves us to follow His will by moving us from within by our own power and we freely subject ourselves to Him in baptism.

[54] *Controversiae*, 'On the papacy', book 1, c. 5.

[55] He notes that Calvin and his other Protestant adversaries accept this.

[56] Ibid. In chapter 8, he argues that there is a special reason for restricting the aristocratic element within the Church: those who are the *optimates* within the Church, namely the bishops and priests, are in danger of corrupting the Church's supreme good, the faith, in a way that has no parallel in temporal society: "Although democracy is absolutely speaking the worst regime, nevertheless, aristocracy seems more dangerous for the Church. For the greatest evil for the Church is heresy, and heresy is stirred up more by the leading men (*ab optimatibus*) than by the common folk. Almost all heresiarchs, after all, have been bishops or presbyters; and so heresies are like factions among the leading men, without which there would be no popular seditions within the Church."

The papal monarchy includes legislative, judicial and executive power. Only the pope has the right to legislate for the whole Church, though he may choose to do so through an ecumenical council: the business of an ecumenical council is determined or approved either by the Roman pontiff in person or by legates acting on his instructions.[57] Again, he has the right to try all legal cases in the Church, and to hear appeals from all lower courts, and the executive power to appoint Catholics to any office or to remove any office-holder.[58] Hence the pope is said to have the *plenitudo potestatis* within the Church, that is, the power to do whatever may be done.[59] The monarchical element within the Church militant is thus, when the Apostolic See routinely chooses to exercise its rights to the full, not only pre-eminent but markedly so.[60]

Why then should we not speak of the Church as a pure monarchy? Usually, if a ruler were bound only by natural and divine law, as the pope is, we should call him a pure monarch. However, in the case of the papacy, the very divine

---

[57] While the pope undoubtedly possesses the power to do alone whatever the episcopate may do corporately, it does not follow that this ought to be the manner in which the pontiff routinely acts. The episcopate enjoys, in addition to the charism of infallibility when united with its head, a positive guarantee that no part of the deposit of faith will ever perish from within it: "the charism of truth, which certainly is, was, and always will be in the succession of the episcopacy from the apostles", as the *Oath Against Modernism* has it. This union of the positive and negative guarantees (absent in merely authentic papal teaching) is why Bishop Gasser said in his *Relatio* at Vatican I that "the most solemn judgment of the Church in matters of faith and morals is and always will be the judgment of an ecumenical council, in which the Pope passes judgment together with the bishops of the Catholic world who meet and judge together with him". Conversely, this is perhaps why the Council of Florence felt the need to justify the Holy See's unilateral insertion of the *Filioque* into the creed as arising "from imminent need", the apparent implication being that the Holy See should not define unilaterally except from imminent need.

[58] John Paul II, *Homily for the Inauguration of his Pontificate*, 22nd October 1978: "Perhaps in the past, the tiara, this triple crown, was placed on the Pope's head in order to express by that symbol the Lord's plan for his Church, namely that all the hierarchical order of Christ's Church, all 'sacred power' exercised in the Church, is nothing other than service, service with a single purpose: to ensure that the whole People of God shares in this threefold mission of Christ and always remains under the power of the Lord; a power that has its source not in the powers of this world but in the mystery of the Cross and Resurrection."

[59] The phrase was first used by St Leo the Great, but became standard only from the 13th century; Brian Tierney, *Foundations of the Conciliar Theory* (Cambridge, 1955), 143. It is used by St Thomas in *Contra errores Graecorum*, II.34.

[60] The Holy See may be shown to have possessed 'universal ordinary jurisdiction' since the beginning of the Church, as the actions of Ss Clement I and Victor I witness, but it may be said to have elected to use this jurisdiction only 'extraordinarily' in the first millennium. It has exercised this jurisdiction on a routine basis only since the pontificate of St Leo IX (1049-1054).

law to which he is subject obliges him to uphold the ordinary authority of the bishops, and the disciplinary autonomy of the Eastern Churches.[61] Thus he cannot suppress the universal episcopate, or the patriarchates of apostolic foundation.[62] The bishops and patriarchs form an aristocratic element in the Church which is part of her divine constitution. Nor can the pope suppress the radical eligibility of all baptised males to the papacy and episcopacy, and hence the democratic element within the Church is also divinely ensured.[63]

A plenitude of spiritual power must belong to the pope given Christ's decision to make St Peter and his legitimate successors the visible guarantors of the Church's infallibility. For while there is a duty for the sake of the truth to remain united to St Peter and his visible successors, yet if he did not have supreme legislative authority in the Church, others could as supreme legislators require the profession of doctrines that might be false; if he did not have supreme judicial authority, others might lawfully depose him for teaching the truth; if he did not have supreme executive authority, others might appoint bishops whose teaching might drown out the truth.

By contrast it will rarely be desirable for a temporal monarchy to include a civil *plenitudo potestatis*. Since divine and natural law do not establish any aristocratic or democratic institutions as obligatory within the earthly city, such a ruler would be a pure monarch, with the disadvantages such a role is likely to occasion.

Aristotle on the best city

Aristotle points out that by asking which is the best constitution, we may mean, "which is superior simply", κρατίστην ἁπλῶς, that is, abstractly the best?[64] However, such a polity, he holds, will be best in practice only for that city which has no previous disadvantages, for example, a shortage of raw materials, meaning that it must make a large place for trade and for merchants.

---

[61] 2nd Vatican Council, *Orientalium Ecclesiarum*, 5; *Unitatis redintegratio*,16.

[62] John Paul II, *Euntes in mundum*, 10.

[63] The original method for the election of bishops, including the bishop of Rome, was strikingly democratic, although with a strong aristocratic element as well, and has been set aside incrementally only by ecclesiastical positive law. Were this law ever frustrated by some sort of dark age in which communication with Rome was again severely restricted, the patristic order would presumably revive *ipso facto*. Nor, from their remarks on this question, does it appear the Fathers would have approved of its gradual suppression. Cf. St Leo I, Epistle 14.

[64] *Politics*, IV.1.

Analogously, a regime of physical training which in the abstract is best will in practice suit only that man "whose body is naturally the finest and is most finely equipped". Secondly, therefore, the question of the best constitution may mean which is best for *this* city or realm, such as Athens or Belgium, taking into account, for example, its history, its site and its natural resources. This question lies beyond the scope of the present enquiry. Finally, we may mean which polity will be a good fit for the greatest number of realms or cities, given that all may not be likely to be capable of that which is abstractly the best.[65]

We can consider first his answer to the question about what is best 'simply speaking'. Whereas St Thomas in his discussion of polities began with the final cause, asking "what arrangement of the offices can best promote the city's end?", Aristotle apparently approaches the question by way of the formal cause. His underlying question is "what arrangement of the offices will give the city a just structure?", and his answer is that it will be when the power of a given citizen within the city is in proportion to his relevant qualities or endowments.[66] Yet since these qualities or endowments are relevant precisely insofar as they enable the city to attain the end for which it exists, the two questions come to the same thing.[67]

Aristotle summarises his position in these lines:

> The political community must be regarded [...] as being for the sake of noble actions, not for the sake of living together. Hence those who contribute most to a community of this sort have a greater part in the city than those who are equal or greater in freedom and descent but unequal in political virtue, or those who outdo them in wealth but are outdone in virtue.[68]

He takes it for granted that those who are themselves disposed for noble actions will be best able to effect these in others, and hence concludes that the city will be just to the extent that its offices belong to those who excel in prudence and the moral virtues. This does not mean that all other qualities

---

[65] Ibid. He also notes a fourth possible meaning to the question, namely, what is the best city 'according to a hypothesis'. In other words, assuming that a city intends to have a polity of a certain kind, for example, one that gives most power to the wealthy, or one that gives equal power to all citizens, what more precise form should it take?

[66] Hence he writes in the *Eudemian Ethics*, VII.9: "Every constitution is a kind of justice", αἱ δὲ πολιτεῖαι πᾶσαι δικαίου τι εἶδος. By this he has in mind a kind of distributive justice; cf. D. Keyt, 'Supplementary Essay', in R. Robinson, *Aristotle, Politics III and IV*, 133.

[67] We assume here for the sake of following Aristotle's argument that the end of the temporal city is man's end simply speaking though this is not in fact the case.

[68] *Politics*, III.9.

must be rigorously excluded, since other attributes can be pre-conditions or instruments of virtuous action: "It is reasonable", he writes, "that the well born, the free, and the wealthy lay claim to honour".[69] For since a part, though only a secondary part, of the city's excellence lies in its repute, freedom, and wealth, citizens who especially cause it to possess these qualities may also receive "a greater part", that is, greater power, within it.

Despite St Thomas's citation of Aristotle as a supporter of a democratic element in the best constitution, this is true only in the most formal sense. Certainly, in describing "the kind of city that one should pray for" the Philosopher remarks that "all the citizens take part in the regime", that is, take an active part in governing.[70] Yet previous to this he has excluded most of the people within its territory from citizenship. Not women and slaves only, but all those engaged mainly in manual work or immersed in thoughts of money are deemed by Aristotle unsuitable to have a true part in the city:

> The citizens should not live a worker's or a merchant's way of life, for this sort of way of life is ignoble and contrary to virtue. Nor indeed should those who are going to be citizens in such a regime be farmers; for there is a need for leisure both with a view to the creation of virtue and with a view to political activities. [...] For the worker element does not share in the city, nor any other type that is not a "craftsman of virtue".[71]

He seems to have thought that this arrangement could be achieved by having the larger merchants physically separated from the city at a port,[72] and by having slaves to farm the land, and perhaps to perform other manual tasks.[73]

It would be easy to dismiss these remarks as the result of a deplorable prejudice in favour of one's own social class. Before doing so, however, one might reflect that Aristotle was a peerless observer of reality, not least of human nature. Yet the nature he observed was fallen and unredeemed. Where the gospel's

---

[69] Ibid. III.12. 'Honour', τιμή, as commonly in Aristotle, includes the sense of 'office' or 'magistracy'. For the relevance of other qualities to virtue, cf. *Nicomachean Ethics* I.9: "We have said that happiness is a certain sort of activity of the soul in accord with virtue; of the other goods, some are necessary conditions of happiness, while others are naturally useful and co-operative as instrument." See also *Nicomachean Ethics* I.8.

[70] *Politics*, VII.13.

[71] Ibid., VII.9.

[72] Ibid., VII. 6.

[73] Ibid., VII.9; cf. I.13, where he writes that "the manufacturing artisan is under a special sort of slavery".

teaching of man's divine vocation is unknown or unaccepted, it is indeed possible that most men are too busy keeping themselves and their families in existence, or seeking and enjoying sensual pleasures, to aspire consistently to any more common good. 'Leisure' allows for reflection, so that higher ideals of civic virtue, statesmanship and magnanimity may enter the mind, even though these do not purify the heart and may leave their possessor still further from the Kingdom of God than the pagan labourer. Where the Incarnation and the universal call to be perfect as our Heavenly Father are accepted, the heart is cleansed and even those who are immersed in the world of matter or money may be able to raise their eyes to consider the spiritual and temporal good of their homeland.

More fundamentally, in this order of providence the aptitudes necessary for the government of temporal affairs are skills not virtues because the end of the temporal city is not the end of man.[74] Its cause is not necessarily righteous, its glory is not necessarily honourable. It is no *more* impossible for a man to be a good statesman and a bad man than it is for him to be a good chemist and a bad man. Only in the heavenly city do rank and virtue coincide.[75] In fact, it is worse than that. The temporal commonwealth is precisely the community constituted by the end proportionate to man's nature, and Satan's rebellion, as we have seen, consisted precisely in the claim that the absolutely final end is proportionate to the nature of every intellectual creature; that created persons are owed beatitude by God, and should not have to receive it as a gift on God's terms. Aptitude and zeal for office in the temporal city may therefore often be a sign of sympathy for his cause.

Contingent factors undoubtedly played a decisive role in the rise of the hereditary principle and the concept of representative democracy in mediaeval Christendom but they both have a fitting place there. For a healthy and natural (or rather supernatural) suspicion must always in Christian eyes attend those drawn to temporal statesmanship. It is a worthy and honourable task but, as with the episcopate, just because a man who desires the office of a statesman, desires a noble task, this does not mean that the one who desires it or the desire itself is always or even often noble. It was natural that Christians should, while

---

[74] Although these aptitudes are largely intellectual in character, they also include corollaries of the moral virtues which it sounds odd to call skills, and which might simply be described as 'useful habits'. Cf. STh 1a 2ae 65, 2. See also A. Pinsent, *The Second-Person Perspective in Aquinas's Ethics* (Routledge: Abingdon, 2012).

[75] Cf. St Thomas's statement in *Quaestiones quodlibetales*, VIII.4, 1 that provided a candidate for episcopal office have charity it is not the man who is better simply speaking, but the one who is more endowed with the qualities that will be used in ruling, such as discretion, energy and knowledge, who should be made bishop.

167

desiring competence in the ministers of temporal power, nevertheless place checks upon these men from those who either do not seek or do not hold such power.

Aristotle's ideal as it gradually emerges from the pages of his treatise may most naturally be called a mixed aristocracy. Virtue is the principal qualification for power. Yet since there is no obvious test by which degrees of virtue may be nicely discriminated, having excluded those classes whom he judges incapable of more than virtue's rudiments, he would have office available to all, once they have received a liberal education favourable to the acquisition of virtue[76] and have then served in the army.[77] It would presumably be left to the judgement of the citizens to discern worth when they come to fill those offices requiring election rather than lot. Certain offences against the moral law, such as adultery, are to be punished with a proportionate loss of civic rights.[78] From the passages in III.12 mentioned above, we can suppose that he would also have favoured granting to those of the *aristoi* who most helped the city to prosper financially, or who adorned it by their distinguished pedigree, the exclusive right to fill certain of the less important offices.

What then of kingship? The Philosopher recognises monarchy as "the first and most divine regime", doubtless because of its resemblance to God's rule over creation.[79] In the *Nicomachean Ethics*, he had likewise said that of the three correct polities, monarchy is best and timocracy the least good.[80] Yet in so speaking he is thinking of an absolute monarchy (παμβασίλεια), with an undivided sovereignty and independent of all human laws. Such a thing, he observes, would be just only if a man should arise who so excels all the citizens even taken collectively that he can no longer be regarded as part of the city.

> There is considerable question about what ought to be done if there happens to be someone who is outstanding not on the basis of pre-eminence in the other goods such as strength, wealth, or abundance of friends, but on the basis of virtue. For surely no one would assert that such a person should be expelled and banished. But neither would they assert that there should be rule over such a person: this is almost as if they should claim to merit ruling over Zeus by splitting

---

[76] Ibid., VIII.2

[77] Ibid., VII.9.

[78] "Let the person be punished with a loss of honour appropriate to his errant behaviour"; ibid., VIII.16.

[79] Ibid., IV.2. St Thomas makes the same comparison in *De Regno*, I.3.

[80] *Nicomachean Ethics*, VIII.10.

the offices. What remains – and it seems the natural course – is for everyone to obey such a person gladly, so that persons of this sort will be permanent kings in their cities.[81]

So unpredictable an occurrence cannot be taken into account when framing a constitution.[82]

Elsewhere, speaking of kingship among the Spartans, he recognises the possibility of a city's laws being decided by an assembly but one man having some executive power over the whole city.[83] There is no mention of such an element in Books VII and VIII of the *Politics*, which in fact have little to say about any of the organs of government. Yet while Aristotle could hardly have denied the force of St Thomas's arguments in the opening pages of the *De Regno*, he would have insisted that barring the arrival of the godlike man, such a monarchical office, like the other public offices, should be held only for a short period, so that as far as possible all the citizens should in turn be rulers and ruled. For:

> Among similar persons nobility and justice are found in ruling and being ruled in turn, for this is something equal and similar: to assign what is not equal to equal persons and what is not similar to similar persons is contrary to nature, and nothing contrary to nature is noble.[84]

Aristotle's answer, then, to his question about the regime which is simply speaking best, while formally compatible with the principles of St Thomas and St Robert Bellarmine, breathes a different spirit: he does not speak of monarchy and endorses a severely restricted democracy.

As we have seen, the Stagirite asks one question which we do not find in the two Christian doctors: "Which polity will be a good fit for the greatest number of realms or cities, given that all cities are not likely to be capable of that which is abstractly the best?" It is in this context that Aristotle speaks of a 'mixed polity', meaning, however, by this phrase a stable mixing of the social classes

---

[81] *Politics*, III.13. Lord understands the phrase 'splitting the offices' to refer to rotation in office.

[82] And indeed, as such a man already lives and reigns over the faithful as citizens and the sinful as subjects from the empyrean heaven, we need look to no other.

[83] Ibid., III.14-15.

[84] Ibid., VII.3.

of freemen within the city.[85] He holds that this mixing, if judiciously done, could give rise to a timocracy. Such a regime is one of the legitimate kinds, since power within it is dependent on virtue; yet it is the least good of the three legitimate kinds, since power is based not on heroic or godlike virtue,[86] as in a pure monarchy, nor on complete virtue, as in the ideal city of books VII-VIII, but on military virtue:

> Where more are concerned, it is difficult for them to be proficient with a view to virtue as a whole, but some level of proficiency is possible particularly regarding military virtue, as this arises in a multitude. In this regime, the warrior element is the most authoritative, and it is those possessing heavy arms who take part in it.[87]

In other words, for the pagan philosopher, what is likely to be within the reach of most cities is something which we might naturally describe as the excellence of a military-minded democracy. Without sanctifying grace, it is perhaps only a great and shared danger, the common life of the camp, and comradeship under arms, which can stably unite people across a city for a noble end.

Hereditary and life-long rule

The French revolutionaries asserted the illegitimacy of hereditary rule. And if no man could justly govern another except as having been appointed by him, it would be, as Desmoulins said, "a crime to be a king".[88] But if the author of nature has given to families the power to unite to achieve ends which they

---

[85] IV.9. This chapter contains Aristotle's only use of the phrase "mixed polity", πολιτεία μεμειγμένη, and the commentators dispute whether he is using the word 'polity' in the generic or specific sense. Cf. R. Robinson, *Aristotle, Politics III-IV*, 90. Despite Robinson's argument, the latter seems more likely.

[86] Cf. *Nicomachean Ethics*, VII.1: "The contrary to bestiality is most suitably called virtue superior to us, a, heroic, indeed divine sort of virtue (ἡρωικήν τινα καὶ θείαν)."

[87] Ibid., III.7. The same definition of a citizen in this regime as the one who possesses heavy arms is given in IV.13.

[88] Camille Desmoulins (1760-94) was prominent among the French revolutionaries. At the trial of Louis XVI, he memorably asserted the doctrine of the rulers as delegates of the people: "It is a crime to be a king. It was even a crime to be a constitutional king, for the nation had never accepted the constitution. There is only one condition on which it could be legitimate to reign; it is when the whole people formally strips itself of its rights and cedes them to a single man, not only as Denmark did in 1660, but as happens when the entire people has passed or ratified this warrant of its sovereignty. And yet it could not bind the next generation, because death extinguishes all rights."

cannot otherwise conveniently obtain, thus creating a society of a new nature in which there is by divine right a distinction between the ruled and the ruling parts, then any sovereign, whether king or senate or populace, who efficaciously promotes the end for which that society exists may lawfully govern it. Hence as the common sense of mankind intuits, it is no crime to be a king; though it is a great crime to be a tyrant, whether as a hereditary monarch or as an assembly of the people.[89]

Neither St Thomas nor St Robert Bellarmine, however, advocate hereditary rule. The angelic doctor, as we have seen, is silent on the matter; the Jesuit doctor, without rejecting heredity as a possible qualification for office contrasts it unfavourably, as we have also seen, with elevation by merit. The arguments against it are sufficiently obvious: why should the chance of birth fit anyone for power?[90] Does it not incline the ruler to see the realm as his own possession, due to him by inalienable right? On the other side of the scales, however, sits the testimony of history. Not only has hereditary rule in fact been frequent, something which by itself might be attributed to the inordinate love of rulers for their offspring, it seems also to have been regarded by mankind as a sufficient arrangement. And since this judgement is both widespread and yet hardly flattering to those who make it, it seems to derive not from fallen nature, but simply from nature, and hence must as far as it goes be true. Again, while because of the need to manifest the truth that Israel was God's possession in a special way He did not at first give them any ruler called a king,

---

[89] Cf. St Thomas Aquinas, *De Regno*, I.12: "If the man who despoils a single man, or casts him into slavery, or kills him, deserves the greatest punishment (death in the judgment of men, and in the judgment of God, eternal damnation), how much worse tortures must we consider a tyrant deserves, who on all sides robs everybody, works against the common liberty of all, and kills whom he will at his merest whim? [...] Such men rarely repent; but puffed up by the wind of pride, deservedly abandoned by God for their sins, and besmirched by the flattery of men, they can rarely make worthy satisfaction. When will they ever restore all those things which they have received beyond their just due? Yet no one doubts that they are bound to restore those ill-gotten goods. When will they make amends to those whom they have oppressed and unjustly injured in their many ways? The malice of their impenitence is increased by the fact that they consider everything licit which they can do unresisted and with impunity. Hence they not only make no effort to repair the evil they have done but, taking their customary way of acting as their authority, they hand on their boldness in sinning to posterity. Consequently, they are held guilty before God, not only for their own sins, but also for the crimes of those to whom they gave the occasion of their sin."

[90] Aristotle points out the danger in *Politics*, III.15.

yet when a kingship was later conceded to them, it was by divine decree hereditary[91]; which could not have been, were such a polity contrary to reason. The father's possession, in the absence of other arrangements, of political power over his adult children probably explains the instinct for hereditary rule. Various things may seem to justify the inclusion of some hereditary element within a constitution: the future office-holder can be trained for his duties from boyhood up; he is not corrupted by the pursuit of office, promising unjust favours to the many or to the rich; he is liable, if he is decent, to be the more emulous of the good examples of his predecessors[92] and the more chastened by their bad ones, as touching him more nearly.[93] Once in office he has time to gain experience: those who take turns to govern, remarks Bellarmine, must often put down the reins before they have fully understood their task, while a king, having always the same office, "though he may sometimes be somewhat slow of mind, yet by long experience often surpasses many others".[94] This last advantage, clearly, can be enjoyed by anyone ruling for life, even if he does not hold his office by right of birth. Again, other things being equal, the hereditary ruler is liable to take more thought for the common good of his country as it will be after his death, since it will then be the charge of his offspring. This suggests that where there is some hereditary power in a constitution, it should be directed especially to those acts that seem likely to affect a people's fortunes

---

[91] Ps. 131:12: "If thy children will keep thy covenant, and these my testimonies which I shall teach them: Their children also for evermore shall sit upon thy throne."

[92] "Then, again, who does not see how empty, how foolish, is the fame of noble birth? Why, if the nobility is based on renown, the renown is another's! For, truly, nobility seems to be a sort of reputation coming from the merits of ancestors. But if it is the praise which brings renown, of necessity it is they who are praised that are famous. Wherefore, the fame of another clothes thee not with splendour if thou hast none of thine own. So, if there is any excellence in nobility of birth, methinks it is this alone - that it would seem to impose upon the nobly born the obligation not to degenerate from the virtue of their ancestors." St Severinus Boethius, *The Consolation of Philosophy*, III.6.

[93] Some words of Chesterton, though speaking of the papacy, suggest how the sense of responsibility increases as the ruler is conscious of his bond with his predecessors: "Then he [Pius XI] made a motion and we all knelt; and in the words that followed I understood for the first time something that was once meant by the ceremonial use of the plural, and in a flash I saw the sense of something that had always seemed to me a senseless custom of kings. With a new strong voice, that was hardly even like his own, he began "Nous vous bénissons," and I knew that something stood there infinitely greater than an individual; I knew that it was indeed 'We'; We, Peter and Gregory and Hildebrand and all the dynasty that does not die"; G. K. Chesterton, *The Resurrection of Rome*, (London: Hodder & Stoughton, 1934), 319.

[94] *Controversiae*, 'On the papacy', Bk. 1, c. 2.

irrevocably or for many years to come, as a declaration of war, or a change in the constitution itself.

Finally, the custom of Christendom is to anoint the monarch who is to rule for life, whether appointed by birth or by election. Such a rite is more than a ceremonial installation: it constitutes him before God a sacred person. It thus gives him a new excellence which allows him to rule without unfittingness over those who are his equals or superiors in knowledge and virtue.[95]

Suffrage

St Thomas and St Robert Bellarmine advocate an element of democracy within constitutions in order to foster peace. Can this simple policy be reconciled with Aristotle's requirement that power within the city be proportioned to one's possession of civic merit? Yes, if we reflect that each person simply in virtue of bearing the image of God has a certain capacity for virtue and hence, equal in that respect, is fittingly given some basic equality of power. But this does not exclude citizens who excel in various ways from receiving additional power, including greater right of suffrage.

In a Greek *polis*, laws and other public measures could be voted on by a gathering of the citizens. Most modern societies restrict such direct democracy to occasional referenda, and practise representative democracy instead. In either case, the questions arise, 'who may vote?' and 'should the voice of each voter bear the same weight?' If civil society is a union of families, then if we desire with St Thomas to have a democratic element within civil society, each family must be represented. If both parents are living, the father represents it within society and thus votes. If he dies, his widow takes his place at the family's head, and she represents it and votes. If both husband and wife were to vote, the family itself would no longer be represented, and their votes might mutually nullify themselves. As when fulfilling any important responsibility on behalf of his family, the husband must desire counsel of his wife. If the family were to have merely a single vote this would have the perverse effect of diminishing the influence of those with greater responsibility. Otto von

---

[95] "It would be much more rational to abolish the English monarchy. But how if, by doing so, you leave out the one element in our State which matters most? How if the monarchy is the channel through which all the *vital* elements of citizenship - loyalty, the consecration of secular life, the hierarchical principle, splendour, ceremony, continuity - still trickle down to irrigate the dust-bowl of modern economic Statecraft?"; C. S. Lewis, 'Myth Became Fact' in *God in the Dock: Essays on Theology and Ethics*, ed. W. Hooper (Eerdmans: Michigan & Cambridge, 2014), 56.

Habsburg has suggested that parents should exercise the vote on behalf of their minor children until the age of majority. The influence of the family would then correspond to the magnitude of its responsibilities. An unmarried adult, being in himself or herself a new family *in radice* may fittingly exercise a single vote.

Yet while families alone are necessary for the being of society, many artificial juridic persons are necessary for its well-being. Desirable then is an arrangement by which these also may speak, through themselves or through their representatives: guilds, unions, associations of employers, and universities may fittingly elect representatives to the legislature, or have some direct right to vote on measures that concern them. Such groups will in any case use their power to influence law and policy, and hence to avoid corruption it is desirable that they do this in a public manner. Provided that the process of election and legislation does not by its very complexity obstruct good government, "the regime that is composed out of more is better".[96]

As we have seen, a mixed regime can be said to have an element of aristocracy simply from the fact that only a small number of citizens at any time are exercising legislative, judicial or executive power over their fellow citizens. Yet to be a true aristocracy, these must be selected by reason of moral and intellectual virtue as well as other qualities relevant for the specific office. Every moral virtue is requisite in a ruler, since any kind of vice will incline a man to use power for private ends. Among the intellectual virtues, although he need possess, apart from faith and the gifts of the Holy Ghost, only those directly relevant to his office, he must at least have a correct grasp of the hierarchy of knowledge.[97] Further aristocratic elements may be introduced in many ways: active voice[98] and passive voice[99] may be limited, as regards some offices, to those who excel in any way that is relevant for the excellence of the society, for example in land-holdings, number of persons employed, offspring sired, taxes paid, hereditary rank, military service or education. Again, a form of suffrage could easily be contrived that would realise the ideals of democracy and aristocracy, if each citizen in electing representatives had a basic vote worth one unit, and if his vote were increased in value according as he possessed more of these secondary excellences. For example, in Britain, the masters of certain ancient universities (and Edinburgh) were given the right to send

---

[96] *Politics* II.6.

[97] They must thus recognise the superiority of philosophy and theology over the inductive and hypothetical sciences.

[98] That is, the right to vote for those who are to hold office.

[99] That is, eligibility for office.

representatives to parliament in addition to voting in their geographical constituency, and the owners of businesses possessed an additional vote in the circumscription where they were based. What is necessary is that these secondary excellences are not given more weight than virtue itself.

Shadow polities

We have seen that to every good polity there corresponds a 'deviation', which occurs when those with power pervert it to private ends. In such cases, however, those who exercise power are still its official depositaries. By a shadow polity is meant a state of affairs in which the official possessors of power are not those who exercise it in reality. Aristotle speaks of various devices, προφάσεις, by which this may be done, for example, a city where power is supposedly spread evenly among the different social classes may in fact incline toward the rich by fining only them for not attending the assembly, thus making it more likely that the rich rather than the poor will vote.[100]

Various names exist for such shadow polities. The term 'plutocracy', already used by Xenophon,[101] conveniently expresses the state of affairs in which the wealthy seek to over-ride or subvert a constitution which does not yet grant them the power they desire. Since riches of themselves tend to cause vain glory,[102] and "all things obey money",[103] this is the state to which all human societies tend, and which rulers must constantly strive to prevent.

'Kritarchy' (or 'kritocracy'), literally 'rule by judges', is used to describe the process by which judges legislate under colour of interpreting the law. It is liable to arise when the mentality of the better educated part of society has drifted too far from that of the mass of the people, but when the official legislators are selected by widespread suffrage.

---

[100] *Politics* III.13.

[101] *Memorabilia*, 4.6.12. According to this author the word was used by Socrates to refer to a city in which there is a property qualification for office.

[102] STh 2a 2ae 188, 7.

[103] Eccl. 10:19.

The term 'bureaucracy', as its hybrid form attests, is not an ancient one.[104] It was apparently coined by a French economist in the early 18th century.[105] It well expresses a state of affairs where the multiplication of small rules makes transactions between citizens, or between citizens and rulers, unduly burdensome, giving unofficial power to the civil servants, "no longer servants and no longer civil",[106] who are supposedly mere intermediaries for expediting these transactions.

The term 'pornocracy', literally, 'rule by harlots', apparently dates from the 19th century, though used to denote a much earlier time, namely the period in the 10th century when the city of Rome and the papacy were dominated by the female members of the family of the counts of Tusculum.[107] It may be more generally used to refer to a state of affairs where the exercise of power is habitually corrupted by lust. As such it is also a perennial danger.

Finally, Plato coined the term 'theatrocracy' to describe a city where poets had corrupted the judgements of the citizens by vicious music. We may borrow the word and use it more generally to describe a state of affairs where men are ruled by those who possess the means of mass communication, and who by dint of frequent repetition cause them to believe whatever these rulers desire, even the most absurd or shameful things.[108]

It will be noticed that all these forms of shadow polity may co-exist.

Conclusion

"The queen stood on thy right hand, in gilded clothing; surrounded with variety".[109] Speaking of a choice between different polities, St Thomas wrote

---

[104] H. W. Fowler, *Modern English Usage* (Oxford: Clarendon Press, 1926): "The formation is so barbarous that all attempt at self-respect in pronunciation may perhaps as well be abandoned."

[105] Jacques de Gournay, 1712-59. The word was used in English by J. S. Mill as early as 1837, in the *Westminster Review*, to describe the contemporary situation in France.

[106] Winston Churchill, speech of 4th June, 1945.

[107] This period is also known in Church history as the 'dark age' or *saeculum obscurum*.

[108] Cf. J. H. Newman, *Loss and Gain: the Story of a Convert* (London: Burns and Oates, 8th Edition, 1881), 167: "My father never could endure newspapers - I mean the system of newspapers; he said it was a new power in the State." Naturally, it is desirable that the media diffuse information which it will benefit the citizenry to know.

[109] Ps. 44:9.

that "danger looms on either side". [110] For the same reason, however, advantages lie on each side. We have made suggestions for a mixed polity which appear to agree with experience and with the sayings of the wise. But these suggestions could be implemented in many ways, in accordance with the possibilities and traditions of a given people.

St Augustine tells that when he was still looking longingly toward the house of God from the outside, "I saw a full Church, and saw how one lived in one manner, another in another". [111] The same legitimate variety belongs also to the Church in her temporal aspect, that is, to the polities and provinces of Christendom.

---

[110] *De Regno*, I.5.
[111] *Confessions*, VIII.2.

Theses

(i)   Differences in the subject of temporal power give rise to three 'pure' kinds of polities, each of which is legitimate, and each of which admits of many species of constitution.

(ii)   The pure polities are distinguished in virtue of the independence, complete, partial or non-existent, of the sovereign over the subjects.

(iii) In a pure monarchy, the sovereign alone enjoys temporal power.

(iv)   In a pure aristocracy, sovereignty pertains only to an elite body, but other citizens possess some temporal authority.

(v)   In a pure democracy, all temporal power is possessed equally by all the citizens.

(vi)   Tyranny is the exercise of temporal power for private ends.

(vii) Pure monarchy, pure aristocracy and pure democracy is each a lawful regime.

(viii) Pure monarchy and pure democracy are 'limiting cases' among men.

(ix)   A mixed polity exists when a society possesses discrete bearers of authority, whose jurisdiction and ability to limit each other is defined by human positive law.

(x)   Mixed polities are named monarchic, aristocratic or democratic insofar as the sovereign element, or the most formal part of the sovereign element, is one man, an elite body, or the whole people.

(xi)   In the abstract, a monarchy is the best of the pure polities, since it is best able to secure the intrinsic common good, namely, peace.

(xii) In the abstract, the best polity is one that is mixed from all three elements, with the monarchic predominating in the executive, the aristocratic in the judiciary and the democratic in the legislature.

(xiii) Each person, equal in bearing the image of God, is fittingly given some basic equality of power, although this does not exclude those who excel in various ways receiving additional power, including greater right of suffrage.

(xiv) Temporal authority should be possessed in proportion to a person's aptitude for office, and conferred upon those who possess prudence and the moral virtues, and, in Christendom the profession of the true faith, and secondarily any kind of distinction relevant to the excellence of a given society.

(xv)   The capacity to judge the worthiness of a potential wielder of temporal power depends on the virtue of the one judging.

(xvi)   Since the family is the unit of society, it is fitting that the family as such have a voice in the person of its head.

(xvii)   It is desirable that the artificial juridical persons that conduce to the well-being of society be represented in the counsels of the realm.

(xviii) The witness of mankind suggests the wisdom of including some element of hereditary power within a constitution.

Chapter 9
Political Economy

Feoh byþ frofur fira gehwylcum;

sceal ðeah manna gehwylc miclun hyt dælan

gif he wile for drihtne domes hleotan.[1]

The origin of property

All the goods of the earth are given to the human race as a whole in order to provide for the needs of their bodies. "And God blessed them, saying: Increase and multiply, and fill the earth, and subdue it, and rule over the fishes of the sea, and the fowls of the air, and all living creatures that move upon the earth."[2] The obligation to make this provision falls upon the individual, the family and the temporal power as the three juridical persons of natural law.[3] "Let every

---

[1] From the opening stanza of the Anglo-Saxon rune poem: "Wealth is a comfort to all men; yet must every man bestow it freely, if he would gain honour in the sight of the Lord."

[2] Genesis 1:28. Cf. 2nd Vatican Council, *Gaudium et spes*, 69: "God intended the earth with everything contained in it for the use of all human beings and peoples. [...] Whatever the forms of property may be, as adapted to the legitimate institutions of peoples, according to diverse and changeable circumstances, attention must always be paid to this universal destination of goods." One consequence of this principle is that one may not so use the earth as to render it uninhabitable or seriously degrade its value for one's neighbour or descendants and successors. Such vandalism is also an offence against the Creator and a violation of His command to 'tend and keep' the earth.

[3] Wealth is the total objective value of all material goods owned by a given individual or group. The objective value of material goods is established by their utility for man, and objective utility is established by human nature (i.e. the means of which it has need for subsistence and perfection). There is therefore a just price for all goods but it cannot easily be ascertained in the abstract or in advance of actual exchange. Cf. STh 2a 2ae 77, 1: "The just price of things is not fixed with mathematical precision, but depends on a kind of estimate, so that a slight addition or subtraction would not seem to destroy the equality of justice." The civil power is not equipped to determine prices and must limit itself to the elimination of factors which might empower one party to an exchange to yield less than the true worth of some good due to the weakness or desperation of the other party. Cf. ibid.: "If the one man derive a great advantage by becoming possessed of the other man's property, and the seller be not harmed through being without that thing, the latter ought not to raise the price, because the advantage accruing to the buyer, is not due to the seller,

soul be subject to higher powers: for there is no power but from God: and those that are, are ordained of God."[4] Artificial juridical persons, such as clubs, regiments, unions, companies, and guilds, may be confected by individuals and families subject to the judgment of the temporal power that the aims of such artificial juridical persons are not inimical to the common good.[56] Divine law, which the individual, the family and the temporal power are commanded by the natural law to recognise and obey,[7] constitutes a fourth juridical person of divine right: the Church, whose public acts are determined by the spiritual power.[8] The spiritual power has the same right to approve and constitute artificial juridical persons, such as abbeys or dioceses, as the temporal power. Neither the spiritual power itself nor the artificial juridical persons it generates[9] are subject to the temporal power.[10] The rights concerning property delineated

---

but to a circumstance affecting the buyer. Now no man should sell what is not his, though he may charge for the loss he suffers." Cajetan in his commentary on this article defines the just price as "that which can now be obtained from buyers, common knowledge being presupposed, and deceit and coercion excluded".

[4] Romans 13:1.

[5] In addition to such confection, public authority may also create juridical persons of its own; cf. A. Ottaviani, *Compendium Iuris Publici Ecclesiastici*, 31, n. 1.

[6] Leo XIII, *Rerum novarum*, 50-52: "Private societies, then, although they exist within the body politic, and are severally part of the commonwealth, cannot nevertheless be absolutely, and as such, prohibited by public authority. For, to enter into a society of this kind is the natural right of man; and the *civitas* has for its office to protect natural rights, not to destroy them; and, if it forbid its citizens to form associations, it contradicts the very principle of its own existence, for both they and it exist in virtue of the like principle, namely, the natural tendency of man to dwell in society.".

[7] Ps. 71:11.

[8] Pius XI, *Divini illius Magistri*, 11. "[T]here are three necessary societies, distinct from one another and yet harmoniously combined by God, into which man is born: two, namely the family and civil society, belong to the natural order; the third, the Church, to the supernatural order."

[9] The episcopate is of divine law and is not generated by the Holy See. Nevertheless, the creation of new dioceses and the delineation of their frontiers is a power reserved by divine law to the papacy and the other apostolic patriarchates.

[10] Cf. Matt 17:23-25: "And when they were come to Capharnaum, they that received the didrachmas, came to Peter and said to him: Doth not your master pay the didrachmas? He said: Yes. And when he was come into the house, Jesus prevented him, saying: What is thy opinion, Simon? The kings of the earth, of whom do they receive tribute or custom? of their own children, or of strangers? And he said: Of strangers. Jesus said to him: Then the children are free." St Robert Bellarmine comments: "When the sons of kings are exempted from taxes, not only their own persons, but their servants and ministers and indeed their whole households are exempted. And it is certain that all clergy properly pertain to the

below thus apply without qualification to the spiritual power and the rights over the property of artificial juridical persons in temporal society enjoyed by the temporal power are enjoyed by the spiritual power over the artificial juridical persons it generates.[11]

In order to render the goods of the earth actually useful for human subsistence it is ordinarily necessary[12] to apply labour to them.[13] In this way, they are transformed into the property of the juridical persons in question.[14] "For the

---

household of Christ, who is the Son of the king of kings"; *Controversiae*, 'On the members of the Church', bk. 1, ch. 28, and see chapters 28-30 for a full discussion and defence of the immunity of clergy from taxation by the temporal power.

[11] Pius IX, *Quanta cura*, 5: "Others meanwhile, reviving the wicked and so often condemned inventions of innovators, dare with signal impudence to subject to the will of the civil authority the supreme authority of the Church and of this Apostolic See given to her by Christ Himself, and to deny all those rights of the same Church and See which concern matters of the external order. For they are not ashamed of affirming ' ... that the excommunication pronounced by the Council of Trent and by Roman Pontiffs against those who assail and usurp the Church's rights and possessions, rests on a confusion between the spiritual and temporal orders, and (is directed) to the pursuit of a purely secular good; that the Church can decree nothing which binds the conscience of the faithful in regard to their use of temporal things; that the Church has no right of restraining by temporal punishments those who violate her laws; that it is conformable to the principles of sacred theology and public law to assert and claim for the civil government a right of property in those goods which are possessed by the Church, by the Religious Orders, and by other pious establishments'."

[12] Leo XIII, *Rerum novarum*, 9: "Truly, that which is required for the preservation of life, and for life's well-being, is produced in great abundance from the soil, but not until man has brought it into cultivation and expended upon it his solicitude and skill. Now, when man thus turns the activity of his mind and the strength of his body toward procuring the fruits of nature, by such act he makes his own that portion of nature's field which he cultivates - that portion on which he leaves, as it were, the impress of his personality; and it cannot but be just that he should possess that portion as his very own, and have a right to hold it without any one being justified in violating that right."

[13] Genesis 2:15; 3:19.

[14] It is of course also possible to acquire property that is simply unoccupied (a notion, unfortunately, open to abuse). Pius XI, *Quadragesimo anno*, 52: "That ownership is originally acquired both by occupancy of a thing not owned by any one and by labour, or, as is said, by specification, the tradition of all ages as well as the teaching of Our Predecessor Leo clearly testifies. For, whatever some idly say to the contrary, no injury is done to any person when a thing is occupied that is available to all but belongs to no one; however, only that labour which a man performs in his own name and by virtue of which a new form or increase has been given to a thing grants him title to these fruits."

scripture saith: Thou shalt not muzzle the ox that treadeth out the corn: and, the labourer is worthy of his reward."[15] As St Thomas explains,

> If this field be considered absolutely, it contains no reason why it should belong to one man more than to another, but if it be considered in respect of the possibility of cultivating it, and the unmolested use of the land, it has a certain commensuration to be the property of one and not of another man.[16]

The existence of private property is thus not a matter of regret or a necessary evil but an institution proportionate to and indeed "pre-eminently in conformity with human nature",[17] and the concomitant of any order of providence, at least, in which man is not preserved from the mortality consequent upon his bodily existence by some preternatural or supernatural gift.

> The fact that God has given the earth for the use and enjoyment of the whole human race can in no way be a bar to the owning of private property. For God has granted the earth to mankind in general, not in the sense that all without distinction can deal with it as they like, but rather that no part of it was assigned to any one in particular, and that the limits of private possession have been left to be fixed by man's own industry, and by the laws of individual races. Moreover, the earth, even though apportioned among private owners, ceases not thereby to minister to the needs of all, inasmuch as there is not one who does not sustain life from what the land produces. Those who do not possess the soil contribute their labour; hence, it may truly be said that all human subsistence is derived either from labour on one's own land, or from some toilsome art, which is paid for either in the produce of the land itself, or in that which is exchanged for what the land brings forth.[18]

---

[15] 1 Tim. 5:18.

[16] STh 1a 2ae, 57, 3.

[17] Leo XIII, *Rerum novarum*, 11.

[18] Leo XIII, *Rerum novarum*, 8. Cf. STh 2a 2ae 66, 2: "This is necessary to human life for three reasons. First because every man is more careful to procure what is for himself alone than that which is common to many or to all: since each one would shirk the labour and leave to another that which concerns the community, as happens where there is a great number of servants. Secondly, because human affairs are conducted in more orderly fashion if each man is charged with taking care of some particular thing himself, whereas there would be confusion if everyone had to look after any one thing indeterminately.

This right of property comes with a corresponding duty upon the owner to use the property to provide for the subsistence of all his dependants.[19] "But if any man have not care of his own, and especially of those of his house, he hath denied the faith, and is worse than an infidel."[20] If the owner has no unprovided for dependants, he has a duty to dispose of at least the *use* of his surplus property to someone who does need it in order to provide for himself and/or his own dependants. This disposal may be accomplished either *gratis* or for a consideration.

> A workman's wages should be sufficient to enable him to support himself, his wife and his children. 'If through necessity or fear of a worse evil the workman accepts harder conditions because an employer or contractor will afford no better, he is made the victim of force and injustice.'[21]

If it is disposed of for a consideration the same obligation will apply to this additional property.[22] This obligation is a moral duty which cannot be enforced

---

Thirdly, because a more peaceful state is ensured to man if each one is contented with his own. Hence it is to be observed that quarrels arise more frequently where there is no division of the things possessed." Aristotle for his part noted that the proposals made in his day by certain proto-socialists for excluding private property, while having 'an attractive face', would not only create friction, but would remove the possibility of exercising the virtue of liberality, as well as excluding the legitimate pleasure of ownership; *Politics*, II.5.

[19] Leo XIII, *Rerum novarum*, 13: "That right to property, therefore, which has been proved to belong naturally to individual persons, must in like wise belong to a man in his capacity of head of a family; nay, that right is all the stronger in proportion as the human person receives a wider extension in the family group. It is a most sacred law of nature that a father should provide food and all necessaries for those whom he has begotten; and, similarly, it is natural that he should wish that his children, who carry on, so to speak, and continue his personality, should be by him provided with all that is needful to enable them to keep themselves decently from want and misery amid the uncertainties of this mortal life. Now, in no other way can a father effect this except by the ownership of productive property, which he can transmit to his children by inheritance."

[20] 1 Timothy 5:8.

[21] John Paul II, *Centesimus annus*, 8, with internal quotation from *Rerum novarum*, 45.

[22] Pius XI, *Quadragesimo anno*, 50-51: "Furthermore, a person's superfluous income, that is, income which he does not need to sustain life fittingly and with dignity, is not left wholly to his own free determination. Rather, the Sacred Scriptures and the Fathers of the Church constantly declare in the most explicit language that the rich are bound by a very grave precept to practice almsgiving, beneficence, and munificence. Expending larger incomes so that opportunity for gainful work may be abundant, provided, however, that this work is applied to producing really useful goods, ought to be considered, as We deduce from the principles of the Angelic Doctor [cf. STh 2a 2ae 134], an outstanding exemplification of

directly by the temporal power without the temporal power thereby usurping the rights of ownership.[23] It may, however, inform the manner in which the exactions necessary for the functioning of the temporal power are made.[24]

An individual unable to provide for his own subsistence or that of his dependants by any means, and to whom no one will give the immediate means of subsistence, may without the guilt of theft appropriate the surplus property of another to the degree necessary for his survival and that of his dependants, since the fundamental basis of the right of property, namely, provision for the subsistence of mankind, supervenes upon the particular right and suppresses it.

Things which are of human right cannot derogate from natural right or divine right. Now according to the natural order established by divine providence, inferior things are ordained for the purpose of succouring man's needs by their means. Wherefore the division and appropriation of things which are based on human law, do not preclude the fact that man's needs have to be remedied by means of these very things. Hence whatever certain people have in superabundance is due, by natural law, to the purpose of succouring the poor. For this reason, Ambrose says, and his words are embodied in the *Decretals* in distinction XLVII: "It is the hungry man's bread that you withhold, the naked man's cloak that you store away, the money that you bury in the earth is the price of the poor man's ransom and freedom." [25]

Although it may often be preferable to dispose of surplus property *gratis*, it is not necessarily always so, owing to the moral hazard that may result: "If any man will not work, neither let him eat" (2 Thessalonians 3:10). Furthermore, if the consideration that a surplus owner receives in return for the use of his

---

the virtue of munificence (*magnificentiae*) and one particularly suited to the needs of the times."

[23] Pius XI, *Quadragesimo anno*, 47: "That justice called commutative commands sacred respect for the division of possessions and forbids invasion of others' rights through the exceeding of the limits of one's own property; but the duty of owners to use their property only in a right way does not come under this type of justice, but under other virtues, obligations of which 'cannot be enforced by legal action' [*Rerum novarum*, 36]. Therefore, they are in error who assert that ownership and its right use are limited by the same boundaries; and it is much farther still from the truth to hold that a right to property is destroyed or lost by reason of abuse or non-use."

[24] For example, the civil power might tax idle property at a higher rate. Cf. Bunreacht na hÉireann (1937), article 42.2.

[25] STh 1a 2ae 66, 7.

property is in turn furnished to some further persons who need it in order to provide for themselves and/or their dependants (also at a consideration) this may result in a virtuous circle multiplying the useful goods and fruitful labour available to mankind.

So long as the original title to some property is sound there is no injustice in profiting from the sale of its use[26] (or from the employment of persons to gather its fruits) because the ultimate title is grounded upon labour and the labourer would not truly receive the fruits of his industry if he were not able to dispose of both the dominion and use of the property thus obtained, whether this disposal occurs by sale, inheritance or gift.[27] For ownership essentially consists in these rights.[28]

---

[26] When the thing is not by its very nature consumed in use; see below.

[27] Pius XI, *Quadragesimo anno*, 57: "[T]he riches that economic and social developments constantly increase ought to be so distributed among individual persons and classes that … the common good of all society will be kept inviolate. By this law of social justice, one class is forbidden to exclude any other from sharing in gains. Hence the class of the wealthy violates this law no less, when, as if free from care on account of its wealth, it thinks it the right order of things for it to get everything and the worker nothing, than does the non-owning working class when, angered deeply at outraged justice and too ready to assert wrongly the one right it is conscious of, it demands for itself everything as if produced by its own hands, and attacks and seeks to abolish, therefore, all property and returns or incomes, of whatever kind they are or whatever the function they perform in human society, that have not been obtained by labour, and for no other reason save that they are of such a nature." The temporal and spiritual powers may also, by reason of necessity and with due compensation, confiscate the property of their subjects, or simply assign some property to a given person by decree when the question of original title is interminable.

[28] "Since among some learned men it often happens that doubt is again raised as to whether it should be branded as heretical to affirm persistently that our Redeemer and Lord Jesus Christ and His apostles did not possess anything either in particular or even in common, even though there are different and adverse opinions on that question, We, in a desire to put an end to this controversy, declare on the advice of Our brethren by this perpetual edict that a persistent assertion of this kind shall henceforth be branded as erroneous and heretical, since it expressly contradicts Sacred Scripture, which in many passages asserts that they did have some possessions, and since with regard to the aforementioned matter it openly submits that Sacred Scripture itself, by which surely the articles of orthodox faith are approved, contains a ferment of falsehood and consequently, in so far as in it lies, this assertion renders the Catholic faith doubtful and uncertain, by completely voiding the trustworthiness of Scripture, thus annulling that by which this faith is approved. Moreover, in the future to affirm persistently that the right to use these same possessions which Sacred Scripture testifies that they had was by no means appropriate to our aforesaid Redeemer and His apostles, and that they did not have the right to sell or to donate them or to acquire others by means of them, which, nevertheless, Sacred Scripture testifies that they did

The desire of each labourer should always be to obtain the ownership of his own means of production, as self-movement is always more consonant with the dignity of man's nature, for "God made man from the beginning, and left him in the hand of his own counsel" (Ecclesiasticus 15:14). Unimpeded exchange ought in ordinary conditions to suffice to ensure that the consideration demanded by a surplus owner for the use of his property is not so great, or the wages offered for the exploitation of an employer's capital not so meagre, as to preclude the accumulation by the labourer of a capital from the fruits of his labour sufficient to purchase his own means of production within a reasonable time.[29] Should unusual conditions (such as an abundance of labour or a dearth of productive property) conspire to remove this prospect from the labourer it may be necessary for the temporal power to employ its revenues to correct this imbalance.[30] Such measures should be adopted with

---

according to the aforesaid or submits expressly that they could have done - since such an assertion evidently implies unjust behaviour and deeds on their part in the aforesaid matter, something which it is surely wicked, contrary to Sacred Scripture, and to Catholic doctrine to hold about the behaviour, actions, or deeds of our Redeemer, the Son of God, we declare on the advice of our brethren that this persistent assertion shall henceforth be worthily branded as erroneous and heretical"; John XXII, *Cum inter nonnullos*, (1323).

[29] This demand flows from human nature itself. "For man, fathoming by his faculty of reason matters without number, linking the future with the present, and being master of his own acts, guides his ways under the eternal law and the power of God, whose providence governs all things. Wherefore, it is in his power to exercise his choice not only as to matters that regard his present welfare, but also about those which he deems may be for his advantage in time yet to come. Hence, man not only should possess the fruits of the earth, but also the very soil, inasmuch as from the produce of the earth he has to lay by provision for the future. Man's needs do not die out, but forever recur; although satisfied today, they demand fresh supplies for tomorrow. Nature accordingly must have given to man a source that is stable and remaining always with him, from which he might look to draw continual supplies. And this stable condition of things he finds solely in the earth and its fruits. There is no need to bring in the supervision of the State (*respublica*). Man precedes the State (*respublica*), and possesses, prior to the formation of any State (*civitas*), the right of providing for the substance of his body"; Leo XIII, *Rerum novarum*, 7.

[30] "It must likewise be the special care of the State (*qui publice imperant*) to furnish those supports of life without which the commonwealth, however rightly composed, is prone to collapse and to ensure that employment be available, particularly for the heads of families and for the young. To achieve this end demanded by the pressing needs of the common welfare, the wealthy classes must be induced to assume those burdens without which human society cannot be saved nor they themselves remain secure. However, measures taken by the State (*rei publicae moderatoribus*) with this end in view ought to be of such a nature that they will really affect those who overflow with wealth and abundance, and who continue to accumulate them to the grievous detriment of others"; Pius XI, *Divini Redemptoris*, 75.

great caution as the temporal power must never be a respecter of persons (Deuteronomy 1:17).[31] The most extreme distortion of this instinct, still more prejudicial to the common good and contrary to the true understanding of property, would be the assertion of a fundamental prior claim by the temporal power on all property and its disposal, which is the fundamental error of Socialism.[32]

> To consider the State (*rem publicam*) as something ultimate to which everything else should be subordinated and directed, cannot fail to harm the true and lasting prosperity of nations. This can happen either when unrestricted dominion comes to be conferred on the State (*rei publicae*) as having a mandate from the nation, people, or even a social order, or when the State (*civitas*) arrogates such dominion to itself as absolute master, accountable to none. If, in fact, the State (*res publica*) lays claim to and directs private enterprises, these, ruled as they are by principles proper to themselves which tend to the safe realization of their aims, may be damaged to the detriment

---

[31] STh 2a 2ae, 63, 1: "Respect of persons is opposed to distributive justice. For the equality of distributive justice consists in allotting various things to various persons in proportion to their personal dignity. Accordingly, if one considers that personal property by reason of which the thing allotted to a particular person is due to him, this is respect not of the person but of the cause. Hence a gloss on Ephesians 6:9, 'There is no respect of persons with God [Vulgate: 'Him'],' says that 'a just judge regards causes, not persons.' For instance if you promote a man to a professorship on account of his having sufficient knowledge, you consider the due cause, not the person; but if, in conferring something on someone, you consider in him not the fact that what you give him is proportionate or due to him, but the fact that he is this particular man (e.g. Peter or Martin), then there is respect of the person, since you give him something not for some cause that renders him worthy of it, but simply because he is this person. And any circumstance that does not amount to a reason why this man be worthy of this gift, is to be referred to his person: for instance if a man promote someone to a prelacy or a professorship, because he is rich or because he is a relative of his, it is respect of persons. It may happen, however, that a circumstance of person makes a man worthy as regards one thing, but not as regards another: thus consanguinity makes a man worthy to be appointed heir to an estate, but not to be chosen for a position of ecclesiastical authority: wherefore consideration of the same circumstance of person will amount to respect of persons in one matter and not in another. It follows, accordingly, that respect of persons is opposed to distributive justice in that it fails to observe due proportion. Now nothing but sin is opposed to virtue: and therefore respect of persons is a sin."

[32] John Rawls tacitly holds this position in *A Theory of Justice*, by assuming that it is the task of the State to distribute property to all according to the most just criterion discoverable. See Robert Nozick's criticism of Rawls's position in *Anarchy, State and Utopia*, ch. 7.

of the public good, by being wrenched from their natural surroundings, that is, from responsible private action.[33]

A surplus owner may retain the use of his surplus property and employ servants to make that property productive, paying them in exchange for their labour a proportion of the fruits of that labour. As with the disposal of the use of the property itself, the danger exists that unusual conditions (such as an abundance of labour or a dearth of productive property) may conspire to preclude the accumulation by the labourer of a sufficient capital to purchase his own means of production within a reasonable time.[34] The apostolic warning applies:

> Come now, you rich, weep and howl for the miseries that are coming upon you. Your riches have rotted and your garments are moth-eaten. Your gold and silver have rusted, and their rust will be evidence against you and will eat your flesh like fire. You have laid up treasure for the last days. Behold, the wages of the labourers who mowed your fields, which you kept back by fraud, cry out; and the cries of the harvesters have reached the ears of the Lord of hosts.[35]

This danger is graver in this instance of paid employment as the labourer is more likely when directed to the ends of another to lack the experience to undertake autonomous labour on his own property. In addition, a serious disparity between his remuneration and the cost of emancipation will be harder to discern than when a labourer employs the use of a determined property for a consideration which may be directly compared to the market value of dominion over a similar property.

When questions of complexity and scale preclude the ownership of some form of productive property by the family or the individual whose labour renders it fruitful (because the labour of many families or individuals is required to

---

[33] Pius XII, *Summi Pontificatus*, 60.

[34] "It is surely undeniable that, when a man engages in remunerative labour, the impelling reason and motive of his work is to obtain property, and thereafter to hold it as his very own. If one man hires out to another his strength or skill, he does so for the purpose of receiving in return what is necessary for the satisfaction of his needs; he therefore expressly intends to acquire a right full and real, not only to the remuneration, but also to the disposal of such remuneration, just as he pleases. Thus, if he lives sparingly, saves money, and, for greater security, invests his savings in land, the land, in such case, is only his wages under another form; and, consequently, a working man's little estate thus purchased should be as completely at his full disposal as are the wages he receives for his labour. But it is precisely in such power of disposal that ownership obtains, whether the property consist of land or chattels"; Leo XIII, *Rerum novarum* 5.

[35] Jas. 5:1-4.

exploit the property in question),[36] then in order to avoid the transformation by means of unusual conditions of an unduly large section of the population into the paid servants of the owners of such surplus capital, the temporal power may, in the exaction of the tax revenues necessary for its proper functions, favour the common ownership by artificial juridical persons constituted by the labourers themselves of their own means of production.

The organisation of employed labourers into unions in order to defend their legal and natural rights against their employers (if necessary by withdrawing their labour) is entirely legitimate but much less desirable than the cooperative ownership by the same of their own means of production. The proliferation of such unions is a sign that the temporal power has failed to prevent the owners of surplus property from misusing exceptional conditions to withhold from the non-owning labourer a just proportion of the fruits of his labour.[37]

The organisation of society based on the self-ownership and self-regulation of spontaneous and essential elements in that society's productive capacity is a natural and fundamental element in the composition of any healthy temporal polity. Indeed, St Thomas identifies the 'vicus', where are concentrated all 'those things which belong to one craft', as a key intermediary stage in the growth of human perfection (i.e. self-sufficiency) between the family and the city. Although he is using the term 'vicus' in a specifically urban context, to

---

[36] "As history abundantly proves, it is true that on account of changed conditions many things which were done by small associations in former times cannot be done now save by large associations. Still, that most weighty principle, which cannot be set aside or changed, remains fixed and unshaken in social philosophy: just as it is gravely wrong to take from individuals what they can accomplish by their own initiative and industry and give it to the community, so also it is an injustice and at the same time a grave evil and disturbance of right order to assign to a greater and higher association what lesser and subordinate organizations can do. For every social activity ought of its very nature to furnish help to the members of the body social, and never destroy and absorb them"; Pius XI, *Quadragesimo anno*, 79.

[37] "First and foremost, the State (*res publica*) and every good citizen ought to look to and strive toward this end: that the conflict between the hostile 'classes' be abolished and harmonious cooperation of the 'orders' (*'ordines'*) be encouraged and promoted. The social political art, therefore, must devote itself to the re-establishment of the 'orders'. In actual fact, human society now, for the reason that it is founded on 'classes' with divergent aims and hence opposed to one another and therefore inclined to enmity and strife, continues to be in a violent condition and is unstable and uncertain"; ibid. 81-82. By 'orders' Pius XI means an organic element in society such as all those engaged in the production of one particular good or set of similar goods who ought to be united in mutual assistance and fraternity, not divided adversarially into owners and employees.

mean a quarter occupied by the members of one guild, the word also refers to a relatively self-sufficient agricultural community.[38]

Distortion of the market

The sale of the use of money is a form of fraud, as the use of money is not distinct from its alienation and therefore one may enjoy only dominion over currency and not its use:

To take usury for money lent is unjust in itself, because this is to sell what does not exist, and this evidently leads to inequality which is contrary to justice. In order to make this evident, we must observe that there are certain things the use of which consists in their consumption: thus we consume wine when we use it for drink and we consume wheat when we use it for food. Wherefore in such like things the use of the thing must not be reckoned apart from the thing itself, and whoever is granted the use of the thing, is granted the thing itself and for this reason, to lend things of this kind is to transfer the ownership. Accordingly if a man wanted to sell wine separately from the use of the wine, he would be selling the same thing twice, or he would be selling what does not exist, wherefore he would evidently commit a sin of injustice. In like manner he commits an injustice who lends wine or wheat, and asks for double payment, viz. one, the return of the thing in equal measure, the other, the price of the use, which is called usury.

On the other hand, there are things the use of which does not consist in their consumption: thus to use a house is to dwell in it, not to destroy it. Wherefore in such things both may be granted: for instance, one man may hand over to another the ownership of his house while reserving to himself the use of it for a time, or vice versa, he may grant the use of the house, while retaining the ownership. For this reason a man may lawfully make a charge for the use of his house, and, besides this, revendicate the house from the person to

---

[38] *De Regno* I.2. The concept of the 'vicus' as an irreducible element in society makes a shadowy appearance in the sixth amendment of the U.S. Constitution in the so-called 'Vicinage Clause' which prevents a jury from being assembled far from the place of the alleged crime. This reflects mediaeval English usage from which the colonists felt the government in Westminster had illegitimately departed in their regard, e.g. by holding treason trials on the other side of the Atlantic; William Blackstone, *Commentaries*, IV.27.

whom he has granted its use, as happens in renting and letting a house.

Now money, according to the Philosopher (Ethic. v, 5; Polit. i, 3) was invented chiefly for the purpose of exchange: and consequently the proper and principal use of money is its consumption or alienation whereby it is sunk in exchange. Hence it is by its very nature unlawful to take payment for the use of money lent, which payment is known as usury: and just as a man is bound to restore other ill-gotten goods, so is he bound to restore the money which he has taken in usury.[39]

As the value of any given unit of currency is determined by the value of the goods available for a consideration by means of that currency divided by the number of units in circulation, the sale of the pseudo-use of money multiplies the number of units in nominal circulation and so constitutes theft from every person in possession of that currency. The toleration of this form of theft by the temporal power is a very great evil and, by causing a dearth of productive property available to a labourer, constitutes the normalisation of extraordinary conditions by which the owners of surplus property may render impossible the acquisition by non-owning labourers of their own means of production. The great wealth obtained by such usurers is invariably employed by them to exert influence over the temporal power to ensure the continuation of the evil by which they enrich themselves.[40]

The lending of money at interest to an individual is not usurious if the liability of that individual is limited to some designated collateral, because what the borrower has done in this case is sell a future interest in that property reserving a time-limited right of redemption, the exercise of which becomes more expensive with time (in recognition of the use the borrower makes of that collateral in the interval). This is a genuine exchange of goods and not the sale of a non-existent commodity. For example, one may lend a man 1000 florins to buy a house and demand in return after ten years 1200 florins in recognition of the use of the house over those ten years with the understanding that the

---

[39] STh 1a 2ae, 78, 1.

[40] Usury is condemned by the First Council of Nicaea, the Second and Third Lateran Councils, the Second Council of Lyons, the Council of Vienne, and the Fifth Lateran Council. It suffices to quote the Council of Vienne, canon 29, whose condemnation is most strident: "If indeed someone has fallen into the error of presuming to affirm pertinaciously that the practice of usury is not sinful, we decree that he is to be punished as a heretic; and we strictly enjoin on local ordinaries and inquisitors of heresy to proceed against those they find suspect of such error as they would against those suspected of heresy."

house (up to the agreed value) reverts to the lender if the money is not paid. One may not, however, after default and upon discovering the house is now (after ten years) worth only 900 florins demand a further 300 florins from the borrower after the sale of the house. The lending of money at interest to a corporation such that the liability of the corporation is limited to its assets and not the private fortunes of the natural persons who compose it is thus never usurious. Unlimited recourse interest-bearing loans to natural juridical persons are always usurious.[41]

A just ruler must eliminate usury from his dominions and ensure that the laws and institutions of the territory over which he rules, while allowing for paid employment, always favour the ownership by the labourer of the means of his own production, where possible as an individual or family and failing that cooperatively.[42]

As the essential functions of the temporal power consist in the preservation and facilitation of those spontaneous activities of its subjects which take place neither *gratis* nor within the precincts of the family,[43] and as all such activities require the means of exchange, the distinction between dominion and use in

---

[41] Benedict XIV, *Vix pervenit* (1745). Cf. T. Dickson (ed.), *Usury* (Zippy: Saint Paul, 2017).

[42] "First of all, those who declare that a contract of hiring and being hired is unjust of its own nature, and hence that a partnership-contract must take its place, are certainly in error and gravely misrepresent Our Predecessor whose Encyclical not only accepts working for wages or salaries but deals at some length with its regulation in accordance with the rules of justice. We consider it more advisable, however, in the present condition of human society that, so far as is possible, the work-contract be somewhat modified by a partnership-contract, as is already being done in various ways and with no small advantage to workers and owners. Workers and other employees thus become sharers in ownership or management or participate in some fashion in the profits received." Pius XI, *Quadragesimo anno*, 64-65.

[43] Inheritance tax is thus contrary to the natural law and void. Death is not a service rendered to the individual or the family by the civil power. "The natural right itself both of owning goods privately and of passing them on by inheritance ought always to remain intact and inviolate, since this indeed is a right that the State cannot take away: 'For man is older than the State,' (*Rerum novarum* 12) and also 'domestic living together is prior both in thought and in fact to uniting into a polity' (*Rerum novarum* 20)"; Pius XI, *Quadragesimo anno*, 47. Cf. St Thomas, *Scriptum super Sententias*, lib. 4 d. 33 q. 2 a. 1: "I reply that it should be said that matrimony, from the intention of nature, is ordered to the education of the children, not for a certain time only, but rather for the entire life of the children (which is the reason why, by the law of nature, parents are to lay up wealth for their children, and children should inherit from their parents). For that reason, since children are a common good of husband and wife, it is necessary according to the dictum of the law of nature that that association remain perpetually undivided. Thus, the inseparability of matrimony is based on the law of nature." See also above, p. 59 n. 66.

the means of exchange does exist in regard to the temporal power. That is, the temporal power owns and its subjects use the means of exchange. The just exactions of the temporal power (taxation) may therefore be correctly described as a charge for the use of the means of exchange (Matthew 22:21; Mark 12:17; Luke 20:25).[44]

The temporal power may not justly impose taxes beyond what is necessary to preserve this order.[45]

Co-operation

So long as the temporal power retains an equitable concern for the welfare of all its subjects it may legitimately empower corporations of all members of a particular profession to examine the proficiency of persons intending to practice that profession and grant or withhold license to do so.[46]

> Labour, as Our Predecessor explained well in his Encyclical, is not a mere commodity. On the contrary, the worker's human dignity in it must be recognized. It therefore cannot be bought and sold like a commodity. Nevertheless, as the situation now stands, hiring and offering for hire in the so-called labour market separate men into two divisions, as into battle lines, and the contest between these divisions turns the labour market itself almost into a battlefield where, face to face, the opposing lines struggle bitterly. Everyone understands that this grave evil which is plunging all human society to destruction must be remedied as soon as possible.[47] But complete cure will not come until this opposition has been abolished and well-equipped organs of the social body - the 'orders', that is, - are constituted in which men may have their place, not according to the position each has in the labour market but according to the respective social functions which each performs. For under nature's guidance it comes to pass that just as those who are joined together by nearness of habitation establish towns, so those who follow the same industry

---

[44] STh 1a 63, 2 ad 2: "Avarice, considered as a special kind of sin, is the immoderate greed of temporal possessions which serve the use of human life, and which can be estimated in value of money".

[45] 1 Kings 10:14.

[46] Such entities should not be so subsumed into the temporal power as to become its extension or to prevent freedom of association; Pius XI, *Quadragesimo anno* 83-87; 91-96.

[47] The fact that this division is now obscured behind a thousand veils of ownership by funds and trusts does not make it any less real.

(*artem*) or profession - whether in the economic or other field - form guilds (*collegia*) or associations (*corpora*), so that many are wont to consider these self-governing organizations, if not essential, at least natural to civil society.[48]

If the term 'capitalism' is understood to mean a juridical order in which the temporal power maintains equality before the law and allows the free interaction of different juridical persons to determine economic relations subject to the qualifications so far examined, then 'capitalism' is not contrary to the natural or divine law. However, this is a misleading use of the term. If capitalism is used more exactly to mean a usurious market (in which capital necessarily enjoys primacy over labour)[49] then it is most certainly contrary to natural and divine law.[50]

Socialism understood as the doctrine that property is vested ultimately in the temporal power and conceded and resumed upon criteria of social utility to individuals, families and artificial juridical persons is a pernicious error whose application renders the social order at odds with the common good itself.[51]

---

[48] Pius XI, *Quadragesimo anno*. 83.

[49] Labour is the source and title to capital. In capitalism, capital acts as if it were the source of and title to itself.

[50] "[C]an it perhaps be said that, after the failure of Communism, capitalism is the victorious social system, and that capitalism should be the goal of the countries now making efforts to rebuild their economy and society? Is this the model which ought to be proposed to the countries of the Third World which are searching for the path to true economic and civil progress? The answer is obviously complex. If by 'capitalism' is meant an economic system which recognizes the fundamental and positive role of business, the market, private property and the resulting responsibility for the means of production, as well as free human creativity in the economic sector, then the answer is certainly in the affirmative, even though it would perhaps be more appropriate to speak of a 'business economy', 'market economy' or simply 'free economy'. But if by 'capitalism' is meant a system in which freedom in the economic sector is not circumscribed within a strong juridical framework which places it at the service of human freedom in its totality, and which sees it as a particular aspect of that freedom, the core of which is ethical and religious, then the reply is certainly negative"; Pope John Paul II, *Centesimus annus*, 42.

[51] "To remedy these wrongs the socialists, working on the poor man's envy of the rich, are striving to do away with private property, and contend that individual possessions should become the common property of all, to be administered by the State (*qui gerant rem publicam*) or by municipal bodies. They hold that by thus transferring property from private individuals to the community, the present mischievous state of things will be set to rights, inasmuch as each citizen will then get his fair share of whatever there is to enjoy. But their contentions are so clearly powerless to end the controversy that were they carried into effect the working man himself would be among the first to suffer. They are, moreover,

Trade may be an honourable activity but is far more open to corruption than the direct sale of intrinsically useful goods by the producer, because skill in facilitating exchange may yield riches independently of the real value of the things exchanged and the desire for money has no natural satiation.

> Hence trading, considered in itself, has a certain debasement attaching thereto, insofar as, by its very nature, it does not imply a virtuous or necessary end. Nevertheless gain, which is the end of trading, though not implying, by its nature, anything virtuous or necessary, does not, in itself, connote anything sinful or contrary to virtue: wherefore nothing prevents gain from being directed to some necessary or even virtuous end, and thus trading becomes lawful.[52]

It is accordingly preferable that exchange be in the hands of the producer or his servants.

The disorders consequent upon usury and the distortions they effect in social relations lead almost inevitably, especially in the absence of true social philosophy, to a growing popular demand for the civil power to take a greater and greater role in regulating and absorbing economic activity. As the temporal power is not fitted to this task it performs it poorly, which results either in a reaction toward liberal capitalism or in a growing authoritarianism and an increasing respect of persons on the part of the civil power. This final breakdown of civility and the rule of law can be delayed in nations with a long tradition of respect for legal norms by an aggravation of the public debt which allows the socialist to conceal his mistakes and the liberal to reduce the burden of taxation without restraining the public expenditure. It is most unlikely that such fiscal procrastination can be maintained indefinitely, since at some point the danger of default will bring an end to the public credit. As Pius XI foresaw "It belongs to Our Pastoral Office to warn these persons of the grave and

---

emphatically unjust, for they would rob the lawful possessor, distort the functions of the State (*reipublicae*), and create utter confusion in communities (*civitates*)"; Leo XIII, *Rerum novarum* 4. Cf. Pius XI, *Quadragesimo anno* 111-120. Pius XI is most explicit at 120: "If Socialism, like all errors, contains some truth (which, moreover, the Supreme Pontiffs have never denied), it is based nevertheless on a theory of human society peculiar to itself and irreconcilable with true Christianity. Religious socialism, Christian socialism, are contradictory terms; no one can be at the same time a good Catholic and a true socialist"; Pope John XXIII, *Mater et Magistra*, 34: "The supreme pontiff [Pius XI] emphasized that the principles of Christians and of 'Communists', as they are called, are completely opposed; and that neither can Catholic men in any way approve of the teachings of the 'Socialists', who seem to hold a less extreme position."

[52] STh 2a 2ae 77, 4.

imminent evil: let all remember that Liberalism is the father of this Socialism that is pervading morality and culture and that Bolshevism will be its heir."[53]

---

[53] Pius XI, *Quadragesimo anno*, 122.

Theses

(i)   The goods of the earth are given to the human race as a whole in order to provide for the needs of their bodies.

(ii)   The obligation to make this provision falls upon the individual, the family and the temporal power as the three juridical persons of natural law.

(iii)   Artificial juridical persons may be confected by the individual and the family subject to the judgment of the temporal power that the aims of such artificial juridical persons are not inimical to the common good.

(iv)   The spiritual power has the same right to approve and constitute artificial juridical persons as the temporal power.

(v)   Private ownership of objects of consumption and of the means of production is an institution proportionate to and pre-eminently in conformity with human nature.

(vi)   The fundamental title to property is labour.

(vii)   The destination of goods possessed privately remains common; in particular, the right of property comes with a corresponding duty upon the owner to use the property to provide for the subsistence of all his dependants.

(viii)   If the owner has no unprovided for dependants he has a duty to dispose of at least the use of his surplus property, either *gratis* or for a consideration, to someone who does need it in order to provide for himself and/or his own dependants.

(ix)   This obligation is a moral duty which cannot be enforced directly by the temporal power.

(x)   In extreme necessity, a person may appropriate the private goods of another.

(xi)   Derived titles to private ownership are inheritance, gift and contract (and also confiscation by the temporal or spiritual power).

(xii)   The desire of each labourer should, all other things being equal, be to obtain the ownership of his own means of production.

(xiii)   A surplus owner may retain the use of his surplus property and employ servants to make that property productive paying them in exchange for their labour a proportion of the fruits of that labour.

(xiv)   Unimpeded exchange ought in ordinary conditions to suffice to ensure that the consideration demanded by a surplus owner for the use of his property is not so great, or the wages offered for the exploitation of an employer's capital so meagre, as to preclude the accumulation by the labourer of a capital from the fruits of his labour sufficient to purchase his own means of production within a reasonable time.

(xv)   Since private property must be ordered to the common good, the temporal power can regulate the right to private property and to its use, yet without stifling these by excessive taxation.

(xvi)   Where considerations of scale preclude ownership by the individual or family operating the enterprise in question, the temporal power ought, in the exaction of the tax revenues necessary for its proper functions, favour the common ownership by artificial juridical persons constituted by the labourers themselves of their own means of production.

(xvii)   The organisation of employed labourers into unions in order to defend their legal and natural rights against their employers is entirely legitimate but much less desirable than the cooperative ownership by the same of their own means of production.

(xviii)   Usury, that is, the sale of the use of money, is a form of fraud.

(xix)   The facilitation of this form of theft by the temporal power is a very great evil and constitutes the normalisation of extraordinary conditions by which the owners of surplus property may render impossible the acquisition by non-owning labourers of their own means of production.

(xx)   The lending of money at interest to an individual is not usurious if the liability of that individual is limited to some designated collateral.

(xxi)   The appropriation of all goods or all productive goods by the temporal power (i.e. socialism) as a supposed remedy for the distortions caused by usurious lending in a market economy (i.e. capitalism) is a still worse distortion issuing in even more terrible injustice.

199

Chapter 10
International Relations

Unity of mankind

Mankind possesses a certain inescapable unity:

> The human race is bound together by reciprocal ties, moral and juridical, into a great commonwealth (*in universam magnamque* [...] *populorum congregationem*) directed to the good of all nations and ruled by special laws which protect its unity and promote its prosperity.[54]

This unity arises from mankind's common origin in God and in a single ancestor, the first man; from its common dwelling place and means of temporal subsistence, the earth; from its identical, proportionate end drawn from our unity of species, and from our common, supernatural and final end, together with the common means necessary to attain it.[55] The "special laws" which rule the human race are not only those which have been agreed by written treaties, but in the first place those which derive from the customs which all or almost all nations have seen to be good to use in their relations one with another: for example, the immunity of ambassadors, or the right of trade between nations not at war.[56]

For this reason, the various temporal commonwealths existing inside or outside Christendom have duties of justice and charity toward one another, insofar as they enter into at least a transitory relation to each other, as also do, for example a buyer and a seller. "In every community, there seems to be some sort of justice, and some type of friendship also." [57]

---

[54] Pius XII, *Summi Pontificatus*, 72.

[55] Pius XII, *Summi Pontificatus*, 37-38.

[56] Suarez, *de Legibus*, II.XIX.9: "For just as in one city or province, custom (*consuetudo*) introduces law, so in the whole human race, the laws of nations could be introduced by customs (*moribus*)." This positive law of nations arises from the habitual relations of polities, and so from their several legislative powers, not from any sort of natural universal jurisdiction, which does not exist.

[57] *Nicomachean Ethics*, VIII.9. Duties of justice arise from the civic friendship which constitutes any particular society and from the consequent need to preserve some form of equality within a society, lest any member of a society be injured by the fact of belonging to it; duties of charity arise from the common vocation to share in the divine life.

However, nature by itself does not suffice to justify the *concrete* unity of the human race. Without the common supernatural end and the common means necessary to attain it, there would be a certain fittingness, all other things being equal, to the unity of the human race in a single juridical order, but no necessity. Hence natural law does not require a 'society of states' as a third necessary society, in addition to the family and to the law-governed temporal commonwealth.[58] Indeed, as the very purpose of particular commonwealths is the implementation of the natural law there is nothing to be gained by generating an additional tier of temporal authority charged with this task. This would only make sense if this ultimate temporal authority were somehow endowed with infallibility in regard to the natural law, allowing it to correct erring polities. It is not in man's gift to bestow such infallibility. Although God *has* created such a universal and infallible agency it does not belong to the temporal order. Insofar as any such purportedly ultimate temporal authority will be most remote from the natural instincts which generate the temporal order it will be more and not less likely to err in regard to the imperatives of rational nature. Insofar as its very existence is coherent only if there be attributed to it an infallibility that it does not in fact enjoy, such an agency will tend to presume to an inordinate authority over the nations and to exercise a perverse and harmful influence upon human affairs.[59]

This does not imply that the unity of mankind is unnatural, for nature itself demands that we discover from God our end and the means God has appointed to worship Him and to attain that end. In answering that demand of nature, man discovers the truths which complete the unity of the human race in the Church.

That is, in the attainment of his merely proportionate natural end man has no absolute need of a society exceeding the boundaries of his nuclear and extended families, his personal friends and his temporal city, except indirectly in that the true worship of God, required even for the attainment of this proportionate end, will in fact entail the discovery of the universal city, the Church.

> A community of men can be built by ourselves, and yet it can never at any time be a wholly fraternal community, nor overcome its limits;

---

[58] The Italian Jesuit Luigi Taparelli (1793-1862) argued in his work *Saggio teoretico di diritto naturale appogiato sul fatto* that the nations of the world tend naturally to form an international society endowed with the executive, legislative and judicial authority necessary for settling international disputes and codifying international law, and with a military power sufficient for enforcing its decisions.

[59] Pius XI, *Ubi arcano Dei*, 44-46.

that is, it cannot be made by their strength alone into a truly universal community. The unity of the human race, and a fraternal communion that rejects all division, arises from the summoning of the Word of the God who is Love.[60]

Temporal communities and individuals who have not made this discovery ought still to feel the necessity under natural law to honour their word, plighted to other such commonwealths and those within them. It is necessary even for the stable existence of a temporal commonwealth that its neighbours accept its undertakings at some level, for else even the existence of a frontier would be impossible.

However, failure to adhere to divine revelation never occurs in adults without fault,[61] either direct or indirect, and so the word of the *latrocinium* is rightly questioned.[62] Hence comes the endemic state of war between human societies, which are found to be "abandoned to the fatal drive of a private interest and collective selfishness exclusively intent on the assertion of [their] own rights and ignoring those of others".[63]

> Reason, by itself, is capable of grasping the equality between men and of giving stability to their civic coexistence, but it cannot establish fraternity. This originates in a transcendent vocation from God the Father, who loved us first, teaching us through the Son what fraternal charity is.[64]

Nevertheless, since temporal commonwealths must honour their undertakings, [65] their mutually agreed obligations, whether arising from universal or nearly universal custom, or from written compacts between individual countries, create a body of positive law[66] which provides a weak and unstable parallel to the universal society of the Church, and which ought to stand alongside it.

---

[60] Pope Benedict XVI, *Caritas in veritate*, 34.

[61] STh 1a 2ae, 89, 6 and 2a 2ae 10, 1.

[62] The guilt may be indirect, in that it may be, and usually will be, a sin other than direct rejection of divine revelation which leads God to withhold that revelation from the unbeliever.

[63] *Summi Pontificatus*, 76.

[64] Pope Benedict XVI, *Caritas in veritate*, 19.

[65] Even to those with whom they may be at war, notes Cicero; *De officiis*, 1.39.

[66] For an analysis of the development of such ideas (for good or ill), see E. Midgley, *The Natural Law Tradition and the Theory of International Relations* (Paul Elek: London, 1975).

In the realised order of Christendom, a true order of justice between temporal commonwealths obtains and is knowable. An authority capable of enforcing this order where it is in jeopardy could and perhaps ought to be created, arising either spontaneously or from the agreement of Christian nations, but, because of the danger of confusion of functions, always with the agreement and blessing of the highest spiritual power. Such was the Holy Empire created, or restored,[67] by St Leo III on Christmas Day, AD 800.[68][69]

---

[67] "Restored" in the sense that Leo III, justified by the usurpation of the Empress Irene, transferred the legal personality of the Roman Republic from the Empire in Constantinople to the person of the Frankish King and with it, the Empire's supranational functions as lieutenant of the Roman Church. However, the Roman Republic as an individual temporal commonwealth persisted on the Bosporus, though now referred to by Latins as the 'Empire of Constantinople', 'Empire of the Greeks', 'Empire of New Rome' or 'Kingdom of the Greeks' (all titles deeply offensive to the 'Byzantines'). The situation was not resolved until the Council of Florence in 1439 when Eugene IV once more recognised John VIII as Emperor of the Romans (without prejudice to the western title), in the preamble to *Laetentur caeli*; cf. Francisco de Vitoria (c. 1483-1546), *De Indis*, Book II. 25. Cf. also Leo X, *Exsurge Domine* in AD 1520: "We grieve the more that this [the Lutheran 'Reformation'] happened there because We and Our predecessors have always held this nation in the bosom of Our affection. For after the empire had been transferred by the Roman Church from the Greeks to these same Germans, Our predecessors and We always took the Church's advocates and defenders from among them." Also: Innocent III, *Venerabilem*, PL 216: 1065-67.

[68] "But from the time when the civil society of men, raised from the ruins of the Roman Empire, gave hope of its future Christian greatness, the Roman Pontiffs consecrated the political power in a wonderful manner by the institution of the Holy Empire. Greatly, indeed, was the authority of rulers ennobled; and it is not to be doubted that what was then instituted would always have been a very great gain, both to ecclesiastical and civil society, if princes and peoples had ever looked to the same object as the Church. And, indeed, tranquillity and a sufficient prosperity lasted so long as there was a friendly agreement between these two powers. If the people were turbulent, the Church was at once the mediator for peace. Recalling all to their duty, she subdued the more lawless passions partly by kindness and partly by authority. So, if, in ruling, princes erred in their government, she went to them and, putting before them the rights, needs, and lawful wants of their people, urged them to equity, mercy, and kindness. Whence it was often brought about that the dangers of civil wars and popular tumults were stayed"; Leo XIII, *Diuturnum*, 22.

[69] Suarez, *de Legibus*, III.VII.13, says of the emperor: "He shares in the excellence of the spiritual order by his relation to the pontifical dignity [...] And perhaps in relation to that end of defending the Church, he has some authority of convoking or moving Catholic princes, or also a similar authority of settling and ending quarrels between them, when it is needful to avoid war and harm to the Church." It is perhaps in deference to this participation in the spiritual order that the Christian emperors were ordained to the diaconate or subdiaconate at their coronations. See J. Bryce, *The Holy Roman Empire* (Macmillan & Co.: Oxford, 1864), 48.

The difficulty with such institutions lies in their tendency either to seek to repress the proper autonomy of the temporal commonwealths, violating the principle of subsidiarity, or to usurp the spiritual functions of the ecclesiastical hierarchy, or both. This danger was already evident between AD 312 and AD 1806.[70] It is a hundred times more manifest in the behaviour of the secular supranational entities of modern times who, refusing to acknowledge the supernatural basis for human fraternity, tend, because there is no separate and autonomous temporal common good of the whole human race, to suppress and absorb the naturally occurring particular commonwealths of which they are composed, in order to take the latter's natural basis for themselves.[71]

An analogy may be useful here. If two men were both morally certain they had dropped a large banknote on the ground, although one of them erred in good faith, and both went to snatch the single banknote lying there, there would be no means of resolving the disagreement short of a gracious concession on the part of one or violence. It would be impossible for a court to settle the matter subsequently because while *ex hypothesi* one of the two men would be legitimately resisting theft and the other committing it, it would be impossible to prove which was doing which. It might be useful to set up a policeman as arbiter between them but his decision would be necessarily arbitrary and it would also be dangerous to empower a public official to exercise such arbitrary authority. All things considered, it might be better just to let them fight it out.

The desire for universal temporal sovereignty is intrinsically disordered precisely because the merely temporal human good does not require vast

---

[70] That is, from the conversion of Constantine to the abdication of Francis II.

[71] "[St Thomas] also composed a substantial moral theology, capable of directing all human acts in accordance with the supernatural last end of man. And as he is, as We have said, the perfect theologian, so he gives infallible rules and precepts of life not only for individuals, but also for civil and domestic society, which is the object also of moral science, both economic and politic. Hence those superb chapters in the second part of the *Summa Theologiae* on paternal or domestic government, the lawful power of the State or the nation, natural and international law, peace and war, justice and property, laws and the obedience they command, and the duty of taking thought both for the needs of individuals and for public prosperity, both in the natural and the supernatural order. If these precepts were religiously and inviolably observed in private life and public affairs, and in the duties of mutual obligation between nations, nothing else would be required to secure mankind that 'peace of Christ in the Kingdom of Christ' which the world so ardently longs for. It is therefore to be wished that the teachings of Aquinas, more particularly his exposition of international law and the laws governing the mutual relations of peoples, became more and more studied, for it contains the foundations of a genuine 'League of Nations'"; Pius XI, *Studiorum ducem*, 20.

dominions to be realised and is indeed prejudiced by them, as St Augustine observes:

I should like first to inquire for a little what reason, what prudence, there is in wishing to glory in the greatness and extent of the empire, when you cannot point out the happiness of men who are always rolling, with dark fear and cruel lust, in warlike slaughters and in blood, which, whether shed in civil or foreign war, is still human blood; so that their joy may be compared to glass in its fragile splendour, of which one is horribly afraid lest it should be suddenly broken in pieces. That this may be more easily discerned, let us not come to nought by being carried away with empty boasting, or blunt the edge of our attention by loud-sounding names of things, when we hear of peoples, kingdoms, provinces. But let us suppose a case of two men; for each individual man, like one letter in a language, is as it were the element of a city or kingdom, however far-spreading in its occupation of the earth. Of these two men let us suppose that one is poor, or rather of middling circumstances; the other very rich. But the rich man is anxious with fears, pining with discontent, burning with covetousness, never secure, always uneasy, panting from the perpetual strife of his enemies, adding to his patrimony indeed by these miseries to an immense degree, and by these additions also heaping up most bitter cares. But that other man of moderate wealth is contented with a small and compact estate, most dear to his own family, enjoying the sweetest peace with his kindred neighbours and friends, in piety religious, benignant in mind, healthy in body, in life frugal, in manners chaste, in conscience secure. I know not whether anyone can be such a fool, that he dare hesitate which to prefer. As, therefore, in the case of these two men, so in two families, in two nations, in two kingdoms, this test of tranquillity holds good; and if we apply it vigilantly and without prejudice, we shall quite easily see where the mere show of happiness dwells, and where real felicity.[72]

---

[72] St Augustine, *The City of God*, IV.3. Cf. A. Fimister, *Robert Schuman: Neo Scholastic Humanism and the Reunification of Europe* (Peter Lang: Brussels, 2008). For his part, John Henry Newman wrote: "It is happier, I think, for the bulk of a people, to belong to a small State which makes little noise in the world, than to a large one"; *Sermons Preached on Various Occasions*, 'The Pope and the Revolution'.

Movement between commonwealths

"A disposition, in fact, of the divinely sanctioned natural order divides the human race into social groups, nations or States, which are mutually independent in organization and in the direction of their internal life."[73] Since the end proportionate to man's nature, for the attainment of which the temporal commonwealth exists, does not in itself require a universal civil order there are a multitude of such polities. Since the family "is antecedent, as well in idea as in fact, to the gathering of men into a community"[74] the particular temporal commonwealth naturally arises at least in part from common descent.[75] This is not an absolute consideration, as the transition from a kin-based social organisation to a fully formed city is paradigmatically marked by the federation and thus the transcendence of such familial groupings. Therefore, while it may be fitting it is not in itself necessary that all groups sharing common descent form a single commonwealth whether singly or in combination with other such groups.[76]

Again, since the goods of the earth are given to the human race as a whole, richer nations have obligations of justice to nations marked by material privation, analogous to the obligations of the rich to the poor within the same land.[77] More generally, temporal commonwealths have the merely negative duty in justice of not impeding each other from attaining their proper ends.[78]

Just as the individual and the family, so also the temporal commonwealth has a duty to harbour the outcast and must offer refuge according to its capacity to those in mortal need or fleeing unjust persecution.[79] Furthermore, it will

---

[73] *Summi Pontificatus*, 72.

[74] *Rerum novarum*, 13.

[75] Cf. Aristotle, *Politics*, I.2. Hence arises the concept of the nation (from *nasci*, 'to be born').

[76] The unnuanced proclamation of a principle of 'national self-determination' by Woodrow Wilson in his 'Fourteen Points' of 8ᵗʰ January 1918 led to much misery and death in the succeeding decades.

[77] Pope Paul VI, *Populorum progressio*, 49; Pope John Paul II, *Sollicitudo rei socialis*, 9.

[78] A. Ottaviani, *Institutiones Iuris Publici Ecclesiastici*, vol. 2, 154 ff.

[79] In an Apostolic Constitution of 1952, *Exsul familia Nazarethana*, Pope Pius XII quoted these words from a letter he had sent to the American bishops in 1948: "You know indeed how preoccupied we have been and with what anxiety we have followed those who have been forced by revolutions in their own countries, or by unemployment or hunger, to leave their homes and live in foreign lands. The natural law itself, no less than devotion to humanity, urges that ways of migration be opened to these people. For the Creator of the universe made all good things primarily for the good of all. Since land everywhere offers the possibility of supporting a large number of people, the sovereignty of the State,

prejudice its own good if it altogether prohibit the migration onto its territory of persons born elsewhere. However, those without a well-founded fear of unjust persecution or mortal need who seek to settle in a foreign land must accept the judgement of the temporal authorities of that place as to its ability and willingness to offer them the right to resettle in their territory.[80] These authorities may also choose when granting them this right to withhold full citizenship from them and even from their offspring, although it is desirable that this be only a temporary measure. The angelic doctor writes:

> They [sc. non-Israelites wishing to settle in the promised land] were not at once admitted to citizenship: just as it was law with some nations that no one was deemed a citizen except after two or three generations, as the Philosopher says in *Politics* III. The reason for this was that if foreigners were allowed to meddle with the affairs of a nation as soon as they settled down in its midst, many dangers might occur, since the foreigners not yet having the common good firmly at heart might attempt something hurtful to the people. Hence it was that the Law prescribed in respect of certain nations that had close relations with the Jews, namely, the Egyptians among whom they had been born and educated, and the Idumeans, the children of Esau, Jacob's brother, that they should be admitted to the fellowship of the people after the third generation; whereas others, with whom their relations had been hostile, such as the Ammonites and Moabites, were never to be admitted to citizenship; while the Amalekites, who were yet more hostile to them, and had no fellowship of kindred with them, were to be held as foes in perpetuity: for it is written in Exodus 17: 'The war of the Lord shall be against Amalek from generation to generation.' [81]

---

although it must be respected, cannot be exaggerated to the point that access to this land is, for inadequate or unjustified reasons, denied to needy and decent people from other nations, provided of course, that the public need, considered very carefully, does not forbid this."

[80] In moderating such migration, rulers may justly take into account the need to maintain the unity of the commonwealth, fostered by common inheritance, language, and history, as well as by the true religion.

[81] STh 1a 2ae, 105, 3. Of course the preservation of the *mores* of the chosen people required more severe measures when they were formed out of but one beleaguered nation on the earth.

Finally, since the family is prior to the community, the temporal commonwealth may not prohibit its subjects from departing its territory to live abroad unless such migration were to threaten its very subsistence.

Warfare

Temporal commonwealths will from time to time inflict, or attempt to inflict, grave wrongs on their neighbours. Sometimes these wrongs will be so grave that were those charged with directing the injured commonwealth to suffer them in silence, or to offer no resistance, they would themselves gravely fail in their obligations to their subjects. Before declaring war, they ought to seek voluntary restitution.[82] Should this be denied, the great evil of war suggests that they have normally a duty to seek arbitration voluntarily; this can be a very reasonable task for the supreme spiritual power.[83] If one or both refuse such arbitration (and subject to the qualifications already raised), and lesser forms of coercion have failed, recourse to arms may be unavoidable. Although very occasionally, as with our earlier example of the banknote, both parties will be subjectively in the right, objectively only one party can be.[84]

Four conditions are generally laid down for a just war, if negotiation and arbitration fail: right intention, legitimate authority, just cause (*ius ad bellum*) and suitable conduct in battle (*ius in bello*).[85] We need not delay over the first of these conditions, since it is common to all voluntary actions that they must be

---

[82] Deut. 20:10-12: "If at any time thou come to fight against a city, thou shalt first offer it peace. If they receive it, and open the gates to thee, all the people that are therein, shall be saved, and shall serve thee paying tribute. But if they will not make peace, and shall begin war against thee, thou shalt besiege it"; Cicero, *De Officiis*, 1.34: "In the case of a state in its external relations, the rights of war must be strictly observed. For since there are two ways of settling a dispute: first, by discussion; second, by physical force; and since the former is characteristic of man, the latter of the brute, we must resort to force when we may not avail ourselves of discussion."

[83] This would be without prejudice to the Supreme Pontiff's native authority to intervene in temporal matters *ratione peccati*, and to furnish a temporal ruler when the temporal power is frustrated. See below, 'The Two Swords'.

[84] It is possible that neither is, as when two countries fight over the territory of an independent third country.

[85] St Robert Bellarmine, *Controversiae*, 'On the members of the Church', bk. 3, ch. 15. For the first three intentions, see STh 2a 2ae 40, 1.

directed to virtue, and not performed for vainglory or under the sway of passion.[86]

The legitimate authority is that which has charge of the commonwealth which is to fight:

> It is not the business of a private individual to declare war, because he can seek for redress of his rights from the tribunal of his superior. Moreover, it is not the business of a private individual to summon together the people, which has to be done in wartime. [...] For this reason Augustine says (*Against Faustus,* XXII.75): "The natural order conducive to peace among mortals demands that the power to declare and counsel war should be in the hands of rulers."[87]

The just cause is of course some grave fault in the enemy which is harmful to oneself or to another. Here again the common doctor quotes the bishop of Hippo:

> A just war is customarily defined as one that avenges wrongs, when a nation or state has to be punished (*plectenda*), for refusing to make amends for the wrongs inflicted by its subjects, or for refusing to restore what it has seized unjustly.[88]

The distinction drawn here by St Augustine was treated more systematically by later thinkers, and led to the classification of wars as either defensive or offensive.[89] According to this classification, a defensive war is fought to repel an enemy seeking to harm or engross lands, goods or people, or to dispossess an enemy who has taken unjust possession of the same.[90] An offensive war seeks to vindicate violated rights, for example, to punish an enemy who has killed one's citizens while they were sojourning in his land, or who has destroyed the goods of one's merchants. In practice, a war is likely to exhibit both features: the treaty of peace signed after a victorious 'defensive' war may

---

[86] Bellarmine observes that should this condition be lacking and the others present, the war is rendered not strictly unjust, but simply bad; 'On the members of the Church', bk. 3, ch. 15.

[87] STh 2a 2ae 40, 1.

[88] *Questions on the Heptateuch,* Book VI.10; quoted in STh 2a 2ae 40, 1.

[89] St Thomas explains likewise that the two acts of the virtue of *vindicatio,* a potential part of justice, are defending and avenging; STh 2a 2ae 108, 2. However, he understands this to be a virtue of a private individual; the ruler as such exercises justice simply speaking (ibid., ad 1).

[90] St Robert Bellarmine, *Controversiae,* 'On the members of the Church', bk. 3, ch. 15; see also Francisco Suarez, *De charitate,* disp. XIII.I.6.

require satisfaction to be made by the erstwhile enemy for the loss of life and goods which the victorious side suffered in the conflict, while an 'offensive' war is liable to be fought at least in part as a means to ward off future outrages similar to those already received.

The possibility of a just, defensive war derives from the natural inclination which each thing has to preserve itself in being.[91] Since in accordance with this natural inclination even an individual man may by his private authority fight off an unjust aggressor, much more may a republic do this, the good of its continued existence being greater than the good of one man's. This natural duty of defending the commonwealth implies that a private man may even fight off an invader without waiting for public authority to declare war, provided that that authority has not determined otherwise.[92]

Whence comes the right to fight the so-called offensive war? It is sometimes objected that neither side has jurisdiction over the other, and hence may not seek to punish the other, just as a private man, though he may repel an aggressive fellow citizen even to the point of lethal force if need be, may not punish him or take satisfaction from him by his own authority, since he has no jurisdiction over him, but must instead go to the courts. It is also objected that an offensive war would make the party that declares it judge and plaintiff in the same cause.[93]

Nevertheless, lest the strong should with impunity abandon themselves to rapine and bloodshed, it appears necessary for the human race, and hence a matter of natural right, that a gravely wronged commonwealth may claim satisfaction and, other means failing, take it by force.[94] Although the ruler of one republic is not the ordinary judge of others, writes Bellarmine, yet by reason of necessity he is made in a certain way the judge of those who have wronged his own people, and may punish them with the sword.[95] Again, to be

[91] STh 2a 2ae 64, 7.

[92] St Robert Bellarmine, *Controversiae*, 'On the members of the Church', bk. 3, ch. 15.

[93] See J. Murphy, 'Suarez, Aquinas and the Just War: Self Defense or Punishment?', in H. Justenhoven and W. Barbieri (ed.) *From Just War to Modern Peace Ethics*, Arbeiten zur Kirchengeschichte Book 120 (De Gruyter: Berlin/Boston, 2012).

[94] Cf. Suarez, *De Charitate*, disp. XIII.IV.7.

[95] *Controversiae*, 'On the members of the Church', bk. 3, ch. 15. Moses orders this to be done to the Madianites for having lured the Israelites into idolatry; Num. 25. Suarez, likewise, remarks that when a ruler declares war on another ruler or commonwealth, he exercises jurisdiction over that ruler or commonwealth, since the offending party has made himself subject to that ruler by reason of his crime, *ratione delicti ei subditur*; *De charitate*, XIII.2.1. An alternative theory which some authors draw from the work of Francisco de Vitoria

judge and actor in one's own cause is not wholly forbidden, being lawful when there is no other judge to whom one may turn; thus in a trial of lèse-majesté, the monarch is both judge, by his representative, and also the party seeking redress.[96]

Alternatively, one could see all apparently offensive wars as being in reality defensive: the party which has unjustly seized the merchandise or harmed the persons of another country may be said to have usurped some of the jurisdiction of that country, as surely as if it had invaded and occupied a part of its land. In seeking to vindicate its violated rights, the injured country is defending itself against this usurpation just as much as if it was seeking to prevent an enemy from occupying its territory, or to dislodge the enemy after occupation. By understanding things in this way, one avoids the difficulties raised against the concept of offensive war, and one does not need to have recourse to the theory of a jurisdiction of the wronged party over the party responsible for the crimes.[97] It follows that no war, unless expressly mandated by God or His vicar, can be strictly described as punitive, since punishment presupposes jurisdiction.

If, nevertheless, we retain the notion of 'offensive war', then the punishment of delinquent states, like that of delinquent citizens, would aim principally at restoring the violated social order by the expiation which the offender makes. Secondarily, like the punishment of citizens, it would also be emendatory, exemplary, expiatory and preservative: seeking, that is, to improve the morals of the offender, to set an example to other states, to remove the stain from the name of the offending polity and to preserve the international social order from future harm. Again, as with the punishment of individual citizens, the restorative end must limit the other ends, since no one may be punished beyond his due even for a good purpose, for evil may not be done that good may come. Still assuming the hypothesis of the punitive war, we may say that

---

proposes that the ruler of the belligerent nation in an offensive war acts by a kind of delegation of the authority of the whole world, in virtue of an international common good; cf. E. Midgley, *The Natural Law Tradition and the Theory of International Relations* (Paul Elek: London, 1975), 89-90. However, the concept of a natural temporal authority of the whole world has been rejected above.

[96] Suarez notes that God Himself, "to whom the public power is similar", acts as judge in His own cause; *De charitate*, XIII.4.7.

[97] Without wholly abandoning the category of offensive war, T. Ortolan acknowledges that most of the motives commonly adduced for such wars give rise to actions which are in reality defensive, and offensive only in appearance; *Dictionnaire de Théologie Catholique*, 'Guerre: II, "La Guerre et le droit naturel"', 3'. It seems possible to render this claim universal.

per se, if a justly defeated enemy could not sufficiently expiate his crime by the surrender of his possessions, the victorious side might enslave or even kill defeated combatants.[98] This practice however was happily abandoned between Christian nations, whose example later spread to other nations.

In the conduct of war, violence must be restricted in intention to combatants, since these alone are executants of the enemy's injustice. Some harm to non-combatants, proportionate to the good to be achieved, may be foreseen but not intended. "Every operation of war which aims indiscriminately at the destruction of whole cities, or of widespread areas with their inhabitants, is a crime against God".[99] "The fathers shall not be put to death for the children, nor the children for the fathers, but every one shall die for his own sin."[100]

Since a friend is another self, one commonwealth may also fight a war on behalf of another, if that other desires it, and the criteria of justice are met.[101] Indeed, since the duties of charity bind commonwealths no less than individuals, if one country is labouring under some grave wrong, a third party which is able to provide help without great harm to itself is bound to do so from charity, even without being asked.[102] In the case of tyranny, the rulers of one commonwealth do not as such have the right to vindicate wrongs done by the rulers of another commonwealth against the latter's own citizens. Nevertheless, if those wrongs reach such a point that the citizens themselves could justly oust those rulers, even by non-constitutional means,[103] then other states may lend their assistance, if this is desired by those citizens.

To fight a just war, a commonwealth need not judge victory certain or even likely. To the extent that the evils that threaten it are greater, to that extent it may defend itself even as the chances of victory are less.[104] To preserve the

---

[98] Deut. 20:13.

[99] *Gaudium et spes*, 80.

[100] Deut. 24:16. Hence St Ambrose excommunicated the emperor Theodosius for avenging himself for the death of his governor in Thessalonika by a massacre of the citizens. Thomas Hobbes stated that St Ambrose deserved to be put to death for this act; *Leviathan*, chapter 42.

[101] Gen. 14.

[102] Cf. *Syllabus of Errors*, condemned proposition 62: "The principle of non-intervention, as it is called, ought to be proclaimed and observed."

[103] See pp. 96-99.

[104] And its action can be supernaturally meritorious. St Bernard wrote: "Indeed, danger or victory for the Christian are weighed by the focus of the heart, not the fortunes of war. If he fights for a good cause, the outcome of the battle can never be evil; and likewise the

greatest goods - life, liberty, and the true faith - a country should be willing to fight even against overwhelming odds, committing its cause to the One in whose hands are all human things, since the battle is the Lord's: *non est enim vestra pugna, sed Dei*.[105] Even when resistance is doomed, it may still be better to offer it, since easy conquest may encourage further injustices, while even doomed resistance may be an act of charity to other potential victims.[106] Yet when the purpose of a war is to vindicate particular violated rights, it will not normally be prudent to offer battle unless there is a greater chance of success than of failure, for otherwise the enemy will be uselessly emboldened. Again, the difficulty of ensuring a merely proportional vindication of rights increases with the increasing power of arms.[107]

*　　*　　*

It is not enough that the temporal polity proclaim the truth of the Catholic Faith in its public law. The Catholic Church, the City of God, is the only society perfect by its own native power for "there is no justice save in that republic whose founder and ruler is Christ".[108] The Lord has instructed her to preach the Gospel to all nations, teaching them to obey all that He has commanded and baptising them in the name of the Father and of the Son and of the Holy Spirit, and her children may never renounce or even suspend the ambition and intention that she be identified with the whole of organised society. The temporal commonwealth must be reconstituted as the community of the baptised. Yet even outside the Church the authority of temporal rulers is real and must be respected, while within its walls the rights afforded the unbeliever by natural law must remain inviolate. God has mercy on whom He will have mercy and the use of violence to secure adherence to the heavenly city is a

result can never be considered good if the cause is evil and the intention is unrighteous"; St Bernard of Clairvaux, *In Praise of the New Knighthood* (Cistercian Publications: Kalamazoo, 2000), 35.

[105] 2 Par. 20:15.

[106] Before the fall of Constantinople on May 29th 1453, Blessed Constantine XI addressed his troops in the following words: "I am imploring you to fight like men with brave souls, as you have done from the beginning up to this day, against the enemy of our faith. I hand over to you my glorious, famous, respected, noble city, the shining Queen of cities, our homeland. You know well, my brothers, that we have four obligations in common, which force us to prefer death over survival: first, our faith and piety; second, our homeland; third, the emperor anointed by the Lord; and fourth, our relatives and friends."

[107] Hence, Pope John XXIII judged matters thus in *Pacem in terris*, 127: "In this age of ours, which boasts in atomic power, it is unreasonable (*alienum est a ratione*) for war to be still a suitable way of restoring violated rights."

[108] *City of God*, II.21.

forbidden blasphemy. The Church enjoys the native right to employ coercive penalties against those of her children who err and, in Christendom, to employ the temporal power to do so. Those outside the pale of baptism are not so subject and to use such means to bring them in is an insult to the sovereignty of God's grace. More than merely violence directed against man, it constitutes violence against God Himself. God has handed over to men the power to become children of God in the form of baptism and in *this* way the Kingdom of God suffers violence but no one comes to the Lord unless the Father draw him[109] and God is not mocked.[110] It is therefore forbidden to invade other lands simply on the basis that their peoples are non-believers or in order to compel adherence to the Gospel.[111]

---

[109] John 6:44.

[110] Galatians 6:7. In a democratic society the task of conforming the civil order to Christ's Kingship and the task of converting the people consequently differ only in idea not in fact.

[111] 'Alcuini Sive Albini Epistolae', no. 111, ed. E. Dummler, in *Monumenta Germaniae Historica*, Epp. II (Hannover, 1892), 159-162; S. Allott, *Alcuin of York: his life and letters* (Sessions: York, 1987), 74.

Theses

(i) Temporal commonwealths have duties of justice and charity to each other, arising from natural and divine law, custom, and written treaty.

(ii) While it is fitting that there be some juridic order between temporal commonwealths, it is unnecessary and unwise to seek to constitute an international political society.

(iii) Within Christendom, an authority capable of enforcing the duties of justice between its provinces may but need not be erected, with the blessing of the spiritual power.

(iv) It is not necessary but may be fitting that all the members of a nation belong to the same civil society.

(v) Owing to the universal destination of goods richer republics have duties of justice to poorer ones.

(vi) Although civil society possesses an obligation to provide refuge to the outcast, it may not admit immigrants who by their numbers or qualities are liable to corrupt its own common good.

(vii) A temporal commonwealth may defend itself by war when other means have failed, when it has a right intention, just cause, and observes proportionate means.

(viii) The so-called 'punitive' war is better understood as a particular case of defensive war.

(ix) If one country is labouring under some grave wrong, a third party which is able to provide help without great harm to itself is bound to do so from charity, even without being asked.

(x) When it is fighting for the highest goods, a commonwealth need not judge victory certain or even likely.

(xi) It is forbidden to invade other lands simply because their inhabitants are non-believers.

Chapter 11

The Two Swords

He said to them: 'When I sent you without purse, and scrip, and shoes, did you want anything?' But they said: 'Nothing.' Then said he unto them: 'But now he that hath a purse, let him take it, and likewise a scrip; and he that hath not, let him sell his coat, and buy a sword. For I say to you, that this that is written must yet be fulfilled in me: *And with the wicked was he reckoned.* For the things concerning me have an end.' But they said: 'Lord, behold here are two swords.' And he said to them: 'It is enough.'[1]

The two powers

We have argued that 'the State', conceived as a perfect society generated by men independently of divine revelation, is a false category. There is but one society which is intrinsically perfect, that is, which does not depend for its existence on any other perfect society. This society is the City of God or the Catholic Church, and its end is beatitude. When it includes within itself the temporal power which belongs to it by right, a power which can in such circumstances also direct men to natural happiness in the present life, its members form Christendom.[2] This is why rather than speaking of 'the relations of Church and State', we have spoken of the relations of the spiritual and temporal power.

We have seen that the temporal power must subordinate itself to the spiritual, because the goods at which they respectively aim are related as penultimate and

---

[1] Lk. 22:34-38.

[2] Cf. C. Journet, *The Church of the Word Incarnate*, tr. A. Downes (Sheed & Ward: London and New York, 1955), 243, on the mediaeval use of the term 'Christendom': "It always connoted, whether directly or indirectly, proximately, or remotely, the Church herself. But it directed attention rather on her lay elements, her relations with the world of culture, her temporal interests, her social activities and embodiments, the organized political whole she was trying to sanctify." The same author quotes with approval the words of another 20th author, Jean Rupp: 'If the *Ecclesia* is the society of Christians as under the jurisdiction of the hierarchy, the *Christianitas* is the society of Christians as subject to the jurisdiction of temporal rulers"; ibid., n. 2.

final end, and to the order of ends corresponds the order of agents.[3] Yet more than this, the two are related as flesh and spirit. The temporal good, that is, must not only be directed toward the spiritual good but can itself only exist by the latter's power. Not only must the body's health be put at the service of the soul's health; the body itself cannot exist as a human body, absent the soul. Just as a body which becomes detached from the soul must die, so if men seek their common temporal good apart from their common immortal good, they will never reach it: secularisation is death.[4]

Mixed matters

Matters which relate directly to both the spiritual and temporal power, but under different aspects, are described as 'mixed'.[5] Each power may legislate about such things, in regard to that aspect of the thing which is relevant to it. Here we must make various distinctions.

Some things are said to be mixed by nature. For example, we have seen that marriage falls as a sacrament within the scope of the spiritual power, and as something necessary for the continuance of the commonwealth within that of the temporal. Other matters mixed by their nature include the protection of public morality, the instruction of the young, and the care of the poor. The mission of the Church obliges her at all times to be concerned for such things.

Other things are said to be mixed only in given circumstances. For example, farming is in itself a matter for the temporal power, since it is an activity that exists directly only for the sake of man's natural life. Yet since wheat and grapes, for example, are necessary for the sacraments to exist, if the continued existence of these crops in a given region were imperilled, the Church would then rightly concern herself with agricultural law. Or again, building regulations are in themselves a matter for the temporal power, but insofar as they apply to the building of churches they are in those circumstances something mixed.

---

[3] See above, 'Temporal authority (I): its origin'.

[4] *Tametsi futura*, 8: "When Jesus Christ is absent, human reason fails, being bereft of its chief protection and light"; ibid. 11-12: "Once the hope and expectation of eternal happiness is taken away, temporal goods will be greedily sought after. Every man will strive to secure the largest share for himself. Hence arise envy, jealousy, hatred. The consequences are conspiracy, anarchy, nihilism. There is neither peace abroad nor security at home. Public life is stained with crime. So great is this struggle of the passions and so serious the dangers involved, that we must either anticipate ultimate ruin or seek for an efficient remedy".

[5] Cf. A. Ottaviani, *Compendium Iuris Publici Ecclesiastici*, 382 ff.

Again, some mixed things are natural by essence, while others are supernatural. For example, fire regulations concern a merely natural reality, preserving buildings against conflagration. A Corpus Christi procession, on the other hand, as a homage to the Eucharistic Lord, is inconceivable except in relation to the supernatural order. Akin to supernatural things are so-called 'supernaturalised ones', which although they have a natural essence have been so elevated by some positive act that they now have the character of supernatural ones. For example, marriage exists by nature, but has been elevated by Christ into a sacrament of the New Law when contracted between the baptised.

A final distinction to be drawn is between the separable and inseparable effects which a thing brings with it. An inseparable effect follows from the nature of a thing, while a separable effect occurs as a result of some positive act of the law-giver. For example, religious vows necessarily bring with them an obligation to practise the evangelical counsels, but they do not necessarily and by their nature entail the loss of a right to vote.

Having posited these distinctions, we may state the following principles:

(i) In legislating about mixed matters, whether they are such by nature or by contingent fact, the two powers should work in concord,[6] while safeguarding the superior rights of the Church: since heavenly beatitude is a greater good than earthly happiness, the temporal power must cede to the spiritual where the latter judges that its goal would otherwise be impeded. Hence the temporal power cannot forbid something which the spiritual power commands or counsels, nor command something which she forbids. For example, clergy may not assume seats in the legislature, if their king commands them and ecclesiastical authority forbids them.[7]

(ii) Without prejudice to (i), each power may legislate about natural things, and about the separable effects of supernatural ones. For example, each power may concern itself with the building of new churches, the temporal power considering, for example, the safety of the structure and whether it fits well in its surroundings, the spiritual power considering the spiritual needs of the local

---

[6] Leo XIII, *Immortale Dei*, 35: "In matters, however, of mixed jurisdiction, it is in the highest degree consonant to nature, as also to the designs of God, that so far from one of the powers separating itself from the other, or still less coming into conflict with it, complete harmony, such as is suited to the end for which each power exists, should be preserved between them."

[7] This does not however imply the duty of obeying a holder of spiritual power if he manifestly errs by commanding something which is clearly unrelated or contrary to the end for which he has such power. See below.

population. Or again, the temporal power may decide that religious profession brings with it the loss of active voice in national elections.

(iii) The temporal power can do nothing in regard to supernatural or supernaturalised things, for example, defining the correct structure of the liturgy, or about their inseparable consequences, for example, legislating to allow the temporal power to dissolve an unconsummated marriage which, although possible, is possible only to the spiritual power.[8]

(iv) The temporal power within Christendom can make the transgression of a law concerning some supernatural thing into a civil offence, because of the harm done by the transgression to the well-being of the commonwealth.[9]

We have already spoken of the rights and duties which the temporal power possesses of itself, including its rights and duties in religious matters both inside and outside Christendom.[10] We must now complete this analysis by looking at the matter, so to speak, from the other end: that is, by considering how the superiority of the spiritual power affect the rights and duties of temporal rulers. As before, the demands of clarity suggest that we begin with what is in itself the abnormal situation, that is, the relation of the Church to bearers of temporal power outside Christendom.

The authority of the spiritual power over the temporal power outside Christendom

The Catholic Church claims for herself the right to influence baptised Christians not only by persuasion, but as having a true jurisdiction over them: she claims, that is, the right to legislate for them in view of their supernatural end.[11] Where this jurisdiction of the Church is not recognised by the temporal

---

[8] *Immortale Dei*, 14: "Whatever, therefore in things human is of a sacred character, whatever belongs either of its own nature or by reason of the end to which it is referred, to the salvation of souls, or to the worship of God, is subject to the power and judgment of the Church. Whatever is to be ranged under the civil and political order is rightly subject to the civil authority."

[9] For example, King Charles X of France legislated to make the desecration of the Blessed Sacrament a capital offence.

[10] See: Chapter 6 above.

[11] The existence of this legislative power was defined at the Council of Trent, Session VII, decree 'On Baptism', canon 8: "If any one saith, that the baptized are freed from all the precepts, whether written or transmitted, of holy Church, in such a way that they are not bound to observe them, unless they have chosen of their own accord to submit themselves thereunto; let him be anathema." Cf. *Immortale Dei*, 11: "In very truth, Jesus Christ gave to

power, that is, outside Christendom,[12] logically the Church can nevertheless claim from the temporal power those rights which are due to her under natural law, as they are due outside Christendom to any religious body which does not act or teach contrary to natural law itself.[13] Natural justice obliges rulers to grant these claims, including liberty of worship, teaching, publication, and persuasion. Nonetheless the Holy See does not cease to present herself as a sovereign power simply as such and independently of any temporal dominion she might also wield.

In such circumstances, these rights of the Church are sometimes enshrined within a concordat, that is, a bilateral contract between the spiritual and the temporal power, each presenting itself as an independent sovereign body.[14] Such agreements bear a relation to the proper union of the two powers similar to that which a legal arrangement between estranged spouses about the custody of children and the division of property bears to their joint domestic life. Moreover, such agreements, on the side of the temporal power, are often promises to do only what it is already obliged to do, for example, to guarantee to Catholics liberty of worship, while on the part of the Church they have often involved the giving of favours and privileges, for example, a right to secular rulers to nominate bishops. Nevertheless, even though the terms be thus unfavourable, ecclesiastical authorities are obliged by natural law to honour such agreements once made, while the civil authorities are obliged to honour them by a double title, namely in virtue of a pre-existing, though unacknowledged, obligation and by virtue of their promise to do so.

His Apostles unrestrained authority in regard to things sacred, together with the genuine and most true power of making laws, as also with the twofold right of judging and of punishing, which flow from that power". The position of Marsilius of Padua, according to which no pope or bishop possesses any jurisdiction greater than that of a simple priest, except insofar as this may have been granted by the authority of the emperor, was condemned by Pope John XXII in 1327.

[12] Cf. *Libertas*, 40: "Others oppose not the existence of the Church, nor indeed could they; yet they despoil her of the nature and rights of a perfect society, and maintain that it does not belong to her to legislate, to judge, or to punish, but only to exhort, to advise, and to rule her subjects in accordance with their own consent and will."

[13] We shall see however in the final chapter that such benevolent neutrality is not only gravely imperfect but also not even fully achievable.

[14] Cf. Pius X, *Vehementer Nos*, 5: "The concordat entered upon by the Sovereign Pontiff and the French Government was, like all treaties of the same kind concluded between States, a bilateral contract binding on both parties to it."; see also L. Billot, *Tractatus de Ecclesia Christi* (Prati: Giachetti, 1910) t. 2, 'de Habitudine Ecclesiae ad civilem societatem', Part III q. 19 art. 2, *De concordatis*; A. Ottaviani, *Compendium Iuris Publici Ecclesiastici*, 4th edition (Rome: Vatican Press, 1954), 433 ff.

Since the baptised have received not a spirit of slavery but of adoption as sons of God, it is fitting that they, more than other subjects, be governed without coercion.[15] Yet their rulers must not allege this fittingness as a cloak for laziness or timidity. Since the Church has jurisdiction over the baptised for the salvation of their souls, she may even outside Christendom remind baptised temporal rulers of their duties to God in the very exercise of their office, and, with no infringement of their just liberty, punish them with suitable penalties if they do not fulfil them.[16] In such cases, where the temporal ruler, but not his temporal power, is subject to the Church, she can command him, in his exercise of temporal power, to obey God, to whom all temporal power is by nature subject. For the Church has jurisdiction over the baptised man who bears temporal power, both as to his private and his public acts. *Dixisti peccata Caroli, dic modo peccata Caesaris*, said the Dominican theologian Domingo de Soto after having heard the confession of Emperor Charles V: "You have told me Charles's sins - now tell me Caesar's." Likewise, his confrère Girolamo

---

[15] Cf. St Thomas More, *Selected Writings*, ed. J. Thornton and S. Varenne (New York: Vintage Books, 2003), 89-90: "Turning to Peter separately, He said: 'Put your sword away' – as if to say, I do not wish to be defended with the sword, and I have chosen you for the mission of fighting not with such a sword but with the sword of the word of God. Therefore return the sword of iron to the sheath where it belongs – that is, to the hands of worldly princes to be used against evildoers. You who are the apostles of my flock have another sword far more terrible than any sword of iron, a sword by which a wicked man is sometimes cut off from the Church (like a rotten limb removed from my mystical body) and handed over to Satan for the destruction of the flesh to save the spirit (provided only that the man is of a mind to be healed) and to enable him once more to be joined and grafted into my body – though it sometimes happens that a man suffering from a hopeless disease is also handed over to the invisible death of the soul, lest he should infect the healthy members with his disease. But I am so far from wishing you to make use of that sword of iron (whose proper sheath, you must recognize, is the secular magistrates) that I do not think even that spiritual sword, whose use properly pertains to you, should be unsheathed very often." The Council of Trent was to declare shortly afterwards: "Although the sword of excommunication is the very sinews of ecclesiastical discipline, and very salutary for keeping the people in their duty, yet is it to be used with sobriety and great circumspection, seeing that experience teaches, that if it be rashly or for slight causes wielded, it is more despised than feared, and produces destruction rather than safety"; Session XXV, Decree 'On reform', cap. 3.

[16] Cf. Pius X, *Singulari quadam*, 3: "No matter what the Christian does, even in the realm of temporal goods, he cannot ignore the supernatural good. Rather, according to the dictates of Christian philosophy, he must order all things to the ultimate end, namely, the highest good. All his actions, insofar as they are morally either good or bad, that is to say, insofar as they agree or disagree with the natural and divine law, are subject to the judgment and judicial office of the Church."

Savonarola is said to have refused absolution to Lorenzo de' Medici on his death-bed for refusing to restore the liberty of the Republic of Florence.

Evidently, the spiritual power can only intervene in temporal matters to the extent that a spiritual good is at stake, and only if the danger is sufficiently serious to justify the hostility which its interventions are liable to stir up toward the Church and her children among non-believers. Again, when judgement about some temporal matter requires not knowledge of revelation or of natural law, along with certain other truths evident to all men, but rather, specialised human learning and expertise, the spiritual power may not intervene. It would be ridiculous, for example, and a form of usurpation, to threaten excommunication upon statesmen for choosing to enter or not to enter some commercial union with other countries, or for acting or not acting to seek to change the climate: for here the spiritual power has not the competence to determine which of the alternatives is good and which, if any, is bad.

The right of the spiritual power to intervene is most clear when dogmas of the faith and the commandments of God are directly at stake. Negative duties under divine positive law, which obtain always and everywhere regardless of circumstances, should be enforced upon a Catholic temporal ruler even in a non-Catholic polity by the spiritual power employing all the penalties at his disposal. A bishop, for example, may solemnly remind a baptised judge of his duty not to invoke formulas of a false religion when giving judgment. Positive duties under divine positive law, which obtain only in the right circumstances, should not be enforced upon a Catholic temporal ruler in a non-Catholic polity because the temporal ruler is, in these circumstances, the proper judge of whether these circumstances do in fact obtain, unless the fact that they obtain is notorious. Thus a bishop may not insist that the Catholic ruler of a non-Catholic society adopt the Catholic faith as the religion of the civil community if the ruler considers it inopportune to do so (for example because Catholics are a small minority of the citizenry and such a move would provoke an insurrection). Negative duties under natural law should be enforced upon a Catholic temporal ruler even in a non-Catholic polity by the spiritual power employing all the penalties at his disposal. A bishop, for example, should remind a baptised legislator of his duty not to vote in favour of a right to kill unborn children, and punish a judge or legislator with a proportionate punishment, such as excommunication, if he disobeys the commandments of God which the Church declares. Positive duties under natural law may be enforced upon a Catholic temporal ruler even in a non-Catholic polity where the temporal ruler's ability to fulfil them (and thus his negligence and contempt in not doing so) is truly manifest. A bishop may, for example, insist that the ruler reform the civil law to recognise monotheism as known by natural reason.[17]

The spiritual power also has the right, as we shall see, to inflict temporal penalties, such as fines or the loss of freedom to travel; but outside Christendom, such penalties cannot be enforced, and so *de facto* have to be freely assumed.[18]

The Church's jurisdiction, however, is not confined to the direct violation by public men of revealed truths or divine commandments, but bears also on anything that would tend to undermine these truths and commandments.[19] For example, the institution of so-called 'civil partnerships' between two persons of the same sex, has been condemned by the Church not as directly contrary to revelation but as aping and undermining marriage. For this reason, she has taught baptised statesmen that they are not free to introduce them, and she may punish them with excommunication if they do.[20] Again, the Church may

---

[17] Pope John Paul II, *Message of John Paul II on the occasion of the 1,200th Anniversary of the Imperial Coronation of Charlemagne by Leo III*: "The European Union's effort to formulate a 'Charter of Fundamental Rights' is an attempt at a new synthesis, at the beginning of the new millennium, of the basic values that must guide the coexistence of European peoples. The Church has followed the drafting of this document with keen attention. In this regard, I cannot conceal my disappointment that in the Charter's text there is not a single reference to God. Yet in God lies the supreme source of the human person's dignity and his fundamental rights. It cannot be forgotten that it was the denial of God and his commandments which led in the last century to the tyranny of idols. A race, a class, the state, the nation and the party were glorified instead of the true and living God. In the light of the misfortunes that overtook the 20th century we can understand: the rights of God and man stand or fall together."

[18] They can nevertheless be imposed under enforceable spiritual penalties: for example, a Catholic statesman who co-operated in introducing abortion into his country could be obliged to do penance in a monastery, and excommunicated if he refused.

[19] In the same way, her magisterium has for its object not only truths directly revealed, but also all truths without which the deposit of faith cannot be securely taught.

[20] Cf. Congregation for the Doctrine of the Faith, 'Considerations regarding proposals to give legal recognition to unions between homosexual persons', (2003), 10: "When legislation in favour of the recognition of homosexual unions is proposed for the first time in a legislative assembly, the Catholic law-maker has a moral duty to express his opposition clearly and publicly and to vote against it. To vote in favour of a law so harmful to the common good is gravely immoral." The general principle is expressed by Pius IX, *Quanta cura*, 5: "We cannot pass over in silence the boldness of those who contend that without sin and with no loss of Catholic profession, one can withhold assent and obedience to those judgments and decrees of the Apostolic See whose object is declared to relate to the general good of the Church and its rights and discipline, provided it does not touch dogmas of faith or morals (*fidei morumque dogmata*). But no one can be found not clearly and distinctly

use her jurisdiction over her children to safeguard not only the deposit of faith but her life and good estate more generally: hence if a statesman confiscated ecclesiastical property, for example, by expelling monks from a monastery and billeting soldiers there, he would be liable to punishment.

When an unjust law is passed, the Church does not, outside Christendom, annul it, though she may condemn it[21]; and if it obliges citizens to unjust actions, she teaches that it does not bind in conscience and must not be obeyed.

Since the interventions of the spiritual power in the temporal order for the sake of "feeding, ruling and guiding the universal Church" are *applications* of revealed truth, they do not have the guarantee of infallibility that belongs to doctrinal definitions. In other words, they could on occasion be imprudent or erroneous, for example, if the bearer of spiritual power claims a competence that does not belong to him. While the Catholic ruler or citizen imbued with a spirit of faith will wish to obey any such precept, it is not excluded that he judge in good faith that he cannot do so. In such a case he must follow this judgement of conscience,[22] even if some penalty is imposed upon him.[23]

---

to see and understand how grievously this is opposed to the Catholic dogma of the full power given from God by Christ our Lord Himself to the Roman pontiff of feeding, ruling and guiding the universal Church." Cf. Pope John XXIII, *Mater et Magistra*, 239: "The Church has the right and duty not merely to guard principles pertaining to religion and to the integrity of morals, but also to declare its authoritative judgment when it comes to putting these principles into practice."

[21] For example, Pope Pius X, in the encyclical *Vehementer*, 'reproved' and 'condemned' the French 'Law of Separation', and Pius XI in *Dilectissima Nobis* did the same in regard to the Spanish law laicizing education.

[22] Cf. Cardinal John Henry Newman, *Letter to the Duke of Norfolk*, 'Conscience', 4: "I have to say again, lest I should be misunderstood, that when I speak of Conscience, I mean conscience truly so called. When it has the right of opposing the supreme, though not infallible Authority of the Pope, it must be something more than that miserable counterfeit which, as I have said above, now goes by the name. If in a particular case it is to be taken as a sacred and sovereign monitor, its dictate, in order to prevail against the voice of the Pope, must follow upon serious thought, prayer, and all available means of arriving at a right judgment on the matter in question. And further, obedience to the Pope is what is called 'in possession'; that is, the *onus probandi* of establishing a case against him lies, as in all cases of exception, on the side of conscience."

[23] St Thomas considers the case of a Catholic who has committed bigamy, and who knows that the woman with whom he is living as his wife is not really such, but cannot prove this before an ecclesiastical court. The angelic doctor teaches, contrary to the opinion of Peter Lombard, that if the court commands the man to have normal conjugal relations with the second woman, he must refuse: "Here the Master [Lombard] says something false; for he must rather die excommunicate than be joined to her who is not his wife, since that would

Such crises of conscience are most likely to occur in mixed matters, where both the spiritual and the temporal power have some right to speak, and where their verdicts are each plausible but conflicting. For example, let us suppose that some Catholic country were protecting the faith in a time of widespread persecution, but also making unjust depredations on the territory of a pagan or heretical land. If the latter country were to declare war on the Catholic one, and the pope were to forbid Catholic soldiers to fight against the Catholic country, what should they do? As with other matters which involve clashes between principles that hold good only for the most part and not invariably,[24] the question cannot be decided in the abstract, but only when the reality occurs; for only then is it clothed with all its morally relevant circumstances. In this example, the just action to perform will depend on the degree of the threat to the territory of the non-Catholic land, the extent of the damage which its rulers will to inflict on their enemy, the degree to which the Catholic country's defeat would be harmful for the Church, and the degree to which this is manifest.[25] Such hypothetical questions illustrate the difficulties that may arise in practice in applying the principle of the subordination of the temporal to the spiritual, but they do not tend to put this principle itself in doubt.

Relation of the temporal power to the Church within Christendom

So far we have been considering the situation outside Christendom, where the pope and bishops in shepherding Catholic rulers and citizens must appeal only to the consciences of their subjects, and may enforce only spiritual penalties. Within Christendom, that is, where Christ's kingship is publicly and correctly acknowledged, the acts which spiritual rulers posit in the temporal order for the good of souls have also a legal status in that order, and may be enforced even with temporal penalties. Since this power to act in the temporal order extends as far as the good of souls may require, and hence there is no temporal good which may in principle be excluded from it, it implies, once again a legal subordination of the temporal to the spiritual power. Hence the temporal ruler while retaining as his proper charge the care of the temporal common good

---

be contrary to truthfulness of life, which must not be given up to avoid scandal"; *Scriptum super Sententias*, IV, d. 38, q. 2, a. 4, qc. 3, *exposition of the text*.

[24] In this case, the principles are 'soldiers should fight the wars that their rulers command them to' and 'Catholics should obey the pope when he decrees that a certain course is necessary for the good of the Church'.

[25] This last consideration touches upon the legitimacy of the spiritual power's decision to intervene, as it determines whether such an intervention would or would not be a usurpation of a judgment proper to the temporal power.

comes as a 'minister of the Church'[26] to have a care for an infinitely higher good:

> You must unhesitatingly recognise, that the royal power has not been conferred upon you solely for governing the world, but especially for the protection of the Church, so that by checking criminal boldness, you may both defend whatever is well established and restore true peace to whatever is disturbed.[27]

In this way is fulfilled the promise made before the Incarnation, by the Father to the Son: "And kings shall be thy nursing fathers, and queens thy nurses: they shall worship thee with their face toward the earth, and they shall lick up the dust of thy feet."[28]

It is customary to speak of the subordination of the temporal to the spiritual power within Christendom as 'the doctrine of the two swords'. In Holy Scripture, the sword is the symbol both of the civil power to coerce which arises from nature and reason,[29] and also of the revealed word of God, cutting away from men all that obstructs the salvation of souls, even the highest of natural ties, to prepare the way for the coming of Christ in grace and glory.[30] In one place the apostle compares this word to a double-edged sword, perhaps because it convicts the preacher as well as his flock,[31] and in the Apocalypse it comes forth from the mouth of the conquering Messiah. Elsewhere, in words full of mystery, Christ bade His apostles take two swords with them when they went out into the night.[32] St Peter Damian, a doctor of the Church who died

---

[26] See above, p. 115.

[27] These are the words of Pope St Leo I to Emperor Leo I, urging him to defend the faith defined at Chalcedon, by freeing the Alexandrian church from usurpers and expelling anti-Chalcedonians from the city of Constantinople; Letter 156. PL 54: 1130: "Debes incunctanter advertere, regiam potestatem tibi non solum ad mundi regimen sed maxime ad ecclesiae praesidium esse collatam ut ausus nefarios comprimendo, et quae bene sunt statuta defendas, et veram pacem his quae sunt turbata restituas."

[28] Is. 49:23.

[29] Rom. 13:4.

[30] Eph. 6:17; Lk. 2:35.

[31] Heb. 4:12.

[32] Writing to Charlemagne in the year 799, Alcuin of York had already used this scriptural passage to refer to the defence of the Church, but in a different way: he tells the king that divine power has put two swords into Charles's hand, one being the power inwardly to purge 'the churches of Christ' from heresy, the other being the power to defend them exteriorly from the attacks of pagans; Monumenta Germaniae Historica, *Epistolae Karolini Aevi*, t. 2, ed. E. Duemmler (Berlin: Weidmannsche Buchhandlung, 1895), 282 (letter 171).

in 1072, states that these two swords are the kingship and the priesthood. The sword of the priest, he says, must render more gentle that of the king, while the sword of the king must sharpen that of the priest.[33] It is however to St Bernard of Clairvaux in the following century that we owe a more developed exegesis of this gospel passage. Writing to his spiritual son Pope Eugene III about the need to defend the Christians of the East, he affirms:

> Each sword must now be drawn, in our Lord's passion, as Christ suffers again in the place where He suffered before. And through whom must this happen, if not through You? For each of them is Peter's, the one to be unsheathed at his bidding, the other by his hand (*alter suo nutu, alter sua manu*), as often as there is need. For concerning that sword of which this might seem to be less true, it was said to Peter, *Put up thy sword into its sheath*. Therefore, that one also was his; though not indeed to be drawn by his own hand. The time has come, as I believe, for both to be drawn in defence of the eastern Church.[34]

The mellifluous doctor is assuming the identification of the two swords of the Gospel with the two powers, and asserting that not only the spiritual one, but also the temporal is in some sense at the disposal of the pope. He re-affirms this in a later work addressed to the same recipient:

> He who would deny that the sword belongs to You, has not, as I conceive, sufficiently weighed the words of the Lord, where He said, speaking to Peter, 'put up *thy* sword into the scabbard'. For it is here plainly implied that even the material sword is Yours, to be drawn at Your bidding, though not by Your hand. Besides, unless this sword also pertained to You in some sense (*alioquin si nullo modo ad te pertineret et is*), then when the disciples said to Christ, *Lord, behold here are two swords*, He would never have answered as He did, *It is enough*, but

---

King Edgar of England came closer to St Peter Damian's exegesis. Addressing a council of bishops assembled in Canterbury with St Dunstan in 969, St Edgar the Peaceable declared, speaking of abuses to be remedied within the Church: "I have in my hand the sword of Constantine, and you have that of Peter. Let us join hands, uniting sword to sword, and drive the leper outside the camp to purify the sanctuary of God"; PL 138: 515-16.

[33] Sermon 69, 'On the consecration of a church', PL 144: 900. The *Dictionnaire de Théologie Catholique* truncates the quotation, giving the impression that each sword is to render the other more gentle; *DTC*, 'Pouvoir du Pape dans l'ordre temporelle. II. Le pouvoir du pape en matière temporelle'.

[34] Letter 237; PL 182: 426.

rather, *It is too much*. We can therefore conclude that both swords, namely the spiritual and the material, belong to the Church, and that the latter is to be used for the Church (*pro Ecclesia*), the former by the Church (*ab Ecclesia*); the former by the hand of the priest, the latter by the hand of the soldier, yet at the good pleasure (*ad nutum*) of the priest and the bidding (*iussum*) of the emperor.[35]

This passage gives rise to questions which St Bernard himself did not need to examine: what if the good pleasure of the priest, and especially, of the pope, and the bidding of the emperor should happen not to agree? Can the pope command the soldier to use the sword even against the emperor himself? For now we may simply note the doctrine that both swords belong in some sense to the pope as head of the Church on earth, and clarify this in what follows.

St Bernard's teaching was accepted by the doctors who followed him. Commenting on the assertion that 'the Church has each sword', St Thomas states:

> It must be said that the Church has only the spiritual one as far as the exercise of it by her own hand is concerned; but she has the temporal one also with regard to commanding it, for it is to be unsheathed at her good pleasure, as Bernard says.[36]

Elsewhere, he writes:

> Spiritual as well as secular power comes from the divine power. Hence secular power is subjected to spiritual power in those matters concerning which the subjection has been ordained by God, namely, in matters belonging to the salvation of the soul. Hence in these we are to obey spiritual authority more than secular authority. On the other hand, more obedience is due to secular than to spiritual power in the things that belong to the civic good. For it is said Matthew 22:

---

[35] *On Consideration*, Book IV, chapter 3; PL 182: 776. St Robert Bellarmine believed that this was the allegorical and not the literal sense of the passage; *Controversiae*, 'On the Supreme Pontiff', bk. 5, ch. 5. Yet since the words are spoken by Christ, if He intended them to include this meaning, as Bellarmine allows, it is by definition part of their literal meaning. Can we not also say that Christ Himself drew attention to the presence of a hidden meaning in His words by adding at this very moment that what related to Him *had a purpose*, τὸ περὶ ἐμοῦ τέλος ἔχει? Even if the literal sense is taken at the most mundane it is a command to assume the resources of temporal coercion, and the jurisdiction of the Apostles over matters spiritual is not in dispute.

[36] *Scriptum super Sententias* IV dist. 37, q.2 a. 2 exposition of the text: *The holy Church of God does not have the sword* etc. St Bonaventure gives the same teaching, commenting on the same passage in the *Sentences*.

Render unto Caesar the things that are Caesar's. A special case occurs, however, when spiritual and secular power are so joined in one person as they are in the Pope, who holds the apex of both powers (*qui utriusque potestatis apicem tenet*), that is, spiritual and secular. This has been so arranged by Him who is both Priest and King, Priest eternal after *the order of Melchisedech, King of Kings and Lord of Lords, whose dominion shall not pass away, and his kingdom shall not be destroyed for ever and ever.*[37]

Boniface VIII famously confirmed this exegesis by the solemn teaching of the bull *Unam sanctam*, where he puts forward the same exegesis of the gospel passage as St Bernard, almost word for word. The spiritual sword, he concludes tersely, is "of the priest", while the material one "is by the hand of kings and soldiers, but at the good pleasures and sufferance (*ad nutum et patientiam*) of the priest". Noteworthy, however, is the pope's omission of the phrase "and at the bidding of the emperor". St Bernard, who was writing to restrain his spiritual son from temptations to grandeur, wished to remind him that his good pleasure would hardly suffice to put the solder in motion without the support of some great temporal power, and especially of the greatest: Boniface, responding to the hostile acts of a great temporal ruler, the King of France, restricted himself to teaching the abstract doctrine of the spiritual ruler's right to direct the temporal sword for the good of the Church.

The Hierarchy's power over temporal matters within Christendom: in general

We have heard St Bernard declare that both swords pertain to the Pope in some way. But in what way? Christ is the king of the Christian people, and His universal vicar on earth is the Roman pontiff, who therefore has jurisdiction over the perfect society which this people form. Hence, when temporal power itself has been brought within this society, as a body vivified by its proper soul, that is, when the Christian people have become Christendom, this power itself is subject to the pope as head on earth of the City of God. In this sense, even the temporal sword, that is, power over earthly things that find their purpose in this world and are destined to pass away with it, belongs to the pope by right.

However, as previously explained, on account of human sinfulness, and to manifest the distinction of heavenly and earthly things, the pope is normally

---

[37] *Scriptum super Sententias*, II dist. 44, exposition of the text, ad 4. St Thomas is not speaking here of the pope's sovereignty over the papal states, which would not place him at the 'apex' of temporal power, higher than any other sovereign.

forbidden to exercise the temporal sword, except within his own domains.[38] It is not he, but lay rulers, who must normally exercise legislative, executive and judicial power over temporal matters.[39] Yet because even the temporal sword is his by right, only one who receives it with his blessing exercises it with full legitimacy; he can correct one who uses it to turn Christian souls from their true end of beatitude; and if he perceives that it is being obstinately so used, he may take it from one person and give it to another. More generally, we can say that the apostolic hierarchy of the Church can use the temporal power but (except as regards their personal property or the property belonging to the juridic persons of their dioceses) only in case of necessity, that is, where it is morally certain that otherwise grave harm would be done to souls.

Hence, St Paul required that judges be established to try disputes between Christians even over temporal matters (βιωτικά), lest Christians bring the name of Christ into disrepute by wrangling before pagan tribunals.[40] Much later, Pope Innocent III would likewise claim the right to exercise temporal jurisdiction, not continuously but rather *casualiter*, that is, 'as occasion requires'.[41] Intervening in a dispute between the King of France and the King of England, he justified his action by his power "to judge concerning sin, the punishment of which certainly pertains to Us, a punishment which We can and must exercise over any person".[42] Pope Innocent IV, likewise, in the context of his struggle with Emperor Frederick II, stated that "the Roman pontiff can exercise his pontifical judgement on any Christian, whatever may be his condition, at least as occasion requires (*saltem casualiter*), and especially by reason of some sin (*maxime ratione peccati*)."[43] The latter phrase, *ratione peccati*,

---

[38] That is, today, the Vatican City; formerly, central Italy.

[39] Hence it does not belong to the pope to establish laws determining the succession of temporal power from one person to another within a given province of Christendom: the designation of the temporal power is itself an exercise of temporal power.

[40] 1 Cor. 6:1-4. Bellarmine insists that the judges established at the apostle's command had true jurisdiction over the faithful, not simply the power to express an opinion, even though this jurisdiction would of course not be recognised by the authorities of the pagan empire; *De Potestate Summi Pontificis in Temporalibus, adversus Guielmum Barcleium*, c. XXI.

[41] Epistle 5, PL 214:1132. Innocent writes: "Not only in the patrimony of the Church [i.e. the papal states], where we have full power in temporal things, but also in other regions when certain cases come to light, we exercise temporal jurisdiction as need requires (*temporalem jurisdictionem casualiter exercemus*)."

[42] Epistle 163; PL 215:180.

[43] *Aeger cui lenia*. Historians consider that this document expresses Innocent IV's thought, though it is apparently not an official pontifical act; see J. A. Watt 'The Papacy' in *The New Cambridge Medieval History*, volume 5, c.1198-c.1300 (CUP: Cambridge, 1999), 142 n. 90.

became a standard one to explain the circumstances in which a pope could lawfully intervene in temporal affairs.[44]

St Robert Bellarmine, moved by the fact that the pope may only act on the temporal order of Christendom for the sake of a spiritual good, spoke of the pope's temporal power as indirect, and many authors in the modern period have followed him.[45] Yet this phrase does not seem to do justice to the unity proper to the Christian people. The Church is the faithful who are also the citizenry of the temporal community within Christendom which is a community of the baptised. Certain members of the faithful constitute the powers which govern that community under its temporal aspect (like the sensitive powers in the human person); others constitute the powers that govern that community under its spiritual aspect but which also govern that community simply and indeed are able to survive the destruction of the psychosomatic unity. The soul is not in the body as a pilot in a ship but is the form of the body: "By it man is man, and animal, and living, and body, and substance, and being. Soul, therefore, gives man every essential degree of perfection. It communicates to the body, furthermore, the act of existence whereby it itself exists."[46] If a 'Christian state' were related to the Church as one intrinsically perfect society to another, and the 'Church'[47] were related to it as an extrinsic agent, then the pope's jurisdiction over temporal matters might well be called indirect. But in fact the Church is one perfect society (which we call 'Christendom' under its temporal aspect), in which the temporal is related to the spiritual as body to soul; the temporal is both constituted by and serves the spiritual. Now the spiritual powers of the soul do not rule in the composite 'indirectly' as if they were something external to it, but directly, and likewise, within Christendom, that which is spiritual rules that which is

---

[44] Since good is to be pursued even more than evil is to be avoided, this papal power must be strictly speaking defined in reference to the salvation of souls: it is a power that may be exercised to promote the salvation of souls, especially when rulers are inducing their subjects so to sin in a way as to imperil that salvation. The reason the phrase *ratione peccati* is most commonly used is because it implies a need for the Pontiff to identify the violation of a *negative* precept of natural or divine law and hence provides greater legal certainty for determining the circumstances when papal intervention would be appropriate.

[45] More precisely, he says that the pope has 'supreme temporal power' indirectly, that is, in virtue of something else; *Controversiae*, 'On the Supreme Pontiff', bk. 5, ch. 7. Elsewhere he writes: "Properly speaking, we say that the pontiff has power in temporal matters, but that he does not have temporal power insofar as he is pontiff"; *De Potestate Summi Pontificis in Temporalibus, adversus Guielmum Barcleium*, c. XII.

[46] *Postquam sanctissimus*, 'Twenty-Four Thomistic Theses', Sacred Congregation of Studies, 1914, thesis 16.

[47] Understood in practice as the clerical hierarchy.

temporal directly. Since within the spiritual part of Christendom, the papacy is that which is most 'formal', i.e. that which causes the other elements of the spiritual part to pertain to the Church, the pope can rightly be said to rule the whole of Christendom.[48]

Some more recent authors, recognising that the pope acts, in certain circumstances, directly in temporal matters have preferred to speak of the pope's spiritual power in the temporal order.[49] Yet a right to dispose of temporal matters *is* temporal jurisdiction. For this reason, we say that the vicar of Christ has a direct spiritual and temporal jurisdiction over Christendom, although he can only exercise the latter on rare occasions. This way of speaking, though it has become unusual in modern times, seems to correspond best to St Thomas's assertion that the Roman pontiff "holds the apex of both powers, that is, spiritual and secular". It also corresponds to Bellarmine's own insistence that the unity of Christendom be conceived on the model of the unity of a human being, with temporal and spiritual matters in Christendom related as body and soul in man. Likewise, the assertion that the pope has a direct spiritual and temporal power over Christendom, while being able to exercise the latter only *ratione peccati*, is in practice equivalent to Bellarmine's statement that "the pope as pope, has a supreme power of disposing of the temporal things of all Christians, to order them to spiritual good."[50]

Coercion of the baptised

The right of the successors of the apostles to rule baptised temporal rulers for spiritual ends extends as far as the rights of the Church herself. But among these rights is that of using coercion, that is, the threat and application of

---

[48] While it is fitting for the sake of his impartiality that he also have his own domain in which he can exercise the temporal sword freely ('the patrimony of the Church'), and that this be a temporally self-sufficient society, he does not possess such domain by divine right. The domain which the popes in fact possess, they have acquired in a human way, as any ruler might. Nevertheless, if it were urgently necessary or highly expedient to do so there would seem to be no barrier to the pope assuming to himself such a dominion by his own decree.

[49] C. Journet, *Church of the Word Incarnate*, 186-87.

[50] *Controversiae*, 'On the Supreme Pontiff', bk. 5, ch. 6: "Asserimus Pontificem ut Pontificem... habere in ordine ad bonum spirituale summam potestatem dispondendi de temporalibus rebus omnium Christianorum."

punishment backed up by force, over the baptised.[51] The Council of Trent, in its seventh session, defined this as a point of dogma:

> If anyone says, that those who have been thus baptized when children, are, when they have grown up, to be asked whether they will ratify what their sponsors promised in their names when they were baptized, and that, if they should answer that they will not, they are to be left to their own will, and are not to be compelled meanwhile to a Christian life by any other penalty (*nec alia interim poena ad christianam vitam cogendos*), save that they be excluded from the participation of the Eucharist, and of the other sacraments, until they repent; let him be anathema.[52]

That the Church has the right to impose both temporal as well as spiritual penalties has been definitively upheld by the magisterium,[53] and by the 20th century codes of canon law.[54]

---

[51] This right was foreshadowed in the Old Law by the penalties to be inflicted on the Jews who had gone over to idolatry, the high priest having the right to judge in difficult matters; Deut. 13:17-18; 17:1-13. St Robert Bellarmine remarks in this connexion: "There is hardly any difference between our heretics and the false prophets of that time"; *Controversiae*, 'On the members of the Church', bk. 3, ch. 20.

[52] Decree 'On Baptism', canon 14. Since exclusion from the sacraments is the highest of spiritual penalties, the further penalties which Trent envisages as legitimate will evidently be temporal ones of some kind.

[53] John XXII, in the constitution *Licet*, promulgated in 1327, taught that the use of bodily force (*corporalis coactio*) has been entrusted to the Church by Christ. Benedict XIV, in the brief *Ad assiduas* of 1755, also condemned the view that Church has no temporal penalties. This latter document was quoted by Pius VI in *Auctorem fidei*, 5: "In that part in which the proposition insinuates that the Church 'does not have authority to demand obedience to its decrees otherwise than by means which depend on persuasion; in so far as it intends that the Church has not conferred on it by God the power, not only of directing by counsel and persuasion, but also of ordering by laws, and of constraining and of forcing the inconstant and stubborn by exterior judgment and salutary punishments' – leading toward a system condemned elsewhere as heretical." In *Quanta cura*, Pius IX condemned those who "are not ashamed of affirming [...] that the Church has no right of restraining by temporal punishments those who violate her laws" (*QC* 5). Cf. *Syllabus of Errors*, 24th condemned proposition: "The Church has not the power of using force (*vis inferendae potestatem*)."

[54] The 1917 Code of Canon Law stated in canon 2214 §1: "The Church has the native and proper right, independent of any human authority, to coerce those offenders subject to her with both spiritual and temporal penalties." This teaching is maintained in the more recent code. Cf. 1983 Code, canon 1311: "The Church has the innate and proper right to coerce (*coercere*) offending members of the Christian faithful (*christifideles*) with punitive sanctions

Since spiritual power by itself does not enable its bearer to enforce such penalties in person, and since it is in vain that a sentence be passed which cannot be executed, the spiritual shepherd may call upon the temporal power to enforce these penalties. This right of the hierarchy to command the secular power to assist it in governing the baptised has been upheld by ecumenical councils.[55]

Outside Christendom, some of the temporal powers of the ecclesiastical hierarchy lapse; others become unusable in practice.[56] This is a sign that where Christendom is not, the Church is not in a normal state, but is akin to a soul separated from the body, immortal indeed but unable to exercise all the powers of which she remains radically possessed.[57]

The Fathers of Trent said that the secular arm could be obliged to assist the pastors in maintaining 'a Christian life' among the baptised. This broad

---

(*poenalibus sanctionibus*)"; also canon 1312§2: "The law can establish [...] expiatory penalties which deprive a member of the Christian faithful of some spiritual or temporal good and which are consistent with the supernatural purpose of the Church." For clerics these sanctions may include a form of imprisonment, such as an order to reside in a monastery; cf. canons 1364 and 1336.

[55] 4th Lateran Council, canon 3: "If, however, a temporal lord, required and instructed by the church, neglects to cleanse his territory of this heretical filth, he shall be bound with the bond of excommunication by the metropolitan and other bishops of the province. If he refuses to give satisfaction within a year, this shall be reported to the supreme pontiff so that he may then declare his vassals absolved from their fealty to him"; Council of Constance, *Inter cunctas*, 'Questions to be proposed to the Wycliffites and the Hussites', 32: "Whether he believes that with the growing disobedience or contumacy of the excommunicated, the prelates or their vicars in spiritual matters have the power of oppressing and of oppressing him again, of imposing interdict and of invoking the secular arm; and that these censures must be obeyed by his inferiors."

[56] As the temporal community severed from Christendom is no longer a community of the baptised, the excommunication of one of its temporal officers no longer results *ipso facto* in his deposition. The authority of the hierarchy to arrest and imprison a delinquent member of the faithful remains but it would be opposed and indeed seen as a criminal act by the secular polity and therefore is not employed.

[57] St Thomas Aquinas, Cf. *Disputed questions on the Soul*, a. 19, 'Whether the sentient powers remain in the soul when it exists apart from the body', ad 2: "Powers of this kind are said to remain in the soul as in their root, when it exists apart from the body, not because they are actually present in the soul, but because the separated soul is of such virtue that, if it is united to a body, it can again cause these powers in the body, just as it causes life to be in it." The intellectual powers in a separated soul on the other hand remain but are impeded in their exercise by the absence of the phantasms through which they normally operate; cf. STh 1a, 89, 1.

expression covers not only faith but also morals.[58] Speaking of women who continued to live in concubinage after three admonitions, the same council decreed: "They shall be cast forth from the city or diocese, if the Ordinaries shall think fit, calling in the aid of the secular arm, if need be."[59]

The Church's power over temporal matters within Christendom: in particular

The pope may exercise the temporal sword within Christendom, Bellarmine specifies, on the persons, laws and judgements of secular princes; or, as we could also put it, on the bearers of executive, legislative and judicial power. The Jesuit doctor considers each case in turn; we shall first summarise his thought, before considering more closely the supreme example of such an exercise of authority, namely, the deposition of sovereigns.

First, papal action on the bearers of power themselves:

> The pope as pope cannot ordinarily depose temporal rulers even for a just cause in the way in which he can depose bishops, that is, as their ordinary judge; he can nevertheless exchange realms, taking them from one man and giving them to another, as the supreme spiritual ruler, if that is necessary for the salvation of souls.[60]

This power touches only rulers. In Christendom, the pope may for a grave cause depose a sovereign king or a president, or declare a sovereign parliament dissolved, but he cannot act thus toward some lesser temporal officers, for example, expel a minister of the crown. For the lesser officer has the higher

---

[58] Although the public power of the Church does not directly command merely internal acts, it can require external acts to be performed in a human way, and hence as requiring certain internal acts. For example, while the internal act of faith is not directly coerced, the profession of faith may be, and this profession by its nature presupposes the internal act. In a similar way, even the civil power can require that when someone makes a contract, he make it with a sincere intention of obliging himself; A. Ottaviani, *Compendium Iuris Publici Ecclesiastici*, 154-55. Cf. Innocent XI's condemnation of the proposition that one satisfies the precept of Holy Communion by a sacrilegious reception, 2nd March, 1679.

[59] Session 24, 'On the Reformation of Matrimony', c. 8. The council also ordained severe punishments for Christian men who maintained concubines, but these penalties did not include expulsion, presumably because of the unintended consequences in regard to proprietary rights that this might have entailed.

[60] *Controversiae*, 'On the Supreme Pontiff', bk. 5, ch. 6. He speaks of 'the pope as pope' to exclude his power as sovereign of the papal states.

temporal officer as his proper judge, and so for a pope to attempt to act on him directly would be a usurpation.

St Robert considers next the papal power with regard to law:

> The pope as pope cannot ordinarily establish (*condere*) a civil law, or confirm them, or nullify (*infirmare*) the laws of rulers, since he is not himself a political ruler of the Church [*sic*]; nevertheless, he can do all these things if some civil law is necessary for the salvation of souls, and kings do not wish to establish it, or if another law is harmful to souls, and kings are unwilling to abrogate (*abrogare*) it.[61]

While Bellarmine speaks of a pope establishing laws, it seems more exact to speak of him as insisting on their establishment, since he acts directly on, not as, the legislator. Again, if a pope is spoken of as nullifying or abrogating laws, yet since he can do this only in regard to measures which by reason of their perversity lack the power to be true laws, it is more accurate to say that he declares them to be null and void of themselves.[62]

The case in question must be one of true necessity, not of mere usefulness. For example, if, in a given province of Christendom sacrilegious public entertainments were routinely held, the pope could insist under threat of deposition that the legislator introduce a law against blasphemy. But he could not insist that the legislator introduce a law requiring every town to build a library for the study of Church history. To do would be to attempt to wield the temporal sword outside of necessity, which positive divine law forbids, and hence the temporal legislator could ignore such a demand.

The third case concerns the pope's temporal power in regard to judicial matters:

> The pope as pope cannot ordinarily judge about temporal things, for Bernard rightly says to Eugene in *On Consideration*, book 1 "[…] Your power regards crimes and not possessions." And yet where this is necessary for the salvation of souls, the pontiff can take up even temporal cases, that is, when there is no one else who can judge, as when two sovereign kings are litigating, or when they can and should judge, but are not willing to pass a verdict.[63]

---

[61] Ibid.

[62] Cf. A. Ottaviani, *Compendium Iuris Publici Ecclesiastici*, 4th edition, (Rome: Vatican Press, 1954), 157.

[63] *Controversiae*, 'On the Supreme Pontiff', bk. 5, ch. 6.

If two provinces of Christendom, for example, are disputing over the ownership of some territory, and no secular court exists to adjudge such matters, the pope may judge the case by divine right and not simply by the consent of the disputants. Or again, if no judge could be found willing to try some Mafia-style boss, against whom there was good evidence that he was leading many people into a life of crime, such a person could on this principle be tried by a civil magistrate appointed by the pope, and if found guilty punished with the customary civil penalties.[64]

In summary: while the temporal sword belongs to the spiritual ruler as of right, he is forbidden to use it except in case of necessity. Thus, when the sword cannot be used by the lay person to whom it is assigned either because of his obstinate sinful misuse of it or because the question of his identity is interminable (as in a territorial dispute between two lay rulers with no temporal superior, or the simple collapse[65] of all government), then the temporal sword defaults to the spiritual ruler to be immediately reassigned to a lay person worthy and capable of wielding it for the good. In a sense, therefore, the pope's temporal interventions are undertaken in order to avoid exercising the temporal power when it has been, through sin or misfortune, returned to him.

So far we have spoken of the pope. Yet other bishops also regularly possess jurisdiction, including the right to excommunicate delinquent Catholics under their charge, including temporal rulers.[66] If such a ruler within Christendom is excommunicated by his diocesan bishop, or other ordinary, he loses his legal right to govern; though if he appeals against his sentence of excommunication to a higher ecclesiastical power, especially to the Pope, then the sentence and its consequences may be suspended while the appeal is considered. This is implied by Boniface VIII's words in *Unam sanctam:* "If the terrestrial power err, it will be judged by the spiritual power; but if a lesser spiritual power err, it will be judged by a superior spiritual power".[67] The bishop also has a power over

---

[64] Ibid.

[65] Cf. Adrian IV's Bull *Laudabiliter* which in 1155 assigned lordship over Ireland to Henry II of England on the implied grounds that Ireland was ungoverned space and his presence was needed for the purpose of "enlarging the borders of the Church, setting bounds to the progress of wickedness, reforming evil manners, planting virtue, and increasing the Christian religion".

[66] A. Ottaviani, *Institutiones,* vol. 2, 170.

[67] The historic practice of the Church in this regard was reflected in the later codification of her law. Canon 1557 of the 1917 Code limits to the pope the right of judging or correcting princes and their children and heirs. Canons 1401 and 1405§1 of the 1983 Code lay down that only the Roman Pontiff may judge "those who hold the highest power in the

laws passed by a legislature which falls wholly under his jurisdiction. Hence if some realm within Christendom is co-extensive with a diocese, he can insist that some law necessary for souls be passed, or declare null some law which is seriously harmful to souls. Finally, in the same circumstances, he can also judge in a case where the refusal of civil judges to hear the case is seriously harmful to souls.

Deposition of temporal rulers within Christendom

By deposition of temporal rulers is meant not the physical act of depriving a ruler of his domains, but the authoritative declaration that he has lost his authority, that is his right to exercise power. As mentioned above in regard to tyranny, such a declaration may be made in a time of crisis by the highest legitimate body which has some charge of the common good. Within Christendom, the body that moves to free itself from a tyrant extra-judicially must seek the confirmation of its action, after the fact if necessary, from the sovereign pontiff; and he may also take the initiative in declaring the tyrant's loss of authority.[68]

Should we speak of a declaration or a deposition?[69] Either expression may be used: the ruler has already deprived himself of the right to rule,[70] but the

---

city *(eos qui supremum tenent civitatis magistratum)*", in cases which regard spiritual matters, and those connected to spiritual matters.

[68] In 1690, Pope Alexander VIII declared void the first Gallican article, which had claimed: "By the command of God, kings and princes cannot be subject to ecclesiastical power in temporal affairs, nor can they be deposed by the authority of the keys of the Church, either directly or indirectly; nor can their subjects be released from loyalty and obedience and be freed from fulfilling their oath of allegiance." James I of England required English Catholics to swear an oath of allegiance, which denied, among other things, the papal power of deposition. Pope Paul V condemned it in 1606, saying: "It cannot be taken, as it contains many things evidently contrary to faith and salvation", but without specifying what those things were. In his *Dictatus Papae*, St Gregory VII asserts that "of the pope alone all princes shall kiss the feet ... it may be permitted to him to depose emperors ... by his command and consent, it may be lawful for subordinates to bring accusations ... [and] that he may absolve subjects from their fealty to wicked men." Indeed, the emperors Justin, Justinian II, John V and John VIII all prostrated themselves before the popes of their day.

[69] Cardinal Ottaviani discusses the question and prefers the former term; A. Ottaviani, *Institutiones Iuris Publici Ecclesiastici*, 4th edition, 1958, vol. 2, 175, n. 57.

[70] Cf. the words of Pope Paul III to Emperor Charles V concerning Henry VIII of England: "Se ipse ille regno et regia dignitate privavit, ita ut sola declaratio privationis adversus eum superstit ("he has already deprived himself of the kingdom and of the royal dignity, so that all that remains is the declaration of this loss"), quoted in ibid., 172.

declaration of the Church gives this fact a binding legal status. On the other hand, even if the ruler had not so deprived himself *ipso facto*, it appears that the spiritual power would have the right to punish him with deposition on account of his crime.[71]

This papal power, as being the most serious intervention in the temporal order, requires for its just exercise some exceptionally grave cause. The most evident such cause is public and obdurate heresy in a ruler, as with the deposition of Elizabeth Boleyn by St Pius V.[72] Bellarmine notes that such interventions were foreshadowed in the Old Testament, for example by the intervention of the high priest Jehoiada who commanded the deposition and even the execution of Queen Athaliah, so that the worship of Baal might be overthrown.[73] The legitimacy of this action in turn rested on the provision in the Law of Moses forbidding the choice of a non-Jew as monarch, lest the people be led into idolatry. He also cites the example of King Uzziah, who in accordance with the Levitical law requiring lepers to be separated from the people at the judgement of the priest left the city after having contracted leprosy, his sons ruling in his stead.[74] This doctor of the Church concludes: "If on account of bodily leprosy, a priest was once able to judge a king and deprive him of a kingdom, why will he not now be able to do the same on account of spiritual leprosy, that is, heresy?"[75] While Christendom, unlike ancient Israel, is not a 'theocracy' if by this term we mean a realm where God Himself directly determines the form of government, it is a continuation and flowering of ancient Israel, as a realm where legitimacy requires profession of the true faith. In such a realm, it is not lawful for Christians to tolerate a publicly infidel or heretical king.

Apart from the general argument for this power based on the subjection of the temporal to the spiritual power, St Robert Bellarmine offers the analogy of

---

[71] Hence, speaking of apostate rulers, Suarez says: "The Church has a direct power over [these] *per se*, and by reason of baptism, and so can deprive them of their power as a punishment for infidelity and heresy"; *de Legibus*, III.X.6.

[72] *Regnans in excelsis*: "Resting upon the authority of Him whose pleasure it was to place us, though unequal to such a burden, upon this supreme justice-seat, we do out of the fullness of our apostolic power declare the aforesaid Elizabeth to be a heretic and favourer of heretics, and her adherents in the matters aforesaid to have incurred the sentence of excommunication and to be cut off from the unity of the body of Christ. And moreover, we declare her to be deprived of her pretended title to the aforesaid crown and of all lordship, dignity and privilege whatsoever."

[73] 2 Chronicles 23.

[74] Lev. 13; 2 Chronicles 26.

[75] *Controversiae*, 'On the Supreme Pontiff', bk. 5, ch. 7. St Augustine describes leprosy as a figure of heresy; *Diverse questions on the gospel*, II.40.

marriage. The tradition of the Church allows for separation from a heretical spouse who seeks to draw the believing spouse from the faith; so why, he asks, should not a faithful people be liberated from the yoke of an unfaithful king who would draw them to infidelity?[76]

St Thomas explains that the Church deposes once-Christian rulers who have abandoned the faith both to punish them and to protect their people:

> She can pass sentence of punishment on the unbelief of those who have received the faith: and it is fitting that they should be punished by being deprived of the allegiance of their subjects: for this same allegiance might conduce to great corruption of the faith, since, as was stated above 'a man that is an apostate with a wicked heart deviseth evil, and soweth discord' (Prov. 6) in order to sever others from the faith. Consequently, as soon as sentence of excommunication is passed on a man on account of apostasy from the faith, his subjects are *ipso facto* absolved from his authority and from the oath of allegiance whereby they were bound to him.[77]

Pope St Gregory VII famously invoked his authority against Emperor Henry IV in the course of the dispute over the right to invest bishops. Although this is itself a question that pertains to the faith, the pope appealed especially to the honour of the Church to justify his bold action. In a council of 1076, invoking the power of binding and loosing promised St Peter, he absolved the emperor's subjects of their oath of fidelity to Henry, and forbade them to serve him as their king, stating: "It is right that he who attempts to lessen the honour of the Church should lose the honour which he seems to have".[78] In 1080, excommunicating Henry for the second time, the pope expressed his sentence still more plainly: "I take from him all royal power and rank".[79] The pope declared to his council that being able to bind and loose in heaven, they could also take and grant on earth "empires, kingdoms, dukedoms, marquisates, counties and the possessions of all men in accordance with the merits of each".[80] In general, however, it seems unlikely that a ruler will be able to harm

---

[76] *Controversiae*, 'On the Supreme Pontiff', bk. 5, ch. 7.

[77] STh, 2a 2ae 12, 2. In the same article he explains that this was not done to Julian the apostate because "at that time the Church was but recently instituted, and had not, as yet, the power of curbing earthly princes" (ad 1).

[78] PL148: 790.

[79] PL 148: 818: "Omnem potestatem et dignitatem illi regiam tollo."

[80] Ibid. While Gregory VII's action is often cited as the first example of a pope claiming the power of deposition, Bellarmine also adduces the action of Pope Gregory II in regard

the Church so much as to fall under the papal sentence of deposition without also being a tyrant who could outside Christendom have been declared deposed by merely natural right.[81]

Deposition of temporal rulers outside Christendom

"It does not pertain to the Church to punish unbelief in those who have never received the faith."[82] Nor is infidelity simply incompatible with temporal authority:

> The divine law, which is the law of grace, does not do away with human law, which is the law of natural reason. Wherefore the distinction between faithful and unbelievers, considered in itself, does not do away with dominion and authority of unbelievers over the faithful.[83]

Yet the Church possesses a certain power even over unbaptised persons ruling over the baptised outside Christendom. She has the radical right, St Thomas holds, to declare such rulers deprived of their authority, if not exactly as a punishment, then at least as a deserved censure:

> This right of dominion or authority can be justly done away with by the sentence or ordination of the Church who has the authority of God (*potest* [...] *iuste per sententiam vel ordinationem Ecclesiae, auctoritatem Dei habentis, tale ius dominii vel praelationis tolli*), since unbelievers in virtue of their unbelief deserve to forfeit their power over the faithful who are converted into children of God.[84]

A Christian Roman emperor, therefore, would not have wronged the Persian emperor if, following such a sentence of the Church, he had deprived the Persian emperor of his kingdom, even if the latter had not been persecuting

---

to the iconoclast emperor Leo III in the 8th century; by forbidding the emperor to gather taxes in Italy, the pope in effect deprived him at least temporarily of part of his empire; *Controversiae*, 'On the Supreme Pontiff', bk. 5, ch. 7.

[81] A. Ottaviani, *Institutiones*, 176.

[82] STh 2a 2ae 12, 2.

[83] Ibid., 10, 10. The opinion that pagan rulers possess no kind of jurisdiction was referred to by the 15th century Polish jurist Paweł Włodkowic (Paulus Vladimiri) as the 'Prussian heresy', in his criticism of the activities of the Teutonic Knights; S. Belch, *Paulus Vladimiri and his doctrine concerning International Law and Politics*, vol. 2 (Mouton & Co.: The Hague, 1965), 1114-15.

[84] STh 2a 2ae 10, 10. The right remains in its root, *in radice*, without coming to fruition.

the indigenous Christians within his realm. Yet in practice, St Thomas notes, the Church does not exercise this right:

> The Church has not claimed this right against those unbelievers who are not temporally subject to her or her members, although she could rightfully exercise it. This she does to avoid scandal. In the same way, our Lord showed (Mt. 17) that He could be excused from paying the tribute, because 'the children are free,' and yet He ordered the tribute to be paid in order to avoid giving scandal. Thus Paul too, after saying that servants should honour their masters, adds, 'lest the name of the Lord and His doctrine be blasphemed'.[85]

The scandal in question is the danger that the infidel ruler or his subjects might hate the Christian name after such an invasion. Nevertheless, the principle stated by the angelic doctor is noteworthy: the Church, as 'having the authority of God', would have the right to give judgement even about unbaptised rulers, in virtue of her care for her baptised children.

The case is different, however, when a usurper seizes a province of Christendom by force or guile and attempts to detach it from the Church. We saw in a previous chapter that usurpation gives no general title to rule, and that to gain such a title, the usurper would have to be accepted by the heads of households, and then only after the *de iure* ruler has lost all realistic hope of regaining *de facto* power. If this happens, that land thereby severs itself from Christendom, and the pope has no right over its ruler beyond the merely radical right, already mentioned, which he does not use. If the infidel ruler is not welcomed, then for however long the usurpation continues, the Church considers that land as still a portion of Christendom, and so the pope may call on Christian princes to take arms against the usurper, as during the Crusades.[86]

Again, if a ruler outside Christendom is preventing the preaching of the gospel, or the free practice of the Catholic religion, the Church may declare him a tyrant, and encourage or even oblige some other baptised person to take arms against him.[87] For as a perfect society the Church has the power to resist

---

[85] Ibid.

[86] Cajetan notes that in such a case, if the ruler whose territory was usurped has no heir living, the Roman Church has the right to provide a ruler *in favorem fidei* ('for the sake of the faith'); *Commentary* on STh 2a 2ae, 66, 8 ad 2.

[87] STh 2a 2ae, 10, 8: "It is for this reason that Christ's faithful often wage war with unbelievers, not indeed for the purpose of forcing them to believe, because even if they were to conquer them, and take them prisoners, they should still leave them free to believe, if they will, but in order to prevent them from hindering the faith of Christ." St Robert

enemies both internal and external.[88] Should a Christian[89] ruler encounter a non-baptised ruler obstinately engaged in promoting or commanding gross violations of the natural law he may (under the usual conditions for a just war) remove him and seek the confirmation of the *de facto* sovereignty acquired over his dominions from the supreme spiritual power.[90]

Objections from non-Catholics

Thomas Hobbes objected to the argument from the subordination of ends to the subordination of powers. No doubt the art of saddle-making is subordinate to that of horse-riding, he observes sarcastically, and yet we do not say that every saddler must obey every rider; so why would a king be obliged to obey the pope?[91] The objection is sophistical. First, a horse-rider as such has no kind of jurisdiction over anyone, and so there can be no question of anyone's having to obey him, whereas the pope has a jurisdiction over the baptised for spiritual ends. Nevertheless, if a given saddler comes to be related to a given horse-rider, though for the sake of pay and not as subject to his jurisdiction, then he must indeed 'obey' the latter, that is, accomplish his wishes; and this because of the subordination of one art to the other.

Again, if there were but one rider in the world, every saddle-maker would be obliged to govern his work according to that rider's ends, if he wished to use his art for good. Likewise, every temporal ruler, insofar as his work is related to the Kingdom of God, is obliged to direct it to the ends of the spiritual power, whose fullness exists in the Roman pontiff. The great difference between the two cases is that while in saddle-making there is little scope for variation within the needs of horsemanship, men may be governed in temporal matters in many ways without interfering with the superior interests of the Church.

This last point enables us to answer the objection made by John Locke, that *every* temporal matter has reference to spiritual ends: what then comes of the claim of Innocent III that this papal power is exercised only 'as occasion

---

Bellarmine agrees that the Roman pontiff can deprive infidels of their dominion over the faithful when they try to subvert the faithful; *Apologia for Reply to the Book of King James of Great Britain*, c.3.

[88] Suarez, *de Legibus*, III.X.6; cf. A. Ottaviani, *Compendium Iuris Publici Ecclesiastici*, 72.

[89] Or, indeed, non-Christian.

[90] This seems to be Francisco de Vitoria's understanding of the basis for Pope Alexander VI's donations in *Inter caetera* (1493). See Francisco de Vitoria, *De Indis*, Book III.9-15.

[91] *Leviathan*, chapter 42, 'Of power ecclesiastical'.

requires'? It might seem that the temporal ruler can be no better than a lackey in his own dominions. In his *Letter concerning Toleration*, Locke argues that the power attributed to the pope by Catholics would be "power to persuade the members of his Church to whatsoever he lists, either as purely religious, or in order thereunto [...] on pain of eternal fire".[92] For example, if a ruler within Christendom wished to build a new road uniting two cities, could not the pope overrule him, declaring that the money would be better spent on a new cathedral? And if the ruler refused to divert the money to this end, could not the pope depose him? Or again, since any case at law by definition involves a question of right, and since to violate right puts one's soul in danger, could not the pope claim the authority to hear appeals in every case, for the good of souls?

We have seen the principles that answer this objection: first, there must be a great spiritual good to be gained and a great spiritual evil to be avoided for the spiritual power to make use of his rights over the temporal power. While it is true that every temporal thing can be used for a spiritual end, this does not mean that some great spiritual good is at stake whenever a decision about temporal things is made. "Whether you eat or drink or whatever you do", says St Paul, "do all to the glory of God." A man may drive along a road or visit a theatre and in either case be advancing toward heaven or hell; and so the pope and bishops have no authority to say whether public money should be used to build motorways or to subsidise the arts. Nor is it the case that the use of money for a spiritual end, such as a new cathedral, will always be of more spiritual benefit for a people, than its use for a temporal end, since one must have food to pray. Secondly, when a decision requires specialised human knowledge, the hierarchy of the Church again has as such no competence to speak. The spiritual power has no special competence to make judgements of fact in the temporal order. Thus, while the hierarchy have every right to denounce a denial of right in the abstract, it has no ability or competence to judge whether a given temporal tribunal has upheld or surrendered right in the concrete.

A pope who continually acted on the temporal order of Christendom, for small or uncertain spiritual gains, would in effect be claiming ordinary temporal authority: he would thus be usurping the temporal sword, contrary to the

---

[92] This objection was renewed in the 20th century by Henri de Lubac and Benito Mussolini, writing separately. Cf. H. de Lubac, 'Le Pouvoir de l'Eglise en matière temporelle', *Revue des sciences religieuses*, 1932 12/3, 329-354. On p. 333, n. 1, de Lubac states that Bellarmine's account offers no clear criterion of what would be a reasonable and legitimate intervention in temporal affairs. For a summary of Mussolini's opposition to the doctrine of the pope's power over the temporal order, see A. Ottaviani, *Compendium*, 359.

teaching of *Unam sanctam*, and contrary to the teaching of Pope St Nicholas I and his predecessors that Christ does not will that the Roman Pontiff possess the imperial power.[93] Positive divine law, therefore, prevents a pope from turning a temporal ruler in Christendom into a cipher of his own will. If a temporal ruler in Christendom were continually governing in ways that clearly rendered the salvation of his subjects much more difficult, then a pope would be permitted if all else failed to declare him deposed and call for assistance to replace him; he is not permitted to govern his realm in his stead.

If it should ever happen that a pope abused his power by insisting on the making or unmaking of laws without claiming that the salvation of souls was at stake, or by claiming this without any show of plausibility, or by declaring a ruler deposed for not acting in accordance with such unjust demands, then the ruler would not be obliged to yield, just as no subject is *per se* obliged to submit to any abuse of power.[94] If the matter is such that the pope declares the salvation of souls to be at stake, but where the question turns on a point of doctrine has not yet been defined by the Church, it seems that the ruler may require that the doctrine be first defined before complying with a papal insistence. For example, if a pope in a restored Christendom required a Catholic ruler to strike down laws permitting the artificial production of human beings *in vitro*, the ruler might himself require that the immorality of such artificial production be first defined by the supreme authority of the pope. For it does not appear that the temporal ruler is obliged to lay down his own authority, albeit temporarily, if the spiritual ruler is not ready wholly to engage his own.

---

[93] Epistle 86 *Proposueramus quidem* to Emperor Michael in 865: "The same mediator of God and man, the man Christ Jesus, by His own acts and distinct dignities, has so decreed the duties of each power, wishing His own to be lifted up by His salutary humility, not to be submerged again by human pride, so that Christian rulers for eternal life may need pontiffs, and that pontiffs may use imperial laws only for the course of temporal affairs; because spiritual action differs from carnal efforts"; PL 119:960. Pope Nicholas is quoting Pope Gelasius I.

[94] To such distressing circumstances would apply the quotation which Newman takes from Bellarmine: "In order to resist and defend oneself no authority is required ... Therefore, as it is lawful to resist the Pope, if he assaulted a man's person, so it is lawful to resist him, if he assaulted souls, or *troubled the state* (turbanti rempublicam), and much more if he strove to destroy the Church. It is lawful, I say, to resist him, by not doing what he commands, and hindering the execution of his will"; quoted in Newman's *Letter to the Duke of Norfolk*, 'Conscience', 4.

Objections from Catholics

One would not, of course, expect Protestant writers such as Hobbes and Locke to uphold the power of the pope over temporal things outside the papal states. But if the doctrine, traditional though it is,[95] appears strange also to some Catholic writers, this is perhaps for two reasons. The first is a failure to realise that by the nature of things it exists only within Christendom. It is not only that a pope would vainly try to exert this power outside Christendom, but that the attempt would lack a legal basis. Only those rulers who have formally subjected their power to Christ can be judged as rulers by the vicar of Christ, and where necessary, in virtue of the intrinsic subordination of temporal to eternal good, have their acts over-ruled or even their power removed. Where rulers have not formally subjected their power to Christ in this way, even though they may have thus sinned gravely by omission, the pope must in a sense apply the words of St Paul: "What have I to do with judging outsiders?"[96] Although the rulers themselves may not be outsiders, for they may be baptised, and hence both their public and private acts fall under the animadversion of the Church, yet their rule itself remains outside.[97]

A second reason why Catholic writers may be reluctant to recognise the power of the pope in temporal matters is a failure to grasp the nature of Christendom, which is not simply a collection of states, each of which acknowledges the true faith, but a single commonwealth. "Kings and pontiffs", Bellarmine writes, "clergy and laity do not make two republics, but one, that is, one Church; for we are all one body."[98] The Church does not cease to be one body because

---

[95] A. Ottaviani states that the doctrine of the ecclesiastical power over the temporal order, being substantially contained "in the acts of the popes and of the ecumenical councils, in the writings of the Fathers and in the treatises of the doctors of the Church" must be recognised as certain; *Compendium Iuris Publici Ecclesiastici*, 356. Pius XII refers in the encyclical *Mystici Corporis Christi* to the "the solemn teaching of Our predecessor of immortal memory Boniface VIII in the Apostolic Letter *Unam Sanctam*". For his part, Bellarmine states that the view that the pope has by divine law no power to deprive guilty temporal rulers of their realms is not so much an opinion as a heresy, *non tam sententia quam haeresis*; *Controversiae*, 'On the Supreme Pontiff', bk. 5, ch. 1.

[96] 1 Cor. 5:12.

[97] Pope Pius IX, speaking of the deposition of monarchs by some of his predecessors, noted that the right to do this "was a consequence of the public law then in force"; *Allocution*, 20th July, 1871, quoted in *DTC*, 'Pouvoir du Pape dans l'ordre temporelle. II. Le pouvoir du pape en matière temporelle'. He stated in the same allocution that this right "had absolutely nothing in common with pontifical infallibility".

[98] *Controversiae*, 'On the supreme pontiff', bk. 5, ch. 7. Cf. St Ambrose, *Commentary on the gospel of St Luke*, c. 11: "The mystery of the Church is clearly expressed, who in the Ninevites

different groups of people within her also comprise distinct earthly provinces with temporal ends. The rulers of each of these provinces are obliged to prefer the good of the Church to that of their own province[99]; and this, as Bellarmine observes, is not simply because the Church is a better society than that which they rule, since there is no general obligation for the rulers of a given society to change their way of ruling in order to benefit some other, better society: it is because the part must prefer the good of the whole to its own good.[100]

We may argue similarly from the nature of the Church as a perfect society. Bellarmine's syllogism is ineluctable:

> The Church must have every power necessary to attain its end; but the power of using and disposing of temporal things is necessary for attaining the spiritual end, since otherwise evil rulers could support heretics with impunity, and overturn religion; therefore, she has this power too.[101]

But if the Church has this power by divine right, that is, if it is the duty of her sons to give it to her when they can, then this power is possessed by the supreme pontiff, who has the *plenitudo potestatis* within the Church.

Some authors object that it is sufficient to attribute to the Church a power to command in temporal matters in a way that binds her children in conscience, without attributing to her a power to act directly on the temporal order, by declaring legislation to be null, judging and deposing.[102] On this view, if a ruler within Christendom were, for example, to decree a right to abortion for all pregnant women, or a duty for doctors to put to death mentally handicapped adults, or were to forbid the offering of Mass, the pope would simply order him to retract his decrees, and if he failed to do so, the pope would excommunicate him and remind his subjects that they must not obey these unjust laws. To desire to do more, these authors say, evinces a lack of faith, as

---

by penance and in the Queen of the South by a zeal for wisdom is gathered from the ends of the whole earth to learn the words of the peaceful Solomon. Truly is she a Queen, whose kingdom is undivided, and who arises from distinct and separated peoples into one body."

[99] Cf. *Syllabus of Errors*, 42nd condemned proposition: "In a conflict of laws between the two powers, the civil law prevails."

[100] *Controversiae*, 'On the supreme pontiff', bk. 5, ch. 7.

[101] Ibid.

[102] Cf. H. de Lubac, 'Le Pouvoir de l'Eglise en Matière temporelle'. This author moreover does not distinguish clearly between the situation inside and outside Christendom.

if one feared that the Church could otherwise fail of her mission; it would even be to tempt the Church as the devil tempted Christ.[103]

Yet in fact it is for the good of souls that the Church have a power to declare evil legislation null, and to declare pertinacious legislators deposed, since she thereby makes subjects bolder in resisting evil, and disposes the way for the replacement of the tyrant. To ascribe such power to her does not betoken a lack of faith in Christ's promise to the Church of indefectibility, a promise which after all does not guarantee her continuance in any given place: it is, rather, to recognise the realism of the inspired text which says: "What manner of man the ruler of a city is, such also are they that dwell therein."[104] The devil in the wilderness strove to make Christ adore him and thus gain power over the kingdoms of the world: this is not quite the same as for theologians to recognise, in accordance with the teaching of the popes and doctors, that the Church has a certain power over the kingdoms of the world by divine right, which she may use to promote the worship of the true God and the devil's overthrow.[105]

Certainly, Christ's power is made perfect in weakness: hence, when divine providence does not permit the exercise of any of the natural or supernatural powers which God has given to His children, they must abandon themselves to that providence, confident that this very impotence will in those circumstances redound to God's glory more than the exercise of their powers would have done. Yet this does not licence us by our own initiative to deprive ourselves of such powers. God may intervene miraculously to free me from a conflagration; but I should not for that reason fail to summon the fire-brigade.

---

[103] Ibid. 340-42. "The theologians who claim for the Church a jurisdiction over the temporal order", wrote de Lubac, "do not perceive [...] that they tempt her, as Satan once tempted Christ in the wilderness." These theologians, as we have seen, include St Peter Damian, St Bernard, St Thomas Aquinas, St Bonaventure, and St Robert Bellarmine.

[104] Ecclesiasticus 10:2.

[105] Cf. Blessed John Henry Newman, *Essays on Miracles*, essay II, 5.6, 'The Sudden Death of Arius': "St. Peter's denunciation of Ananias and Sapphira was followed by their instantaneous deaths; St. Paul's denunciation of Elymas, by his immediate blindness. These instances, moreover, suggest that our Lord's earthly ministry might probably be conducted on different laws from those which belonged to His risen power, when the Spirit had descended, and light was spread abroad; according to the text in which blasphemy against the Son of man and blasphemy against the Spirit are contrasted". As we argue in the following section, however, penalties such as death and blinding are not ones that the spiritual power imposes either directly or through the intermediary of the temporal power. Hence St Thomas held that St Peter was prophesying and not imposing a sentence when he told Sapphira that she would die as her husband had done; STh 2a 2ae 64, 4 ad 1.

Spiritual and temporal punishments

We spoke above of 'mixed matters'. Under this heading fall certain actions which both the spiritual and the temporal power have a native right to prohibit, though for different ends. *Per se*, any external, vicious act is subject to such prohibition by each power, since every such act harms or impedes both the common temporal good and the common spiritual good of the city of God. On the other hand, in our order of providence "man is not ordained to the political community, according to all that he is and has",[106] and consequently "it is not necessary that all of his acts earn a reward or punishment in reference to the political community".[107]

The temporal ruler in Christendom, therefore need not make all infractions of canon law, for example, into civil offences: he may well choose to manifest the infinite elevation of the supernatural end of his citizens by not incorporating into the law of the land some of those acts which are only wrong because they are contrary to that supernatural end, for example, neglect of the holy days of the Church. Yet even these acts may in principle be punished by him, since, as we have often said, the citizenry cannot be rightly directed even toward their temporal end if they are averted from their ultimate one.[108] And when it comes to crimes against the supernatural end which are seriously destructive of the temporal peace and good of Christendom, such as public heresy and blasphemy, the temporal ruler would neglect his duty were he not to forbid them. Nevertheless, the judgement about whether or not a crime has been

---

[106] STh 1a 2ae 21, 4 ad 3. Thus sanctifying grace is not given to us *for the sake* of perfecting the temporal community, even though without such grace fallen man cannot fulfil his duties to this community. Henri Grenier remarks however that if man had been assigned a merely natural end, he would then have been ordained to his political community according to all that he had and was; H. Grenier, *Cours de Philosophie*, vol. 2, 349.

[107] Note that St Thomas says it is "not necessary" (*non oportet*) that they be so rewarded or punished, not that it is necessary that they should not be.

[108] Charlemagne made all infractions of canon law into civil offences, in his *Capitularies*, tit. 1 cap. 2, observing: "In no way are We able to understand how they can be faithful to Us, who have shown themselves unfaithful to God and disobedient to their priests." This was recalled and praised by Benedict XIV in *Providas Romanorum* in 1751, and by Leo XII in *Quo graviora* in 1826. A. Ottaviani states: 'Civil law can *in the name of the Church* punish the laity for transgressing the laws of the Church in spiritual matters. [...] Indeed, the republic can also *in its own name* punish the laity for these faults or even omissions, when from such a transgression of ecclesiastical law harm follows in the civil order itself'; *Compendium*, 391.

committed against the supernatural end belongs to the ecclesiastical tribunal, not to the secular one.[109]

It is not unjust if each power should punish numerically the same crime, inasmuch as the same crime is contrary to both the temporal and the eternal good of the citizenry. Yet the distinction of orders will be clearer if crimes are punished in reference to the good against which they directly offend. For example, the public blasphemer in Christendom will more suitably be punished by an ecclesiastical tribunal, and the thief by a lay tribunal, even though each offender could without injustice be punished by both.[110]

The lay or temporal tribunal has at its disposal only temporal sanctions: fines, confiscations, loss of temporal office, imprisonment, exile, corporal and capital punishment. It cannot impose spiritual punishments, for example, partial or complete exclusion from the sacraments or sacramentals of the Church, deprivation of ecclesiastical burial, or suspension from or loss of ecclesiastical office. The spiritual tribunal has these spiritual penalties at its disposal, and uses them by preference, as most fitting to its own nature. Yet, as we have just seen, the Church claims for the spiritual power a right to use temporal punishments also on her wayward children.

In the first place, she can impose temporal penalties on willing subjects, both inside and outside the sacrament of penance. A penitent in confession, for example, may be obliged to donate money to some worthy cause. A member of a religious order may be given a non-sacramental penance by his superior.[111] Secondly, within Christendom, she can call on the help of the 'secular arm', that is, the temporal power. The spiritual power does not necessarily possess what is called the *vis armata*, that is, public physical force for coercing unwilling subjects. But it possesses the right to be aided by the *vis armata* of the temporal

---

[109] In the case of heresy this tribunal would be diocesan, subject to appeal to the Holy See. In many periods this process was foreshortened by the institution of the Holy Office of the Roman and Universal Inquisition and various other regional inquisitions. See: Paul III, *Licet ab initio*, 21st July 1542.

[110] Cf. 1917 Code of Canon Law, 2198: "A crime which offends only the law of the Church, by its nature, is prosecuted only by ecclesiastical authority, though at times, where this authority judges it necessary or opportune, by requiring the help of the secular arm; a crime which only offends the law of civil society, civil authority punishes by its own right, without prejudice to canon 120, although the Church also has competence in regard to this crime insofar as it is a sin (*ratione peccati*); a crime which offends the law of each society can be punished by each power." Canon 120 of this code affirmed the need for clergy to be tried before an ecclesiastical court for all cases, unless in some place other provision had been legitimately made.

[111] The *Rule of St Benedict* provides for the beating of unruly monks.

power. Hence, if someone has been sentenced to imprisonment for breaking an ecclesiastical law, the bishop in Christendom may call on the police to enforce the sentence.

The temporal penalties inflicted for a given crime may well differ, depending on whether the temporal authority is acting in its own name, or as the instrument of the spiritual power. In the former case, they will tend to be more severe.[112] The temporal power punishes not only for correction, good example and deterrence, but also for the sake of restoring the order of justice in this life; for the proper end of the temporal power is by definition to be achieved here below. The spiritual power is ordered to the hereafter, and seeks the just order among the members of the Church militant insofar as this helps them to their eternal end. The punishments inflicted by the spiritual power therefore are never inflicted merely to restore the order of justice[113] within the Church but always with a view to the future life. From this point of view, a punishment is sufficient when it corrects the guilty and protects the good of others.[114] Asked by St Augustine, Archbishop of Canterbury, what should be done to Englishmen caught stealing from churches, Pope Gregory the Great replied in these terms:

There are some who commit theft though they have resources, and there are others who transgress in this matter out of want. Hence it is needful that some should be corrected by fines, but some by beating, and some more severely, but some more lightly. And, when any one is somewhat severely dealt with, he should be dealt with in charity, and not in anger; since to the man himself who is corrected, the punishment is assigned lest he should be given up to the fires of hell. For we ought so to maintain discipline towards believers as good fathers are wont to do towards their sons, whom they both smite

---

[112] Cf. St Augustine, *Letter* 134 to Apringius the pro-consul, 3: "The cause of the province is one thing, that of the Church is another; the governance of the former must awe men into submission; the gentleness of the latter should win acceptance by kindness" ("alia causa est provinciae, alia est ecclesiae: illius terribiliter gerenda est administratio; huius clementer commendanda est mansuetudo.")

[113] Indeed, were the Church to seek to inflict the punishment owed to her offending children in strict justice she would have to execute all baptised persons guilty of actual mortal sin in order to ensure their eternal damnation, which would rather frustrate the purpose of her own existence - the salvation of souls.

[114] Cf. F. Cavagnis, *Institutiones Iuris Publici Ecclesiastici* (Rome: Desclée & Lefebvre, 1906), 191-93.

with blows for their faults, and yet seek to have as their heirs the very persons on whom they inflict pain.[115]

The temporal power may use bloody means, even capital punishment, when acting on its own authority: within Christendom it may also do this against spiritual offences like heresy if they gravely harm the common temporal good.[116] Theologians have disputed about whether the spiritual power also possesses the *ius gladii*,[117] and hence can require the temporal power to execute delinquents.[118]

It appears more reasonable to deny this. True, other things being equal, the faith should be defended *more* vigorously because of its role in bringing man to eternal life than because of its role in contributing to man's happiness in this world.[119] Yet capital punishment has never been included in canon law. The

---

[115] Book XI, Epistle 64.

[116] Leo X, *Exsurge Domine* (1520) 33. Permission to employ such means (*relinquere iudicio saeculari*) is however dependent on the spiritual power whose prudential judgement in this matter looks to the spiritual good of the offender and the community. "If in order to save an earthly life it is praiseworthy to use force to stop a man from committing suicide, are we not to be allowed to use the same force — holy coercion — to save the Life (with a capital) of many who are stupidly bent on killing their souls?" St Jose Maria Escrivá, *The Way*, 399. From the perspective of the spiritual power the use of the final sanction, however, is ordered principally to the salvation of other members of the Church; cf. STh 2a2ae 11, 3: "If he is yet stubborn, the Church no longer hoping for his conversion, looks to the salvation of others, by excommunicating him and separating him from the Church, and furthermore delivers him to the secular tribunal to be thereby driven from the world by death." The same principle applies to other extremely grave offences committed by persons primarily subject to the canonical tribunals; cf. Pius V, *Horrendum illud scelus*, 30th August, 1568.

[117] 'The right of the sword', i.e. the right of a person or institution to order capital punishment.

[118] Cf. F. Cavagnis, *Institutiones* 198-209; C. Journet, *The Church of the Word Incarnate*, 250-54. Cavagnis says that by far the greater number of doctors deny that the Church possesses the *ius gladii*, *Institutiones*, 200. This consensus is reflected in the *Decretum Gratiani*, which quotes the 11th Council of Toledo: "His a quibus Domini sacramenta tractanda sunt, iudicium sanguinis agitare non licet" ("those who are to handle the Lord's sacraments may not carry out the judgement of blood.") We prefer to say rather that it is the spiritual power, rather than the Church, which lacks it. See above, p. 231, n. 47.

[119] Hence, if a Christian land must fight a defensive war against an infidel nation, the soldiers may motivate themselves not only by the thought that victory will make it easier for their children to be good citizens, but still more by the thought that it will make it easier for them to be saved. In defending the institution of military religious orders, St Thomas affirms that soldiering may be motivated not simply by the safety of the commonwealth, but also by "the conservation of divine worship"; STh 2a 2ae 188, 3.

clergy themselves may not shed blood: thus they are more conformed to Christ, whose Passion they represent at the altar, and as the ministers of the New Testament, they manifest the truth that this Testament does not offer temporal rewards or make temporal threats.[120] Since it is fitting that the clergy show forth the meekness of Christ more visibly than others, it is also fitting that this meekness be infused even into such temporal means as they employ.

Yet the Church can remind the bearers of temporal power of their duty to deal with criminals in the manner proper to the temporal power, just as she can remind anyone of their duties, for example, surgeons of their duty to do no harm. Even if the duty in question were a duty of capital punishment, the execution would still not be performed in the name of the Church, just as surgeons who have been reminded of their duties do not therefore heal in the name of the Church.[121] Pope Leo I recognised that the Church was helped by such means, even without requesting them.[122]

***

---

[120] STh 2a 2ae 64, 4. The Church of God is not to be defended like a camp, said St Thomas Becket, as he prepared for martyrdom.

[121] Cf. F. Cavagnis, *Institutiones Iuris Publici Ecclesiastici*, 205-6; C. Journet, *The Church of the Word Incarnate*, 251-53; A. Ottaviani, *Institutiones Iuris Publici Ecclesiastici*, 358-59. It is in this sense that one may interpret St Thomas when he speaks of wars being waged "by the authority of rulers or of the Church"; STh 2a 2ae 188, 3 ad 4. Although the chivalry of Europe were summoned to the banner of the Cross and the liberation of Jerusalem by Bl. Urban II and encouraged by him through the endowment of the Crusade with a singular indulgence, yet that campaign and by implication the subsequent expeditions were undertaken formally at the request of the temporal ruler of the Levantine Christians: Alexios I Komnenos and thereafter the rulers of the Crusader territories established at the end of the First Crusade.

[122] Epistle 15, to Turribius, concerning the suppression of Priscillianism: "Even the leaders of the world so abhorred this profane folly that they laid low its originator, with most of his disciples, by the sword of the public laws. For they saw that all desire for honourable conduct was removed, all marriage-ties undone, and the divine and the human law simultaneously undermined, if it were allowed for men of this kind to live anywhere under such a creed. And this rigorous treatment was for long a help to the Church's law of gentleness which, although it relies upon the priestly judgment, and shuns blood-stained vengeance (*sacerdotali contenta iudicio, cruentas refugit ultiones*), yet is assisted by the stern decrees of Christian princes as men in fear of bodily punishment have recourse to the spiritual remedy." In the previous century, St Optatus invoked the example of Moses in defence of the capital punishment meted out to some members of the violent Circumcellion sect, while noting that it happened without any request from the bishops; *De Schismate Donatistarum*, III, cc. 6-7.

It is fitting that those who rule be not themselves unruly. [123] While the necessities of a fallen world require men to obey sinful rulers, this would scarcely be tolerable if we did not know that these rulers will themselves be judged on the last day. Of God's servants the clergy it will be asked whether they made fructify the spiritual wealth entrusted to them, a wealth unfailingly fruitful if some evil will on the part of its stewards does not intervene; of the holders of temporal power, citizens of the Church militant, it will be asked whether they sought to submit their sceptres to His reign.

A certain nobleman went into a far country, to receive for himself a kingdom, and to return.

And calling his ten servants, he gave them ten pounds, and said to them: Trade till I come.

But his citizens hated him: and they sent an embassage after him, saying: We will not have this man to reign over us.

And it came to pass, that he returned, having received the kingdom: and he commanded his servants to be called, to whom he had given the money, that he might know how much every man had gained by trading.

And the first came, saying: Lord, thy pound hath gained ten pounds.

And he said to him: Well done, thou good servant, because thou hast been faithful in a little, thou shalt have power over ten cities.

And the second came, saying: Lord, thy pound hath gained five pounds.

And he said to him: Be thou also over five cities.

And another came, saying: Lord, behold here is thy pound, which I have kept laid up in a napkin; for I feared thee, because thou art an austere man: thou takest up what thou didst not lay down, and thou reapest that which thou didst not sow.

He saith to him: Out of thy own mouth I judge thee, thou wicked servant. Thou knewest that I was an austere man, taking up what I laid not down, and reaping that which I did not sow: And why then didst thou not give my money into the bank, that at my coming, I might have exacted it with usury?

---

[123] Jn. 8:7.

And he said to them that stood by: Take the pound away from him, and give it to him that hath ten pounds.

And they said to him: Lord, he hath ten pounds.

But I say to you, that to everyone that hath shall be given, and he shall abound: and from him that hath not, even that which he hath, shall be taken from him.

But as for those my enemies, who would not have me reign over them, bring them hither, and kill them before me.[124]

---

[124] Lk. 19:12-27.

Theses

(i)   Outside Christendom, the Church claims from the temporal power those rights which are due to her under natural law.

(ii)   Mixed matters are those which, under different aspects, relate directly to both the spiritual and temporal end of society.

(iii)   Both powers should legislate about mixed matters in a harmonious way which safeguards the superior rights of the spiritual power.

(iv)   A concordat between the spiritual and temporal power, presenting themselves as sovereign and independent bodies, is an abnormal arrangement, but produces obligations mutually binding under natural law.

(v)   It is fitting that the baptised be governed without coercion.

(vi)   Nevertheless, the Church has the right to impose both temporal and spiritual penalties upon the baptised so that they will lead a Christian life.

(vii)   Outside Christendom, the Church may remind baptised temporal rulers of their duties to God and to herself in the very exercise of their office, and punish them if they disobey, either with spiritual penalties, or with temporal penalties that, however, must be freely assumed by the guilty party.

(viii)   Outside Christendom, the Church reprobates rather than nullifies immoral laws.

(ix)   The spiritual power cannot enjoin temporal rulers to accomplish duties whose existence may be discerned only by specialised human learning and competence.

(x)   If the bearer of spiritual power claims a competence that does not belong to him, the bearer of temporal power is not obliged to obey him.

(xi)   Within Christendom, the acts which spiritual rulers accomplish in the temporal order for the good of souls have also a legal status in that order.

(xii)   Since the pope and the other Catholic bishops govern the spiritual kingdom which is the Catholic Church, when the temporal power itself belongs to this kingdom, that is, in Christendom, this power is itself under their authority.

(xiii) The apostolic hierarchy of the Church can declare null some use of, or reassign possession of, the temporal power but only in case of necessity, that is, where it is morally certain that grave harm would otherwise be done to souls.

(xiv) Within Christendom, the Church has the right to command the secular power to assist in enforcing the penalties mentioned in (vi) above.

(xv) The pope may *ratione peccati* in case of spiritual necessity declare a sovereign deposed and institute a replacement.

(xvi) The pope may in case of objective and grave negligence insist upon the passing of a law by temporal rulers, or declare some law previously passed by them to be null through conflict with natural or divine law.

(xvii) The pope may in case of spiritual necessity exercise judicial power about some temporal matter, when there is no competent temporal judge, or none who is willing to act.

(xviii) Other bishops have similar powers in the case of rulers subject to their jurisdiction, of legislatures which govern a people entirely subject to that bishop's jurisdiction, and of law-suits between people subject to his jurisdiction.

(xix) Within Christendom, it is not lawful for Christians to tolerate a publicly infidel or heretical king.

(xx) Within Christendom, the body that moves to free itself extra-judicially from a tyrant must seek the confirmation of its action, after the fact if necessary, from the sovereign pontiff.

(xxi) The distinction between faithful and unbelievers, considered in itself, does not do away with dominion and authority of unbelievers over the faithful.

(xxii) Nevertheless, the Church possesses the radical right to declare deposed unbaptised persons ruling over the baptised outside Christendom, simply because they are unbaptised.

(xxiii) To avoid scandal, the Church does not exercise this right.

(xxiv) As a perfect society the Church has the power to resist external as well as internal enemies; hence if a ruler outside Christendom is preventing the preaching of the gospel, or the free practice of the Catholic religion the Church may declare him a tyrant, and encourage or even oblige some other baptised person to take arms against him.

(xxv) Should a Christian ruler encounter a non-baptised ruler obstinately engaged in gross violations of the natural law he may (under the usual conditions for a just war) remove him and seek the confirmation of the *de facto* sovereignty acquired over his dominions from the supreme spiritual power.

(xxvi) The rulers of each province of Christendom must prefer the good of the Church to that of their own province, as every part must love the whole more than itself.

(xxvii) The temporal ruler in Christendom can, but need not, make infractions of canon law into civil offences.

(xxviii) The temporal penalties inflicted for a given crime are likely to differ, depending on whether the temporal authority is acting in its own name, or as the instrument of the spiritual power.

(xxix) The spiritual power does not shed blood, either acting directly or through the medium of the temporal power, yet its bearers can remind the bearers of temporal power of their duties, even when these include the duty to shed blood.

Chapter 12
The Two Cities

I saw heaven opened, and behold a white horse; and he that sat upon him was called faithful and true, and with justice doth he judge and fight. And his eyes were as a flame of fire, and on his head were many diadems, and he had a name written, which no man knoweth but himself. And he was clothed with a garment sprinkled with blood; and his name is called, the Word of God. [...] And I saw the beast, and the kings of the earth, and their armies gathered together to make war with him that sat upon the horse, and with his army.[1]

While reason by itself teaches the need for a perfect society in which any distinct temporal power will be subject to the spiritual one, our principal guide in politics must be revelation. Holy Scripture, especially in its final book, instructs us that history's theme is the honour of God. Hence a perpetual and personal conflict between Jesus Christ, with those who belong to him, and the fallen spirits, with those who belong to them. No political philosophy or statesmanship which is ignorant of or rejects this revealed truth can be called realistic or well founded.

For as in the time of Augustine, so even now, two loves are still making two cities, the love of God to the contempt of self, and the love of self even to the contempt of God. It cannot be otherwise, since every rational being either loves God or himself above all else: for whatever it may be that turns a man aside from the natural inclination of all creatures to love their Creator more than themselves, it is for love of himself that he aspires toward that thing:

As Augustine says in Book XIV of the *City of God,* just as love of God makes the city of God, so the disordered love of oneself makes the city of Babylon; and just as in the love of God, God himself is the final end to whom all things are directed which are loved with right love, so in the love of one's own excellence is found an ultimate end, to which all other things are directed. For the man who seeks to

[1] Apoc. 19:11-19.

abound in wealth, or in science, or in places of honour, or in any other things whatsoever, aims, through all these things, to excel.[2]

These two cities are not merely metaphors, as if they were two multitudes which had their unity only in the mind. They are warring forces, though mortals may hardly discern the progress and issue of their engagements.

Whence do they receive their unity? Christ is the head of mankind, principally in regard to men's souls, insofar as these have received or can still receive His grace and glory,[3] but secondarily in regard to their bodies,[4] for those who will be glorified at the end of time. Yet His headship has different modes as it relates to different men:

> If we take the whole time of the world in general, Christ is the head of all men, but diversely. For, first and principally, He is the head of such as are united to Him by glory; secondly, of those who are actually united to Him by charity; thirdly, of those who are actually united to Him by faith; fourthly, of those who are united to Him merely in potentiality, which is not yet reduced to act, yet will be reduced to act according to divine predestination; fifthly, of those who are united to Him in potentiality, which will never be reduced to act, as with those men existing in the world who are not predestined, who, on their departure from this world, wholly cease to be members of Christ, as being no longer in potentiality to be united to Christ.[5]

His headship over this mystical body, which is the Church, is both external and internal. It is external: for He exercised it personally while on earth, and since the Ascension He has exercised it through the teachings, laws, and precepts given by apostles and pastors in His name, through Christian parents, and rulers within Christendom, accomplishing their vocation, and through any other supernatural solicitations to good which one man offers to another. It is internal, as regards the grace that flows from God to man, since Christ's humanity, "through its unity with the Godhead, has the power to justify".[6] In

---

[2] *De Malo*, 8, 2; cf. *De Malo*, 8, 1 ad 19: "As the philosopher says in *Rhetoric* II, to love is to will good to someone. Therefore insofar as a man aspires after any kind of good things, he seems to love himself. [...] All the roots and sources of the vices enclose a disordered love of oneself."

[3] STh 3a 8, 2.

[4] Ibid.

[5] Ibid. 8, 3.

[6] Ibid. 8, 6.

the first sense, others, especially the popes, patriarchs and other bishops, share to some limited degree, for a time, and by His authority, in the headship of Christ over the Church. In the second sense, to be head is proper to Him, since among all created things, only the humanity of Christ, in virtue of the hypostatic union, can touch the soul directly.

The devil apes Christ's headship. Yet being a creature, he cannot exercise a headship by action directly upon the soul. Hence, he is called the head of all the wicked "in virtue of external governance alone."[7] The unity of Babylon thus resembles that of God's city as a corpse jerked by a puppet-master might resemble a living man. The devil exercises this headship through enticement to evil: false teaching, evil laws, bad examples, and every other illecebration. Not that every sin need follow directly from a diabolic initiative, for the power and knowledge of the fallen spirits, though great in comparison to ours, is limited and fallible. Yet just as a commanding officer might set his whole army on the march, not by speaking to each man in turn, but by causing the standard to be carried before it, so Satan has set the example of his revolt, and of all the revolts that flowed therefrom, in front of the human race, "which some imitate at his suggestion, and others spontaneously, without any suggesting".[8] This intention of the first and highest fallen angel that as many persons as possible follow his apostasy gives to his city such unity as it enjoys, or rather, as it endures: "The purpose of the devil is the aversion of the rational creation from God."[9] He thus becomes the head of all who put themselves knowingly or unknowingly beneath his sway.

All this is the doctrine of the two cities, taught by Scripture,[10] familiar to theologians and spiritual writers,[11] and recalled by Pope Leo XIII in 1884:

> The race of man, after its miserable fall, "through the envy of the devil", from God the Creator and giver of heavenly gifts, separated into two diverse and opposite parts, of which the one steadfastly contends for truth and virtue, the other for those things which are contrary to virtue and to truth. The one is the kingdom of God on earth, namely, the true Church of Jesus Christ; and those who desire

---

[7] Ibid. 8, 7.

[8] Ibid.

[9] Ibid.

[10] James 4:4: "Adulterers, know you not that the friendship of this world is the enmity of God? Whosoever therefore will be a friend of this world becometh an enemy of God."

[11] Among spiritual writers, see for example St Ignatius of Loyola, *Spiritual Exercises*, 'The Fourth Day – Meditation on Two Standards', and St Francis de Sales, *Introduction to the Devout Life*, I. 18, 'On how the soul chooses the devout life'.

from their heart to be united to it, so as to gain salvation, must needs serve God and his only-begotten Son with their whole mind and with an entire will. The other is the kingdom of Satan, in whose possession and control are all whosoever follow the fatal example of their leader and of our first parents, those who refuse to obey the divine and eternal law, and who have many aims of their own in contempt of God, and many aims also against God. [...] At every period of time each has been in conflict with the other, with a variety and multiplicity of weapons and of warfare, although not always with equal ardour and assault.[12]

The City of God is the Catholic Church, laity and clergy together.[13] Some among the baptised - all those in mortal sin - are not citizens of that city, but no one who is wholly outside her pale belongs to it.[14] The other city is the multitude of temporal polities existing outside the Catholic Church, that is, outside Christendom. Some among the citizens of these polities – all those with living faith in Christ - are not citizens of the city of man; but these polities themselves, by not submitting themselves to the incarnate Word, are by that fact in opposition to Him. "He who is not with me is against me": these words apply not only to the heart of man but also to the institutions which have come out of his heart, and hence to the temporal power itself.[15] Writing to a pagan magistrate who imagined that Christian and non-Christian might be united in the temporal objective of furthering the good of their homeland, St Augustine rejects this idea:

---

[12] *Humanum genus*, 1-2.

[13] More precisely we can say that while the Church and the City of God are the same society, having the same end and the same rulers, 'the Church' denotes this society as composed of those who profess the true faith, share the same sacraments and acknowledge the same spiritual rulers, while 'the City of God' denotes it as embracing all those who are effectively tending toward eternal life.

[14] Boniface VIII, *Unam sanctam*. "Urged by faith, we are obliged to believe and to hold that the Church is one, holy, catholic, and also apostolic. We believe in her firmly and we confess with simplicity that outside of her there is neither salvation nor the remission of sins, as the Spouse in the Canticles proclaims: *One is my dove, my perfect one. She is the only one, the chosen of her who bore her,* and she represents one sole mystical body whose head is Christ and the head of Christ is God. In her then is one Lord, one faith, one baptism. There had been at the time of the deluge only one ark of Noah, prefiguring the one Church, which ark, having been finished to a single cubit, had only one pilot and guide, namely Noah, and we read that, outside of this ark, all that subsisted on the earth was destroyed."

[15] Matt. 12:30; Lk. 11:23.

These things I have said, [Augustine corrects him] because of your having written that the nearer you come to the end of life, the greater is your desire to leave your country in a safe and flourishing condition. Away with all these vanities and follies, and let men be converted to the true worship of God, and to chaste and pious manners: then will you see your country flourishing, not in the vain opinion of fools, but in the sound judgment of the wise; when your fatherland here on earth shall have become a portion of that Fatherland into which we are born not by the flesh, but by faith, and in which all the holy and faithful servants of God shall bloom in the eternal summer, when their labours in the winter of time are done.[16]

Indeed, since the Fall there has been a tension between the pursuit of temporal and spiritual goods. Hence just as even a righteous man living on earth must refrain from "carnal desires which war against the soul" (1 Pet. 2:11), so too even within Christendom, the temporal polity must be continuously checked by the spiritual power lest it follow its fallen tendency to rejoin the city of man. "The whole world is the Church, and the whole world hates the Church. The world hates the world: the world in enmity, the world reconciled; the condemned world, the saved world; the defiled world, the purified world."[17]

Since the devil is *the prince of this world*, it follows that even were it not necessary for the temporal power to be subjected to Christ in virtue of His universal kingship, or in virtue of the subordination of man's temporal to his spiritual end, or in virtue of his inability to reach even his temporal end without the gospel, it should be done from simple prudence, as protection from a powerful and malevolent foe who would use every means to damn human souls. Nor may one attain some 'stable equilibrium' of the holy and the demonic within society; the conflict must be renewed each morning. *Militia vita hominis super terram.*[18]

---

[16] St Augustine, Letter 91.6 in J. G. Cunningham (trans.) *Nicene and Post-Nicene Fathers*, First Series, vol. 1 (Buffalo, NY: Christian Literature Publishing Co., 1887).

[17] St Augustine, *Tractates on the Gospel of St John*, 87.2: "Totus ergo mundus Ecclesia est, et totus mundus odit Ecclesiam. Mundus igitur odit mundum, inimicus reconciliatum, damnatus salvatum, inquinatus mundatum"; PL 35: 1853.

[18] Job 7:1.

Lessons of experience

The doctrine of the two cities, and the consequent need for Christendom, which comes to us by revelation and theology, is confirmed by the experience of the Church.

When the Son of God came into the world, He came to die, and offered no resistance to those who crucified Him. Christians are called to the imitation of Christ, and this imitation is most striking in martyrdom. Any Christian ruler therefore naturally feels some reluctance to make use of force in defending supernatural truth. Yet should he refuse to do so on principle he would wrong both God and his own subjects. Christ did not come to exercise temporal authority over men,[19] or to bid others use it on His behalf while He lived,[20] but to teach them and die for them. It was fitting that as a divine Person, He should thus establish His Father's kingdom by wholly divine means. Yet those who govern this Kingdom on earth spiritually and temporally must according to their possibilities make some use of coercion to preserve its good estate, as of a means connatural to human government.[21]

The experience of St Augustine illustrates well both this reluctance and this duty. When the Catholic emperors desired to assist the Church in her struggle with the Donatists in Africa, the bishop of Hippo wished at first to receive nothing more than protection against the material violence of these schismatics. Preaching alone, he thought, should be used to recall them to unity with the Church. His mind was changed by seeing that financial penalties imposed by the Roman laws occasioned sincere and lasting conversions. Writing to Vincentius, a Donatist who had complained about these laws as contrary to Christian tradition, the bishop of Hippo unfolded his thought at some length:

---

[19] Lk. 12:13-14: "One of the multitude said to him: Master, speak to my brother that he divide the inheritance with me. But he said to him: Man, who hath appointed me judge or divider over you?"; Jn. 6:15: "Jesus therefore, when he knew that they would come to take him by force and make him king, fled again into the mountains, himself alone."

[20] Matt. 26:53-54: "Thinkest thou that I cannot ask my Father, and he will give me presently more than twelve legions of angels? How then shall the scriptures be fulfilled, that so it must be done?"

[21] Cf. St Robert Bellarmine, *Controversiae*, 'On the members of the Church', bk. 3, ch. 22: "It was fitting that Christ, who had come to be judged and not to judge, should not avenge injuries personally (*per se*), but should leave them to be avenged by His spiritual sons; of this we have the figure in David, who whilst he lived was never willing that Semei, who had cursed him, should be killed, but nevertheless in death commanded Solomon that his sin should not be left unavenged, 3 Kings 2."

We see not a few men here and there, but many cities, once Donatist, now Catholic, vehemently detesting the diabolical schism, and ardently loving the unity of the Church; and these became Catholic under the influence of that fear which is to you so offensive, by the laws of emperors. [...] Originally my opinion was, that no one should be coerced into the unity of Christ, that we must act only by words, fight only by arguments, and prevail by force of reason, lest we should have those whom we knew as avowed heretics feigning themselves to be Catholics. But this opinion of mine was overcome not by the words of those who controverted it, but by the conclusive instances to which they could point.

For, in the first place, there was set over against my opinion my own town, which, although it was once wholly on the side of Donatus, was brought over to the Catholic unity by fear of the imperial edicts, but which we now see filled with such detestation of your ruinous perversity, that it would scarcely be believed that it had ever been involved in your error. [...] For how many were already, as we assuredly know, willing to be Catholics, being moved by the indisputable plainness of truth, but daily putting off their avowal of this through fear of offending their own party. How many were bound, not by truth – of which you had not the possession - but by the heavy chains of inveterate custom. [...]

How many supposed the sect of Donatus to be the true Church, merely because ease had made them too listless, or too conceited, or too sluggish, to take pains to examine Catholic truth! How many would have entered earlier had not the calumnies of slanderers, who declared that we offered something else than we do upon the altar of God, shut them out. How many, believing that it mattered not which party a Christian belonged to, remained in the schism of Donatus only because they had been born in it, and because no one was compelling them to forsake it and pass over into the Catholic Church.[22]

In a letter to the imperial official, Boniface, St Augustine replies to various objections which were made then as now to the use of force in defence of the truth. The first is that the true Church can only have penalties inflicted on her,

---

[22] Epistle 93: 16-17. The whole letter should be read.

and not inflict penalties on others. In reply, he appeals both to Scriptural allegory and to reason:

> If the true Church is the one which actually suffers persecution, not the one which inflicts it, let them ask the apostle what Church Sarah was a type of, when she inflicted persecution on her hand-maid. For he declares that the free mother of us all, the heavenly Jerusalem, that is to say, the true Church of God, was prefigured in that woman who afflicted her hand-maid (yet if we investigate the story further, we shall find that it was rather the handmaid who persecuted Sarah by her pride, than Sarah who persecuted the handmaid by her severity: for the handmaid was doing wrong to her mistress, and the mistress was only imposing a discipline to her pride.)
>
> [...]
>
> There is a persecution of unrighteousness, which the impious inflict upon the Church of Christ; and there is a righteous persecution, which the Church of Christ inflicts upon the impious. She therefore is blessed in suffering persecution for righteousness' sake; but they are miserable, suffering persecution for unrighteousness. Moreover, she persecutes in the spirit of love, they in the spirit of wrath; she that she may correct, they that they may overthrow: she that she may recall from error, they that they may drive headlong into error.[23]

Again, he considers the objection that it is better for the baptised who have rebelled against the Church to be recalled simply by the preaching of the truth:

> It is indeed better, as no one would deny, when men are led to worship God by teaching, than when they are driven to it by fear of punishment or by pain; but it does not follow that because the former men are better, that those who are not such should be neglected. For many have benefitted, as we have experienced and are still experiencing, in being first compelled by fear or pain, so that they might afterwards be taught, and might carry out in deed what they had already learned by word.[24]

---

[23] Epistle 185.11. In modern English usage, it is paradoxical to use word 'persecute' in anything other than a pejorative sense. We retain it here in order to preserve the connexion with the beatitude which St Augustine quotes; otherwise, it would be clearer to translate *persequor* as 'penalise'.

[24] Ibid. 21.

A third argument of his opponents leads St Augustine to affirm that Scripture had prophesied that the temporal weakness of the faithful in the first days of the Church would be replaced by the temporal strength of Christendom:

> As to the argument of those men who are unwilling that their impious deeds should be checked by the enactment of righteous laws, when they say that the apostles never sought such measures from the kings of the earth, they do not reflect that that time was other than this, and that all things are done in their season. For what emperor had as yet believed in Christ, so as to serve Him in the cause of piety by enacting laws against impiety, when that prophetic word was still being fulfilled: *Why have the Gentiles raged, and the people devised vain things? The kings of the earth stood up, and the princes met together, against the Lord and against his Christ?* For that was not yet happening which is spoken a little later in the same psalm: *And now, O ye kings, understand: receive instruction, you that judge the earth. Serve ye the Lord with fear: and rejoice unto him with trembling.* How then are kings to serve the Lord with fear, except by preventing and chastising with religious severity things done against the commandments of the Lord? For a man serves God in one way in that he is a man, in another way in that he is also king.[25]

Here again the saint recalls that he had initially desired that the Donatists be simply prevented from doing violence to Catholics. Yet he remarks that even at that time, his judgement had been contradicted by older and more experienced men, who had seen in other places that laws obliging heretics and schismatics to give up their conventicles had borne good fruit. St Augustine came to share their opinion, when he perceived that in matters of religion as in other moral duties, there exists in some men a "hardness which cannot be softened by words, but yet admits of softening through some little severity of discipline",[26] and that such discipline tends to produce not false brethren, but a strong and genuine Christendom, *firma et vera Catholica.*[27]

At the Last Supper the Lord Himself instructed the disciples to obtain the means of temporal coercion warning them that "this that is written must yet

---

[25] Ibid. 19. Internal quotations are from Psalm 2, a psalm which St Augustine very often uses in this sense.

[26] Ibid. 25-26.

[27] He is speaking not of coercing men to baptism, but of inducing the baptised to fulfil their Christian duties. It is also clear that the 'discipline' of which he speaks could not be rightly applied if it were likely to provoke resistance equivalent to a civil war.

be fulfilled in me: And with the wicked was he reckoned."[28] He thereby implied that the implacable hostility of the world to Christ and His mystical body necessitates the appropriation by the Church through spiritual means of the temporal power lest she succumb to the temptation to cast herself from the temple parapet and presume upon the providential protection of her Saviour.

St Robert Bellarmine, speaking more than a thousand years after St Augustine, affirms that experience teaches that it is not possible adequately to resist the forces that would dissolve Christendom without maintaining the ultimate sanction.

> For the Church has gone forward trying all remedies, one after the other. First, she only excommunicated; then she added the punishment of fines; then exile; finally, she was forced to come to the penalty of death. For heretics despise excommunication, calling it an empty punishment.[29] If you threaten them with fines, they fear neither God nor man, since they know that foolish men will not be lacking to support them. If you put them in prison, or send them into exile, they corrupt their neighbours with their words, and they corrupt those afar off with their books. Hence the only remedy is to send them promptly to their own place.[30]

It would be strange not to tremble at such words: but if *the devil, as a roaring lion, goeth about seeking whom he may devour,* who will say that they are untrue?

A secular Christendom?

Since man has immediate knowledge of reality through his senses alone, sensible realities make a deeper impression on him than intelligible ones. Hence any great and prolonged fact is liable to appear to him as also a necessary one. But since he is by nature inclined to what is good, he readily persuades himself that what appears to him as necessary is also good.

For these reasons, no doubt, there have not been lacking Catholic authors who have taught that the destruction of Christendom, even if achieved by men with evil intentions, is a good, or at least a means toward a good greater than would

---

[28] Luke 22:37.

[29] *Frigida fulmina,* lit. 'cold bolts of lightning'.

[30] *Controversiae,* 'On the members of the Church', bk. 3, ch. 21. Cf. St Thomas More, *The Yale Edition of the Complete Works of St. Thomas More,* L. A. Schuster, Richard C. Marius, James P. Lusardi (ed.), vol. 8, I-III, *The Confutation of Tyndale's Answer* (Yale: Yale University Press, 1973) 16-17.

be achieved by its preservation or restoration.[31] Such authors wish to unite the principle of secularisation championed by the French Revolution to Catholic doctrine and sound philosophy.[32]

The principal proponents of this latter view in the 20th century were Jacques Maritain and Charles Journet. While not denying that the union of the temporal and spiritual powers, with the legal subordination of the former to the latter, had been a good in its time, and that the doctrines on which it rested remained immutably true, [33] they referred to this political order as a 'sacral' or 'consecrated' Christendom, and declared that the time had now come for a 'lay', 'secular', or 'profane' Christendom. This they described as a society where the gospel, as taught by the Catholic Church, would be in fact the principal source of inspiration for the citizens and the institutions of the society, without the Church herself enjoying by law any privileged place within it.[34] Moreover, they held that such a 'secular Christendom' was not to be regretted as a second best, but would constitute a moral progress. For in such a society, temporal values will be more perfectly "distinguished from spiritual realities, not in the least to be withdrawn from their influence, but on the contrary to achieve a dependence that is to be more conscious of itself, and more conformable to the respective nature of either". This will benefit the Church, they argued, allowing her "to appear all the more clearly to the world as the Body of Christ, as the Kingdom not of this world".[35]

---

[31] Again, those who write on questions of theology and political philosophy are liable to delight in abstract reasoning more than does mankind as a whole, and hence easily attribute to such reasoning an excessive part in our race's acquisition and retention of religious truth.

[32] These trends of thought are summarised in J. Rao, 'He Who Loses the Past, Loses the Present: Putting *Dignitatis Humanae* in its Full Historical Context' in T. Crean and A. Fimister (ed.), *Dignitatis Humanae Colloquium*: Dialogos Institute Collection, vol. 1 (Dialogos Institute: 2017).

[33] For example, in his 1927 work *Primauté du Spirituel,* Maritain defended the papal right of deposition taught by Boniface VIII in *Unam sanctam.*

[34] Maritain put forward his proposal especially in *L'Humanisme Intégrale,* published in 1936, and in *Man and the State,* published in 1951. For Journet, see especially, *The Church of the Word Incarnate,* tr. A. Downes, (Sheed & Ward: London and New York, 1955), 214-330.

[35] *The Church of the Word Incarnate,* 220-21; cf. J. Maritain, *True Humanism,* 4th ed. (London: Centenary Press, 1946), 170: "By virtue of a process of differentiation normal in itself (though vitiated by the most erroneous ideologies) the secular order has in the course of the modern age built up for itself an autonomous relation with regard to the spiritual or consecrational order [...] In other words, it has come of age. This is again a historic gain, which a new Christendom must know how to preserve." Henri de Lubac used similar language in 'Le Pouvoir de L'Eglise en matière temporelle'.

These noble aspirations masked a fallacy. Certainly, it is more conformable to the nature of the Church *simply as such* when the pastors use only spiritual means and spiritual penalties in tending the flock of Christ, and hence have no need of a secular arm. But as St Augustine might have asked, what of "those who are not such"; of those, that is, who will not let themselves be helped by such means? Are they to be allowed to perish when they might have been saved, simply to avoid Pharisaic scandal?[36] Since the Church is a Mother who wishes to save her children by all lawful means, it is more conformable to the nature of the Church *as existing among fallen men*, harried by "the rulers of the world of this darkness",[37] to have temporal power also at her disposal. And, conversely, it is far more conformable to the nature of the temporal power for it to be united to and not separated from the spiritual one, since it cannot reach its own end otherwise. The temporal power that does not tell the citizens where the sources of grace are to be found and defend them against attack, will not be able to accomplish its native duty to God, nor to defend natural law and human dignity in a stable and integral way.[38] Nor would its shortcomings be purely negative. The civil order separated from the Church cannot but perceive her as a dangerous rival. As John Henry Newman observed, the world will always say of the Church: "It is a natural enemy to governments external to itself; it is intolerant and engrossing, and tends to a new modelling of society."[39] And they will turn their wrath against her.

---

[36] That is, the malicious judgement that the pastors of the Church desire temporal power for its own sake, and for their own self-aggrandizement.

[37] Eph. 6:12.

[38] The secular Christendom of Maritain and Journet depended on their acceptance of some form of 'anonymous Christianity', i.e. the view that men can be justified, and able to fulfil the moral law, without explicit faith in Christ as the Redeemer who has been sent into the world from God. On this basis, these authors were able to suppose that the Church could adequately look after the souls of her children, and temporal rulers adequately look after their societies, while renouncing all enforceable temporal penalties which might help to maintain explicit faith in Christ. In his late work *On the Church of Christ*, Maritain asked: "Who would dare to say [...] that there are more saved among the Christians than among the non-Christians?"; J. Maritain, *On the Church of Christ: the Person of the Church and her Personnel*, trans. Joseph Evans (University of Notre Dame Press: Notre Dame, Indiana, 1973), chapter X, section II. 3. See also T. Crean, 'Maritain's anonymous Christianity', *New Blackfriars*, 99 (1081), May 2018, 287-97. For his part, Journet affirmed that a secular Christendom "implies at least the *practical* and *implicit* recognition of high spiritual values, such as the existence of God, the sanctity of truth, the value and necessity of goodwill, the dignity of the person, the spirituality and immortality of the soul, *no matter what theoretical doctrines may be explicitly professed on these points*", *The Church of the Word Incarnate*, 218, our italics.

[39] John Henry Newman, *Essay on the Development of Christian Doctrine* (Longmans, Green, and Co.: London, 1909), 208.

A secular Christendom is thus a chimaera, which is perhaps why today the very phrase has apparently disappeared. If it is possible to divine from revelation anything about the 'movement of history', it is that the absence of the secular arm will be felt not as an 'historic gain', but with increasing keenness as a grievous loss, as the years go by. For the devil rages the more, as he perceives that his time grows short.[40] *L'antéchrist approche toujours plus,* wrote St Francis de Sales, *ce n'est merveille si ses troupes s'avancent plus dru.*[41]

The witness of the popes

Small wonder, then, that while Christendom stood, the popes reminded Catholic rulers unflaggingly of their duties to God and to the Church.[42] Writing to Emperor Theodosius II, St Celestine I praises him for his part in assuring the success of the council of Ephesus in 430; but noting that Nestorius was still spreading his doctrine, he enjoined the emperor thus: "Let Your Clemency separate him from the company of men, that he may no longer have the opportunity of destroying any."[43] We have already seen Leo the Great tell his namesake in Constantinople that imperial power was given him principally for the protection of the Church.[44] After him, Pope St Gelasius warned the emperor of his day, Anastasius I, that as he valued his salvation so he must protect Christ's Church against heresy: "With what confidence, I ask, will you seek for rewards from Him there, whom you do not keep from loss here?"[45] St Gregory the Great, in a letter to the Emperor Maurice, used words that would become famous:

> For power over all men has been given by heaven to my Lordships' piety for this reason, that those who seek good things may be given help, that the path to heaven may be opened more widely, and that

---

[40] Apoc. 12:12.

[41] "The antichrist draws ever nearer, no wonder if his troops come on apace"; from his work *The Standard of the Holy Cross.*

[42] Cf. T. Pink, 'The Interpretation of Dignitatis Humanae: A Reply to Martin Rhonheimer', *Nova et Vetera*, English Edition, Vol. 11, No. 1 (2013), 93: "It is just historical fantasy to suppose that Catholic endorsement of religious coercion at the magisterial level was peculiar to a 'few isolated popes' of the nineteenth century."

[43] Letter 23; PL 50: 546: "Clementia vestra ab omni societate removeat, ut facultatem aliquos perdendi non habeat." The pope was, of course, requesting that Nestorius be exiled, not executed.

[44] See p. 226.

[45] PL 59:43: "Qua fiducia, rogo te, illic eius praemia petiturus es, cuius hic damna non prohibes?"

the earthly realm may be in service to the heavenly kingdom (*terrestre regnum coelesti regno famuletur*).[46]

A life-time later, in 680, it was the turn of Pope St Agatho to remind the emperor of his day, Constantine IV, of his principal duty. Having defined the doctrine of the two wills in Christ, and besought the emperor to permit this doctrine to be freely confessed at the council that had been convened in Constantinople, St Agatho continued:

> Nor could anything be found more likely to commend the clemency of Your unconquerable fortitude to the divine majesty, than that those who err from the rule of truth should be repelled and the integrity of our evangelical and apostolic faith should be everywhere set forth and preached.[47]

Such citations could be multiplied indefinitely. It suffices, however, to note that the teaching which had characterised the centuries of Christendom was maintained even as mortal blows rained upon the Christian realms. Though admired by Voltaire, Benedict XIV would write: "Sovereign rulers are chosen by God, to be defenders of the faith, and protectors of the Church".[48] A generation after the French revolution, Gregory XVI summed up the perennial doctrine of St Peter's successors:

> May Our dear sons in Christ, the princes, support these Our desires for the soundness of both sacred and public affairs (*pro rei et sacrae et publicae incolumitate*) with their resources and authority. May they understand that they received their authority not only for the government of the world, but especially for the defence of the Church. They should diligently consider that whatever work they do for the welfare of the Church accrues to their rule and peace. Indeed,

---

[46] PL 77:663. The pope was requesting that Maurice reconsider a law forbidding soldiers to leave the army for the monastic life before they had served out their allotted time. It is noteworthy that the pope describes himself as subject to the emperor's bidding (*iussioni subiectus*) in this matter: the law requiring that the soldiers serve out their time was not in itself unjust. Yet he warns him that if he does not revoke the law, he will have to explain himself before the just Judge. The pope uses the plural form, because the emperor had made his son Theodosius co-emperor.

[47] PL 87:1212. The emperor in this case decreed that clergy who did not accept the Council's definition concerning the two wills of Christ would be deposed, while government officials would be dismissed, and private persons exiled.

[48] *Providas Romanorum*, a letter of 1751, against Freemasonry.

let them be convinced that the cause of the faith is of greater weight than that of their kingdom.[49]

A century later, even after the 'breaking of nations' in the Great War, Pius XI would speak in the same way. "If the rulers of nations wish to preserve their authority, to promote and increase the prosperity of their countries, they will not neglect the public duty of reverence and obedience to the rule of Christ."[50]

This teaching was repeated, albeit quietly, at the most recent of the councils. The bishops declared that they were leaving intact, *integer*, "the traditional Catholic doctrine on the moral duty of men and societies toward the true religion and toward the one Church of Christ."[51] Whatever his private views, the pope of the day did not instruct the Christian people, nor could he, that they should never again hope to put flesh on the bones of this doctrine.[52] He judged, however, that the growth of secularism had become so great by his time that Catholic temporal rulers would not succeed in subjecting their power to Christ and the Church in the formal and explicit way that had formerly constituted Christendom, and he declined to ask them to do so. Whether he judged rightly is not our present business. Then the Catholic doctrine was put away, as once the high priest put away the sword of David with which the giant had been slain, against the day when he should call for it anew:

---

[49] *Mirari vos*, 23, an encyclical written in 1832. The quotation from Pope St Leo I's letter to the emperor will be noted; it would be repeated by Pius IX in *Qui pluribus*, 34. For his part, Leo XIII addressed these paternal words to the American republic: "[T]hanks are due to the equity of the laws which obtain in America and to the customs of the well-ordered Republic. For the Church amongst you, unopposed by the Constitution and government of your nation, fettered by no hostile legislation, protected against violence by the common laws and the impartiality of the tribunals, is free to live and act without hindrance. Yet, though all this is true, it would be very erroneous to draw the conclusion that in America is to be sought the type of the most desirable status of the Church, or that it would be universally lawful or expedient for State and Church to be, as in America, dissevered and divorced. The fact that Catholicity with you is in good condition, nay, is even enjoying a prosperous growth, is by all means to be attributed to the fecundity with which God has endowed His Church, in virtue of which unless men or circumstances interfere, she spontaneously expands and propagates herself; but she would bring forth more abundant fruits if, in addition to liberty, she enjoyed the favour of the laws and the patronage of the public authority"; *Longinqua*, 6. See also Alexis de Tocqueville, *Selected Letters on Politics and Society*, ed. Roger Boesche (University of California Press: Berkeley, 1985), 50-51.

[50] *Quas primas*, 18.

[51] *Dignitatis humanae*, 1.

[52] It is well known that Giovanni Battista Montini, Paul VI, had been deeply influenced in his youth by the 'integral humanism' of Maritain. See Philippe Chenaux, *Paul VI et Maritain: Les Rapports du 'Montinianisme' et du 'Maritanisme'* (Studium: Brescia, 1994).

David came to Nobe to Achimelech the priest: and Achimelech was astonished at David's coming. And David said to Achimelech: Hast thou here at hand a spear, or a sword? The priest said: Lo, here is the sword of Goliath, the Philistine, whom thou slewest in the valley of Terebinth, wrapped up in a cloth behind the ephod: if thou wilt take this, take it, for here there is no other but this. And David said: There is none like that, give it me.[53]

---

[53] 1 Sam. 21.

Theses

1. Two loves form two cities, which have unity from their head and which are necessarily in conflict.
2. Christendom is necessary to protect the Church against the city of the world.

Postscript: *What the Law does not tell you*

And behold a certain lawyer stood up, tempting him, and saying, Master, what must I do to possess eternal life? But he said to him: What is written in the law? how readest thou? He answering, said: Thou shalt love the Lord thy God with thy whole heart, and with thy whole soul, and with all thy strength, and with all thy mind: and thy neighbour as thyself. And he said to him: Thou hast answered right: this do, and thou shalt live. But he willing to justify himself, said to Jesus: And who is my neighbour?

And Jesus answering, said: A certain man went down from Jerusalem to Jericho, and fell among robbers, who also stripped him, and having wounded him went away, leaving him half dead. And it chanced, that a certain priest went down the same way: and seeing him, passed by. In like manner also a Levite, when he was near the place and saw him, passed by. But a certain Samaritan being on his journey, came near him; and seeing him, was moved with compassion. And going up to him, bound up his wounds, pouring in oil and wine: and setting him upon his own beast, brought him to an inn, and took care of him. And the next day he took out two pence, and gave to the host, and said: Take care of him; and whatsoever thou shalt spend over and above, I, at my return, will repay thee.

Which of these three, in thy opinion, was neighbour to him that fell among the robbers? But he said: He that shewed mercy to him. And Jesus said to him: Go, and do thou in like manner.

Human beings spontaneously seek the highest realisation of their nature available to them. They call this state 'happiness'. False beliefs about the character of happiness are the principal cause of unhappiness in man. Being finite they seek to transcend their natural limitations through friendship – willing the good of another for the other's own sake.[1] The highest good available to man in virtue of his nature alone is the contemplation of God but it is scarcely available. Objectively, the highest form of friendship available to man is the civic friendship which unites all the citizens of a commonwealth.[2] The life of a great statesman falls within man's grasp and may be realised to a

---

[1] See pp. 15-16.

[2] See pp. 29-30.

very high degree, but it falls short of man's more exalted potential. The life of a philosopher is the most exalted available to unaided nature, but it is only very imperfectly within man's grasp. The duties of a statesman and the solitude of the philosopher make the simultaneous pursuit of both ideals impossible. Such persons as Ss Thomas More and Severinus Boethius present exceptions because their lives were transformed by the supernatural power of grace and yet the violent if glorious ends in which those lives concluded express the ineradicable tension which persists between these ideals in the world. Plato and Marcus Aurelius illustrate the point from the pagan perspective: the former was a disastrous politician and the latter was a very inferior philosopher.

Nature alone therefore presents man with an insoluble conflict between two ideals.[3] This is not surprising, as a state of pure nature devoid of any positive revelation could never exist.[4] It is impossible to know man's end merely by introspective consideration of human nature. While it is possible to know man's proportionate end in this way, it is not thereby possible to know his actual end in this order of providence.

It therefore follows as a necessary consequence of the divine justice itself that even if God had made us only for the end proportionate to our nature he would have revealed this to us.[5] Nor does He deny man this revelation even in his fallen state save as a result of personal sin.

> Granted that everyone is bound to believe something explicitly, no untenable conclusion follows even if someone is brought up in the forest or among wild beasts. For it pertains to divine providence to furnish everyone with what is necessary for salvation, provided that on his part there is no hindrance. Thus, if someone so brought up followed the direction of natural reason in seeking good and avoiding evil, we must most certainly hold that God would either reveal to him through internal inspiration what had to be believed, or would send some preacher of the faith to him as he sent Peter to Cornelius (Acts 10:20).[6]

So while it may seem to fallen man that he has but the resources of nature to guide him, this is in fact a result of his sin in failing to follow the direction of natural reason by seeking good and avoiding evil. The irrational denial that

---

[3] This is illustrated by Aristotle's inconclusive discussion in *Politics* VII.1-3.

[4] See p. 10.

[5] STh 2a2ae 2, 3.

[6] St Thomas Aquinas, *De Veritate* 14, 11 ad 1.

anything more than reason is required for human life (rationalism) is a proud denial of man's moral failure, a failure of which he is quite aware.

But rationalism has disastrous moral consequences. Without revelation man seeks friendship, a friendship that is in itself altruistic - but he seeks it for selfish reasons. It is not desired for its own sake but in order to transcend man's finitude.[7] A man who could live without society would either be a beast or a god, Aristotle observes.[8] Man may not wish to be a beast but he would not spurn divinity. Not being sought for its own sake, friendship without revelation and grace has quasi-natural limits. Like the lawyer who questioned Christ, Aristotle, the model of natural reason, does not know who his neighbour is. Man seeks the friendship of his kin, of his spouse, of his personal companions and of his fellow citizens but there his desire comes to rest. He has no need to exert himself to seek the good of the distant stranger for his own sake. He has much to lose from offering friendship to his enemies and much to gain from withholding it from his slaves. Friendship with God, it would seem to the rationalist, is impossible. The first mover has no finitude to transcend. There is an essential selfishness to Aristotle's friendship. We seek it in order to expand out of ourselves. We seek it out of need and from the desire for our own happiness. I love my kindred, I love my spouse, I love my comrades and I love my fellow citizens but I need go no further. I cannot love God, he does not love me, I hate my enemies, I use my slaves[9] and all other things being equal I am indifferent to foreigners. Man knows by natural reason that he should love his neighbour as himself but he does not know who his neighbour is.

In any world that God might have created He would have revealed to His rational creatures their end precisely because this knowledge cannot by its nature be discerned through reflection on nature. This essential communication in our world consists in the revelation of God's supernatural providence: that He offers His friendship to man. For the rationalist this is impossible. It causes man to recognise that friendship is not, as enclosed reason would suppose, a mixed perfection which implies finitude in its holder but a pure perfection which can and therefore must exist in the Pure Act.[10] In revealing this to us God already reveals implicitly the dogma of the Trinity[11] and in thereby telling us something that exceeds not only the natural knowledge

---

[7] STh 1a 32, 1 ad 2.

[8] *Politics* I.2. See above p. 16.

[9] See discussion on p. 68 n. 19.

[10] See p. 15.

[11] St Thomas Aquinas, *De Potentia* IX.9.

of man but of every creature that has been or even could be made, God causes us to share in His knowledge of Himself, and so in the divine sonship.

> I will not now call you servants: for the servant knoweth not what his lord doth. But I have called you friends: because all things whatsoever I have heard of my Father, I have made known to you.[12]

In so doing, Christ destroys the boundary erected by man's self-enclosed and fallen reason between himself and God, between himself and his enemies, his slaves and the stranger. "You have heard that it hath been said, Thou shalt love thy neighbour, and hate thy enemy. But I say to you, Love your enemies: do good to them that hate you: and pray for them that persecute and calumniate you that you may be the children of your Father who is in heaven." He thereby generates the true human city, the City of God, "the people made one with the unity of the Father, the Son and the Holy Ghost".[13]

---

[12] Jn. 15:15.

[13] St Cyprian of Carthage, *On the Lord's Prayer*, 23; PL 4:536.

Index

authority: 32-35. *See also 'auctoritas* and *potestas',* 'spiritual power', 'temporal power'

Averroes (Ibn Rushd): 10

baptism: confers citizenship in Christendom, 117; coerced unlawful, 117-18, 162, 214; of infants in danger of death, 52; jurisdiction of the Church and, 52, 117, 220, 233, 239, 267; rulers and, 79, 83; of society, 115

Barclay, William (jurist): 230-31

Becket, St Thomas: 81, 253

Bede, St: 137

Bellarmine, St Robert: Adam as temporal ruler, 75; apostles able to establish true (civil) judges, 230; baptism obliges temporal ruler to subject his rule to Church, 79; not fitting that Christ should have used coercion, 264; nature of Christendom, 246-47; Church as perfect society, 247; civil power may not be indifferent to religious truth, 107; clergy, in relation to civil laws, 127, and to taxation, 181; punishment of heretics, 233, 268; 'indirect power' of pope, 231-32; seven basic polities, 150, compared, 157-58, 160-62; pope (and bishops), when able to use temporal authority, 229-30, 232, 235-41, 247, and theological note of this doctrine, 246; origin of temporal authority 89, in a sense spiritual, 109; sense of 'two swords' in St Luke, 228; union of spiritual and temporal power in one man lawful, 76-77; war, 209-10

Benedict XIV (Pope): children of Jews, whether to be baptised, 52; duties of rulers to Church, 249, 272; temporal penalties inflicted by Church, 233; usury, 193

Benedict XV (Pope): 106

Benedict XVI (Pope): reason unable to produce universal community, 202

Bernard of Clairvaux, St: on Christian knighthood, 212-13; on the two swords, 227-29

Bessette, Joseph: 126

Billot, Louis: 220

bishops: aristocratic element within Church, 154, 162; and temporal sword, 237. *See also* 'Church', 'spiritual power'

Blackstone, William: 191

body-soul relation: *See* 'soul-body relation'

Boethius, St Severinus: 172, 277

Boleyn, Elizabeth: 48, 239

Bonaventure, St: 228

Boniface VIII (Pope): 74, 81, 229, 237, 262

Bracton, Henry de: 70

Bryce, James: 203

Byzantium: 76-77, 138-39, 203, 213

Cajetan, Thomas de Vio: 100, 181, 242

Calvin, John: 40, 45, 109, 162

canon law: relation to civil law, 130, 249-50. *See also* 'Code of Canon Law (1917)', 'Code of Canon Law (1983)'

capitalism: 195-96

Carolingian Empire: 76, 223, 226, 249

Catechism of the Catholic Church: capital punishment, 125; Cicero on natural law, 123; armed resistance to unjust rulers, 98; rulers as representatives of God, 88; societies not recognising Redeemer become totalitarian, 80

Catechism of the Council of Trent: 126

Cavagnis, Felice: 251-53

Celestine I (Pope): 271

Cessario, Romanus: 53

charity: 15, 278. *See also* 'revelation'

Charles I (King of England): 57, 142-43

Charles X (King of France): 219

Dionysius the Areopagite: 10, 74

Dionysius Cato: 127

Divini illius Magistri: 10, 17, 54, 181

Duhamel, P. Albert: 19

Edgar (King of England): 227

education: 50-55, 124; belongs primarily to Church and to family, 53; to Church by double title, 20, 52; family has inalienable right, 51-52; supervisory role of temporal power, 54, 111. *See also 'Divini illius magistri'*

epikeia: 136-37

Epistle to Diognetus: 83

equality: 57, 59, 70, 173

equity: 93, 139-40. *See also 'epikeia'*

Erastus (Lieber), Thomas: 77

Escriva, St Jose Maria: 252

European Union: 223

Eusebius of Caesarea: 116

excommunication: civil effects of, 117, 234, 240, 247-48, 252

executive power: 90-95, 161, 235-36. *See also 'ius'*

fall of the devil: to private good, 25; by claiming proportionate end as ultimate, 167

fall of man: need for non-patriarchal rule derives from, 56-57; creates distinction in title to temporal and spiritual power, 75

family: 40-60; divorce, 46-48; headship of father, 42-43; natural society, 40-41, 44-45; relation to temporal society, 44-45, 48-54; unit of temporal society, 57-59, 173

Fascism: 51

Feser, Edward: 126

Filmer, Robert: 57

Florence, Council of: 122, 163, 203

Fowler, Henry: 177

Francis II (Emperor): 205

friendship: 14-15, 278-79; children's need for exemplar of 40, 46; between commonwealths, 200, 212; as foundation of society, 15, 25, 27-28; goal of rulers, 28; contrary to 'instrumentalization', 25; a pure perfection, 15. *See also 'revelation', 'servitude'*

Funck, Johann Nicolaus: 66

Gallican articles: 238

Garrigou-Lagrange, Réginald: 26

Gasser, Vincent: 163

Gaudium et spes: 26, 69, 180, 212

Gelasius I (Pope): 34, 72, 76-77, 245, 271

Giles of Rome: 83

Gilson, Etienne: 22

Gonzalez, Irenaeo: 30

Gournay, Jacques de: 176

Gredt, Joseph: 32

Gregory I (Pope): 251; principal duty of emperor, 271-72; servitude, 56-57, 69;

Gregory II (Pope): 240-41

Gregory VII (Pope): 238, 240

Gregory XVI (Pope): 272-73

Grenier, Henri: 11, 16, 32, 249

guilds: *See 'labour'*

Habsburg, Otto von: 173

Henry IV (emperor): 240

Henry VIII (King of England): 48, 238

Marx, Karl: 41

means of production: *See* 'private property'

Melchizedek: 75, 83, 229

Midgley, E.B.F.: 202, 211

Mill, John Stuart: 73, 176

'mixed matters': 217-19, 225, 249

mixed polity: 150-52; Aquinas on, 142-43, 158-60; Aristotle on, 168-69; Bellarmine on, 160-62; Charles I on, 143; possible variations, 152-54

monarchy: 57, 142-43, 146-49, 161, 167-68, 214; absolute, 168-69; anointing of monarch, 83, 173; the constitution of the Church, 157, 162-64; whether hereditary licit, 170-73; best of pure regimes, 155-58

Montesquieu (Charles-Louis de Secondat): 90

More, Thomas: 19, 221, 268, 277

Moses: 210, 262; possesses both swords, 75-76, 129; monarch, 157, 159, 162

Murphy, James: 210

Mussolini, Benito: 244

nationhood: 206

natural law: 91-93, 122-23. *See also* 'law', 'necessary society'

Nazianzen, St Gregory: 82

necessary society: 12; authority in, 33-34; civil society as, 84-86; the family as, 40- 41; 'society of states' is not, 201

Newman, John Henry (Cardinal): 176, 205, 248; origin of kingdoms, 98-99; papal authority, 224, 245; the two cities, 270

Nicaea, Council of: 192

Nicholas I (Pope): 245

Noah: 63, 85

non-constitutional change of rulers: 95-98, 212

Nozick, Robert: 87, 188

Octavian Augustus: 72, 138, 161

Optatus, St: 253

'order of providence': 10

Orientalium Ecclesiarum: 164

Ortolan, T.: 211

Ottaviani, Alfredo (Cardinal): 12, 21, 32, 49, 90-91, 181, 220, 235; cause of authority, 33-34, its subject, 89; deposition of rulers, 235-39, 242; international relations, 206; mixed matters, 217, 249; papal power in temporal realm, 244, 246; punishment, 125, 253; right, 36; separation of powers, 94

'patrimony of the Church': 230, 232

Paul III (Pope): 238, 250; on slavery 68-69

Paul V (Pope): 238

Paul VI (Pope): 135, 206, 273; Church as perfect society, 18

peace: as aim of ruler, 27, 157, 159, though not sole, 107, 116

perfect society: 16-18, 20, 259; Church alone intrinsically so, 20-22, 72, 216, 229-31; consequences, 220, 242, 247

Peter of Tarentaise: 44-45

Philip Augustus: 84

Philip of Macedon: 9

Pink, Thomas: 108, 271

Pinsent, Andrew: 167

Pius V (Pope): 239, 252

Pius VI (Pope): 233

religion, 115; duty of worship, 105-7. *See also* 'temporal power', 'polity'.

Rupp, Jean: 216

Sagues, Joseph: 45

salary: *See* 'wage'

Sales, St Francis de: 116, 261, 270

Savonarola, Girolamo: 10, 222

Scruton, Roger: 140

secular societies: 105-13, 219-25; death as analogy for secularization, 217; how disposed to become Catholic, 114-15; of short duration, 106. *See also* 'Christendom', 'rulers'

'separation of powers': 94-95

servitude: 63-70; Aristotle, 43-44, 68; chattel slavery, 64-65, 67; usury a form of, 70; war and, 69

Sheed, Frank: 10

Shestak, Eduard: 48

Sicut Iudaeis: 118

simony: 77, 130

Sixtus V (Pope): 98

social contract: 86-90. *See also* 'society'

social kingship of Christ: 78, 104-5, 117, 273

socialism: 184, 188-89, 195-97

society: nature and division of, 11-13; reason for 13-16. *See also* 'common good', 'perfect society'

society of states: 201

sodomy: 41, 109, 141

Sola, Francis: 45, 49

Soto, Domingo de: 222

soul-body relation: analogy for relation of Church and temporal commonwealth, 82-83; immaterial powers of soul analogous to the spiritual power, 231; sensitive powers of soul-body composite analogous to the temporal power, 231; subsistence of separated soul analogous to state of Church outside Christendom, 234

sovereignty: 151-52, 207; and legislative power, 94

spiritual power: authority over temporal power, 77-79, 130, inside Christendom, 229-48, and outside 219-225; need for in all orders of providence, 18-19, 259

'State': 21, 216

Suarez, Francisco: 18, 127, 136, 239; Church's right of self-defence, 242-43; custom, 133-35; Holy Roman emperor, 203; international law, 200; 'merely penal' law, 132-33; unjust law, 132; war, 209-211

subsidiarity: 113, 204

suffrage: 173-75

Supreme Court of the United States: 51

Syllabus of Errors: 21; authority, 84, 95, 112; international relations, 212; marriage, 47, 49; spiritual power in relation to temporal order, 76, 116, 233, 247

Tacitus: 135

Taparelli, Luigi: 201

tax: 190; inheritance unlawful, 59-60, 193; as remedy for injustice, 185, 194

temporal power: 72-100, 103-119; Bellarmine's account of origin, 89; dislocated outside Christendom, 80; distinction from spiritual, 75-77, 129-30; division of, 90-95; before the Fall, 74-75; institution by spiritual, 80-84; not just material force, 84; origin outside Christendom, 84-90; exercised by pope or bishop from necessity, 76-77, 237; purpose of, 72-74, 103-4; not the source of all rights, 112; when exercised as 'secular arm', 115, 234-35, 250; subordination to spiritual, 77-79, 130-31. *See also 'auctoritas* and *potestas'*, 'non-constitutional change of rulers', 'rulers', 'social contract', 'usurpation'

Tertullian: 98

theocracy: 239

Theodosius I (Emperor): 212

Theodosius II (Emperor): 271

Thomistic theses, twenty-four: *See 'Postquam sanctissimus'*

Tierney, Brian: 163

Tocqueville, Alexis de: 94, 273

toleration: 110, 117-119

trade: 60, 196, 200

trade unions: 190

Trent, Council of: 19, 182; clerical exemption, 127; coercion, 116, 221, 233, 235; Church's jurisdiction, 117, over marriage, 49; legislative power of Church, 220

two swords: 216-255; doctrinal note, 246; foreshadowed in Old Testament, 239; 'sword' in Holy Scripture, 226; both swords belong to Peter, 227-30; use of temporal sword by spiritual ruler exceptional, 237. *See also* 'spiritual power'. 'temporal power'

tyranny: 95-98, 142-43, 156-57, 159, 171, 212; deposition of tyrant within Christendom, 238-41, and outside, 241-43

Unam sanctam: 229, 237, 245-46; Maritain on, 269; rule through intermediaries, 74; no salvation outside Church, 262

unhappiness: 74, 276

Urban II (Pope): 253

usurpation: 98-100, 242; of spiritual matter by temporal ruler, 76, 97, 116, 182, 204; of temporal matter by spiritual ruler, 130, 222, 225, 236

usury: 191-93; inverts proper relation of capital and labour, 195; condemned by Church, 192-93; evil consequences of, 196; form of slavery, 70; unjust power obtained by, 192

Victor I (Pope): 163

Vienne, Council of: 192

Villey, Michel: 35, 37

virtue: aim of education, 50; aim of laws, 124, which inculcate it gradually, 128; moral, necessary for office, 174; excellence in administering temporal affairs not virtue *simpliciter*, 167

Vitoria, Francisco de: 203, 243; theory of just war, 210-11

voluntary society: 12-13, 33-34, 41, 86

wage: lawful to hire a worker for, 185-65, 189, 193; living, 46, 184

warfare: 208-13; endemic, 202. *See also* 'crusades'

Wilson, Woodrow: 206

Wlodkowic, Pawel: 241

world government: 92; desire for disordered, 204-5. *See also* 'society of states', 'Vitoria, Francisco de'

Wormuth, Francis: 150

Xenophon: 175